T0320609

Second Edition

The Complete Guide for

CPP

Examination Preparation

Anthony V. DiSalvatore
CPP, PSP, PCI, CFE, CLSD

CRC Press
Taylor & Francis Group
Boca Raton London New York

CRC Press is an imprint of the
Taylor & Francis Group, an **informa** business

CRC Press
Taylor & Francis Group
6000 Broken Sound Parkway NW, Suite 300
Boca Raton, FL 33487-2742

© 2016 by Taylor & Francis Group, LLC
CRC Press is an imprint of Taylor & Francis Group, an Informa business

No claim to original U.S. Government works

Printed on acid-free paper
Version Date: 20150611

International Standard Book Number-13: 978-1-4987-0522-6 (Hardback)

Library of Congress Cataloging-in-Publication Data

DiSalvatore, Anthony V.
   The complete guide for CPP examination preparation / Anthony V. DiSalvatore. -- 2nd edition.
      pages cm
   Earlier edition authored by James P. Muuss and David Rabern.
   Includes bibliographical references and index.
   ISBN 978-1-4987-0522-6 (hardcover : alk. paper) 1. Private security services--United States--Examinations, questions, etc. I. Muuss, James P. Complete guide for CPP examination preparation. II. Title.

HV8291.U6M88 2015
363.28'9076--dc23

2015021734

Visit the Taylor & Francis Web site at
http://www.taylorandfrancis.com

and the CRC Press Web site at
http://www.crcpress.com

I dedicate this book to my parents, Beverly and Remo; my brothers, Joe, Fred and Remo; my children, Andriana and Remo; and to my wife, Beth. They teach me something new about life every day and make the world a better place.

Contents

Preface

It has been an honor and a privilege to author the second edition of *The Complete Guide for CPP Examination Preparation*. For those who wish to advance their knowledge, professionalism, and integrity in security-related fields, the CPP designation is a must-have. While I was transitioning from law enforcement to the private sector, those who were recognized and respected in the private sector stressed the importance of the CPP designation.

I have found that employers, agencies, and associates accept and recognize the knowledge, professionalism, and expertise of those who have attained the CPP designation. They readily accept that security practitioners who have attained the CPP have a mindset and understanding that security is an ever-expanding, maturing discipline that requires constant vigilance in keeping abreast with the latest technologies, legal aspects, and best practices.

I remember when I studied for the CPP there were many different materials, methods, and sources available. Since everything seemed so diverse and scattered, it was confusing and made it difficult to determine what materials and sources were important. I was, therefore, very excited when contacted to work on this book. I believe it is a clear, concise study tool with the resources needed to prepare properly for the CPP certification examination.

In the past, many viewed the security profession as a necessary, non-revenue-generating discipline that had to be tolerated. World events have driven home the fallacy of that belief. In these turbulent times, where the forces of evil are making unprovoked attacks on societies, businesses, and individuals, properly trained, dedicated, and proven security professionals are needed more than ever. Businesses and governments have come to understand the importance of an effective security program and the impact it makes on the lives and well-being of everyone. The CPP designation has come to be recognized as the benchmark of a serious practitioner who has demonstrated dedication and expertise in the security field.

As you take the journey toward the CPP designation, take the corresponding test questions that are provided after completing each of the required areas of study. These are not the questions that will be on the actual exam, but they will convey the principles and concepts that will be seen on the exam helping to determine if you have mastered the required information.

My hope is that you learn and find the material contained in this book useful, helpful, and informative in your quest. Once you attain your certification, you will have set yourself apart from the rest of the security field as a serious, professional practitioner who has mastered the domains of the CPP designation.

Acknowledgments

It has been an honor and a privilege to be involved in the publication of this book. In my opinion, the CPP certification is one of the most recognized and universally accepted certifications in the security industry. It truly is a measuring stick of one's knowledge of this field. I am grateful to have had the opportunity to be in security-related positions for over 30 years and have worked shoulder to shoulder with so many fine people. I have been truly blessed and am grateful to have been gifted with a passion for helping others and trying to make a positive difference, with security-related organizations as my conduit. Amazingly, my passion grows stronger every day, and I hope that readers are fortunate enough to have found their niche and are able to achieve success while helping others.

Author

Anthony V. DiSalvatore, CPP, PSP, PCI, CFE, CLSD, possesses over 30 years of experience in security-related positions. He has been involved in the opening of numerous casinos, hotels, and entertainment complexes. DiSalvatore served as a state trooper for the New Jersey State Police and received a Distinguished Service Award for actions taken.

Anthony has also been recognized for actions taken while working at large properties in South Florida, New Jersey, and New York City. DiSalvatore performed an integral role during hurricanes Frances and Wilma in South Florida, hurricane Sandy in New Jersey, and the largest power outage in US history in New York City by ensuring that business continuity and disaster recovery plans were executed.

Anthony holds an associate degree in arts and science from Gloucester County College, a bachelor's degree in law justice from Glassboro State College, and master's degrees in education administration from Seton Hall University and criminal justice from Rutgers University. DiSalvatore is a member of the American Society for Industrial Security (ASIS) International and the Gaming and Wagering Protection Council; has previously held membership in the Crime and Loss Prevention Council, Business Management and Business Continuity Council; and has been recognized by ASIS as a Triple Crown recipient by being a Certified Protection Professional (CPP), Physical Security Professional (PSP), and Professional Certified Investigator (PCI).

Anthony is also a Certified Fraud Examiner and Certified Lodging Security Director and has presented at numerous venues across the country. He has also been treasurer of the Las Vegas Security Chiefs Association and the gaming subsector lead in the Department of Homeland Security Commercial Facilities Coordinating Council and possesses a Secret Level Clearance.

1 Introduction

This chapter is designed to give you an overview of the Certified Protection Professional (CPP) exam, an appreciation for the journey the CPP designation has made from a concept to what it has come to represent today, an idea of what you will be required to know and do, and some useful hints in preparing for and taking the exam.

WHY SHOULD I TAKE THE CERTIFIED PROTECTION PROFESSIONAL EXAM?

One question the security professional asks when considering taking the CPP exam is why he or she should take the time and exert the effort to prepare to take the exam. The answer is that as a security professional, it is in your own best interest to attain the CPP designation. In the past several years, the Professional Certification Board (PCB) has coined a descriptive phrase to define the CPP designation. That phrase is "board certified in security management."

The CPP designation began when a group of security contractors in the defense industry came together to form what was to be the American Society for Industrial Security (ASIS). This group of defense contractors was committed to improving the security industry as a whole. Among this group was Loren Newland, CPP. He suggested that a professional certification for the security industry be created whereby the knowledge of security professionals could be measured. Thus began the long journey of the CPP certification.

It was not an easy task to create a designation that was a viable measure of the security professional's knowledge and that was accepted by the industry. As in a lot of professions, the security industry encompasses a wide range of security knowledge, technical expertise, and various disciplines and applications of that knowledge.

Of course, there are many areas that overlap into many of the security disciplines. A person working in the banking industry would be required to have a great deal of knowledge about safes, vaults, alarm systems, and closed-circuit television (CCTV) applications. So, too, would the security practitioner in the retail industry need to know the same information, but he or she would have to master the security requirements of dealing with, for example, shoplifters.

The concept of one designation that would encompass all of the required skills was a daunting task. With hard work, vision, and dedication to the concept, the CPP designation became a reality. In the almost three decades that the CPP designation has been around, it has grown into the industry's primary designation and a designation that is recognized and respected around the world.

The CPP designation has become the benchmark by which the industry and the corporate executive who hires the security professional judge the candidate's ability to perform his or her job functions. They realize that the designation has proven the individual's ability and dedication to improving knowledge and professional skills. The CPP also has the experience required to perform the needed job functions.

The security director/manager is tasked with much more than overseeing some security officers or doing some background investigations. He or she must have the ability to deal with all levels of company management; local, state, and federal law enforcement; and complex legal issues. He or she must also conduct investigations, administer contracts, formulate budgets, and perform myriad other tasks not directly related to security.

The CPP exam covers the job functions a CPP is called upon to perform in the real world of business. In your preparation for the exam, you will learn new information, master new skills, and gain a new appreciation for the job you are striving for.

A few years ago, you started to see "CPP preferred" in employment ads. Now the CPP designation is mandatory for most mid- and high-level management positions.

In today's highly competitive business world, the CPP designation marks you as a professional worthy of consideration and respect by your peers and the business community.

EXAM REQUIREMENTS

Once you have made the most important decision—that is, to pursue the CPP certification—what do you do next?

The first thing you need to ascertain is whether you meet the requirements to sit for the exam. The PCB has set minimum standards in training and experience for anyone wishing to attain the CPP designation. These qualifications have been established to maintain the viability of the designation and to assure the candidate that he or she can take and successfully pass the exam. The PCB has determined that a candidate should have either of the following:

- A minimum of 9 years of experience in the security industry, with at least 3 of those years in responsible charge of a security function

- A bachelor's degree or higher and 7 years of security work experience, with at least 3 of those years in responsible charge of a security function

Responsible charge is defined as having direct responsibility over the personnel and outcome of a specific task.

Factoring in educational degrees can modify the requirement mandating 9 years of experience. If you have a 2-year degree, you only need 7 years of experience. A 4-year degree lowers the experience requirement by another 2 years. A master's degree lowers the requirement to only 3 years of experience, and a doctorate will require you to have 2 years of experience. In all of these cases, you need at least 3 years in responsible charge of a security function.

If you are claiming educational credits, the PCB will require you to submit official transcripts with your application to take the test.

Applicants cannot have any criminal convictions, which would reflect negatively on the security profession or ASIS.

Your application to take the exam must be endorsed by a CPP in good standing who certifies that you have made complete and accurate statements on the application. The endorser also certifies that in his or her judgment, you have met all of the requirements to sit for the exam.

PREPARING TO TAKE THE EXAM

SELF-EVALUATION

Once you have determined you meet the minimum requirements, the next step is to objectively evaluate your strengths and weaknesses. A problem many candidates run into is that they may be highly proficient in their chosen area of security but the CPP exam is a broad-spectrum exam that evaluates knowledge in many disciplines. You may know a great deal about alarms, CCTV, lighting, and access control, but you may not be well versed in guard force management or investigative techniques. An honest evaluation of these weaknesses will allow you to determine where most of your study efforts must be placed.

AVAILABLE RESOURCES

Once you have determined which areas you may require special help with, you need to locate the resources available to you. This is not as hard as it may seem. Your first resource is ASIS International. ASIS is extremely dedicated to the CPP program and to helping you obtain the designation. A call to ASIS customer service at 703-519-6200 or connecting through the Internet at www.asisonline.org will give you access to a great deal of information on the CPP exam, test dates, research material, general information on the exam, and much more.

On the local level, you can contact a CPP chapter liaison. This is a member who has volunteered to run chapter-level efforts to aid persons wishing to pursue the designation and who promotes the CPP program among the ASIS members and the business community. He or she has access to all of the information and resources you require.

Many chapter liaisons have set up formal training programs presented by other CPPs. These classes can be a great deal of help in your preparation for the exam. If your chapter does not have a liaison, speak to the chapter chairperson. He or she can help direct you to local assistance. Check other chapters in your area (especially in larger, metropolitan areas). If all else fails, contact your assistant regional vice president for CPP matters or the regional vice president for assistance and information. A call to ASIS headquarters will give the name and phone number of these officers.

Once you have started your training program, set up a small study group among the CPP candidates in your chapter. A study group can be a great resource. Try to have persons engaged in various areas of security in your group. This way, you will obtain the benefit of the members' varied work experiences.

The expertise of the chapter members cannot be undervalued. Members need not be CPPs. I have found that most members are more than willing to share their knowledge and time to help you. By networking with these members, you can find new friendships and business resources as well.

SETTING UP YOUR STUDY PROGRAM

The CPP exam covers almost the entire spectrum of the security industry. You must know security management, physical security, investigation techniques, guard force management, substance abuse problems, legal issues, personnel protection, protection of sensitive information, interfacing with public-sector law enforcement, and much more.

As mentioned previously, no one segment of the security industry prepares you to address all of the areas necessary to be successful in taking the CPP exam. Therefore, a realistic, comprehensive, and measured approach must be taken when setting up your study program. Many CPP candidates fail to set up a realistic study program, or they inadequately prepare for the examination. These two shortfalls will doom many test takers to failure or a substandard test performance.

There should be three separate and distinct parts to your study program. The first is an individual study program. This must be a regular part of your schedule. It is a mistake to cram too much information into your head in too short a period of time. Put aside a portion of your lunch hour or a set time each evening to study. The time you choose to study can be important. If you try to study late in the evening when you are tired, you will not benefit from your efforts. Likewise, getting up early may be good for you, but give yourself time to wake up and have breakfast. Trying to study when your energy is low is also not a good idea. Do not try to do too much in one sitting. Consistency is the watchword when it comes to this portion of your study program.

The second part of your study program should take a more formal, educational approach. This is where your chapter CPP liaison or chairperson will be most helpful. Find out when and where your chapter's CPP preparation classes are held. If they do not have one, push to get a program started. Check with other nearby chapters; they may have one that you can attend. Attend all of the preparation classes, even the ones in which you believe yourself to be competent. You may be surprised that you can learn something even in these areas.

The third part of your program should be setting up a small study group. Try to find other candidates who can agree on a set day and time. It would be best if each member of the group had expertise and experience in varied segments of the security industry. You do not necessarily want four retail security experts in one study group.

HELPFUL HINTS

The following are some hints that can help you in studying for and taking the CPP exam.

1. Do not allow interruptions during either your study group or your private study. Turn off your cell phone and pager. Interruptions break up your concentration and make your efforts less productive.
2. In your studies, do not skip over areas you find difficult or boring. These are most likely the areas in which you will need the most help.
3. Keep your study efforts focused. Do not jump around. Pick a subject and scrutinize it until you have mastered the information you are required to know.
4. Be methodical and consistent in your efforts. A carefully laid-out approach to your study will be much more productive.
5. Take some planned breaks in your study. Preparing for the CPP exam is usually a long-term effort. Do not make it a marathon. Giving yourself time to relax and to digest the information you have gained will help you to retain the information better and will help prevent study burnout.

6. Seek out CPPs and ask for their advice. Many times, they will be able to give you valuable insights into taking the exam and answer technical questions on the subjects you are studying.
7. Be confident in your abilities. A defeatist attitude will doom you to failure.
8. Do not be in a rush to take the exam. Many candidates rush into taking the exam, setting themselves up for a failing score. This leads to a loss of self-confidence. There are many candidates who have never taken the exam a second time because of the first failure.
9. Plan a set time to do your studying and stick to it as much as possible. Do not try to study late at night when you are overly tired or early in the morning when you are not fully awake and your energy is low.
10. Periodically evaluate your progress and test yourself. This will give you an opportunity to determine how well you are understanding and retaining the material you are studying.
11. Remain focused on your eventual goal. Do not let yourself become discouraged. Eliminate unnecessary distractions.
12. *Do not* cram the night before the test. Rest and get a good night's sleep. If you do not know the material by then, you should reevaluate whether you should take the test at that time.
13. Have a good breakfast before taking the exam so your energy level will be high.

By setting up a balanced, focused, methodical study program, you will find that you enjoy your efforts more and retain more of what you learn. You will also vastly improve your chances of being successful in passing the exam.

THE TEST AND ADDITIONAL STUDY MATERIALS

EXAM STRUCTURE AND CONTENT

The CPP exam consists of 200 scored multiple-choice questions and may contain 25 "pretest" (unscored) questions randomly distributed throughout the examination, for a total of 225 questions. The time allowed takes into consideration the review of pretest items.

The exam covers tasks, knowledge, and skills in eight broad domains that have been identified by CPPs as the major areas involved in security management. All exam questions come from the official reference books. No questions on the exam are taken from any other source.

Domain 01: Security Principles and Practices (19%)

Task 01/01: Plan, organize, direct, and manage the organization's security program to avoid and/or control losses and apply the processes necessary to provide a secure work environment

Knowledge of
01/01/01—Principles of planning, organization, and control
01/01/02—Security theory, techniques, and processes

Task 01/02: Develop, manage, or conduct threat/vulnerability analyses to determine the probable frequency and severity of natural and man-made disasters and criminal activity and their effects on the organization's profitability and/or ability to deliver products/services

Knowledge of
01/02/01—Quantitative and qualitative risk assessments
01/02/02—Vulnerability analyses

Task 01/03: Evaluate methods to improve security and loss prevention systems on a continuous basis through the use of auditing, review, and assessment

Knowledge of
01/03/01—Cost–benefit analysis methods
01/03/02—Available security-related technology
01/03/03—Data collection and trend analysis techniques

Task 01/04: Develop and manage external relations programs with public-sector law enforcement or other external organizations to achieve loss prevention objectives

Knowledge of
01/04/01—Roles and responsibilities of external organizations and agencies
01/04/02—Methods for creating effective working relationships
01/04/03—Techniques and protocols of liaison

Task 01/05: Develop and present employee security awareness programs to achieve organizational goals and objectives

Knowledge of
     01/05/01—Training methodologies
     01/05/02—Communication strategies, techniques, and methods

Domain 02: Business Principles and Practices (11%)

Task 02/01: Develop and manage budgets and financial controls to achieve fiscal responsibility

Knowledge of
     02/01/01—Principles of management accounting, control, and audits
     02/01/02—Business finance principles and financial reporting
     02/01/03—Calculation and interpretation of return on investment (ROI)
     02/01/04—The life cycle for budget planning purposes

Task 02/02: Develop, implement, and manage policies, procedures, plans, and directives to achieve organizational objectives

Knowledge of
     02/02/01—Principles and techniques of policy/procedure development
     02/02/02—Communication strategies, methods, and techniques
     02/02/03—Training strategies, methods, and techniques
     02/02/04—Preventive and corrective maintenance for systems

Task 02/03: Develop procedures/techniques to measure and improve organizational productivity

Knowledge of
     02/03/01—Techniques for quantifying productivity/metrics/key performance indicators (KPIs)
     02/03/02—Data analysis techniques and ROI

Task 02/04: Develop, implement, and manage staffing, leadership, training, and management programs in order to achieve organizational objectives

Knowledge of
     02/04/01—Interview techniques for staffing
     02/04/02—Candidate selection and evaluation techniques
     02/04/03—Job analysis processes

02/04/04—Principles of performance evaluations, 360° reviews, and coaching

02/04/05—Interpersonal and feedback techniques

02/04/06—Training strategies, methodologies, and resources

02/04/07—Human capital management

Task 02/05: Monitor and ensure a sound ethical climate in accordance with the laws and the organization's directives and standards to support and promote proper business practices

Knowledge of

02/05/01—Good governance standards

02/05/02—Guidelines for individual and corporate behavior

02/05/03—Generally accepted ethical principles

02/05/04—Confidential information protection techniques and methods

Domain 03: Legal Aspects (7%)

Task 03/01: Develop and maintain security policies, procedures, and practices that comply with relevant elements of criminal, civil, administrative, and regulatory law to minimize adverse legal consequences

Knowledge of

03/01/01—Criminal law and procedures

03/01/02—Civil law and procedures

03/01/03—Homeland or national security procedures

03/01/04—Privacy laws and regulations

03/01/05—Information resources and methods of conducting legal research

Task 03/02: Provide coordination, assistance, and evidence such as documentation and testimony to support legal counsel in actual or potential criminal and/or civil proceedings

Knowledge of

03/02/01—Statutes, regulations, and case law governing or affecting the security industry and the protection of people, property, and information

03/02/02—Criminal law and procedures

03/02/03—Civil law and procedures

03/02/04—Employment law (e.g., wrongful termination, discrimination, and harassment)
03/02/05—Investigation processes
03/02/06—Preservation and rules of evidence
03/02/07—Fact-finding processes and techniques
03/02/08—Interview/interrogation processes and techniques

Task 03/03: Provide advice and assistance to management and others in developing performance requirements and contractual terms for security vendors/suppliers and establish effective monitoring processes to ensure that organizational needs and contractual requirements are being met

Knowledge of
03/03/01—Key concepts in the preparation of and/or response to requests for proposals
03/03/02—Contract law, indemnification, and liability insurance principles

Task 03/04: Provide assistance to management, legal counsel, and human resources in developing strategic and tactical plans for responding to labor disputes, including strikes

Knowledge of
03/04/01—Federal laws governing labor relations, including union and management issues

Task 03/05: Develop and maintain security policies, procedures, and practices that comply with relevant laws regarding investigations

Knowledge of
03/05/01—Laws pertaining to developing and managing investigative programs
03/05/02—Laws pertaining to the collection and preservation of evidence
03/05/03—Laws pertaining to managing surveillance processes
03/05/04—Laws pertaining to managing investigative interviews
03/05/05—Laws related to the rights of employees and the employer in conducting an investigation

Task 03/06: Develop and maintain security policies, procedures, and practices that comply with relevant laws regarding personnel security

Knowledge of
- 03/06/01—Laws pertaining to managing the background investigation process
- 03/06/02—Laws pertaining to personnel protection programs, methods, and techniques to provide a secure work environment
- 03/06/03—Laws pertaining to executive protection programs
- 03/06/04—Laws, government, and labor regulations regarding organizational efforts to reduce employee substance abuse

Task 03/07: Develop and maintain security policies, procedures, and practices that comply with relevant laws regarding information security

Knowledge of
- 03/07/01—Laws and regulatory requirements pertaining to protection requirements for proprietary information and intellectual property

Domain 04: Personnel Security (12%)

Task 04/01: Develop, implement, and manage, background investigations to validate individuals for hiring, promotion, or retention

Knowledge of
- 04/01/01—Background investigations and employment screening techniques
- 04/01/02—Information source quality and types

Task 04/02: Develop, implement, manage, and evaluate policies, procedures, programs, and methods to protect individuals in the workplace against harassment, threats, and violence

Knowledge of
- 04/02/01—Protection techniques and methods
- 04/02/02—Threat assessment analysis
- 04/02/03—Intervention and response tactics
- 04/02/04—Educational and awareness program design and implementation
- 04/02/05—Travel security programs

Task 04/03: Develop, implement, and manage executive protection programs

Knowledge of
>04/03/01—Executive protection techniques and methods
>04/03/02—Risk analysis
>04/03/03—Liaison and resource management techniques
>04/03/04—Selection, costs, and effectiveness of proprietary and contract executive protection personnel
>04/03/05—Travel security programs

Domain 05: Physical Security (25%)

Task 05/01: Survey facilities in order to manage and/or evaluate the current status of physical security, emergency, and/or restoration capabilities

Knowledge of
>05/01/01—Types and applications of, and protection offered by, protection equipment
>05/01/02—Survey techniques
>05/01/03—Building plans, drawings, and schematics
>05/01/04—Risk assessment techniques

Task 05/02: Select, implement, and manage security processes to reduce the risk of loss

Knowledge of
>05/02/01—Fundamentals of security system design
>05/02/02—Countermeasures
>05/02/03—Budgetary projection development process
>05/02/04—Bid package development and evaluation process
>05/02/05—Vendor qualification and selection process
>05/02/06—Final acceptance and testing procedures
>05/02/07—Project management techniques
>05/02/08—Cost–benefit analysis techniques

Task 05/03: Assess the effectiveness of the security measures by testing and monitoring

Knowledge of
>05/03/01—Protection technology and systems
>05/03/02—Audit and testing techniques

Domain 06: Information Security (8%)

Task 06/01: Survey information facilities, processes, and systems to evaluate current status of the following: physical security, procedural security, information systems security, employee awareness, and information destruction and recovery capabilities

Knowledge of
> 06/01/01—Security survey and risk assessment methodology, qualitative and quantitative risk analysis, and cost–benefit analysis of protective measures
> 06/01/02—Protection technology, equipment, and procedures
> 06/01/03—Current methods used to compromise information
> 06/01/04—Building and system plans, drawings, and schematics

Task 06/02: Develop and implement policies and standards to ensure that information is evaluated and protected against all forms of unauthorized/inadvertent access, use, disclosure, modification, destruction, or denial

Knowledge of
> 06/02/01—Principles of management
> 06/02/02—Information security theory and terminology
> 06/02/03—Laws pertaining to protection requirements for proprietary information and intellectual property
> 06/02/04—Protection measures, equipment, and techniques, including information security processes, systems for physical access, data control, management, and information destruction

Task 06/03: Develop and manage a program of integrated security controls and safeguards to ensure confidentiality, integrity, availability, authentication, nonrepudiation, accountability, recoverability, and auditability of sensitive information and associated information technology resources, assets, and investigations

Knowledge of
> 06/03/01—Information security theory and systems methodology
> 06/03/02—Threat and vulnerability assessment analysis and mitigation
> 06/03/03—Systems integration techniques

06/03/04—Cost–benefit analysis methodology
06/03/05—Project management techniques
06/03/06—Budgetary projection development process
06/03/07—Vendor evaluation and selection process
06/03/08—Final acceptance and testing procedures, information systems, assessment, and security program documentation
06/03/09—Protection technology, equipment, investigations, and procedures
06/03/10—Training and awareness methodologies and procedures

Domain 07: Crisis Management (8%)

Task 07/01: Assess and prioritize risks to mitigate potential consequences of incidents

Knowledge of
07/01/01—All hazards by type, likelihood of occurrence, and consequences
07/01/02—Cost–benefit analysis
07/01/03—Mitigation strategies
07/01/04—Risk management and business impact analysis methodology
07/01/05—Making the business case to management

Task 07/02: Prepare and plan how the organization will respond to incidents

Knowledge of
07/02/01—Resource management techniques
07/02/02—Emergency planning techniques
07/02/03—Communication techniques
07/02/04—Training and exercise techniques
07/02/05—Emergency operations center (EOC) concepts and design
07/02/06—Primary roles and duties in an incident command structure

Task 07/03: Respond to and manage an incident

Knowledge of
07/03/01—Resource management techniques
07/03/02—EOC management principles and practices

Task 07/04: Recover from incidents by managing the recovery and resumption of operations

Knowledge of
07/04/01—Resource management techniques
07/04/02—Short- and long-term recovery strategies
07/04/03—Recovery assistance resources
07/04/04—Mitigation opportunities in the recovery process

Domain 08: Investigations (10%)

Task 08/01: Develop and manage investigation programs

Knowledge of
08/01/01—Principles and techniques of policy and procedure development
08/01/02—Organizational objectives and interdepartmental liaison
08/01/03—Relevant sources of investigation
08/01/04—Report preparation for internal and court purposes

Task 08/02: Manage or conduct the collection and preservation of evidence to support postinvestigation actions (employee discipline, criminal or civil proceedings, arbitration)

Knowledge of
08/02/01—Evidence collection techniques
08/02/02—Protection/preservation of crime scene
08/02/03—Requirements of chain of custody
08/02/04—Methods for preservation of evidence

Task 08/03: Manage or conduct surveillance processes

Knowledge of
08/03/01—Surveillance techniques
08/03/02—Technology/equipment and human resources

Task 08/04: Manage and conduct specialized investigations

Knowledge of
08/04/01—Financial and fraud-related crimes
08/04/02—Computer-based and Internet crimes

08/04/03—Proprietary information and industrial espionage crimes
08/04/04—Arson and criminal damage crimes

Task 08/05: Manage or conduct investigative interviews

Knowledge of
08/05/01—Methods and techniques of eliciting information
08/05/02—Techniques for detecting deception
08/05/03—The nature of nonverbal communication
08/05/04—The use of human rights codes for cautioned statements
08/05/05—Required components of written statements

ADDITIONAL STUDY MATERIALS

ASIS Disaster Management, *Emergency Planning Handbook*, 2nd ed., Alexandria, VA: ASIS International, 2003.

ASIS International, *Protection of Assets (POA) Manual*, Alexandria, VA, 2004.

Broder, James F., *Risk Analysis and the Security Survey*, 2nd ed., Waltham, MA: Butterworth-Heinemann, 2000.

Fay, John J., Ed., *Encyclopedia of Security Management*, Burlington, MA: Butterworth-Heinemann, 1993.

O'Hara, Charles E. and Gregory L. O'Hara, *Fundamentals of Criminal Investigation*, 7th ed., Springfield, IL: Charles C. Thomas, 2003.

Purpura, Philip P., *Security and Loss Prevention: An Introduction*, 4th ed., Waltham, MA: Butterworth-Heinemann, 2002.

Robbins, Stephen P., *Managing Today!*, 2nd ed., Englewood Cliffs, NJ: Prentice-Hall, 2000.

Sennewald, Charles A., *Process of Investigation: Concepts and Strategies for Investigators in the Private Sector*, 2nd ed., Burlington, MA: Butterworth-Heinemann, 2001.

Sennewald, Charles A., *Effective Security Management*, 4th ed., Burlington, MA: Butterworth-Heinemann, 2003.

Whitman, Michael E. and Herbert J. Mattord, *Management of Information Security*, Boston: Cengage Learning, 2004.

2 Security Management

More and more today, the security professional must be an accomplished businessperson as well as a security practitioner. The role of the security manager/director has evolved in the past 20 years. He or she must be as comfortable with preparing financial spreadsheets and developing budgets as with conducting investigations and managing security personnel.

Therefore, built into this chapter and, to some extent, other chapters are the key areas of study for these domains. Some of the key areas are developing and managing your department's budget, interfacing with other department heads and upper-level management, and dealing with outside contracts and law enforcement/regulatory agencies.

OVERVIEW

"Security management" is an umbrella term that covers many duties, responsibilities, and tasks. Gone are the days when a security manager simply supervised a few security officers or maybe a receiver on the loading dock. Closed-circuit television (CCTV) and alarm systems were rudimentary, at best. Everything was low tech, and very little management skill was required.

Today, the security profession has grown and evolved into a very sophisticated, high-tech profession. The modern security manager or director wears many hats. He or she must be educated in the planning, layout, and use of alarm systems, CCTV, and access control systems; background investigations, criminal, and civil investigations; the use of undercover operatives; guard force management; criminal and civil law; privacy laws; union rights; the use and implementation of drug-screening programs; interaction with management and the criminal justice system; interrogation techniques; and much, much more.

The security manager must also be able to manage, train, and inspire the employees under his or her direct control. All of this can seem to be an overwhelming task, and it requires training, education, experience, and dedication.

This is why a large number of the questions on the Certified Protection Professional (CPP) exam fall under the general heading of security management. The Professional Certification Board claims the CPP to be board certified in security management in all of its material.

In this chapter, we address the definitions, concepts, and principles you need to study and be familiar with for the security management portion of the test. Other areas, which, in a larger sense, could be viewed as security management topics, will be covered in other, more specific chapters, such as Chapters 3 and 5.

USEFUL DEFINITIONS

The following is a list of commonly used terms and definitions that you will be expected to know for the CPP examination:

1. Line executives: those who are delegated chain-of-command authority to accomplish specific objectives in the organization.
2. Staff functions: functions that are advisory or service oriented to the line executive.
3. As a general rule, the security manager or director serves in a staff capacity when his or her role is as an advisor to a superior executive.
4. When the security manager or director exercises authority delegated by the senior executive to whom he or she reports, he or she is exercising functional authority.
5. The security manager or director exercises full line authority over his or her own department.
6. From an organizational standpoint, security cuts across departmental lines and relates to the activity of the company.
7. Delegation of authority: this is a must. The degree to which a security manager or director is able to delegate responsibility is a measure of his or her leadership ability.
8. The single most common management weakness is the failure to properly delegate responsibility and the authority to carry it out.
9. Chain of command: the path along which authority flows.
10. Span of control: the number of personnel over which any individual can exercise direct supervision effectively.
11. Security management should only directly supervise security personnel.
12. Unity of command: where an employee should be under the direct control of only one superior.
13. There are six basic principles of organization:
    a. A logical division of work
    b. Clear lines of authority as set forth in the organizational chart
    c. Limited span of control
    d. Unity of command
    e. Proper delegation of responsibility and authority
    f. Coordination of efforts through training and communication

14. The two key points to remember about an organizational chart are as follows:
    a. The horizontal plane indicates the division of areas of responsibility.
    b. The vertical plane defines the levels of authority.
15. For an organizational structure to be most effective, it should be flexible.
16. A security director from an effective organizational standpoint should report to the highest-ranking corporate officer possible.

MANAGEMENT THEORIES

In the study of security management there, are several theories involving motivation of employees and styles of management. These will, in some way, be reflected on the exam. It is also important for the security manager or director to be familiar with them.

MASLOW'S THEORY

Dr. Abraham Maslow developed a five-step process that describes human behavior in terms of the needs that are experienced. These needs are as follows:

- Basic needs, such as food and shelter
- The need for safety, such as security, protection, and avoidance of harm and risk
- The need to belong, such as membership and acceptance by a group and its members
- The need for ego status, such as achieving some special recognition
- The need to self-actualize, such as being given assignments that are challenging and meaningful and allow for creativity

MOTIVATION–HYGIENE THEORY

Frederick Herzberg's motivation–hygiene theory is another of the basic management theories that are relevant to the exam.

Herzberg defines two different categories of needs, independent of each other. The two categories are as follows:

1. Hygiene factors:
   - Salary
   - Fringe benefits
   - Security

- Rules and regulations
- Supervision
2. Motivators:
   - Challenging assignments
   - Increased responsibilities
   - Recognition for work
   - Individual growth

Herzberg believed that hygiene factors do not produce growth in the individual or increase work output but that they do prevent losses in performance.

On the other hand, Herzberg felt that motivators had positive effects on employees, resulting in increased job satisfaction and increased total output capacity.

There is a close relationship between Herzberg's theory of motivation and Maslow's theory. Herzberg's theory is also known as the "work motivation theory" in that genuine motivation comes from work itself and not from so-called hygiene factors.

THEORY X

Theory X was developed by Douglas McGregor. McGregor believed that traditional managers have certain basic assumptions, which he labeled as Theory X. He defined them as follows:

- It is management's role to organize resources in a structure, which requires close supervision of all employees and brings about maximum control.
- It is management's responsibility to direct the efforts of the personnel of the agency, to keep them motivated, to control all their actions, and to modify their behavior to fit the needs of the organization.
- If management does not take an active part in controlling the behavior of the employees, they will be passive to the needs of the organization.
- The average employee is naturally lazy and will work as little as possible.
- The average employee lacks ambition, dislikes responsibility and authority, and prefers taking orders to being independent.
- The employee is basically self-centered, has no feeling for organizational needs, and must be closely controlled.
- By nature, the average employee resists change.
- The average employee does not have the ability to solve problems creatively.

Theory X is not an unpopular theory today. Theory X managers motivate employees by attempting to satisfy basic and safety needs.

THEORY Y

Theory Y, also developed by Douglas McGregor, has the following assumptions:

- It is management's role to organize resources to reach organizational goals.
- Work can be an enjoyable part of one's life if the conditions are favorable.
- People are not naturally lazy, passive, or resistant to the needs of the organization but have become so as a result of their experiences working within the organization.
- Management does not place the potential for development within the employee. It is management's responsibility to recognize the potential that is present within each individual and allow the individual the freedom to develop his or her abilities.
- People possess creativity and can solve organizational problems if encouraged by management.
- The essential task of management is to develop organizational conditions and operational procedures so the individual can attain his or her goals by directing efforts toward organizational goals and objectives.

Security officers in a Theory Y organization achieve satisfaction for their ego and self-actualization needs. The assumptions of Theory Y produce an environment that truly motivates employees.

IMMATURITY–MATURITY THEORY

Chris Argis developed the immaturity–maturity theory.

Argis listed seven changes that should occur in the employee's personality if he or she is to develop into a mature person and be an asset to the organization:

1. From passive to active
2. From restrictive behavior patterns to diversified behavior
3. From dependence to independence
4. From erratic shallow interests to deeper and stronger interests
5. From short-term perspective to long-term perspective
6. From subordinate position to an equal or superior position
7. From lack of self-awareness to awareness and control over self

The prime point in this theory is that there is a challenge to management to provide a work climate in which every employee has the opportunity to mature.

Autocratic Theory

The autocratic theory dates back to the Industrial Revolution of the 1750s. The manager's position under this theory is one of formal and official authority. Under this theory, management has complete control over the employee. This theory gets results up to a point but does nothing to develop the potential of the employee.

Custodial Theory

This theory's aim is to make the employee happy and contented through the wealth of the company, which provides economic benefits to the employee. This theory does not adequately motivate the employee. Employees look in areas other than the job to secure fulfillment or challenge.

Supportive Theory

The prime element of this theory is leadership; managers think in terms of "we" rather than "they." Little supervision is required, as employees will take on added responsibility with the knowledge that support is available from the supervisory level of management.

Ten Deadly Demotivators

The "ten deadly demotivators" formulated by Dr. Mortimer Feinberg in his book *Effective Psychology for Managers* are as follows:

- Never belittle a subordinate.
- Never criticize a subordinate in front of others.
- Never fail to give your subordinate your full attention.
- Never give your subordinate the impression that you are mainly concerned with your own interests.
- Never play favorites.
- Never fail to help your subordinates grow, when they are deserving.
- Never be insensitive to small things.
- Never "show up" employees.
- Never lower your personal standards.
- Never vacillate in making a decision.

Key Qualities of a Successful Security Manager

The key qualities of a successful security manager are as follows:

- Patience
- Wisdom
- Virtue
- Empathy
- Kindness
- Trust
- Knowledge
- Self-control

SELECTION OF OUTSIDE SERVICES

Another critical area, which the security manager or director must be able to handle in an effective manner, is the management of the guard force assigned to the company's facilities.

Depending on the type, size, and number of the facilities, you may be responsible for one or two employees or a staff of a hundred or more employees. This staff may include uniformed officers, investigators, receivers, auditors, shipping order checkers, CCTV/alarm technicians, and, at times, undercover and surveillance specialists.

Very few organizations will have the resources to contain all of these services in-house. Many times, these services will be contracted for with outside providers. The following are some of the ways organizations will use outside suppliers either alone or in conjunction with in-house resources.

Many organizations will contract out the guard force to companies that specialize in supplying such services. The motivating factors behind this decision are mainly financial. Contracting for guards is less expensive when you take into account salaries, benefits, taxes, insurance, recruitment and training costs, overtime, holidays, uniforming costs, and the costs of preparing and auditing payrolls.

Other benefits to the company include more flexibility in the usage of manpower. The company does not have to absorb the cost of recruiting, interviewing, and investigating applicant backgrounds, or training and uniforming replacement officers or temporary officers for emergency situations.

Many companies blend in-house and contract officers. They will contract for the line officers for the cost benefits while using in-house supervisors to keep tighter control over the guard force operations.

There are definite benefits to using contract officers, but there are many problems as well. Establishing some well-defined conditions within the scope of the contract can eliminate many of the problems encountered when utilizing contract officers.

Proper selection of the company to be used is of paramount importance. It is not always important that the company is extremely large or known nationwide to be able to supply a quality service. There are several areas to be checked when considering which company to select:

- Does the company have a reputation for providing a quality service and for living up to its promises?
- What are the professional backgrounds of the persons who own and run the company?
- Does the company have the manpower and financial recourses to fulfill the contract?
- Does the company carry sufficient liability, vehicle, and worker's comp insurance to properly protect the client?
- Is the company properly licensed in the areas in which you require service?
- Can the company provide various ancillary services you may require, or do you have to find other suppliers?
- What procedures does the company use for recruiting, hiring, and screening applicants?
- Will the company allow you to review and possibly sit in on their training programs?
- Are their officers bonded, and do they drug screen their employees?
- If required, can the company provide officers with specialized training (i.e., first aid, cardiopulmonary resuscitation [CPR], computer training, etc.)?

If you can determine in advance the answers to these needs and questions, you will be better able to select a company that will meet your requirements.

Once you have selected one or more companies you may wish to employ, your next step is to interview the highest executive available. Visit their offices; see firsthand if they have the equipment, personnel, and facilities they claim to have. Obtain at least three references, preferably in the same type of service you require, and then check them out.

Monitor their training programs to establish whether or not they meet your needs and if they meet with existing criteria for training of security personnel. If site-specific training will be required, ascertain if the programs can be made to meet those requirements.

Check with whatever state agency regulates the security industry and make sure the company's license is current. Verify their insurance and establish that it meets or exceeds your company's criteria. Ascertain if there are any complaints on record and what those complaints involved; check to see if there has been any disciplinary action taken against either the company or one of their principals. Check with civil records regarding the company to determine if there have been lawsuits filed against the company; if so, find out what the circumstances were and what the outcomes were, if applicable.

In most states, company files are, to some extent, public information. These files will provide you with information about an owner's background and experience. This will help you to decide if the owner's expertise meets your needs. Look not only for experience but also for education and professional certifications, such as holding a CPP designation. Once you have accomplished your due diligence, the cost factor can then be added to your decision making.

There are benefits to having a supplier who can provide a variety of needs, such as guards, background investigations, undercover operatives, surveillance, shopping services, polygraph services, etc. However, do a due diligence on each service you require. Just because a company may be a good guard agency does not necessarily mean that it has the expertise to provide investigative services.

Finally, obtain a copy of their service agreement or have your legal department draw up one for the company to sign. Check it for cost breakdowns, overtime factors for special requests, expense charges, hold-harmless agreements, and insurance limits, and make sure any special requirements you have determined necessary are delineated in the contract.

Once all of your inquiries have been conducted and all pertinent information has been gathered, it will be considerably easier to make a proper selection.

FINANCIAL RESPONSIBILITIES

One of the duties of the security manager or director is to formulate security budgets with which to run his or her operations. Besides salaries and the applicable taxes, there must be money allotted for equipment purchases and upgrades, outside security and investigative services, supplies, and emergency situations that may arise.

It is a sad fact that many companies look upon the security department as a necessary evil, a profit-taking, non-revenue-generating, department. In today's world, security is essential to any company's financial well-being. Besides safeguarding the company's profit, property, and proprietary information, the security department is charged with the protection of the company's greatest asset: the personnel. Without proper financing, these responsibilities cannot be fulfilled. A well-prepared budget presented to the company in a clearly thought-out, logical manner is the best way to ensure proper financing.

Reports that are supplied on a regular basis, are well documented, and outline the security department's activities, goals, and successes can establish the worth of the security operation to upper management.

When formulating a budget, there will be three distinct areas to be considered. The first is your fixed operational costs. This consists of payroll, taxes, and payments on vehicle leases or rental equipment, such as repeater costs or postage machines. The second is costs that are necessary but are not fixed. This covers costs that routinely fluctuate (i.e., fuel costs and the use of outside security and investigative costs). The third area is a capital budget for major capital budget purchases. These would include new vehicles, expensive equipment, and uniforms.

When considering how much is going to be required for funding the fixed-costs portion of the budget, your budget history will be of great help. If you research the past several quarters, you will be able to determine your historical manpower utilization and thereby your projected manpower costs.

Carefully review your overtime costs. Overtime costs can eat up your budget very quickly and cause you to have budget shortfalls. First, analyze why the overtime was necessary. Was the overtime caused when the company encountered problems, which required extra coverage? Was it caused by call-offs due to illness or officers quitting without proper notice? In the case of illness or the loss of personnel, you may be able to hire part-time or on-call workers. This type of employee could be used to eliminate the more costly overtime and can also help if a security problem arises that requires additional coverage.

You must also take into account vacation relief and the requirements that the influx of seasonal obligations has on your payroll. Your budget history can aid you in making these determinations. You need to also project added costs due to predetermined raises, government-mandated costs, or escalating costs of benefits, such as medical insurance, sick leave, tuition reimbursement, etc. Meet with upper management and establish if there is growth projected that will require additional manpower utilization in the upcoming budget. By looking ahead, you can be better prepared to meet the security needs of your employer.

Review the other fixed costs in your budget. Determine if these costs are really necessary or if they are there because "that's the way it has always been done." You need to continually look for better and more cost-effective ways to accomplish what needs to be done. When contracts for outside services or products are due for renewal, investigate other alternatives. You may find that another option is more cost-effective and provides you with better service. However, do not allow yourself to be caught in the low-cost trap. Always opt for quality of service and performance rather than just cost savings.

DISCIPLINARY PROCEDURES

Disciplining employees is difficult for all managers. Everyone likes to be the "good guy" and not the one who hands out punishment or must terminate fellow employees. However, discipline is a vital part of any organization. In order for any organization to operate smoothly and efficiently, discipline is a necessary occurrence.

Before a company's disciplinary policy can be effectively implemented, there must be a written policy that is distributed to all personnel so everyone is aware of exactly what the organization's policies are. Employees should receive a copy of both the policy and the disciplinary procedure and should sign a form acknowledging receipt and their agreement to abide by the policy. This signed form should be retained by the department of human resources in the employee's file.

In order for a disciplinary policy to be effective and not detrimental to the organization, there are several things that it must be:

- The policy must make sense and should be reasonable. It cannot violate either state or federal labor law.
- Discipline must be fairly meted out without favoritism or prejudice.
- Discipline must be proportional to the offense committed.
- Discipline must be progressive.
- Employees must have recourse if they believe they have been disciplined unfairly or too harshly.
- All disciplinary actions taken must be completely documented and reviewed.

It is important that strict control be maintained over who recommends that disciplinary action be taken and who gives final approval for the discipline to be implemented. Either the head of a department or a member of the human resources department must handle termination of employees. The violation should be clear-cut, documented, and the accepted punishment for the offense(s) committed.

Possible disciplinary actions would include the following:

- A verbal warning with or without counseling
- A written warning
- A suspension (the length may vary based on the infraction and the employee's disciplinary history)
- Demotion
- Termination

Another issue that must be considered is whether or not the company has a collective bargaining agreement with a union. This agreement may very well spell out what disciplinary actions may be taken. It will also mandate union representation.

In the case of an investigative interview or interrogation, you may have to permit a union representative to observe the process, but not unless the employee requests such an observer and the representative may not inter-fere in the process. If the representative does intervene, he or she may be excluded from observation.

One more basic principle of effective management is that you always praise in public and reprimand in private. Too many managers criticize and hold employees out for humiliation in front of their peers and, worse yet, their sub-ordinates. This practice only breeds resentment and encourages bitterness and disloyalty from the person punished. It will also adversely affect the other employees who see this happen, many of whom will be offended by what they see and will become unwilling to try to advance or stay with the company, fearing the same type of situation will happen to them. Someone who has suf-fered such a humiliation may also become both a disciplinary problem and a security risk as a desire for revenge takes hold. From this revenge motive come theft, industrial espionage, and the spreading of dissatisfaction and sabotage. It is the security manager's job to prevent these behaviors. Make sure public displays of discipline do not occur in the first place. Do not permit the fertile ground to exist that permits these problems to take root and grow.

DELEGATION OF RESPONSIBILITY AND AUTHORITY

One of the biggest mistakes managers make is to fail to properly delegate both responsibility and authority. Some managers like to micromanage everything that their departments carry out. This stifles the creativity and development of employees. At the same time, always macromanaging everything can cause failure of a project because no one is taking respon-sibility to see that the job gets done properly.

One of a manager's responsibilities is to train those under him or her to be able to replace him or her, if necessary. A good manager encourages those employees who show the ability and initiative to grow and take on more responsibility.

Once you have delegated the responsibility to someone to accomplish a certain goal, you must also delegate the authority he or she will require to accomplish that goal. One always goes hand in hand with the other.

It is a good idea to have meetings with employees on a regular basis. This allows you to monitor the progress of the project and the employees' ability to perform. It also allows the employees an opportunity to ask ques-tions or seek advice should they need to do so.

Some of the major benefits to the company utilizing such a practice are as follows:

- Worthy employees are given an opportunity to grow and expand their capabilities.
- Future management personnel are nurtured and trained.

- The employees see there is opportunity to advance with the company and add to the worth of their employer.
- Many new ideas and processes are developed in such an atmosphere.
- The company prospers under such a program, which in turn helps all employees.
- The ability to have this "backup management" in place provides for continuity in administration in case of illness, death, retirement, or turnover in management personnel. This also gives the manager more opportunities for growth because he or she has trained personnel ready to step up should he or she be promoted. Many times, employees are held back from achieving better positions because properly trained replacements are not available.

MEDIA RELATIONS

There are times when the security manager must deal with the print and electronic media. Some of these times could be the following:

- Your specific company or industry becomes the focus of an investigative story.
- The company is involved in a labor dispute.
- Terrorist activities.
- A natural disaster affects your firm.
- A criminal act highlights your firm.

It is important at these times to handle all interaction with the media in a correct manner. The company should speak with one voice; the outgoing flow of information, especially if it refers to an ongoing investigation, should be carefully considered so the integrity of the investigation and the privacy and constitutional rights of the parties involved are observed.

The company must also consider the public relations aspect when dealing with the media. Unfortunately, some members of the media wish only to sell papers or increase their viewership. At times, stories are sensationalized for those purposes. Therefore, the following program should be set up and personnel trained beforehand so that the media relations program can be immediately and effectively implemented if the need arises.

- An emergency committee should be put together and properly trained. This committee should have, as its chairperson, the highest-ranking corporate officer possible.
- The committee should consist of a media consultant along with representation from the legal department, public relations, security,

human resources, finance, risk management, and the insurance carrier.

- All personnel, especially security, should be briefed and instructed to make no comments but to refer all inquiries to the designated person who will act as the official spokesperson for the company.

A full committee such as this is only for major media situations. For routine interactions with the media, a public relations person should be utilized. A ranking member of management, the security manager, or a human resources representative can also be used. No matter whom the company selects for this responsibility, the media spokesperson should receive specialized training.

TRAINING OF PERSONNEL

As a security manager, it is your responsibility to make sure all of your security personnel are properly trained for their job responsibilities. Inadequate training is one of the reasons most commonly cited in security liability lawsuits. The other reasons are improper screening, hiring of personnel, and inadequate supervision.

Training basically falls into three general areas. They are as follows:

1. *Job- and site-specific training.* This covers company rules and regulations, specific job functions as they relate to that site, training on camera and alarm systems, post orders, patrol functions, etc.
2. *Legal or educational training.* This covers such topics as use of force, criminal law, criminal procedure, search and seizure, report writing, interview techniques, radio procedures, etc.
3. *Weaponry training.* This all-inclusive term would cover the use of items such as handcuffs, batons, chemical agents, and firearms.

It is of the utmost importance that you are fully compliant with any local, state, and federal laws, especially as they relate to the possession and use of the weapons enumerated here. Check and ascertain if the state requires specific training or special licensing for these items.

Make sure that any instructors or lesson plans have been certified and can stand up to challenges in court. All training received should be fully documented and should describe the type of instruction received, the date and location of instruction, and the name of instructor used. A copy of the test should also be retained.

Along with training, there must be a written policy in place outlining when force can be utilized; what weaponry, if any, can be carried; and the rules governing their use. Every officer or investigator should receive this training. A regular program of follow-up training should be given and documented so ongoing training will establish the company's legal position. Any outside vendors that supply the company with these types of services should provide this same level of training and must agree to abide by all company rules, regulations, and procedures. Insist on documentation for all training and licensing of outside personnel.

ARMING OF PERSONNEL

The choice to arm your security personnel is a decision that requires a great deal of thought and consultation with corporate management and the company legal team. It is not a decision that should be entered into rashly or without proper consideration. There is a process that should be used beforehand in making that all-important decision. This process should include answering the following questions:

1. Why do you want to arm the security personnel? Deadly force is not used to protect property, only lives. Some businesses, by virtue of their activities, may require officers to be armed. Some examples are nuclear power stations, power plants, hydroelectric facilities, government facilities, armored car transport units, ATM response units, businesses in high-crime areas, and other businesses engaged in the transport of highly valued merchandise. Your reasons should be carefully considered before you move to arm your personnel. The liability of your company when you arm your personnel goes up tremendously.
2. What is your corporate philosophy relative to the arming of the security force? Many corporations are against firearms as a policy of the corporation. If this is the case, then you will have a major hurdle to overcome.
3. What are the liability issues that arise from arming company personnel? Review all of the legal and financial liabilities. Determine if the need actually outweighs the potential liabilities the company could incur.
4. Will your insurance cover or allow the arming of personnel? Consult with your insurance company. Many insurance companies will not allow the arming of security personnel. If they do, you can expect a drastic rise in premiums to obtain the necessary coverage. Insurance agents may also want to attach special conditions such as specialized training, more extensive background checks, and limitations on calibers or weapons and configuration of bullets.

5. What are the current local and state firearms laws? Check out your local and state laws as they pertain to the use of weapons. There may be licensing requirements, training requirements, and, of course, laws governing the use of both physical and deadly force.

6. Does the company have both a firearms policy and a use-of-force policy in place? After the officers receive training in these areas, it is important that they sign a certificate acknowledging the fact that they were trained in these policies and that they agree to abide by the terms and conditions of these policies. A separate policy regarding makes, calibers, and sizes of weapons that are authorized should also be produced. (You will most likely have to consult with your insurance company about these policies as well.)

7. Is arming personnel a financially viable option? After all of the consultation and research has been accomplished and you have determined the financial impact of these proposed changes, you will then be able to make a considered opinion as to whether or not it is wise to arm personnel.

CONCLUDING THOUGHTS

There are many other areas that a security manager or director must be knowledgeable about and deal with on a regular basis. Some of these issues that have not been mentioned include internal/external investigations, drug use in the workplace, workplace violence, interfacing with all levels of law enforcement, protection of confidential information, and more. I have purposely not addressed these issues, as they will be discussed in more detail in their respective chapters.

There is a great deal of knowledge and expertise that the security manager must possess and master. The entire field of security is an ever-growing and evolving entity. Not only must you master today's concepts and disciplines, but you must also always strive to stay abreast of new technologies, court decisions, and policies. Only by doing so can you truly consider yourself to be a professional.

3 Investigations

The ability to effectively and, above all, legally conduct an in-house investigation is of great importance in the security field. An illegally conducted investigation can spell personal, financial, and professional disaster for all involved. The security professional must have a working knowledge of the laws pertinent to conducting internal investigations, suspects' rights, modern methodology used in these investigations, and the use of outside resources and interaction with the proper law enforcement organizations. The tools of an investigator, also know as the three "I's" will also be explored. They are information, interrogation, and instrumentation. Information is the knowledge that the investigator obtains from other persons; interrogation is the skillful questioning of witnesses as well as suspects; and instrumentation is physical science methods used to detect crime.

This chapter deals with those subjects in a manner that provides guidance not only in the preparation for the Certified Protection Professional (CPP) exam but also for your professional career.

INTRODUCTION

WHAT IS AN INVESTIGATOR?

An investigator is an individual who is resourceful, has good observation skills, and has a desire to learn the truth and follow through to the end relentlessly. An investigator must be unbiased, be unprejudiced, and not allow personal likes and dislikes to interfere with an investigation. An investigator uses street smarts and good listening skills, is polite and respectful, and is adaptable to whatever situation he or she is presented with.

An investigator has high ethical values that guide behavior. An investigator must observe and adhere to the principles of honesty, goodwill, accuracy, discretion, and integrity. He or she must be faithful, diligent, and honorable in carrying out assignments, and must be in charge of professional responsibilities that promote clearly defined standards required of all professional investigators. A professional investigator observes all federal and state laws and does not violate them in any manner. Professionals should be committed to continually endeavoring to maintain integrity and trust in accordance with the highest moral principles.

Since 9/11, the need for professional investigators has increased dramatically to assist in providing additional security everywhere. 9/11 opened the door to a whole new need for investigative services in many areas, which include background checks and investigations of theft, burglary, and vandalism. This list goes on and on. Individuals, corporations, and small businesses have come to realize that investigators are necessary because of their resourcefulness in gathering factual information.

In addition to the environment caused by 9/11, the continual demand for investigators is also due to the increase in population, economic growth and activity, and domestic and global competition. Crime is on the rise, and investigators will be called on more than ever to gather evidence for individuals, companies, and government agencies, including federal, state, and local departments. Law enforcement agencies are also becoming more dependent on the private security industry. A lack of manpower and resources has limited or prohibited their ability to handle the overload.

The future for investigators and for those pursuing private investigations as a career is promising to all. It is the most challenging, interesting, intriguing, romantic, and, ultimately, exciting profession. Today, forensic tools allow more cases to be solved with more certainty than ever before. Modern technologies, such as ballistics, DNA profiling, genetic fingerprinting, blood analysis, and serology, just to name a few, are on the cutting edge and are state-of-the-art tools for the contemporary investigator.

As this trend continues, the investigator now realizes that his or her credentials and abilities can dictate future success. Continued education is mandatory to survive. ASIS stands united in its effort to promote and support all professional efforts to educate the investigator.

CODE OF ETHICS OF THE INVESTIGATOR

The purpose of ethical business practices is to provide, in conjunction with laws, a structure that will promote the greatest interests of the profession and the public and protect them from illegal or unethical performance.

Confidentiality and Privacy

The purpose of confidentiality is to safeguard privileged communication and information that is obtained in the course of business. Disclosure of information is restricted to what is necessary, relevant, and verifiable with respect to the client's right to privacy. An investigator must not disclose, relate, or betray in any fashion the trust placed in him or her by the client, employer, or associate. An investigator's duty is to preserve the client's confidence by protecting confidential information and not breaching confidentiality through the disclosure of private information to anyone without the client's knowledge and consent. Professional files, reports, and records should be maintained under conditions of security with provisions made for their destruction when appropriate.

Truth

Investigators fulfill an obligation of commitment to serve the client's interest and an obligation to determine facts and render honest, unbiased, and complete reports. They support the search for truth and disclose whatever discovery was made to the client.

Keeping Informed

Investigators have an obligation to maintain technical competency at such a level that the client receives the highest quality of services that the investigator can offer. Keeping informed of developments and changes in local, state, and federal laws; public policies; and forensic and technical advances is a top priority.

Business Conduct

Investigators do not engage in illegal or unethical practices. They do not maliciously injure or defame the professional reputation of colleagues, clients, or employers. They support law enforcement and promote fidelity to trust, which is built by character and conduct. They do not become involved in an investigation on behalf of a client with the intent to break the law or unethically use the information obtained. They do not mislead the public by false advertising with personal qualifications that are not possessed or by advertising services not available. They carry professional liability insurance for their own protection and for the protection of clients.

Conflicts of Interest

Investigators refrain from accepting an assignment or employment if the assignment would create a personal or professional conflict of interest with previous or current investigations. They do not engage in work for one client against the interest of another client, and they do not enter into fee arrangements for illegal or improper services or accept gratuities or gifts that would likely create conflicts of interest or influence testimony in any matter.

An investigator must be a professional in everything he or she does, including joining a professional association, treating clients and employees with respect, and providing a quality product for a fair price. There are a lot of private investigators and private investigative agencies; however, the key to success for an investigator is providing good-quality personalized service in his or her specialized area of expertise.

INVESTIGATIVE SERVICES

An investigation is a planned and organized determination of facts concerning specific events, occurrences, or conditions for a particular purpose.

- An investigation requires a purpose, a subject, and an investigator.
- An investigation is a well-planned and controlled operation.

The subject of investigation encompasses a broad variety of material. The following are some examples:

- Criminal and civil investigations
- Incident-type and background-type investigations
- Local area investigations
- National or international investigations
- Telephone, street, and personal interview investigations
- Physical and technical surveillance
- Undercover operations

The investigator is a skilled and prepared person:

- An investigator is a seeker of truth.
- An investigator does not prejudge or make a determination as to the outcome of an investigation until he or she has collected all of the facts possible regarding the investigation.
- An investigator is a professional who keeps alert to and mindful of what he or she is working on at the time, no matter how tedious the assignment.

An investigator works in a dynamic environment:

- People and things change, both in themselves and in relationship to each other.
- It is possible that the subjects of an investigation may become aware that an investigation concerning their interests is in progress and then make positive efforts to deceive or confuse the investigator.
- Awareness of such obstacles and the ability to work through them are critically important items in an investigator's makeup.

Attributes

Without regard to the specific subject, an investigation is characterized by five attributes if it is to be dependable. It must be objective, thorough, relevant, accurate, and current. Meeting these requirements is a practical test of the skill of an investigator.

Objective

Being objective requires that the investigator be willing to accept any fact, regardless of its significance to preconceived ideas. This is achieved by recognizing the investigator's own personal prejudices and compensating for or neutralizing their effects on the work.

Every investigator forms preliminary opinions or impressions of the probable result of the investigation. Such impressions are formed as the investigation moves forward:

- Sometimes, the impressions are conscious, in which case they can be regarded as working hypotheses or "try-on" versions of what the facts might be.
- Many times, the impressions are not consciously formed but accumulate as a fuzzy context for the individual facts that are uncovered.

The professional investigator must be aware that investigative findings are the foundation for the impressions and not the reverse:

- Persisting in accepting a version of the facts contrary to, or unsupported by, the actual findings is a frequent mistake of the amateur or nonprofessional and is a constant danger for the professional.
- Investigators who cannot sort out and identify personal prejudices—about people, places, outlooks, and so on—are likely to miss the mark.

A practice that sometimes prejudices an investigative report is the use of adjectives connoting feeling. The investigator tends to "editorialize" on matters in which he or she has a personal feeling or position:

- One reason that competent investigative reports often appear dull and colorless is the deliberate effort on the part of a skilled investigator to allow the facts to speak for themselves and not to suggest or project significance by the use of loaded adjectives.
- When adjectives are used by persons who are interviewed in the course of an investigation, the use of the exact words used by the persons, coupled with an accurate description of the setting in which the remarks were made, is often very useful in helping to assess or evaluate the meaning of the information developed.

Thorough

A thorough investigation not only checks all leads but also checks key leads more than once to ensure consistency in results:

- When the statement of a witness or informant is critical, the source should be taken over the same ground several times if possible without compromising the investigation.
- Corroboration of important aspects through different sources is another means of achieving thoroughness.

Relevant

Being relevant means that the information developed pertains to the subject of the investigation:

- A fairly frequent problem with investigations is that persons of the same name are confused, either by the clients or by the investigator.
- Another aspect of information being relevant is cause and effect. A developed fact may be the result of some other fact under investigation, or it could be the cause of the original fact.
- Relevance is an important issue when it comes to the management of the investigation. Facts that are not material to the case may cost valuable resources to collect, thus limiting other areas or sources that could be checked.
- A review of the productivity of an investigative effort must be completed to determine the relevance to the investigation and whether or not that effort is cost-effective.

Accurate

A sound investigative technique dictates frequent tests for accuracy. The mental processes that collect and sort data from the physical senses often produce errors:

- If data are subject to physical measurement, they should be measured. As with relevance to an investigation, the accuracy of material or facts collected is critical.
- Valuable resources may be wasted on information that is not accurate.
- Inaccurate information collected and passed on to a client could result in both civil and criminal legal ramifications for the company.

Current

"Currentness" or timeliness requires that the investigation be carried to the latest possible point at which information relevant to the purpose of the investigation might be found. A difficulty frequently encountered in investigations is caused by information not being current:

- Information obtained that has not been thoroughly examined or tested may not be worth anything, especially if the information is not current.
- An example is an individual's work history. Although an individual's history may have been excellent at several previous employers, his or her most current work history may be questionable or derogatory. Obtaining the individual's work history for his or her present job would be the most current information available, although extreme care must be taken so as not to disrupt the individual's employment.

INVESTIGATIVE RESOURCES

Investigators need to constantly develop their resources so that they can obtain information quickly and accurately when needed to conduct an investigation successfully. Records and documents that can be obtained and studied can reveal important facts on incidents and people. There are vast amounts of public and private resources that are available and can provide shortcuts to many investigative problems.

Most investigators primarily utilize public resources obtained from government agencies, such as federal, state, and local offices, and from business organizations. Today, there are many private information resource companies that, for a fee, will provide background information on a subject. This saves the investigator from spending time physically conducting the research and allows him or her to focus on other aspects of the investigation instead.

Some examples of obtaining local records and documents are as follows.

Public Library

The public library is a significant source of information, mostly in the form of directories. Directories can be valuable sources of lead information, and any information from them that is used should be verified before it is reported to the client. If the investigator does not have a computer with direct access to some of the sources listed, the library has computers available for online research, thereby providing assistance through one of the best research tools available. Many employees at libraries routinely access information for research purposes and will assist you in finding what you are looking for. Plus, if they do not have it, they would know where to get it. The following are some examples of what can be found at a library:

- Periodical and newspaper indexes contain insight into the states, cities, and towns in which they are published. ABC, CBS, and NBC also index news programs, which cover the national evening news as broadcasted since 1972.
- *Who's Who in America* and *Who's Who in the World* contain biographies of prominent people and their notoriety and exper- tise. These volumes contain information about the individuals' schooling, writings, awards, origins, and residences. There are also *Who's Who* directories in categories such as dancing, music, art, and others that are compiled by several different publishers.
- *The American Medical Directory* provides listings for the presi- dents and secretaries of medical associations in all countries. The directory also has listings of doctors and their specialties, licenses, schooling, and home and business addresses.
- *The Martindale-Hubbell International Law Directories* is an example of legal directories of lawyers prepared by state bar asso- ciations that contain information on all of the lawyers in the world. Bar associations list attorneys' current addresses if still practicing or the last known if not. These directories may be helpful when inquiring on past divorces, foreclosures, and other legal actions, provided that the attorney knows what you are trying to accom- plish and what relevance the information has to your investigation.
- There are a variety of criss-cross or reverse directories, such as the Thomas directory, R.L. Polk, Bresser's, and other genealogy reference sources. Some use addresses to locate a subject's name and phone number. Other criss-cross directories can be used to find occupation, locate phone numbers by prefixes, and provide a name and address once the telephone number is found. Criss-cross directories can also be useful in locating neighbors for inquiries when trying to find someone. These directories were created to assist collectors, skip tracers, and others in cross-referencing a name to an address, an address to a name, or a name to a phone number. The directories are kept for years and can be useful when no other information exists.
- *Baird's Manual of American Colleges and Fraternities* lists active and inactive fraternities and sororities and their organizations.
- *Lloyd's Register of Shipping* provides listings of all merchant and passenger ships of the world and their owners. There are also Lloyd's registers and directories that contain information on offshore units,

submersibles, underwater systems, shipping indexes, and voyage registers that contain reports on voyages, reported movements, oceangoing trades, etc. on merchant vessels. There is also *Lloyd's Register of Yachts*, which provides names and addresses of owners, as well as descriptions and names of their yachts.

- Business directories that provide a background on businesses are available, like *Dun & Bradstreet, Standard & Poor's*, and *Moody's*. These volumes list information on larger public and private utilities, transportation companies, banks, trust companies, mutual and stock insurance companies, wholesalers, and retailers. Information includes names of corporate officers, locations, phone numbers, annual sales, and number of employees. *Business Periodicals Index* and *Business Publications Index and Abstracts* provide magazine and book reviews of business activities.
- *Directories in Print* contains listings on general business, industries, banking, finance, insurance, real estate, and others.
- *The Corporate Yellow Book* contains listings of subsidiaries and divisions of leading corporations, their leaders, board members, outside affiliations, revenues, addresses, etc.
- *The Encyclopedia of Associations* lists nonprofit organizations, such as educational, religious, business, commercial, trade, and hobby organizations, with their names, addresses, members, and publications.
- General encyclopedias can be used to research topics.
- Maps and atlases show counties, states, and countries.
- *The News Media Yellow Book* provides information on reporters, writers, and editors of national news media organizations.
- *Where's What: Sources of Information for Federal Investigators* directs an investigator to what documents are available and what information can be disclosed.
- *The Congressional Directory* is a listing of almost all higher-level government employees and agencies. This includes those in the judiciary and executive branches as well as information on each member of the Senate, House, and their committees. It also contains a detailed directory of other official governmental committees and subcommittees, officials of the courts, military establishments, federal departments, governors, boards, commissions, and biographies of all congressional members.
- *Baedeker's Guides* are guidebooks on tourism in foreign countries.
- *The Directory of Expert Witness in Technology* lists expert witnesses that have special knowledge, skill, experience, training, or education in a particular subject. This is a very resourceful tool when one needs to find an expert on a certain subject for court.

- Copies of federal government publications are available at most libraries of every document issued by the city, county, and government agencies and departments informing the public of new developments, such as budgets, committee reports, local affairs, etc.

Churches

The library has a list of the main offices of every denomination, including phone numbers that an investigator could use to contact a church to see if the subject belongs to that church.

Telephone Directories

For residential listings, the White Pages give different variations in the spelling of last names as well as phone numbers. In the business section, the Yellow Pages give business information, and the Blue Pages list information on federal, state, and local agencies in the area. Also included in telephone books is information on different time zones and zip codes throughout the country.

Local Newspapers and Magazines

Newspapers keep all back issues stored on microfilm, which can be useful when investigating a subject or activity that has been in the paper. Magazines contain detailed activities of prominent citizens and lists of subscribers, and provide forwarding addresses of those who have a magazine subscription.

City and County Business License and Permit Offices

Each county requires that a business have a permit that includes any "Doing Business As" (DBA) alias the company may have. The permit provides the names, addresses, phone numbers, and type of business on the license. If the subject has or had a business, you can find a lot of useful information on the business application and the suppliers that were used.

County Clerk's Office

This department has and maintains records of those who applied for citizenship, marriage licenses, and decrees for divorce. Marriage licenses provide useful information pertaining to previous marriages and names of the couple as well as the changes in name of the bride, places of birth, ages, and occupations at the time. Divorce records reveal information on dependents, names and ages of children, assets, and vehicles owned, including Vehicle identification number (VIN) numbers, as well as other property and businesses that were acquired during the marriage. Divorce records may also give the investigator insight into the character of the parties and new directions to take. The county clerk's office also maintains records on all businesses filing as DBAs. Records are kept by the owner's name and cross-referenced by the business name, listing the address or any business the subject and registrants are involved in. This is useful if the subject did not want to become incorporated and listed both the home and business address. Weapon permits, as well as death and birth records, can also be found through this department.

Local Law Enforcement

Local law enforcement maintains records on incident reports, accident reports, and criminal reports. All files must be closed before the information can be released, and as long as the criteria are met, access to the records may be permissible under the Freedom of Information Act (FOIA) with the proper written form.

Local Fire Department

This department is responsible for records on all fires reported within the city plus records on fire safety inspections and burning permits. The fire department may also assist in disclosing fire zoning violations of businesses.

Courthouse or Clerk of Courts

The court maintains criminal, civil, and domestic files that are accessible to the public or restricted to those who need to know, such as investigators doing background investigations. Records detail felony and misdemeanor charges pertaining to criminal activities, and civil records contain information on civil suits like bankruptcy, judgments, divorce records, and others. These records can give a criminal or civil history of an individual or organization, domestic violence history, asset information, etc.

City Recorder or Register of Deeds

This office maintains documents relating to real-estate transactions, deeds, mortgages, leases, wills, bankruptcies, military discharges, and financial statements. It may also provide Uniform Commercial Code (UCC) filings and tax liens. Vital statistics are maintained here, such as the records of all births, deaths, and marriages within the county, which is very useful in missing-persons investigations.

County Property or Tax Assessor

This agency has records that contain maps of real properties, including information on dimensions, addresses, owners, location, taxable value, and improvements. Records also show the address where the tax bill is being sent if the property is rented out. This source of information can be helpful in locating a person or determining a person's assets.

Tax Collector

The tax collector gathers names and addresses of who pays property taxes, legal descriptions of properties, amounts of taxes owed or paid out, and the names of former owners. Records also give accurate locations of properties.

Street Department

This department maintains maps of the city and streets, which can assist the investigator in locating someone by looking at the city blueprints.

Building and Surveyor Department

This department maintains blueprints of construction sites, buildings, landmarks, roads, rights of way, etc.

Health Department

The health department investigates local health concerns; it establishes and enforces city health regulations, such as seeing to it that restaurants maintain an acceptable level of cleanliness and provide emergency services.

This department also keeps birth and death certificates on file. These records can be useful in that birth certificates usually reveal the date of birth, correct full name, names of both parents, address at the time of birth, delivering physician or midwife, name of hospital, and other information that can be followed up on in many ways to locate someone. Death records can be used in the same way, as they list the deceased person's full name, social security number (SSN), date of birth, occupation, parents, and mother's maiden name. This information can help the investigator directly contact people who knew the subject.

Coroner's Office

This office contains information on deceased individuals within the county, and the coroner establishes the cause of death in cases where death may have occurred under unusual or questionable circumstances.

City Attorney

The city attorney usually maintains files of complaints made against businesses suspected of fraud. Sometimes, an investigator can obtain records of past depositions from a subject after the case is closed.

County Auditor

The auditor collects information on all county employees, occupations, and rates of pay.

Voter Registration

Voter registration records can reveal a subject's complete name, address, length of time at the address, telephone number, date of birth, and occupation if the investigator has some idea where the subject may be living. Using an election record is mostly useful for finding missing persons.

Human Resource Department

This department provides employment records, dates of hiring, lengths of employment, and disciplinary information.

State Agencies

Department of Motor Vehicles

The Department of Motor Vehicles (DMV) can provide driver's license identification (depending on the state), such as name, address, date of birth, SSN, copy of the subject's signature, physical description, driving history, and lists of vehicles owned. The DMV can also be useful in revealing who owns a vehicle if the investigator only has a license plate number or the VIN to go by. License plates and VINs not only help find persons but can also yield lienholder information.

The Driver's Privacy Protection Act (1944) allows people to ask that their motor vehicle records not be given out to commercial list compilers for use in markets; however, the records of the drivers and owners who assert this right will still be available to debt collectors and to businesses verifying information on job and insurance applications. This exemption does not apply to accident, motor vehicle violation, and driver status records.

Social Service Agencies and State Unemployment Offices

These offices may share information on who applies for or are recipients of public assistance for legitimate investigations.

Professional and Licensing Bureaus

These bureaus contain information from the department of the state, which issues licenses or certificates to individuals who qualify, such as doctors, lawyers, dentists, and the like.

State Comptroller's Office

This office investigates white-collar and fraud crimes reported to the state.

Secretary of State

The secretary provides corporate records that list officer and director information, year of establishment, type of corporation, registering agent, and stock value. UCCs are also filed with the secretary of state. These items document the financial transactions of loans that an individual or business takes out and personal or business assets put up as collateral, while providing a lien notification on items that were financed by the lender. These records also indicate tax liens and judgments against individuals and companies, which are often identified by name, SSN, or taxpayer identification number. Depending on the state, there is a wide variety of services that are available, and one must call to find out what is offered.

Department of Corrections

This department maintains records of inmates, disciplinary actions, parole dates, what the inmate is charged with, and the like.

Workers' Compensation Bureau

This bureau keeps records of job-related injuries, previous employers, dependents, and the subject's address.

State Game Warden

The warden enforces hunting and fishing laws and the issuing of licenses.

Federal Agencies

The FOIA, known as "the public's right to know," has made it possible for the public to gain access to government records. The Privacy Act amended the FOIA in 1974, which further improved the accuracy, completeness, and relevancy of the data collected and stored. This gives people the right to review information about themselves and to dispute the information if incorrect. The two acts allow citizens to access records of all federal agencies with the proper written request.

It may be possible for the resourceful investigator to attain information from the following agencies.

US Postal Service

The postal service has records of forwarding addresses on businesses and individuals. The postal service will no longer furnish this information on an individual, just on businesses, but if the person has moved within the past year, a letter sent to the old address may be returned with a notation in the upper left corner saying "Do Not Forward, Address Correction Requested." Be sure to include a return address. If there is a forwarding address on file, the letter should come back to you with the new address.

Bureau of Immigration and Naturalization

The Bureau of Immigration and Naturalization (INS) maintains records on immigrants who have applied for citizenship or who have attained citizenship, including names, countries of origin, ages, dates of arrival, and much more.

Departments of the Armed Forces

Anyone can obtain a standard form 180, or a letter requesting service records that provide a person's date of birth, service dates, ranks and grade change, awards, decorations, duty assignments, current duty status, dependents, and any court-martial records. The back of the form has a written release authorization that has to be signed by the person only if health records or any detailed part of his or her personnel records is requested that is not part of the service history. List as much on the request as possible with the name, SSN, and approximate dates of service to assist in the search.

National Coast Guard

The Coast Guard requires that all vessels over 25 ft. long be registered with them, and they investigate all offshore smuggling matters.

Drug Enforcement Administration

The Drug Enforcement Administration (DEA) has a listing of names of physicians and pharmacists who are licensed handlers of narcotics.

Federal Bureau of Investigation

The Federal Bureau of Investigation (FBI) maintains fingerprint records, information on America's most wanted, and criminal records and documents on file. It investigates all crimes against the federal government as well as assisting local and state law enforcement.

Social Security Administration

The Social Security Administration (SSA) maintains the name of everyone who has worked and paid into the system since the 1930s. This can help if you have the SSN of an individual, and the agency can give you the last known address of the person. The SSA also has a list of former cardholders who are deceased, which may be helpful in locating someone using the last known address of the parents, relatives, or siblings, whom one can make inquiries about.

SSNs tell about the place where the application for a social security card was filed. In most cases, the state where social security was applied for is also the place of birth and provides a clue on where to search for public records on an individual. This can be especially helpful in conducting a background investigation on a person with limited information and when trying to locate a missing person. Table 3.1 provides a list of the first three numbers of the SSN that identify the state in which it was issued.

TABLE 3.1
Identifying the State That Issued a Social Security Number (Prior to June 25, 2011)

001–003 New Hampshire	268–302 Ohio	503–504 South Dakota
004–007 Maine	303–317 Indiana	505–508 Nebraska
008–009 Vermont	318–361 Illinois	509–515 Kansas
010–034 Massachusetts	362–386 Michigan	516–517 Montana
035–039 Rhode Island	387–399 Wisconsin	518–519 Idaho
040–049 Connecticut	400–407 Kentucky	520 Wyoming
050–134 New York	408–415 Tennessee	521–524 Colorado
135–158 New Jersey	416–424 Alabama	525 New Mexico
159–211 Pennsylvania	425–428 Mississippi	526–527 Arizona
212–220 Maryland	429–432 Arkansas	528–529 Utah
221–222 Delaware	433–439 Louisiana	530 Nevada
223–231 Virginia	440–448 Oklahoma	531–539 Washington
232–236 West Virginia	449–467 Texas	540–544 Oregon
237–246 North Carolina	468–477 Minnesota	545–573 California
247–251 South Carolina	478–485 Iowa	574 Alaska
252–260 Georgia	486–500 Missouri	575–576 Hawaii
261–267 Florida	501–502 North Dakota	577–579 Washington, DC

SSN Randomization

The SSA changed the way SSNs are issued on June 25, 2011. This change is referred to as "randomization." The SSA developed this new method to help protect the integrity of the SSN. SSN randomization will also extend the longevity of the nine-digit SSN nationwide.

The SSA began assigning the nine-digit SSN in 1936 for the purpose of tracking workers' earnings over the course of their lifetimes to pay benefits. Since its inception, the SSN has always comprised a three-digit area number, followed by the two-digit group number, and ending with the four-digit serial number. Since 1972, the SSA has issued social security cards centrally, and the area number reflected the state, as determined by the ZIP code in the mailing address of the application.

There are approximately 420 million numbers available for assignment. However, the previous SSN assignment process limited the number of SSNs available for issuance to individuals by each state. Changing the assignment methodology extended the longevity of the nine-digit SSN in all states. On July 3, 2007, the SSA published its intent to randomize the nine-digit SSN in the Federal Register Notice, *Protecting the Integrity of Social Security Numbers* (docket no. SSA 2007-0046).

SSN randomization affected the SSN assignment process in the following ways:

- It eliminated the geographical significance of the first three digits of the SSN, referred to as the area number, by no longer allocating the area numbers for assignment to individuals in specific states.
- It eliminated the significance of the highest group number, and as a result, the High Group List is frozen in time and can only be used to see the area and group numbers the SSA issued prior to the randomization implementation date.
- Previously unassigned area numbers were introduced for assignment excluding area numbers 000, 666, and 900–999.

These changes to the SSN may require systems and/or business process updates to accommodate SSN randomization.

If you have any questions regarding SSN randomization or its possible effects on your organization, please see the related frequently asked questions or e-mail your question(s) to ssn.randomization@ssa.gov.

Federal Aviation Administration

The Federal Aviation Administration (FAA) operates the same way the DMV does and keeps records of all registered licensed aircraft and of all licensed pilots and their medical certificates. Also, it records any official suspension or revocation of pilot privileges as well as all liens on licensed aircraft.

National Crime Information Center

The National Crime Information Center (NCIC) collects and retrieves data about those wanted for criminal activities and contains criminal history files on criminals. This database is usually only available to law enforcement agencies. An investigator, with the help of the marshal's office or the FBI, can list the name of a missing child or a handicapped adult at the NCIC.

Bureau of Alcohol, Tobacco, and Firearms

The Bureau of Alcohol, Tobacco, and Firearms (ATF) can provide information on establishments that are firearm dealers and on those who possess legal machine guns. Also, the ATF investigates bomb-threat cases.

Federal Bankruptcy Court

Bankruptcy is a federal matter, and the records are public. The petition on file contains SSNs, dates of birth, current and former addresses, bank accounts, stock ownership, employee histories including salaries and benefits earned in the past years, and all property and vehicles owned, including VINs that are exempt from the proceedings. Records are obtained at the place of filing.

Interstate Commerce Commission

This commission regulates all interstate shipments of goods, licensing of truck lines, and railroads.

Federal Communications Commission

The Federal Communications Commission (FCC) monitors all radio transmissions, issues radio licenses, and investigates violations.

Veterans Administration

The Veterans Administration (VA) contains records of ex-military personnel who have been treated in military hospitals.

Federal Trade Commission

The Federal Trade Commission (FTC) investigates charges of false advertising and regulates trade practices.

Private Organizations

Private sources can provide the investigator with enormous amounts of information. Several organizations that can be utilized are listed as follows.

- Telephone companies maintain a library of old directories for the area that can be useful in establishing a prior residency when doing a background investigation.
- Public utility companies provide addresses of subscribers and may collect other personal information.
- Credit reporting bureaus provide financial histories on an individual, but these reports are restricted by the Fair Credit Reporting Act (FCRA) and require a written release from the person, or the investigator must have a legitimate purpose to obtain such information. An investigator must be aware of the FCRA rules or he or she could face fines, jail time, and loss of license.

  Parts of a credit report not regulated by the FCRA are called the header and are used for social security traces or national identifiers. SSN traces can provide verification of current address, date of birth, employment, marital status, whether more than one SSN is used or is valid, and the development of former addresses. National identifiers utilize a name and the last known address to obtain an SSN, and then an SSN trace is performed to get the best results.
- Taxicab companies and car rental and leasing companies may provide records of an individual's trip, travel times, mileage, etc.
- Hospitals may provide information on a patient's illness, injury, etc.
- College and school records, such as yearbooks, provide information on achievement awards, etc., for an individual.

- Jewelers may assist in providing leads on stolen jewelry.
- Pawnshop operators may assist in providing leads and information pertaining to stolen items.
- Shipping and transportation companies maintain records of goods and quantities shipped, destination, etc.
- The Internet has vast amounts of information and is constantly expanding in networks providing communication links and international business links worldwide. Information can be obtained in minutes on almost any subject available.
- Moving companies maintain records of people moving, dates, addresses, etc.
- Travel agencies and airlines maintain records of travel dates, travel itineraries, rental cars, names, and addresses of passengers.
- The local Better Business Bureau lists the history and reputations of businesses and firms and also the names of owners or corporate information.
- Bank and loan companies maintain records on bank accounts, names of loan officers, credit records, etc. To obtain data on bank accounts and credit reports on transactions is illegal at this time, and an investigator needs a subpoena to access the data.

Table 3.2 lists some examples of information/leads and the sources that provide them.

TABLE 3.2
Sources of Information/Leads

Attorneys	*Martindale-Hubbell Law Directory*, Yellow Pages, state bar registry
Addresses of businesses or individuals	Yellow Pages or White Pages, voter registration, criss-cross directories
Banks, officers, or cashiers	Rand McNally international bankers directory
Brand names and trademarks	*MacRAE's Blue Book, Standard & Poor's Register of Corporations*
Business reputations	Local Better Business Bureaus, trade associations, local businesses
Corporations and their officers or executives	State commissioner, county courthouse, *Dun & Bradstreet, Standard & Poor's Register of Corporations*
Financial information	*Dun & Bradstreet*, credit bureaus, county court, recorder's office
Reputation of an individual	Present and former neighbors, work associates, newspaper clippings and magazine articles

INFORMANTS

Information gathered from people is still the best primary resource for gathering data, which can lead to further investigative leads or questions. Investigators should attempt to develop informants whenever the opportunity arises. Most of the time, informants are developed on a personal basis of friendship or by other motivators. Some informants are driven by their own self-interest, and their desire to assist in an investigation depends on what motivates them. All information obtained from informants should be verified before it is used. Some of the motivators include the following:

- Moral and ethical reasons
- Financial gain
- Revenge
- Exposing activities they disapprove of
- Fear of getting in trouble
- Wish to avoid punishment

Informants can be described in the following categories:

- Regular sources
  - Witnesses
  - Eyewitnesses
  - Victims who commonly aid the investigator in answering the "who, what, where, when, and how" questions of an investigation
  - Suspects
  - Accomplices
- Cultivated sources
  - Ordinary citizens: Interviewing citizens in their daily activities who work in a particular area related to the investigation. Bartenders and waitresses in a bar or restaurant, utility workers, cab drivers, motel employees, etc. may reveal information about the subject or the case under investigation
  - Street people
- Paid or confidential informants
  - Those who reveal information not readily available to the general public and have connections to criminal activities: These types of informants do not want their names to become public. The investigator must keep such sources private and confidential so that they do not fall victim to retaliation
  - Organized crime
  - Gang members

- • Prostitutes
- • Drug dealers
- • Specialists and professionals: These are people who have technical knowledge or expertise in a particular subject or field. They can be called in as expert witnesses in court or can be valuable in giving their expertise on the investigation

CONSTITUTIONAL AND LEGAL RESTRAINTS ON SOURCES OF INFORMATION

There are federal, state, and local laws that limit what an investigator can and cannot do, and these are regulated as to what information can legally be obtained.

FREEDOM OF INFORMATION ACT AND PRIVACY ACT OF 1974

The FOIA and the Privacy Act of 1974 protect personal rights by implementing safeguards against invasion of privacy by limiting access to records and documents maintained by public and private agencies. Records kept by the agencies are only collected and maintained for legitimate and lawful purposes.

The FOIA makes things very time-consuming, and processing of a requested document can take up to several weeks. Sometimes, an investigator can get the document through another source that would be more practical if on a short deadline. However, there is a lot of government information that is only available through the FOIA. There are some exemptions that prohibit access to records, such as areas that concern information that could violate national security, private trade secrets, commercial or financial information, the banking industry including stock and commodity exchanges, maps concerning oil wells, personnel and medical files that cause an invasion of personal privacy, records or information complied on criminal and civil investigations, foreign intelligence, and the like.

Most of the records with the proper written form can be released at the government's discretion, leaving it up to the agency to release all or some of the material even if it falls under the exempt records, especially if one can show that it would be in the "public's best interest." Make sure the written request is as precise as possible, indicating what type of record and what type of agency would have the information. The government can refuse if the request is too broad, and most government agencies will not release information. The *Reporters Committee for Freedom of the Press* and other guidebooks are available on how to use the FOIA to obtain information.

Fair Credit Reporting Act

The FCRA protects private citizens by ensuring that parties accessing their personal information are doing so for permissible reasons. Here are the basic guidelines concerning permissible purposes for obtaining a report from the credit bureau:

1. In response to the order of a court having jurisdiction to issue such an order
2. In accordance with the written instructions of the consumer to whom it relates
3. To a person who has reason and
   a. Intends to use the information in connection with a credit transaction involving the consumer on whom the information is to be furnished and involving the extension of credit, review, or collection of an account of the consumer
   b. Intends to use the information for employment purposes in an "investigative consumer report" bearing public information
   c. Intends to use the information in connection with the underwriting of insurance
   d. Intends to use the information in connection with determining the consumer's eligibility for a license or other benefit granted by a government instrumentality required by law to consider an applicant's financial responsibility of status
   e. Otherwise has a legitimate business need for the information in connection with a business transaction involving the consumer
   f. Needs to review the account to determine whether the consumer continues to meet the terms of the account

Rights of the People

The first 10 amendments to the United States Constitution are guidelines in protecting the personal rights of US citizens. The Bill of Rights basically states the following:

- First Amendment: Provides freedom of religion, freedom of speech, freedom of the press, and the rights to assemble peaceably and to petition the government for remedy or compensation of grievances.
- Second Amendment: The right of the people to keep and bear arms.
- Third Amendment: Provides that no soldier shall be quartered in any house without the consent of the owner during peacetime.

- Fourth Amendment: Provides against unreasonable searches and seizures. The Fourth Amendment provides guidance on issuing search and arrest warrants in that the warrant must be based on probable cause, not suspicions, and based on facts. For instance, in the case of *Mapp v. Ohio* (367 U.S. 643, 644 [1961]), evidence was obtained by violating the Fourth Amendment and the exclusionary rule that prohibits police from using illegally seized evidence at a criminal trial. Therefore, evidence key to the case was disallowed and affected the outcome of the trial. The Fourth Amendment protects individuals not only from unreasonable searches and seizures but also from illegal seizures of their persons, meaning illegal arrests.
- Fifth Amendment: Protects those accused of crimes from torture or coercion to extract a confession, and the right to be free from self-incrimination. In *Miranda v. Arizona* (384 U.S. 436 [1966]), the Fifth Amendment was violated because the right to be informed of the right to remain silent before questioning, thereafter known as the Miranda warning, had not been administered. Also, the defendant's right to consult an attorney had not been iterated. The Fifth Amendment also states that no person shall be tried for the same offense twice (double jeopardy) and that the law should be reasonable and applied in a fair manner while upholding the individual's rights during due process of law. No person shall be deprived of his or her property for public use without just compensation.
- Sixth Amendment: Covers the right to a fair trial, right to counsel, and right to a speedy and public trial. In the cases of *McNabb v. U.S.* (318 U.S. 332 [1943]) and *Mallory v. U.S.* (354 U.S. 449 [1957]), the original verdict was overturned as a result of a violation of the Sixth Amendment due to delays in prompt arraignment. The McNabb–Mallory rule states that during "unnecessary delays taking the person apprehended before a judicial officer as required by State and Federal law," a confession or statement made during the delay will not be used. In the case of *Escobedo v. Illinois* (378 U.S. 478 [1964]), it was determined that police were in violation of Escobedo's rights due to failure to allow him to consult with an attorney after he requested one when the investigative interview turned into an accusatory interrogation.
- Seventh Amendment: The right to trial by jury in a civil case.
- Eighth Amendment: Guarantees against excessive bail or fines being imposed and provides protection from cruel and unusual punishment.

- Ninth Amendment: Provides that certain rights contained in the Constitution shall not be denied or find fault with others retained by the people.
- Tenth Amendment: States that "powers not delegated by the Constitution nor prohibited by the States are reserved by the state."

In addition to the Bill of Rights, the following also protect the rights of the people:

- Fourteenth Amendment: The Fourteenth Amendment's due-process clause states that persons charged with state crimes are entitled to rights similar to those of persons charged with federal crimes, such as in *Mapps v. Ohio* and *Brown v. Mississippi* (1936), where a coerced confession deprived the defendant of his right to due process. Due-process amendments are protection of freedom of speech and press, protection from unreasonable searches and seizures, right to counsel, protection from self-incrimination, right to jury in all criminal cases, and protection against double jeopardy.
- Habeas corpus: The appeals process through state and federal courts by writ of habeas corpus, which is a court procedure to bring the detainee before the court to determine the legality of the individual's custody and to determine whether the defendant was fairly provided his or her constitutional rights and protections under the Bill of Rights in court proceedings.

LAW ENFORCEMENT AND PROFESSIONAL INVESTIGATORS

Law enforcement officers have greater powers than investigators do in the methods of arrest, detention, search, and interrogation, which allow them to operate with a wider jurisdiction.

Law enforcement officers are governed by the Constitution, especially pertaining to the Fourth and Fourteenth Amendments, while professional investigators are not. Investigators are limited to the powers possessed by every citizen. Professional investigators and private citizens are not required to advise persons of their legal rights through Miranda warnings or adhere to constitutional prohibitions against unreasonable searches and seizures. Giving Miranda warnings only applies to law enforcement officers in custodial interrogations. For example, the exclusionary rule states that evidence obtained by an illegal search and seizure will not be admissible in a court of law. However, evidence seized by a professional investigator or private citizen with no official knowledge or in conjunction with law enforcement can be used by the prosecution and is not subject to the exclusionary rule.

Some states offer courses and then deputize private investigators, allowing them the additional arrest powers that law enforcement officers have. This can be an advantage for the investigator, although at other times, this additional authority can cause many problems when situations arise, and one can be accused of an erroneous arrest or false imprisonment. Law enforcement officers are protected provided that the arrest was based on probable cause, whereas an investigator must justify and prove that a felony was actually committed.

Investigators and private citizens can arrest for felonies and, in some states, for "breach of peace" misdemeanors committed in their presence. For the most part, people are not aware of their own personal rights. All people have the right to an attorney, and an attorney must be provided if requested; one cannot be coerced into a confession. If an investigator oversteps his or her authority when on an assignment, tort litigation against the investigator can result, and the investigator's employer can also be sued for a legal injury.

Tort Law Applications

A tort is a wrong done to another person. There must be a legal duty owed by one person to another, and a breach of that duty can directly result in a legal injury as a consequence of that action. The injured party may bring a lawsuit for damages against the private investigator caused by "tortious" conduct.

Tortious conduct includes the following:

1. Negligence or absence of due diligence
2. The taking, without permission, of a person's name or likeness to the benefit, gain, or advantage of another (for example, identity theft)
3. Invasion of privacy or trespassing on the seclusion or solitude of the person by invading his or her home or eavesdropping
4. Public disclosure of private facts
5. Publicity that places the person in a false light in the public's eye (for example, surveillance that is performed in an unethical, prolonged, or conspicuous manner causing fright, shame, mental suffering, and humiliation due to what neighbors are observing)
6. Intentional battery, assault, false imprisonment, trespassing on private land, and trespassing on another's personal possessions
7. Defamation of character
8. Malicious prosecution

METHODS OF INVESTIGATION

COLLECTING EVIDENCE

The collection of evidence plays an important role in revealing the facts about a crime. It also establishes a discipline of order when collecting and preserving evidence. An investigator must have adequate knowledge on processing and preserving collected evidence at a crime scene. Evidence collection plays a very important part in building a case. If it is performed improperly, the evidence gathered could become tainted and would not be admissible in court, possibly damaging the case.

Basic Rules for the Proper Collection, Preservation, and Maintenance of Evidence

The basic rules for collecting, preserving, and maintaining evidence must follow the chain of custody to be used in court. The investigator will be asked to prove that the evidence is in the same condition as when it was found at the crime scene. He or she must also be able to properly account for the evidence from the time of discovery until the time it is presented in court. Any break in the chain of custody can suppress the item and its use as evidence:

- Keep the chain of custody as short as possible by restricting handling to a minimum.
- Document thoroughly any contacts or transportation of the evidence until presented in court.
- Document in detail the date, place, and time of discovery.
- Photograph and sketch the crime scene, documenting where each piece of evidence was found; then remove the evidence from the crime scene.
- Mark the evidence with a distinctive mark, being careful not to damage or alter the evidence. Usually, letters, numbers, or combinations of both are used to mark evidence. Always keep a log documenting how the evidence was marked, what was used, and when and where the mark was placed. If the investigator cannot mark the evidence without damaging it, he or she should apply a marked label or package the item first and then mark it. Marking provides a positive identification.
- Place evidence in the proper evidence container, marked with the date, place, and time of discovery along with the identity of the collector. If at all possible, have witnesses present when packaging evidence.
- Place the evidence in a secured evidence locker to avoid its becoming lost, stolen, or tainted until the item can be presented in court.

Basic Rules for Handling Evidence

When handling evidence, each item packaged must have the date, place, time, and condition of the item marked on the container before it is placed in a secured storage locker or sent to a laboratory. Do not allow articles of evidence from the suspect and the victim to contact each other. Each item collected must be packaged and preserved separately to avoid contamination. When sending specimens to the laboratory, use only the labs that are certified and qualified to process the samples provided:

- Biological evidence, such as hair, soil, fingernails, etc., should first be placed in a paper envelope and then put in a plastic bag.
- Specimens of hair should contain at least 50 strands if possible.
- Submit all suspected seminal stains to the laboratory.
- Allow bloodstains to dry naturally before packaging. It is recommended that blood samples be packaged in a paper envelope sealed with tape instead of a plastic bag in case the sample did not dry thoroughly.
- Do not put damp evidence in a plastic bag, because of bacterial or fungal reactions.
- Liquid, oil, and grease should be left in the containers in which they were found. If not found in their original containers, put the samples in clean glass containers to avoid contamination.
- Food and beverages should be left in the containers in which they were found.
- Tightly seal substances that can evaporate.
- Put disks and tapes in plastic bags without folds in the bag.
- Mark bullets at the base. Store lead casing or shells within pieces of paper without touching one another and twist each piece of paper at both ends like a piece of candy to close it.
- Weapons should be placed in a cardboard box, with triggers secured.
- Metal and paint scrapings should be placed in a plastic bag along with a sample of the paint marked for control purposes.
- Fiber evidence should not be placed in an envelope, because fibers are difficult to locate and paper envelopes are made of fiber. Use a plastic bag, vial, or pillbox.
- Charred documents should be delivered in person to a lab after placing them on top of loose cotton in a cardboard box.

Containers Used to Preserve Evidence

- Pillboxes
- Envelopes (for small items or powdery material)

- Bottles
- Vials
- Plastic bags (for small, dry objects)
- Paper bags
- Cardboard boxes

Kinds of Evidence

- Real, physical evidence found at the crime scene: fingerprints, clothing and personal items, photographs, notebooks, credit cards, identification, weapons, burglary tools, guns, tire prints, footprints, etc.
- Scientific evidence found at the crime scene that can be analyzed in a laboratory: blood, hair, and semen samples; soil, metal, and paint scrapings; liquids; etc.
- Circumstantial evidence: any information gathered that is related to the evidence but is not conclusive
- Testimonial evidence: the statements of competent, sworn witnesses, which are used to support the facts related to the real evidence
- Direct evidence: the observations of eyewitnesses

Hearsay Evidence

Hearsay evidence is based not on a witness's personal knowledge but on information revealed to the witness by another person. Generally, hearsay evidence is not admissible in a court of law.

Exceptions to the rule are as follows:

- A voluntary confession in expressed terms made against the interest of the defendant by an accused person shows guilt in itself, and that self-incriminating statement can be relied on as truthful.
- A criminal admission, the evidence heard in rebuttal, or impeachment evidence.
- A dying declaration when the person, at the time the statement was made, knew or thought he or she was dying.
- A spontaneous statement made by the subject, who blurted it out without thinking about what he or she said, that was overheard by someone else. This is admissible in court.

INTERVIEWS AND INTERROGATIONS

Once an incident has occurred, the investigator looks at the physically observable and the written or spoken words of those who witnessed or participated in the act. Two methods that are used are interviews and interrogations. Both methods are useful in gathering information about a case and involve question-and-answer exchanges. Interviews and interrogations should always be recorded, and written statements should follow after. Always inform the person that you are tape-recording the interview.

When interviewing, never be judgmental or form a conclusion; adjust your character traits to blend in with those of the person you are interviewing. Do not ridicule, harass, or abuse anyone you are interviewing or interrogating.

INTERVIEWS

An interview is the questioning of a person who has or is believed to have information of official interest to the investigator. The interviewee is believed to be able to answer all or part of the who, what, where, when, why, and how of a case. At the time of the interview, the witness or any party questioned is not considered to be a suspect or involved in any wrongdoing related to the crime.

During interviews, the investigator should be polite, kind, and attentive while allowing the person to tell his or her story without being interrupted. This will aid the development of a rapport with the individual as well as make him or her feel comfortable. Developing a rapport with the witness allows him or her to view you as a human being open to receiving information. Always start with open questions, letting the person tell what he or she knows or observed. Open questions are narrative in nature and allow witnesses to freely express and emphasize their versions of what they know or think they know. After the witness is finished telling his or her account of events, use direct questions to clarify any questions or open gaps in the statement.

The investigator must decipher the credibility and truthfulness of the interviewee. This can entail a series of evaluations relating to the subject's personality, reputation, attitude, and demeanor. When interviewing witnesses or victims, the investigator must be able to judge their emotional status. Emotions can greatly affect a person's ability to recall events as they occurred. The investigator must assist a witness in recalling and relating the facts exactly as he or she observed them. The investigator does not want to cause more emotional stress and must be able to question in an empathic way without causing more devastating trauma.

The purpose of an investigative interview is to gain information to establish facts of the crime. Examples of basic information an interviewer will want to obtain or confirm with the witness are as follows:

- Verifying statements and the physical evidence given with prior information obtained
- Identifying additional witnesses

- Identifying perpetrators and accomplices
- Securing additional evidence
- Developing background information on the specific crime or offense
- Eliminating suspects and discovering details of other offenses
- Evaluating and verifying all discoveries made

FOLLOW-UP INTERVIEWS

Follow-up interviews can be most beneficial to the investigator because they reaffirm and reestablish the facts of the first interview. They can shed new light on new evidence, jog the memory, or identify other suspects who were missed.

Sometimes, an investigator may want to switch to interrogative questioning if the witness becomes a potential suspect after revealing more information. This also happens when interrogative questioning of a suspect reveals that the suspect is also a valuable witness, thus turning an interrogation into an investigative interview.

INTERROGATIONS

An interrogation is the questioning of a person suspected of having committed an offense or of a person who is reluctant to make a full disclosure of information in his or her possession that is pertinent to an investigation. Interrogation techniques used in questioning are very different from those used in interviews. An interrogation is more aggressive and accusatory. Sometimes, if the suspect is more hostile and uncooperative, close-ended questioning may be better than open-ended questioning. Closed questioning involves questions with yes-or-no answers. A suspect may more readily answer this type of question, therefore providing some useful information rather than providing no answers when questioned in an open-ended and narrative style.

Two techniques most commonly used during an interrogation are as follows:

1. Sympathetic. For example, "I understand how frustrating it must have been for you to see your partner living high on the hog while you barely scraped by. Is there anything you can tell me about who else may be involved?"
2. Logic and reasoning. For example, "Look, we have all the evidence we need to convict you on these embezzlement charges. However, if you tell us who your accomplice was, and turn state's evidence, we're willing to offer you..."

The main approaches used in interrogation are as follows:

- Indirect approach: Used when there is not enough evidence and is presented in an exploratory manner. For example, "Tell me everything you know to be true about what really happened on..."
- Direct approach: The suspect's guilt is reasonably certain. For example, "Look, you and I both know you were there, so what motivated you to do it?"
- Subterfuge approach: This can be used to induce guilty persons to confess when all approaches have failed, for example, playing good cop/bad cop, playing one suspect against the other, hypothetical reenactment of the crime, etc.

The purpose of an interrogation of a suspect is to obtain an admission or confession of wrongful acts. An admission is when the suspect makes self-incriminating statements and admits or acknowledges wrongdoing. A confession is when the suspect confesses to the crime.

An admission or confession should be obtained voluntarily in a written or signed statement. Investigators who are working independently of law enforcement are not required to inform the suspect with the Miranda warning; therefore, statements made by a suspect in response to interrogation can be admissible in court.

Written and Signed Statements

Properly written statements contain the best form of preservation and provide a written record in the case file. Written statements are useful at trials to refresh recollection, impeach witnesses, monitor testimony, and discourage the witness or suspect from changing his or her story.

Whether the statement made is from a witness, an admission, or a confession dictates what elements the statement should include:

- Elements of a statement from a witness.
  - Start time and an end time of the statement.
  - The witness's personal information, such as name, address, telephone number, date of birth, place of employment, and SSN. This information identifies the author.
  - Date, time, and place.
  - The witness acknowledges that the interviewer is an investigator and not a police officer.
  - The statement was given freely and voluntarily, and was not coerced by threats or promises.

- The statement should be in a narrative form, question and answer, or a combination of both, accounting the specific details of the events and observations reported. Be sure the statement is written in the person's own words and manner of speech.
- The statement should state that the witness has read all the contents and made any necessary changes. If changes are made in the statement, the witness needs to initial the changes where the corrections were made.
- In the conclusion, the statement should contain an affirmation that the contents are, in fact, true, correct, and voluntarily provided.
- Signature of the witness.
- Signature of the person who conducted the interview.
- Elements of an admission statement.
  - Date and time of the admission.
  - Admission statements are usually taken at the beginning of the interrogation after verbal admittance of wrongdoing.
  - The suspect writes down in his or her handwriting a simple statement of guilt or culpability.
  - The suspect should sign the statement.
  - The suspect may or may not sign a full statement or confession later on. An unsigned statement may not be as good as a signed one but may be of value.
- Elements of a written confession should be the actual words spoken by the suspect. If the person uses "street talk," record it as it was said, but hold the person to the subject at hand. Do not clean it up or put words in the suspect's mouth to make it sound better. Confessions can be in either a written narrative form or a format taken by a stenographer or tape recorder that is transcribed to reflect exactly what was said.
  - Start time and an end time of the statement.
  - The suspect's personal information, such as name, address, telephone number, date of birth, place of employment, and SSN. This information identifies the author.
  - Date, time, and place.
  - Names of the people present and who conducted the interview.
  - The suspect acknowledges that the interviewer is an investigator and not a police officer.
  - No prescribed format.
  - The statement was given freely and voluntarily, and was not coerced with threats or promises.
  - A written confession is a comprehensive written narrative with details of intent and possible motive. It should be written in a narrative form, question and answer, or a combination of both.

- The statement should state that the suspect has read all the contents and made any necessary changes. If changes are made in the statement, the suspect needs to initial the changes where the corrections were made.
- In the conclusion, the statement should contain an affirmation that the contents are, in fact, true, correct, and voluntarily provided.
- Signature of the suspect.
- Signature of the persons who conducted and witnessed the interview.

NONVERBAL AND VERBAL RESPONSES

Along with having good interviewing and interrogation techniques, it is also important to read the body language of the person being questioned. Nonverbal and verbal responses are indicators of truth or deception. Telling the truth about an incident can lead the suspect to be in fear of being shamed, embarrassed, or punished, and the investigator may need to redirect the approach in questioning if deception is suspected. For example, one could maneuver the suspect into a casual conversation unrelated to what the questioning is about and encourage the suspect to brag, while watching mannerisms and comparing his or her responses to questions when the interrogation starts. The more interviews and interrogations are done, the more the investigator will be able to develop techniques for observing interviewees. Some basic signs that an investigator may notice are as follows:

- Truthfulness can be seen in genuine expressions, confident eyes with more direct contact, a real smile, and a more relaxed appearance.
- Nonverbal responses occur when a person is not comfortable with the questions being asked. Some of the common things seen in detecting deception include the following:
  - Nervousness
  - Dilated pupils (this happens when a person is threatened)
  - Perspiration
  - Increase or decrease in breathing
  - Refusal to shift the body when sitting for long periods of time
  - Rubbing the back of the neck
  - Playing with jewelry or clothes
  - Running fingers through hair
  - Blushing
  - Yawning or stretching
  - Constantly clearing the throat

- Shifty eyes or not making direct eye contact when asked questions
- Closed arms and rigid-looking, tight-lipped appearance
- Exaggerated gestures
- Refusing to respond, being silent
- Sarcastic expressions
- Verbal responses that can indicate deception:
  - Stuttering
  - Repeating one's own words or the question
  - Becoming irrational in speech
  - Saying things like "I swear," "This is a set up," "This is not my style," "I couldn't have possibly done something like that," "I don't have time for this" or other excuses to leave, etc.

During investigations, investigators may also use devices to detect deception. The technology used relies on the skill, technique, and experience of the operator. The polygraph and voice analyzer can only be administered with the permission of the suspect, and they only should be used to enhance an investigation, not replace it:

- Investigative uses
  - Useful in developing leads
  - Verifying statements
  - Checking information
  - Saves money by focusing on specific suspects
  - Occasionally encourages a confession
- The best-known lie detectors
  - Polygraphs or lie detectors record changes in pulse and respiration rate, blood pressure, and skin sensitivity to electricity (galvanic skin response). A polygraph exam is only as good as the examiner administering the test. A number of states prohibit the use of the polygraph.
  - Computer voice analyzers (CVSAs) process speech electronically and provide immediate results for single- or multiple-word answers to questions, record subaudible microtremors in speech on a digital tape, and require no attachments to the person. These tapes can be analyzed weeks to several months later. Some states prohibit the use of a CVSA.
  - Psychological stress evaluations (PSEs) may be used with or without the knowledge of the individual being tested; they record and analyze stress-related components of the human voice and require no attachments to the individual. The PSE has not been admitted as evidence in court and is forbidden for use in employee testing by the Employee Polygraph Protection Act of 1988 (EPPA).

SURVEILLANCE METHODS

Surveillance is an important tool that investigators may use to obtain information by observing directly the activities of persons or places during the course of an investigation. The surveillance can be covert, to avoid discovery, or overt, in which a closed-circuit television (CCTV) camera or the like is placed in a conspicuous place to prevent wrongdoings. Overt surveillance is an open operation, so the subject knows he or she is being followed or is under some type of surveillance activity that will either deter criminal activity or cause the his or her to make mistakes, which may lead to additional information concerning the case.

The majority of surveillances are covert in nature, requiring the investigator to appear inconspicuous in any given situation and location. The purpose of covert surveillance is to conduct secretive and continuous observation to obtain information, develop leads, secure evidence that a crime or deed has been committed, or observe the actual commission of the act. Surveillance is used in all types of investigations, such as domestic, criminal, civil, and fraud.

The following are terms often used in or associated with an undercover operation or surveillance along with a brief definition or description of each phrase:

- Be burnt: To have your subject know that he or she is being followed and who is following him or her. If a subject is lost, he or she can be found again, but if the subject becomes aware that he or she is being followed, the case is finished.
- Be hot: To have your subject suspect that he or she is being followed.
- Be made: To be detected by the subject.
- Bugging: Eavesdropping by electronic means, such as a hidden microphone or radio transmitter.
- Bumper beeper: A battery-operated device that emits radio signals, which permits a vehicle to be tracked by a directional finder-receiver. Also called a beacon, transponder, ground positioning system (GPS), or electronic tracking device.
- Burn the surveillance: When the surveillant's behavior causes the subject to know he or she is under surveillance.
- Cell phone: Placed on silent mode.
- Close or tight surveillance: The subject is kept under constant surveillance. The aim is not to lose the subject even at the risk of being made.
- Convoy: A countermeasure to detect surveillance.
- Loose surveillance: Cautious surveillance because the loss of the subject is preferable to possible discovery.
- Moving surveillance: A surveillant follows the subject.
- Pen register: A device that records all numbers dialed on a telephone.
- Shadow: To follow secretly.

- Stakeout: Also called a plant or fixed surveillance. The surveillant usually remains in one fixed position or location.
- Subject: The party under surveillance.
- Surveillance: The secretive, continuous, and sometimes periodic watching of persons, vehicles, places, or objects to obtain information concerning the activities and identities of individuals. The observation of people is to gather information relevant to an investigation without the subject being aware of the shadowing, which includes watching or following a person.
- Surveillant: The person conducting the surveillance.
- Spy cams: Aid in observing the subject's activities with a hidden camera, which can be located in items such as books, clock radios, teddy bears, miniature wireless pinhole camera systems, and smoke detectors.
- Tail: To follow and keep under surveillance.
- Tailgating: A form of open surveillance in which the subject's vehicle is closely followed.
- Technical surveillance: Surveillance involving the use of electronic devices to enhance tracking of moving objects or observing of the subject's activities.

PRESURVEILLANCE

Certain activities should be carried out before surveillance is started. They are necessary so that the investigator is prepared and thus performs a professional and successful job for the client:

1. Obtain information pertaining to the subject, including a detailed physical description—height, weight, color of hair, eye color, etc.—as well as any other distinguishable characteristics such as tattoos. Obtain a photo if at all possible.
2. Obtain the subject's name, any aliases, address, place of employment, and telephone numbers.
3. Obtain details of vehicles that the subject may use. Locate all possible routes that the subject may take from home to work, to the store, to an acquaintance's home, or to any other place he or she may repeatedly visit. Document entrances and exits that may be used when leaving work or other office buildings or complexes.
4. Make note of habits, mannerisms, places frequented, and hours of employment.
5. Perform a background check for any criminal, civil, or prior activities. Also check the subject's marital status to determine if there is a spouse who may also be living at the residence.

6. Perform relevant surveying or research the area, taking in the target area, including traffic conditions and transportation that could be used by the subject, and record suitable sites for surveillance. Also determine what type of neighborhood the subject lives in, so that the investigator can blend in with the surroundings and dress appropriately.

7. Before surveillance begins, determine how many hours are required, ensure that all shifts are covered and relief is available, and give a briefing on the surveillance activities as the surveillance moves along.

8. Choose an inconspicuous vehicle that blends in or use a rental car, which should be exchanged on a daily basis. The vehicle must always be in good running condition with a full tank of gas.

9. Bring a change of clothes, money, and food and water for extended surveillance.

10. Always have a pretext or cover story ready if asked why you are in a particular place.

11. Always make a positive identification of the subject before hours are sunk into surveillance.

12. Be prepared for stationary or mobile surveillance.

13. The surveillance report should include all presurveillance data that were collected.

SURVEILLANCE EQUIPMENT/TOOLS

- Two 35 mm cameras with a minimum of a 200 mm lens. Other useful lenses available include wide-angle, telephoto, close-up, or macro lenses. One camera should be loaded with film for daytime conditions, and another camera should be loaded with film for reduced-light conditions. Use the appropriate color film for day and nighttime conditions with an electronic flash.

- Digital still camera: These types of cameras are very convenient, allow images to be saved on disks, and provide pictures that can immediately be viewed and edited. You can also easily print your own pictures from your computer, enhance images before printing, and e-mail pictures.

- All cameras must have a built-in time and date stamp.

- A palm-sized camcorder with night capability: This allows you to record and document events as they happen, with sound; it should also be equipped with a zoom lens and a microphone. The investigator can record long-range, midrange, and close-up activities. Video cameras can catch people in the act, whereas the activity may be lost with a camera.

- A voice-activated tape recorder.

- Extra batteries, tapes, and film.

- Binoculars with a minimum of 10× capability.
- A monocular with a minimum of 8× capability.
- A flashlight and a red lens cover.
- A radio, cell phone, pagers, and earpiece can be useful if you are outside of your vehicle.
- Infrared snooper scope for visual enhancement at night.
- Compass.
- Current maps and enhanced maps of known surveillance areas.

TECHNICAL SURVEILLANCE

GPS tracking devices, bumper beepers (attached on a vehicle for tracking), and beepers (attached to a person for tracking) are used in some types of surveillance. Spy cams may be used in aiding an employer to maintain and ensure a safe and secure workplace. An investigator will want to check the federal and state laws with regard to the legality of using such devices and to avoid invasion-of-privacy lawsuits.

TYPES OF SURVEILLANCE

There are two types of surveillance that are used: fixed or moving (or there can be a combination of both). Moving surveillance is the most difficult to achieve and the most vulnerable to discovery. It involves following the subject whenever he or she goes to unknown locations. Moving surveillance can include many different approaches and can be accomplished by foot or by any means available, such as using bicycles, mopeds, motorcycles, helicopters, watercraft, or airplanes.

Foot surveillance involves following the subject through crowded and urban areas.

- Never lose sight of your subject under any circumstances. One investigator alone can perform successful foot surveillance; however, it can be better done with two or more people.
- Keep several people ahead of you and the subject.
- Never stare at the back of the subject's head; many people can sense when they are being watched. Watch the subject from the waist down.
- Never make direct eye contact with the subject.
- Do not act suspicious by peeping around corners or buildings or by hiding behind objects or trees. Act normal and as though you have the right to be there just like anyone else.

Vehicle surveillance involves following the subject in a motor vehicle. Whenever possible, have two or more investigators in separate vehicles with cell phone or radio capabilities on the surveillance to lessen the chances of being burnt.

- Do not take unnecessary chances; adhere to all traffic laws and your safety and that of those around you.
- Use a vehicle with a discreet appearance. Neutral colors, like tan or white, that blend in are best; avoid two-toned vehicles. Do not have identifying decals or bumper stickers on the vehicle or characteristics that stick out, such as chrome, huge lifts, and the like. Even if the surveillance vehicle does blend in with the surroundings, avoid using vehicles with distinguishable grills that the subject may notice in his or her rearview mirror.
- Do not tail the subject; stay a car or two behind. Whenever possible, try to maneuver your vehicle to the right or left side of the subject's vehicle, thus keeping somewhat in the subject's blind spot. Wear a hat to cover your hair and drive with your sun visor down to help conceal parts of your face. Try to parallel them when following them into a turn, keeping as low-key as possible. Another technique that can be used to follow your subject without losing him or her is to purchase small round reflector stickers that match the subject's vehicle color. This way, the sun will hit the reflectors and be a beacon for you. Also, putting a tiny piece of red tape on the taillight will assist at night, creating a distinctive pattern when following the subject.
- With multiple vehicle surveillance, use a decoy vehicle to follow closely, and when the subject turns, the decoy keeps driving, and the other vehicle resumes mobile surveillance. This can throw the subject off if he or she becomes suspicious. Another technique in multiple vehicle surveillance is positioning the vehicles to leapfrog each other. Employ two or more vehicles equipped with communication to follow the subject. The trailing vehicle moves up to the forward position while the lead vehicle drops back to the end at different time intervals. This is done so that the subject never sees the same vehicle for long periods of time or over a great distance.
- Always act relaxed, with an arm draped over the seat or elbow propped on the door when driving. These actions give the appearance of an unconcerned driver.

Stakeouts are from fixed or stationary positions that allow for the visual monitoring of a given location. A stakeout can require the investigator to be parked in a vehicle outside an establishment or to be across the street observing from another building. Stakeouts sometimes require long hours and patience. So relax and be prepared to not leave your position for a long period of time.

- Stakeout trucks are preferred and practical, and allow enough room for surveillance equipment and discretion. Vans or old panel trucks can be used.
- Use one-way glass if at all possible.
- Wear clothing that blends in with the environment.
- It is advisable to let local police know you are in the vicinity by providing them your license plate number and vehicle description so your stakeout may be saved from a nosy neighbor.
- If a police officer does approach you, have your investigator's license and driver's license available. Keep your hands in plain sight, preferably on the steering wheel if at all possible. Advise the police officer immediately that you are an investigator working surveillance. In most states, you are not required to reveal the subject you have under surveillance.

TABLE 3.3
Investigator Surveillance Checklist

Case #: _____   Investigator: _____

Information:
___ Case information packet
___ Investigator information sheet
___ Picture(s) of subject(s)
___ Labeled maps of all addresses listed
Equipment:
___ Two 35 mm cameras
___ Camera lens(es)
___ Binoculars
___ Monocular
___ Mini tape recorder
___ Camcorder
___ Radio
___ Small flashlight with red lens
___ Compass
Supplies:
___ Minimum of four (24-exposure) rolls of 35 mm film for day and nighttime conditions
___ Minimum of four blank videotapes
___ Minimum of four blank audiotapes
___ Adequate fuel level
Investigator surveillance gear:
___ Sun visors, large enough for windshield   ___ Flares
___ Hats   ___ Tool kit
___ Flashlight   ___ Wigs

- If the subject confronts you, never reveal that you been watching him or her. Tell the subject that you do not know what he or she is talking about and leave.

An example of an investigator surveillance checklist is shown in Table 3.3.

RESULTS AND REPORTS

Most investigative reports are written in a narrative style to communicate what happened in the correct chronological order or time sequence in which the events took place. The objective of any report is to create an accurate, detailed, easy-to-understand, and professional account of the events that took place from information obtained from interviews, interrogations, or the investigator's personal observations. In addition to photographs, videos, or recorded tapes, this objective is achieved by writing clear, precise reports that enable the reader to visualize what was seen in the same way the witness or investigator saw or experienced it.

The following are guidelines to follow when writing a report:

1. Style
   a. Reports are to be written in a narrative style. For example, "I arrived at 101 E. Main Street, and I followed the subject into the elevator."
   b. Every sentence should begin with either a noun or a pronoun. For example, "The subject went into the store. She walked over to the men's clothing department."
   c. Abbreviate only where absolutely necessary, for example, "a.k.a." (also known as), "DOB" (date of birth), etc.
   d. Every sentence is to be a complete sentence.
2. Vocabulary
   a. Precise
      i. Correct verb selection. For example, "The crowd shifted," "ran," "scattered," "dissolved," or "turned." All these verbs have radically different meanings. Use the proper verb to describe what was observed.
      ii. Nouns. For example, "The subject was hitting the woman with a musical instrument." Describe the musical instrument in more detail and give the name if possible: "The subject was hitting the woman with a small instrument that looked like a harmonica."
   b. Objective
      i. Objective writing provides information just like it is, with no personal comments added or implied. Writing

objectively is controlled, factual, and direct, and is not subjective. For example, "The subject wore an orange-and-green striped shirt with blue jeans." The following is *not* an example of objective writing: "The subject was wearing an ugly orange-and-green striped shirt with blue jeans that looked like they came from Goodwill."

   c. Accurate

      i. Be accurate in selecting the correct word. For example, was it a Blazer or a Bronco; was it teal or blue? Also be accurate in documenting numbers and time.

3. Content

   a. Always put in the report the five W's and one H: who, what, where, when, why, and how. Concentrate on the facts, and report the correct order of events that took place. The report usually includes a description of how the crime was committed, the motive, financial impact of the crime, and a review of the evidence identifying those either directly or indirectly responsible. For example, if a company's employee committed the crime, the report should include the employee's history with the company. Information such as any disciplinary problems, criminal background, and financial resources should be noted. No matter what the case, surveillance or conducting investigations, the only perception of your work is through the reports that are turned in. Take pride in yourself, your reports, and your company.

4. In addition, spending more time on your report now will save you time later. Proofread your report and make any necessary revisions.

5. Some key points regarding report writing are as follows:

   a. Use short sentences.

   b. Use short paragraphs.

   c. Use simple words.

   d. Be accurate.

   e. Be clear.

   f. Conceal confidential informants.

   g. Do not include your suspicions, opinions, or conclusions in the body of the report, only the facts that you discovered.

   h. Document time segments and chronological order.

An example of an investigator's progress report is shown in Table 3.4.

TABLE 3.4
Investigator's Progress Report

Page___of___

Date_____

Case #_____

Client_____

Mileage: Start_____   Finish_____   Total_____

Surveillance Report

9:40 a.m.	Investigator #10 departed from base en route to 5340 North Miller Avenue in Phoenix, Arizona.
10:03 a.m.	Investigator #10 arrived at 5340 North Miller Avenue in Phoenix, Arizona. The house is a single-level, beige home with brown trim. A green Chevy Blazer bearing AZ license plate #ABF 512 with a Suns bumper sticker on the left side of the bumper was parked in the driveway (video and pictures obtained).
11:12 a.m.	Investigator #10 made a pretext call to confirm that the subject was home.
11:37 a.m.	The subject exited the house and entered the green Blazer. The subject is a white female, approximately 5'5", 115 lbs., with dark brown shoulder-length hair. The subject wore a red T-shirt with blue shorts and brown sandals. The subject proceeded south on Miller Avenue to Elliot Road then west on Elliot Road and pulled into the Ma & Pa's Steakhouse parking lot (video and pictures obtained).
12:01 p.m.	The subject exited her vehicle and entered Ma & Pa's Steakhouse (video and pictures obtained).
12:04 p.m.	Investigator #10 entered Ma & Pa's Steakhouse and saw the subject at a booth in the southwest corner of the restaurant. The subject sat across from a white male with short brown hair and a trimmed mustache. He wore a blue long-sleeved dress shirt. The subject and the male, who was approximately 6'1", 195 lbs., and wearing gray slacks, exited the restaurant (pictures obtained).
12:20 p.m.	The subject entered the green Blazer, and the male entered a black Toyota Camry bearing AZ license plate #LMR 642 (pictures obtained). They both exited the parking lot, the subject following the male. The subject and the male headed west on 48th Street. Both the subject and the male pulled into the Holiday Inn on 48th Street and Van Buren (video and pictures obtained).

(*Continued*)

TABLE 3.4 (CONTINUED)
Investigator's Progress Report

12:40 p.m.	Both the subject and the male exited their vehicles and entered a door on the east side of the hotel (video and pictures obtained). Investigator #10 entered the hotel and lost visual of the subject and the male. Investigator #10 took surveillance position outside the Holiday Inn.
2:51 p.m.	The subject exited the east door and entered her vehicle (video and pictures obtained). The subject then proceeded north on 48th Street to Rosewood Road and east on 64th Street. The subject pulled into Gentle Care Daycare and entered the building (video and pictures obtained).
3:03 p.m.	The subject exited Gentle Care Daycare with a child approximately 3 years old with blonde hair and wearing a pink shirt and pink shorts (video and pictures obtained). The child was placed in a car seat in the back of the subject's Blazer. The subject exited the parking lot and then drove south on 64th Street, turning east on Juniper to Miller Avenue South.
3:19 p.m.	The subject pulled into 5340 North Miller Avenue in Phoenix, Arizona. The subject removed the child from the car seat. The subject carrying the child entered the residence (video and pictures obtained).
3:30 p.m.	Surveillance terminated.
5:00 p.m.	Investigator #10 returned to base and completed and filed this report.

TYPES OF INVESTIGATIONS

BACKGROUND INVESTIGATIONS

Companies or businesses that serve the public are increasingly being held liable for criminal actions and negligent behavior that their employees inflict on third parties. It is the duty of employers to investigate an employee's background to determine if he or she has harmful character traits. Most offenders do not voluntarily offer in the employment interview or document on the employment application that they have a propensity to commit fraud, drink too much, or have violent tendencies. Because they do not want to be disqualified from employment and must work, they take great care in concealing derogatory information to protect their best interests.

For example, an employer hires an employee without performing a background check. The employer then places that employee in a trusted position with access to secure areas or information. The employee also may or may not come into physical contact with clients or customers. The employee commits an illegal act during his or her contact with the client. The business could face a civil litigation, especially if a background check is done after the fact and it was then discovered that the employee had committed a similar act prior to his employment. The business is liable to the injured parties because it had not shown due diligence in hiring.

Improperly done background investigations, such as not confirming that the information on the application is accurate and factual, can show negligence. If the derogatory information becomes known during the course of employment, but the employer keeps the person on anyway, this shows negligent retention and can cause litigation judgments on the business. An example would be a convicted pedophile working in a children's day-care facility or an alcoholic applying for a truck-driving position.

Employers are also responsible for maintaining safe and orderly workplaces that protect employees from real and potential dangers. The workplace must be free from known hazards and risks under federal and state laws, such as the Occupational Safety and Health Administration (OSHA). The employer must try to ensure that the employees are not exposed to those who steal, use drugs or alcohol on the job, hurt people, are dishonest, or display inappropriate behavior in the workplace. Employers also have the legal duty to conduct a thorough and meaningful investigation on any claim of unlawful discriminatory harassment.

Employment Application

A completed employment application is the most important information-gathering tool in an employment-related background investigation. Applications should request and obtain the following information:

1. Name, address, and telephone numbers with any first and last name variations the applicant has used.
2. Citizenship: Was he or she born in the United States, and does he or she have a green card?
3. Military record: Military DD-214, a standard document given to all US military personnel when discharged. The document has the dates of entry and separation, including the job description and reasons for discharge.
4. At least three personal references. The persons provided should not be relatives, nor should the applicant currently reside with them. Along with their names, phone numbers should be provided.
5. Any security clearances.
6. Previous education, listing the name of the school, the years attended, as well as the degree, diploma, or certification that was earned.
7. Former employment including all jobs held in the past 7 years. Names, addresses, and telephone numbers as well as the names of supervisors should be included. If there are gaps in employment, applicants need to explain the reasons for them in detail.
8: Background regarding spouse and relatives.
9. Full, detailed explanations about prior convictions. Questions cannot be asked about prior arrests, only prior convictions.
10. Hobbies.
11. Previous residences.

To overcome restrictions on disclosing data, do the following:

- Have applicants sign a disclosure form stating that they authorize the release of information on credit history, background, and educational history when they fill out the application.
- Include a special clause in the statement that would release the person providing the information from liability.

Employee Screening

The purpose of an employment-related background investigation is to prevent employee theft, lawsuits, and losses to the company. Screening potential employees helps verify the accuracy and completeness of an applicant's statements, develops additional relevant information, and determines suitability for employment or continued employment.

Three common ways applicants falsify applications are as follows:

1. Incomplete application
2. Willful omission of facts or job references, or providing references with the wrong address or references that are nonexistent
3. Misrepresentation of education or employment history

Employee screening should include the following:

1. Check any available local security incidences and police files to reveal if derogatory information exists.
2. Gaps in employment should be explored.
3. Check previous residences.
4. Research the applicant's consumer report and financial status, depending on job requirements.
5. Check civil court records.
6. Check criminal court records.
7. Contact personal references.
8. Verify educational background, including degrees received, training programs attended, and dates.
9. Interview former employees and work associates.
10. Personal contact is the most desirable form of investigation when checking references. A face-to-face interview often leads to more truthful and straightforward talk, and nonverbal clues are more easily detected.
11. Check military history. An investigator can also perform a military search in the National Personnel Records Center in St. Louis, Missouri, if the applicant does not have the standard DD-214 document.
12. Check professional certificates.
13. Check SSNs. An SSN issued prior to June 25, 2011 can reveal the area of the country where the number was issued, in case the applicant omitted his or her previous nationwide address to conceal a derogatory address. The number also supplies a way to check for governmental records indexed under the SSN.

Legal Constraints on Employment-Related Screening

Fair Credit Reporting Act

Employers can obtain an investigative consumer report that reveals the employee's character, general reputation, personal characteristics, or mode of living with the intent to use the information from credit reporting bureaus for employment purposes. The employee must give a written authorization permitting the release of consumer information.

If adverse actions are taken because of the consumer report, the employee is notified in writing, orally or electronically, of the fact that negative public record information is being reported by the consumer-reporting agency. The name of the credit agency along with the name and the address of the person to whom such negative information is being reported is provided to the consumer before an adverse action results.

The employer should maintain strict procedures designed to ensure that whenever public information is likely to have an adverse effect on employment, the information is complete and up to date.

Civil Rights Act—1964

1. Prohibits discrimination in hiring, firing, promoting, or giving raises or other benefits because of an employee's race, religion, sex, or national origin.
2. Prohibits limiting, segregating, or classifying employees in any way that would deprive or tend to deprive any individual of employment opportunities or otherwise adversely affect status as an employee, because of race, religion, sex, or national origin.
3. Job applications cannot inquire about prior arrests, only convictions.
4. Job applications that contain blanks could lead to the applicant's rights being violated.

Age Discrimination in Employment Act—1967

This Act bans discrimination against workers or applicants who are at least 40 years old on the basis of age.

Americans with Disabilities Act

The Americans with Disabilities Act (ADA) prohibits employers from discriminating against a "qualified individual with a disability." An individual with a qualified disability is one who, with or without reasonable accommodation, can perform the essential functions of an assigned position. Employers are allowed, under the ADA, to test for drug use, but they may not discriminate against a person who has successfully completed a drug rehabilitation program and who no longer uses illegal drugs. Current drug users are not protected.

The ADA protects individuals from the following:

1. That which physically or mentally impairs and substantially limits one or more of the major life activities of the individual
2. The individual's impairments being recorded
3. The individual being regarded as having an impairment

National Labor Relations Act

The following are the provisions of the National Labor Relations Act (NLRA):

1. Prohibits discrimination in hiring on the basis of union affiliation.
2. Employees have the right to form, join, and assist unions.
3. Employees have the right to engage in concerted activities (usually collective bargaining to improve work conditions and wages, grievances, on-the-job protests regarding unfair labor practices, picketing, and strikes).
4. Employees have the right to picket their employer's premises but not to trespass on the premises during the strike. Any interference with the picket line, such as restraining or coercing picketers to stop, is a violation of the act and can cause the employer to pay heavy fines and sanctions.
5. The US Supreme Court in the case of *National Labor Relations Board v. Weingarten* (1975) upheld a ruling that a denial of an employee's request to have a union representative present at an "investigatory interview" was an unfair labor practice.
6. Polygraph testing for dishonesty is not an unfair labor practice under the Taft–Hartley Act; however, it is an unfair labor practice if used to learn about union activities or an employee's actions regarding work conditions.

Employee Polygraph Protection Act of 1988

The EPPA restricts the use of lie detectors by most private-sector employers in applicant screenings and, for the most part, with current employees as well. Lie detectors include polygraphs, deceptographs, voice stress analyzers, psychological stress evaluators, or any other similar devices, whether mechanical or electrical, the results of which are used for the purpose of rendering a diagnostic opinion regarding the honesty or dishonesty of an individual. Lie detectors do not include medical tests used to determine the presence or absence of a controlled substance or alcohol in bodily fluids. Also not included are written or oral tests commonly referred to as "honesty" or "paper-and-pencil" tests (machine scored or otherwise), and graphology tests commonly referred to as handwriting tests in regard to the honesty or dishonesty of an individual.

The EPPA also prohibits the employer from discharging, dismissing, disciplining, denying employment or promotions to, or otherwise discriminating against the employee based on the results of a polygraph test or based on the refusal of the employee to take the test, without additional evidence that would support such action. If the employee quits on his or her own, instead of taking the test, the employer cannot give a negative reference to another potential employer in the future.

Exceptions allowing administration of lie-detector tests include the following:

- United States Government employers, any state or local government employers, or employees.
- Public agencies, such as school systems and correctional institutions.
- Private businesses may give certain job candidates preemployment polygraph tests, such as potential employees who will handle large sums of money or engage in security services.
- National defense and security, or any intelligence or counterintelligence functions.

Other exceptions are as follows:

- Employers manufacturing, distributing, or dispensing controlled substances may administer polygraphs to prospective applicants who would have direct access to the manufacture, storage, distribution, or sale of controlled substances and to current employees under criminal or other misconduct investigations involving the same.
- Employers who provide security services to clients that could have a significant impact on the public's health, safety, and security. Examples of this are employees providing protection to electric or nuclear power plants, public water supply facilities, companies that ship or store radioactive or other toxic waste materials, and public transportation. Employers may also provide security services for the protection of currency, negotiable securities, precious commodities or instruments, and proprietary instruments. These employers would provide their clients with armored cars and personnel; persons who would design, install, and maintain security alarm systems; or any other uniformed or plainclothes security personnel.
- Employers conducting investigations of economic loss or injury. The test is administered in connection with an ongoing investigation involving theft, embezzlement, misappropriation, or an act of unlawful industrial espionage or sabotage. There is reasonable suspicion that the employee was involved in the incident under investigation and had access to the property that is the subject of investigation. The "ongoing investigation" cannot be part of a sustained surveillance program, and the loss must have happened and be documented in a report, audit, or initial incident investigation.

When the incident in question is an ongoing, specific investigation, there is an economic loss to the employer, and the employee is subjected to polygraph testing, the following general criteria must be met (obtain a copy of the EPPA guidelines and the Department of Labor regulations from your state to ensure that the testing and requirements are being met):

1. A written notice for the basis of the testing, including a detailed description of the loss or activity under investigation, the specific amount of the loss, and a statement that the employee had access to the property.
2. The basis for the employer's reasonable suspicion, such as inconsistencies between facts, claims, and statements; information from a coworker; and the employee's behavior and conduct.
3. The statement must be signed by a person legally authorized to bind the employee, other than the examiner, and must be retained for at least 3 years.
4. The employee must be provided with advanced notice about the date, time, and location of the scheduled test.
5. Make sure the credentials of the polygraph examiner meet EPPA requirements.
6. After the polygraph test, conduct an interview with the employee prior to any adverse action and provide the employee with a copy of the polygraph report, along with questions, conclusions, and charts.
7. Maintain all records for at least 3 years.
8. Test results can only be released to the employee, anyone the employee specifically chooses, the firm or agency that requested the test, and any others who may require receiving the results through due process of law.

The employee has the right to review all questions in writing prior to the test and may request changes before taking the test. No questions can be asked that are degrading or that inquire about one's beliefs or opinions on religion, race, politics, union affiliation, sexual preference, or anything that needlessly intrudes upon the employee. The employee has the right to terminate the test at any time without adverse actions. The employee has the right to legal counsel before taking the test.

The test is not to be a basis or a condition for employment. The employer cannot terminate, suspend, discipline, deny promotions to, or discriminate against an employee based on a polygraph test or on the refusal to take the test without additional evidence to support such action. Additional evidence, such as an ongoing investigation, access to the property that is the incident under investigation, together with evidence supporting the employer's reasonable suspicion of the employee's involvement, must be attained for the employer to take adverse action, including termination.

Omnibus Crime Control and Safe Street Act of 1968 (Title III)

This prohibits private individuals and employers from intercepting wire or oral communications. Under this title, wiretaps are currently limited to use in investigations of crimes related to drug trafficking, bribery, and currency reporting, and they must be based on probable cause. Some exemptions do apply:

- Wiretapping takes place in a one-party consent state, meaning that only one party to the conversation needs to consent.
- The wiretap is obtained with a court order called an *ex parte* order.
- It is necessary for emergency cases involving national security.

Electronic Communication Privacy Act of 1986

The Omnibus Crime Control and Safe Street Act of 1968 was amended to the Electronic Communication Privacy Act of 1986 (ECPA), which regulates more recent forms of electronic surveillance.

The following are exceptions of the Act:

- Where there is one-party consent to the communication
- When an employer uses a telephone extension to monitor employees in the ordinary courses of business, for example,
  - Training on interaction with the public
  - Determining whether an employee is discussing business matters with a competitor
  - Determining whether an employee is making personal calls
  - Phone company monitoring for mechanical or service checks

Electronic surveillance is the use of electronic devices to covertly listen to a conversation, and wiretapping is the covert interception of telephone communication. Employers should conduct electronic surveillance, including video and monitoring, as unobtrusively and with as little invasion as possible. Surveillance generally should be kept out of areas where employees have a reasonable expectation of privacy such as private offices, restrooms, locker rooms, and break rooms. Civil liability suits claiming invasion of privacy and intentional infliction of emotional distress can arise if electronic monitoring is mishandled.

Invasion-of-privacy issues usually do not arise when employers monitor work activities and do not conduct surveillance of personal and private behavior and communications. As long as employers forewarn their employees that conversations are being monitored, the invasion of privacy does not become an issue.

Electronic surveillance *does not* evoke the Fourth Amendment if monitoring of employees is for the following reasons:

- Evaluating employees and their records of performance and productivity
- Providing a safe and crime-free workplace
- Assisting in avoiding fraudulent workers' compensation claims
- Helping to prevent assault-like behavior and the use of drugs and alcohol
- Deterring employee theft

Another area that involves invasion-of-privacy issues is the monitoring of e-mails and voice mail of employees. Under the ECPA of 1986, the person or entity (employer) providing the wire electronic communication service is not liable for the offense regarding stored communication, such as voice mail and e-mail, that is saved on equipment owned by the employer. For the employer's own protection, it is best to inform employees of the intent to periodically review and monitor e-mails and voice mails to ensure that the services and computers are restricted to business use. If at all possible, it is best to obtain written consent to avoid any invasion-of-privacy issues.

Some states require all parties to consent when electronic surveillance and wiretapping are involved. "If you want to be sure your recording is not in violation of the law, get the consent of both parties to the conversation, which really just means giving notice. The consent is inferred from the parties' willingness to participate in the conversation once notice is given that it is being recorded."

Undercover Investigations

An undercover investigation is one where the investigator assumes a role or identity to make observations or acquire information. The major distinction between undercover and other covert operations, such as surveillance, is that the undercover investigator does not conceal his presence or attempt to pass unnoticed; he or she conceals his or her true identity. Undercover investigations at the workplace provide management with skilled eyes and ears to observe employees on the job.

The investigator can observe employees under normal working conditions without stirring up employee suspicion or resentment. He or she is also able to partake in the activities of the target group or individual, providing a complete overview of the employee(s). The undercover investigator can give management a moral picture and work evaluation of all employees, thus providing insight into why there is a decline in business, which may be due to stealing, gambling, sleeping instead of working, excessive overtime, lax supervisors, and unauthorized computer use.

This means of security is invaluable. Undercover operations have actually saved companies from going out of business. Undercover investigators are usually called in to gather evidence instead of police officers because there is enough reliable information on criminal activity or asset losses but not enough information that a crime has been committed.

Every undercover operation should include the following:

- A qualified investigator. The consideration here is to ensure that the investigator will not be known to any of the persons likely to be in the target population. Generally, the undercover investigator should come from outside the employer or organization, typically from an investigative agency.
- Fitting the assignment. The investigator should be a logical "fit" in the proposed assignment. Factors such as sex, age, education, ethnic origin, etc. are extremely important. If the position is within an unskilled labor force, one typically filled by persons with less than a high school education, the investigator needs to fit that profile. Therefore, an undercover investigator whose style or mannerisms indicate a college education, or whose spending habits suggest greater resources than are typical for such jobholders, will cause red flags. The undercover investigator will be visible immediately; he or she will become the object of wonder and suspicion, making it difficult to establish casual contact with coworkers.
- Agent preparation. For example, if the investigator must apply to a personnel office and undergo a battery of tests of some kind, then he or she must see those tests beforehand to pass them with the required performance grade. Also, the investigator must know as much as possible about the work assignment and the names and descriptions of key people, including the suspects.
- Plausible cover story. The cover story is the explanation of the investigator's identity and how he or she came to be in the job. Generally, the more intimate the personal association between the investigator and members of the target group, the greater depth will be required for the cover story. The cover must not only explain the investigator's qualifications for the particular job but also offer a convincing account of how the job was obtained and what the agent's past life has been. Routine documents are provided to support cover. No document of actual identity is to be carried.

- Carefully thought-out emplacement and extortion techniques.
- Becoming friendly with coworkers and the suspects. This is accomplished through undercover "roping," which is the art of gaining the trust and confidence of a suspect to the point where the suspect will disclose to the investigator his or her criminal activities or at least lower his or her guard when around the investigator.
- Determining loopholes in operations, such as exits, layouts, shipping and receiving, and procedures in billing.
- Knowing the types of personnel employed, the day(s) salaries are paid, and the problem that the business is mainly concerned about.

The technical meanings of theft or stealing are as follows:

- Larceny: The wrongful taking and carrying away of the personal property of another with intent to convert or to deprive the owner of its use and possession by stealth.
- Robbery: The action of robbing a person or place by force or fear.
- Burglary: Illegal entry into a building with the intent to commit a crime such as theft.
- Motor vehicle theft: The object stolen is a vehicle.
- Fraud: Wrongful or criminal deception intended to result in financial or personal gain.
- Embezzlement: The fraudulent appropriation of property by a person to whom it has been entrusted. The major difference between larceny and embezzlement is that in larceny, the theft never had permission, whereas embezzlement does.

In conducting undercover theft investigations, consider the following:

- A complete description of items
- Ownership data
- Date the loss was noted and who discovered the loss
- To whom the loss was reported
- Area the loss occurred in
- Circumstances (i.e., forced entry)
- Extent of search
- Internal security measures contributing to theft
- Review of security to ensure that it is up to date
- How oriented the employees are to security
- Timeliness of security measures
- Implementing controls

Ways for the investigator to gather information, leads, and facts to assist in presenting and proving the case are as follows:

- Physical surveillance: recording what is observed with a camera, photographs, or video recorder
- Electronic surveillance: recording with CCTV or computer programs that record keystrokes
- Searches to locate and preserve physical evidence, including e-mails
- Research and audit: reviewing and examining all documents and records
- Forensic analysis: drug testing, polygraphs, and handwriting samples
- Working undercover: posing as an employee
- Interviewing on a selective basis: information gathering
- Use of informants

During undercover investigations, the investigator should not engage in activities in violation of rights created by the NLRA, such as those regarding union activities or concerning protected collective bargaining activities, and actions that could constitute a basis for civil actions such as invasion of privacy. Among the activities restricted or prohibited by the NLRA include interference or restraint through the use of surveillance or investigations into the actions of workers in exercising their collective bargaining rights. The actions of workers protected, including attending, organizing, or otherwise meeting with others to discuss the attitudes and sentiments of the workers being organized, as well as picking up and reading organization literature, are considered collective bargaining rights.

If the undercover investigator observes any of these activities and reports them to the employer, it constitutes prohibited restraint or interference. Even if the employer did not request such information but accepts it when offered by the investigator, the results are the same. It is very important that the investigator in any collective bargaining environment be aware not to report or note protected collective bargaining activities.

Areas of concern with undercover investigation are that under some circumstances, a failed or exposed undercover operation could lead to damage actions against the employer, if persons can establish tortious conduct toward the investigator. The tort most likely to be established would be some invasion of privacy, generally from an intrusion at a time and in a place where there was reasonable expectation of privacy because it was not public or readily available to the public. The fact that the place is on the premises of the employer does not automatically make the expectation of privacy unreasonable. For example, dressing rooms, restrooms, workers' automobiles, medical examination rooms, and the like have been held to be places in which an employee has a reasonable expectation of privacy.

Also, a complaining employee who could show a public disclosure of private fact may also prevail if such disclosure would be offensive to a reasonable person.

1. This could be enough, even if the actual invasion of a private place could not be shown.
2. The employee must not have given express or implied consent to the invasion or the disclosure. However, if the employer talks freely in an employee locker room in which the undercover investigator is among the listening coworkers, there is an implied consent to listening by all present.
3. With regard to the public disclosure of matter offensive to the complaining employee, it must also be a public or general disclosure, not a private or limited one.
4. A disclosure by the investigator to the employer would not be a public disclosure if it were made only to the employer in a private, discreet fashion.

A reasonable investigation does not in itself constitute an invasion of privacy unless it is carried to extremes or used for impermissible purposes. The employer bases the investigation techniques and methods used on an adequate and lawful interest. For example, the protection of assets against a known or suspected threat of an unlawful or otherwise improper nature is an adequate and lawful interest by the employer.

EMPLOYEE INVESTIGATIONS

Workplace investigations are undercover and confidential so that the development of evidence on theft, embezzlement, bribery and kickbacks, harassment, sabotage, or substance abuse can be detected.

Employee misconduct investigations are usually for one or more of the following purposes:

- To determine if company rules and policies have been violated
- To determine if state and federal laws have been violated

Sexual Harassment

The Equal Employment Opportunity Commission (EEOC) has defined two conditions of sexual harassment: (1) *quid pro quo* (Latin: "something for something") harassment, where a claim arises that a supervisor conditions employment opportunities on the return of sexual favors from the employee and (2) hostile environment harassment, where a claim arises that an employer created or allowed a pattern of conduct pertaining to sex that causes an unpleasant, or hostile, work environment. Also included is ongoing sexual harassment that the employer had actual or constructive knowledge of and failed to take immediate and appropriate corrective action on. The following are the basic criteria from the EEOC for determining whether action constitutes unlawful behavior:

- If submission to the conduct is either an explicit or implicit term or condition of employment
- If submission to or rejection of the conduct is used as a basis for an employment decision affecting the person rejecting or submitting to the conduct
- If the conduct has the purpose or effect of substantially interfering with an affected person's work performance or creating an intimidating, hostile, or offensive work environment

Every company or business should establish a zero-tolerance sexual harassment policy and post the policy to discourage sexual harassment and to let employees know that such incidents will be promptly and independently investigated. All employees should be made aware that when a complaint has been made, whoever assists in the investigation will not be subjected to any form of retaliation, and all matters regarding the case will be confidential.

Individuals found to have committed sexual harassment will be subjected to appropriate disciplinary measures. Investigators handling the case should provide well-written reports and complete records of the investigation, especially if the investigation led to a disciplinary termination and the person tries to seek legal action, or the claimant files a sex discrimination lawsuit.

Employers should train employees to avoid harassing others and create safeguards to prevent incidents of sexual harassment, as well as offer remedies to injured parties.

Theft Investigations

Employee theft accounts for billions of dollars of loss for businesses every year. Smaller and medium-sized businesses are more apt to become victims than larger businesses, primarily due to lack of direct supervision. Smaller-sized businesses consider and rely on employees' trustworthiness and therefore provide employees with more freedom of movement. Policies, procedures, and practices that are lacking and not followed in the company create an opening for dishonest employees that allows them to steal from their employer.

Employees steal for many reasons, including lack of loyalty to the company, feelings of being underpaid and unappreciated, feeling disgruntled, revenge, greed, excessive lifestyles, gambling, substance abuse problems—the list goes on and on. Some people are kleptomaniacs and have a compulsive need to steal from other people to feel a deep satisfaction about themselves. Others rationalize their behavior and believe that their motives are for a just cause. Most employee thefts are private matters that occur when employees seize an opportune moment and believe that they could and can just get away with it. The more theft is tolerated, the more it will occur and accelerate over time.

Theft prevention involves the quality of people we hire by (1) preemployment screening, (2) the environment that the employees are placed in, (3) the quality of management supervising that environment, and (4) having strict guidelines and procedures. There is more to be gained by taking action rather than setting aside financial reserves and adjusting prices to cover the burden of internal crime. The creation of additional internal security departments can reduce theft through preventive efforts coupled with a direct attack on the thieves themselves.

Indications of theft include variances and inventory shortages, evidence or other clues discovered during company inspections, or information received from informants. All businesses are different and have different operations. Some examples of guidelines and indicators of theft are as follows:

- Records of openings and closings: An alarm system monitored by an independent agency can provide times that the business has been opened or closed outside of normal operation hours. These records are useful in looking for a particular pattern of unusual entries or exits at the company.
- Employee locker inspections: Although it is unusual to find any hard evidence of theft in such locations, other indications of violations of company rules and regulations may be found, such as evidence of gambling paraphernalia or alcohol and drug use. Sometimes, evidence of theft can be found, like packaging materials or a product that was used for personal reasons. Inspecting employees' lockers does not constitute an invasion of privacy as long as the employer put the employees on notice that lockers are subject to inspection.
- Workstations: Employee workstations, over time, tend to collect personal effects. Desk drawers, file cabinets, or other containers should be inspected for any contraband, falsified documents, and the like.
- Waste containers: These should be checked for discarded evidence of theft or violations of the company's rules and regulations.
- Concealed areas: Crawl spaces, elevator pits, stairwells, etc., are all potential hiding places used to conceal theft by storing contraband for later pickup. They can also be utilized for sleeping on duty, which is stealing money by claiming hours not worked.

Major factors in employee theft are the lack of proper security measures or a control program. If there is no strict policy against theft or disciplinary measures that management goes by, then the employee will think that the worst that can happen when getting caught is to lose his or her job. Controls and deterrents are more for those who are basically honest employees, and these employees are kept that way by not giving them the opportunity. A dishonest employee just does not care and will always find ways around security.

An effective loss control program should emphasize the following:

- Carefully designed safeguard measures and preventive aids, such as security inspection checklists.
- Physical inventory inspections of goods and merchandise: Vulnerable areas to be considered are shipping and receiving zones, warehouses and storage areas, stockrooms, tool storage, fenced areas, and parking lots.
- Integrity or honesty testing: Checking the employee by posing as a customer making purchases, thereby observing his or her job performance.
- Employee education and motivation: Training seminars, reward and incentive programs, face-to-face meetings, and bulletins.
- Suggestion or grievance box: Employees know a great deal of what is going on within a business, including illicit activity, and are reluctant for reasons of their own to become involved openly. Providing a suggestion box allows effective communication with management in exposing dishonesty, other job-related problems, or suggestions. The suggestion or grievance box should provide assurances of confidentiality or anonymity when used.
- Daily audits with prompt reporting of missing items.
- Taking immediate steps toward apprehension and recovery.
- Prosecution.
- Remedial action.

Employee Absenteeism

Employee absenteeism is a subtle form of thievery that causes losses to a business. Absenteeism costs businesses millions of dollars each year because companies do not receive full value for pay received by absent employees. Ways to reduce absenteeism and motivate employees to feel pride and care about their work are as follows:

- Develop ways to make the employee feel important and significant to the company—that he or she is not just a number.

- Personalize the relationship. For example, go down to the workplace and address the employee, asking how he or she is doing, if he or she has concerns, etc.
- Proper training, clear instructions, assistance, and understanding. Employees want fair treatment and to be recognized for excellence and dedication.

SABOTAGE INVESTIGATION

Industrial sabotage is another form of thievery that causes loss. Sabotage is any willful act designed to hinder or obstruct the purposes for which a company operates. Common motivations for sabotage include the following:

- Disgruntled employees
- Union problems
- Dissatisfied outside contractors
- Penetration by organized crime
- Foreign manipulation
- Rioting

The following are key points to remember about sabotage:

- It is very difficult to identify and prove sabotage.
- If sabotage is strongly suspected, notify the FBI and preserve evidence.
- Arson is a common method of sabotage because it is very effective and tends to destroy evidence.

DRUG ABUSE INVESTIGATIONS IN THE WORKPLACE

Another large cost to companies is the use of alcohol and drugs in the workplace. Many companies are striving to provide a drug-free workplace because of the concern over economic costs, increased health care costs, absenteeism, increased on-the-job accidents, fear of liability for injuries, and the belief of increased employee theft. Employers want to control and manage the conduct of employees, thus providing a safe working environment for everyone. Rules for drug and alcohol testing are changing continually to provide a drug-free workplace.

Employees who use alcohol and drugs while working are more likely to create and have the following:

- Unnecessary safety risks for themselves and those around them
- More on-the-job accidents

- Missed work and more sick days
- Increased health care costs
- Filing for workers' compensation
- Stealing
- Garnished wages
- Decreased work productivity
- Higher turnover rates
- Friction among coworkers
- Damage to equipment
- Poor decisions
- Damage to the company's public image

An investigator should consider the following checks when conducting alcohol and drug abuse analysis:

- Attendance and absenteeism from work
- Financial problems
- Dysfunctional relationships
- Arrests
- Health and accident records
- Nearby bars: interviewing the bartender, waitresses, and even the "regulars" may provide useful information

When conducting drug and narcotic investigations, one should consider the following:

- Drugs can be carried in a number of ways, including within prescription bottles, fountain pens, toothpaste tubes, etc.
- The best approach is that a suspect is innocent until proven guilty.
- Chronic drug use generally indicates mental or emotional illness.
- Drug abusers commonly feel they cannot manage without drug support.
- Drug abusers commonly have a social maladjustment history and have difficulty getting along with others.

Common symptoms of an addict are a peculiar glistening look in the eyes, trembling hands, sallow skin, and wan cheeks; redness or ulcers in his or her nose, if drugs are being sniffed; and a rash on the skin from needle use.

Drug cravings can manifest as runny nose and eyes, frequent yawning and sneezing, continual itching of arms and legs, and dilation of pupils.

The Drug-Free Workplace Act of 1988 requires that all businesses contracting with the federal government, as well as those receiving federal financial assistance, certify that they have in place policies and procedures for addressing workplace substance abuse and also have taken certain steps to create and maintain a drug-free workplace. The Act prohibits employees from engaging in the unlawful manufacture, distribution, dispensation, possession, or use of controlled substances. Drug-free workplace rules also allow federal agencies to conduct preemployment drug testing.

Although private companies are not subjected to the Fourth Amendment like federal, state, county, and city governments, which must show a compelling reason, they too must guard against invasion of privacy. The OSHA states that an employer is obligated to provide a safe workplace. Company policies should be established regarding drug and alcohol use, and the company must be familiar with state and federal laws. Private companies only need to show that legitimate business interests or needs justify the invasion of privacy. For example, reasonable suspicion of drug and alcohol use in safety-sensitive positions, postaccident testing following certain types of accidents involving the loss of human life, and situations where a driver receives a citation under state or local laws for a moving traffic violation are examples of times where invasion of privacy is justifiable.

Random testing is probably the most effective means of detecting and deterring drug and alcohol use in the workplace, and it is the most controversial. So far, only a few states currently allow the use of random testing in non-safety-sensitive positions. Employee drug testing that is regularly scheduled, and preemployment testing imposed as a condition of employment, must be recognized as a legitimate need, and the policy and procedures must be suitable and reasonable according to the following standards:

- Advanced notice is given.
- Proper chain of custody is utilized.
- Confidentiality is guaranteed.
- Samples are tested at a certified laboratory.
- Follow-up reports are given to the applicants.
- Applicants have the opportunity to challenge and question test results.

DRUG CLASSIFICATIONS

Controlled Substances Act, Title II of the Comprehensive Drug Abuse Prevention and Control Act of 1970

This is the consolidation of numerous laws regulating the manufacture and distribution of narcotics, stimulants, depressants, hallucinogens, anabolic steroids, and chemicals used in the illegal production of controlled substances. The DEA and the Food and Drug Administration (FDA) are responsible for enforcing the provisions of the Controlled Substances Act (CSA). Any business that wants to handle one of these controlled substances, such as manufacturers, pharmacies, hospitals, doctors' offices, etc., must register with the DEA, receive an identifying number, and maintain records of their transactions.

Schedules of the CSA and their descriptions are as follows:

- Schedule I: High potential for abuse and has no current accepted medical use in the United States. There also is a lack of accepted safety of use of the drug or substance under medical supervision. Examples are heroin, LSD, marijuana, and methaqualone.
- Schedule II: High potential for abuse, which may lead to severe physical and psychological dependence, but has a current accepted medical use in the United States with restrictions. A written prescription by a practitioner is required and cannot be phoned into the pharmacy unless in an emergency. No refills are allowed. Examples are morphine, cocaine, methadone, and methamphetamines.
- Schedules III and IV: Less potential for abuse than schedules I and II, but abuse may lead to moderate or low physical dependence or high psychological dependence. Schedule IV substances have less potential for abuse than schedule III with some degree of physical and psychological dependence. There is a current accepted medical use in the United States. The prescription can be written or called into the pharmacy with up to five refills within a 6-month period. Examples include anabolic steroids, codeine, Tylenol with codeine, some barbiturates, Darvon, Valium, Violin, and XENIX.
- Schedule V: Low potential for abuse, even less than schedule IV. There is a current accepted medical use in the United States. There is still some degree of physical dependence and psychological dependence with abuse in this class. The purchaser must be 18 years of age and is entered in a log kept by the pharmacist. Schedule V substances includes many of the over-the-counter medications, such as low-strength prescription cold and pain medicines.

Repeated use of any drug can result in a buildup of tolerance as well as physical and psychological dependence.

- Drug dependence: Results from the repeated use of the drug, creating an ever-increasing tolerance, thus requiring larger doses for the desired effect.
- Physical dependence: Alteration of normal bodily functions, which necessitates the continual presence of the drug or substance in order to prevent withdrawals.

- Psychological dependence: Even after the physical need for the drug has passed, the addict still psychologically needs the drug or substance.

For brief descriptions of some of the scheduled drugs or substances, see Chapter 5.

GAMBLING INVESTIGATIONS

Gambling is a form of employee misconduct that is costly to a company. Gambling takes the employee away from his or her job duties for games of chance. Gambling on the job can have stakes as high as the employee's paycheck, which, if lost, could cause him or her to neglect his or her personal needs, such as paying rent or buying food, and he or she may well succumb to the temptation, if the opportunity arises, to commit theft.

Gambling in the American industry has been around for a long time, has a theft-influencing factor, and has ties to organized crime. This does not include the occasional office lottery but, rather, the larger forms, such as placing worldwide bets on horse or dog tracks etc., which are linked with organized crime.

Gambling investigations should consider the following:

- Use of undercover operators
- Evidence of gambling items: Records of paraphernalia found in employee lockers or workstations such as IOUs, rosters of players within the gambling pool where identification numbers are being used, or various athletic or payroll check pools
- Cooperation with local, county, or state law enforcement agencies
- Use of scientific devices such as fluorescent powder
- Use of concealed cameras
- Use of handwriting and fingerprint experts to examine documentary evidence

The following are some guidelines to prevent theft:

- Drug-free workplace
- Preemployment screening
- Loss awareness
- Employer–employee communications

EMBEZZLEMENT INVESTIGATIONS

Unlike external theft, which is immediately known to management, an internal theft, being stealthy, often goes undetected until large losses have occurred. Embezzlement is something that is usually ongoing, often escalates, and is worked alone. However, organized theft rings do occur and can bankrupt a company very quickly. Employee dishonesty is very serious and dangerous to a business because it makes it difficult to create accurate estimates of the probable loss.

Embezzlement occurs when persons who hold a position of trust find themselves with an unshakable problem, usually of a financial nature, that they think can be resolved by "borrowing" the funds from an employer. For example, an employee may borrow from the employer to tide over his or her financial need and then turn to gambling to recoup the funds that were borrowed, meaning additional financing. The losses become so large that they cannot be concealed, and the person is unmasked.

Embezzlement is the misappropriation of money and wrongful conversion of merchandise. The legality of embezzlement is the breach of trust or fiduciary responsibility of someone who is authorized, whereas larceny is the wrongful taking and carrying away of personal property with intent to convert or deprive the owner from use that is not authorized. Without a confession, it is hard to prove that a white-collar crime was willfully committed. The investigator must also prove other factors in conjunction with the embezzlement, larceny, or fraud to supplement the charge, such as employment misconduct behaviors, education, experience, training, and years at the job.

Key factors and motivators contributing to employee embezzlement are the product of economic need, revenge, or psychological reasons. The elements can be described as follows:

- Extravagance in one's lifestyle and living beyond one's income
- Heavy or chronic gambling
- Undesirable associates
- Alcohol and drug addictions
- Personal financial problems at home
- Playing Robin Hood to take from the rich and give to the poor
- Rationalization of dishonest actions to avoid creating anxiety
- Lack of management and inadequate establishment of controls, such as poor systems of accounting and lack of checks to the person in the trusted position

Opportunity for embezzlement arises in a business when the following are present:

- Inadequate rewards established for employees of the organization
- Lack of checks and balances of persons in positions of trust
- No audit trails or separation of duties

- Lack of operational reviews and follow-ups on audits, inspections, and policy and procedures
- Inadequate orientation and training on company policies and legal, ethical, and security issues
- Lack of employee education
- Failure to monitor and enforce policies of honesty and loyalty

Suspicious activities that are common in embezzlement include the following:

- Change in spending habits.
- Increase in standard of living.
- Apparent devotion to work, such as working later hours or refusing to take vacations, because of not wanting to be exposed.
- Account discrepancies or questionable transactions such as "padding" to cover up or "skimming" before cash entries are made. Most common in small businesses are fake entries and documents for purchases in the books, and fake credits and refunds.
- Complaints or allegations of misconduct by coworkers, customers, contractors, and informants.
- Noticeable behavior changes.
- Objection to a procedural change leading to closer supervision.

A disciplined environment with appropriate checks and balances combined with other safeguards is one of the most effective countermeasures against embezzlement. Some ways to detect theft include the following:

- Separation of duties and audit trails
- Periodic financial and operational audits
- Gathering information on lifestyles and personal habits of the employee
- Interviewing coworkers
- Searching e-mails
- Conducting quality checks on company phones
- Investigating suspicious activities and behavior

Embezzlement by Computer

Almost all companies and businesses today have computers that are taking the place of handwritten records and journals. Computers have taken the place of many job functions in the workplace and are built to do whatever the operator directs them to do. Computer embezzlers can fleece the company and fool its auditors through instructing a software program to write fictitious checks and send them to a home address or to program the computer to report abnormally high inventory losses as normal merchandise breakage, thus allowing the theft of good merchandise without it being noticed after one instructs the computer to remove the evidence.

Safeguards against computer theft include the following:

- Do not let the computer programmer actually operate the machine.
- Segregate computerized check-writing operations from the departments that authorize the checks, making it difficult for the embezzler to convert fudged data into actual payouts.
- Transfer computer operators and programmers to different machines and programs. This way, the person will not be working on the project long enough to rig the computer to steal and get large sums of money.
- Immediately investigate irregularities.
- Feed test data into the computer and determine whether anything interfered with the program.
- Management should conduct audits and internal spot checks.

In the private sector, access to targeted computers can be investigated without a search warrant. However, if there is no policy and procedure or foundation that exists, the employer can be sued for violation of privacy. The employee handbook and policies and procedures should contain and explicitly state that the company owns the computers that are used by employees and staff members. Also advise employees that there is no reasonable expectation of privacy in using company machines; if they choose to use the computer for personal communication or for other purposes, they do so at their own risk.

Fraud Investigations

Rarely during a fraud investigation does one see only one kind of fraud being committed. Theft and embezzlement are both considered fraudulent acts and are committed together. Fraud can be defined as the improper obtaining of an asset or item by providing or disseminating false information. There are many types of fraud:

- Corporate fraud: Any fraud perpetrated by or against a business corporation.
- Computer fraud: Use of a computer with the intent to commit a fraudulent act. In other words, any misappropriation of funds or embezzlement accomplished by tampering with computer programs, data files, operations, equipment, or media, which results in losses sustained by the business whose computer was manipulated,

is considered computer fraud. This also includes knowingly accessing or otherwise using a computer without authorization or exceeding authorization limits with intent to commit a fraudulent act.

- Medical fraud: Fraud against Medicaid, insurance companies, and other health care organizations.
- Theft of intellectual property rights or counterfeiting: Selling knockoff or copycat goods that are protected by trademarks, patents, or copyrights.
- Financial fraud: Material representation of a financial fact intended to deceive another to his or her detriment while the person committing financial fraud experiences an economic gain.
- Credit card fraud.
- Economic fraud: Fraudulent schemes such as the pyramid scheme, chain referral, short weighing products, and phony going-out-of-business sales, just to name a few.
- Personal injury and vehicular accidents: Phony or exaggerated claims of personal injury or material injury suffered from accidents.
- Fraudulent income, such as disability claims.

Fraudulent acts occur in a variety of forms in the workplace; some examples include time-card falsification, employment application falsification, injury claim falsification, fraudulent accident/injury claims, check fraud by employees, misuse of company credit cards, and expense account abuse.

Some guidelines to prevent fraud are as follows:

- Managerial controls
- Employee screening
- Forensic account
- Financial controls

WORKERS' COMPENSATION

Workers' compensation is required by law in all states that mandate employers to provide for all injuries and diseases arising out of or occurring in the course of employment. Workers' compensation makes employers liable to the disabled employee without regard to the matter of fault or negligence, unless the acts are proved willful, such as disobeying safety rules or being intoxicated by alcohol or another drug while at work. Benefits may include medical expenses and compensation for disability or death.

Workers' compensation is the claim of an injury from a work-related action that progresses to a disability. Investigators are often effectively used to gain evidence to prove the claim fraudulent and that the claimant is not suffering or disabled from any work-related injury.

Methods used to gain evidence include the following:

- Stakeouts
- Photograph and video surveillance
- Activity checks
- Interviews
- Medical documentation of injuries and sites of injuries
- Neighborhood checks
- Previous employment and background checks
- Well-written reports that are accurate, detailed, and precise

ESPIONAGE INVESTIGATIONS

Many businesses and corporations do not adequately identify and protect their businesses' information or computer telecommunication systems with proper security or policy and procedures, thereby leaving their employees unaware of their responsibility to protect proprietary information. The company could stand to lose a great deal should a competitor gain possession of information pertaining to items such as formulas, processes, clientele, production capacity, future plans for expansion, market research, bids for contracts, and research and development.

The greatest hazard to a company's sensitive information is its own employees. They present a risk to proprietary information primarily either through loose talk when they do not realize the confidential nature of the information they are discussing or possessing or through having an "it's nothing worth stealing" attitude. Employees may also disclose information as the result of bribes, blackmail, or the desire for revenge after being passed over for a promotion, being underpaid, and so on, or the employee may have secured the job for the sole purpose of securing information.

Economic or industrial espionage is the unethical practice of one company attempting to learn its competitors' secrets. Espionage may occur between two US firms or internationally between a foreign firm or government and a US firm.

Types of data most firms keep private are as follows:

- Research and development
- Pricing
- Products and promotions
- Facility expansion or relocation
- Style changes

- Management changes
- Competitive bidding
- Finance
- National defense matters
- Employee data
- Client lists

Methods used to conduct industrial espionage are as follows:

- Burglary
- Infiltration to get past protective barriers, such as moles and spies
- Moles using existing employees as one of the strongest interlinks to gather information
- Electronic surveillance methods, such as bugs and wiretapping
- Bribery and extortion
- Blackmail
- Trash search (dumpster diving)

Internal leaks can be minimized by the following:

- Carefully screening all prospective employees.
- Postemployment screening of employees. If the employee is living above his or her means and is placed in a sensitive area, he or she may be susceptible to bribes; a drinker or drug user may be vulnerable to extortion.
- Screening subcontractors such as cleaning crews.
- Training and selling employees on the need to protect company secrets.
- Enforcing a need-to-know policy. If they do not need it, they should not possess it.
- Enforcing the clean desk policy. employees should clean and lock desks during absences.
- Listening to talkative employees.

Security should consider the following steps to protect company secrets:

- Compartmentalize classified information. Handle on a need-to-know basis.
- Sensitive data should be well secured against unauthorized and unnecessary access.
- Safeguard all documents with confidential information by placing them in secured and locked areas.
- Shred and destroy all discarded documents.
- Regularly check phones for wiretaps.

- Sweep conference rooms for bugs such as hidden microphones and radio transmitters.
- Contact the FBI if there is evidence of a spy.

Economic Espionage Act of 1996

For many years, federal law has protected intellectual property through patent and copyright laws. Congress has extended the vital federal protection to another form of proprietary economic information—trade secrets.

Theft of trade secrets, in general, refers to the following: (1) There is the intent to convert a trade secret that is related to or included in a product that is produced for or placed in interstate or foreign commerce. (2) Economic benefit is gained through the theft of the trade secret, by anyone other than the owner. (3) It is done with the intent or knowledge that such an offense will injure any owner of that trade secret. (4) A person still knowingly steals, takes or conceals without authorization, or obtains such information through fraud or deception; without authorization, copies, sketches, draws, photographs, downloads, uploads, alters, destroys, replicates, transmits, delivers, sends, mails, or communicates such information; receives, buys, or possesses such information, knowing the same to have been stolen or obtained without authorization; and attempts to commit or conspire with one or more persons to perpetrate any offense previously described above.

Trade secrets may consist of all forms and types of financial, business, scientific, technical, economic, or engineering information, including patterns, plans, compilations, program devices, formulas, designs, prototypes, methods, techniques, processes, procedures, programs, or codes, whether tangible or intangible, and regardless of whether or how they are stored, compiled, or memorialized physically, electronically, graphically, photographically, or in writing, if the following are true:

- The owner has taken reasonable measures to keep such information secret.
- The information derives independent economic value, actual or potential, from not being generally known or readily available through proper means to the public.

The following are guidelines that businesses can take to protect their trade secrets and provide proof that the theft of trade secrets was purposeful and not accidental:

- Employees and contractors should sign nondisclosure agreements specific to each trade secret. Blanket statements might not support the intent provisions of the Act.

TABLE 3.5

Penalties under the Economic Espionage Act

Domestic Economic Espionage		
Individual criminal liability	Up to 10 years	Up to $250,000 fine
Corporate criminal liability	N/A	Up to $5000 fine
Foreign Economic Espionage		
Individual criminal liability	Up to 15 years	Up to $500,000 fine
Corporate criminal liability	N/A	Up to $10,000 fine

- Entrance interviews should be conducted with all employees and contractors who may be exposed to any trade secrets. Make sure they understand and agree in writing that they know about the Economic Espionage Act (EEA) and will protect such secrets.
- Exit interviews should be conducted with departing employees and contractors, particularly to remind them of their continuing obligation to avoid disclosure of proprietary information.
- As part of his or her employment contract, each employee or contractor should be required to regularly report back as to his or her future employment. If the previous employer is concerned regarding a specific matter, a letter can be sent to the new employer to put them on notice that their employee possesses protected trade secrets.

Penalties under the EEA are as shown in Table 3.5.

TRAFFIC ACCIDENT INVESTIGATIONS

Investigators most likely will be called on to develop a case to support the client's claim after the accident had already happened. Investigation claims can be from the insurance companies themselves or claims of negligence and great bodily harm from the individuals involved in the accident. If the investigator is called out to the actual accident scene, the following primary emergency actions should be taken:

- Care for the injured.
- Get any fire or other hazards under control.
- Locate drivers, witnesses, and helpers.
- Determine any existing traffic hazards.
- Locate and safeguard physical evidence.

When the emergency steps are under control, take the following actions:

- Conduct preliminary interviews of drivers.
- Gather evidence for identifying any hit-and-run vehicles.
- Interview other witnesses.
- Determine the condition of drivers.
- Question drivers regarding licensing, registration, and their explanations of what happened.
- Determine and report positions and conditions of vehicles involved.
- Photograph skid marks and locations of vehicles.
- Determine and report the place where injured persons and damaged vehicles were found.

Measurements and maps are important in accident investigations. Accident scene measurement equipment should include a tape measure of at least 50 ft., pencil, paper, ruler, clipboard, crayon, flashlight, cameras, template, and written statements from all witnesses and drivers.

There are three kinds of measurements or maps:

1. Urgent measurements to locate things at the scene
2. Measurements of location to make scale maps and diagrams
3. A map drawn from the measurements made and objects or marks located at the scene

Many times, the investigator will be called out to investigate an accident after the fact, where the vehicle and the marks left behind are the only evidence available at the scene. It is difficult to prove a driver's condition or behavior at the time, and statements from those involved in the accident tend to be unreliable. The driver is the primary factor in almost every accident; the driver makes the decisions and controls the vehicle. The investigator must reconstruct the accident and prepare an investigative report. Some of the following items are necessary for full field investigations:

- Obtain medical reports.
- Obtain the accident reports.
- Record any obvious physical handicap of the driver that is not the result of the accident, such as hearing impediments, color blindness, or eyesight problems.
- Determine if the driver has any medical health concerns, like diabetes, previous heart attacks, strokes, etc.

- Locate and interview any outstanding witnesses who may make a statement or suggestion that the driver was intoxicated, fell asleep, or attempted some action that interfered with driving, such as texting, adjusting the radio, eating, talking on a cellular phone, or looking at a map.
- Investigate the vehicle, looking for items such as partially eaten food, unfolded maps, alcohol containers, pill bottles, or over-the-counter medications.
- Determine what the driver was doing, such as leaving a party or bar, or going on a long trip.
- Note any illegal conditions of equipment ownership, registration, etc. that may have contributed to the accident.
- Determine existing weather conditions, such as daylight, dusk, nighttime, rain, or snow.
- Determine visibility conditions, such as sun glare or fogginess.
- Determine road surface conditions, such as whether it was dry, wet, or slippery, or there was loose gravel.
- Determine what traffic control devices were at the scene, such as stop signs, stoplights, right-of-way markings, etc.
- Consider debris at accident scene.
- Examine tire imprints, marks, and skid marks.
- Determine vehicle damage, condition, or some malfunction to show how and why the accident happened; look at the brakes, condition of the tires, speedometer readings, etc.
- Videotape and photograph the scene. Photographs should show the position of vehicles at the time of the accident; damage; angles of collision; marks on the road; paths of vehicles before, during, and after collision; and overall condition of the scene as viewed by the driver.

The most frequent direct causes of traffic accidents are speed, initial behavior, delayed actions and perceptions, and faulty evasive actions. Reconstruction of an accident is usually necessary only when the cause of an accident cannot be satisfactorily determined by available evidence.

CLAIMS INVESTIGATIONS

Claims investigations help insurance companies and the self-insured fight fraudulent claims by detecting fraud and providing detailed reliable reports and admissible evidence. All serious claims investigations should be handled through a personal contact type of investigation.

A claim report serves several purposes:

- Provides a permanent record
- Provides a summary of all claims
- Brings together various parts of a file

The most important elements of a claims investigation are the accident report; information including identification of vehicles, premises, and products; statements of eyewitnesses and "fact" witnesses; insured claimants; and various official reports and records.

Methods that are used in claims investigations include the following:

- Activity checks on the individual in question, such as if the individual claims whiplash and is found to be out waterskiing
- Surveillance
- Interviews with friends, family, and coworkers
- Medical and autopsy reports
- Skip tracing
- Record searches, such as criminal, civil, DMV, etc.
- Previous employment
- Education and professional credentials
- Neighborhood checks

Most claims investigations are usually the following:

- Property and casualty claims
- Workers' compensation claims
- Liability
- Malpractice suits
- Theft
- Accidents

Table 3.6 lists various official reports and records for review in claims investigations.

ARSON INVESTIGATIONS

Arson has been identified as the fastest-growing type of crime in the United States. National statistics indicate that it is the most expensive crime committed when measured on a cost-per-incident basis. Arson is responsible for approximately half of all fire-related property damage in the United States. Crimes involving arson are among the most devastating crimes because they destroy property, disrupt lives, and cause an increasing

TABLE 3.6
Various Official Reports and Records for Review in Claims Investigations

Government	Medical	Media	Visual Aids	Various Experts
Municipal	Doctors	Newspapers	Photos	Handwriting
County	Hospitals	Television	Videotapes	Appraisers
Federal	Labs	Movies	Models	Weather
Police	X-rays		Diagrams	
Fire				
Marriage licenses				
Deeds				
Leases				
Contracts				
Liens				
Motor vehicle registration				
Death certificates				
Birth certificates				

economic burden on citizens. Arson crimes are hard to solve, and arrests do not have high conviction results. Every fire, regardless of size, should be investigated.

Arson can be defined as the willful burning or destruction by explosion of a structure or the personal property of someone by another person or persons, or the destruction of the property by the owner if done for the purpose of defrauding an insurer. The elements of arson are malicious intent, setting fire or burning certain buildings, and aiding in such burnings.

Related areas that apply to arson include the following:

- Burning of nonresidential buildings, railway cars, ships, and vessels
- Burning of wood fences, fields, forests, and vehicles
- Attempted arson
- Burning insured property with the intent to defraud
- Burning of insured vehicles

The investigator must determine whether a fire or explosion was set intentionally or accidentally. All possible accidental causes must be eliminated. This can present a challenge to the investigator because unless all causes can be eliminated, the fire must be declared as accidental or from an unknown origin. The point of ignition or origin must be determined as early as possible in arson investigations, and then evidence must be found to support the theory of arson. Every fire, regardless of size, should be investigated.

Some ways to determine how the fire started can include the following:

- The direction and location of the flames as well as the most heavily damaged or charred areas most often point to where the fire originated. A fire burns in a triangular pattern away from its source, which is usually found on the windward tip of the triangle. The existence of two or more separate blazes or points of origin usually indicates an intentionally set fire.
- The color and height of flames, as well as the odor and color of smoke, can determine if an accelerant or other substances were used, such as kerosene, gasoline, oil, tar, paint solvent, etc.
- Look for any incendiary material or ignition devices, such as unnatural kindling agents, matches, candles, chemicals, or a delayed fuse, timers, or wiring in gas and electrical devices. Other materials to look for are items that can spread the blaze to other areas, such as rope, newspapers, rags, etc. These will need to be tested, as they may have been soaked in an accelerant.
- Look for any evidence of tampering with alarm systems, doors, windows, or sprinkler systems.
- Observe any splatters or burn patterns on the floor.
- Look for any electrical appliances out of place.
- Look for any flammable liquid containers.
- Determine the weather conditions at the time of the fire.
- Interview the owner of the structure or property, any witnesses, firefighters, and dispatch.
- Perform record checks on the owner to determine if he or she has suffered fire losses more than once and to learn of phony ownerships, false claims, and the past history of the property.
- Conduct background checks on everyone, including the person who called in the fire, the owner, and any witnesses.
- Photograph and diagram the scene.
- Collect evidence from the scene, such as ashes, charred paper, matches, and gas containers. The debris most suitable for analysis is absorbent by nature, like padded furniture, carpeting, plasterboard, and flooring. Gas chromatography techniques are used to determine whether or not accelerants or other substances were used to facilitate destruction.
- Locate the owner's insurance carrier to find out if the property is overinsured or has more than one policy.
- Find out if there was any police activity or reports concerning the area, and if any local news stations covered the story.
- Research the general area to see if there had been another fire in the area and, if possible, determine if the fire was arson or

accidental. If the fire was determined to be arson, compare the styles of ignition and any similarities.

Some key motives of arson are as follows:

- Insurance fraud, a common arson-for-profit scheme. The majority of vehicular fires are intentionally set for insurance money.
- Economic gain.
- Political motives.
- Personal satisfaction and revenge against an enemy.
- Diversionary tactics to conceal other crimes.
- Sabotage.
- Destroying corporate or business records.
- Intimidation, extortion, or murder.
- Thrill of setting fires, or pyromania.
- To attract attention to oneself, for example, starting the fire and reporting it by saving lives and property in hopes of being recognized.

BOMB-THREAT INVESTIGATIONS

Bomb threats are often employed to "make a point" with target victims. Work locations, factories, schools, libraries, hospitals, exhibitions and entertainment centers, theaters, arenas and stadiums, and public transport stations and terminals, such as airports or bus stations, are the favorite targets of bomb threats. The major objective of telephoned bomb threats is usually psychological and financial harassment. Some bomb threats are hoaxes, where no actual device had been placed and for whatever reason, the caller wished to disrupt the intended target. Some examples of who may make a fake bomb threat are disgruntled employees, employees looking for a day off from work, students seeking to avoid taking an exam, or thrill seekers with no motivation. Other instances of bomb threats occur when the caller has a more serious purpose and may want media attention.

Bombs are defined as any chemical compound, mixture, or device that functions by explosion to release instantaneous gas and heat. With this in mind, all bomb threats should be treated as the real thing until determined otherwise, and plans and risk assessments made of the area should be established in writing and given to all management personnel in case a bomb threat occurs and the area needs to be vacated. Before evacuation occurs, all designated routes must be searched prior to evacuation and cleared for passage. Evacuees must be removed to a distance sufficient to ensure they will not be injured should a detonation or explosion occur.

Explosion

An explosion is a sudden, violent, noisy eruption, outburst, or discharge by material acted upon with force such as fire, shock, or electrical charge, which causes the solid or liquid material to convert into gas and violently expand or burst.

General rates of explosion are as follows:

- Flash fires, which usually occur in the open where there is an immediate reaction in which fuel is consumed upon ignition. An example of this is when a propane tank explodes.
- Explosions.
- Detonations are instantaneous decomposition of the explosive material, producing a release of heat and causing a pressure-created shockwave. An example of this is when TNT explodes.
- Deflagrations, which are rapid auto combustion explosions.

Basic types of explosions are as follows:

- Boiler
- Flammable gas
- Chemical
- Dust
- Nuclear, implosion-triggered fission bomb
- Sonic

4 Protection of Sensitive Information

One of the most important responsibilities that the security professional has is to protect the company's information from those who should not have access to it. Trade secrets, trade negotiations, business plans, financial reports, and other classified and personal information must be protected. In today's world of industrial spies, computer hackers, and sophisticated thieves, this responsibility has become more vital to a company's well-being.

The security professional must, however, master the ability to create, evaluate, and maintain a viable program to protect these most valuable of a company's assets.

The protection of sensitive information is a very serious problem for many companies. The competitiveness of industry, both nationally and internationally, has caused incidents of information theft and sabotage to increase, almost exponentially, over the years. As a security manager or director, it will fall to you to devise ways and advise company officials on how to identify losses, develop countermeasures, identify and apprehend suspects, and minimize the impact of the loss of company-sensitive information.

First, however, you must understand what constitutes sensitive information. Only after identification of what company information is sensitive and where it is located or stored and determining the vulnerability of the information can an effective and comprehensive program be constructed to prevent its loss.

WHAT CONSTITUTES SENSITIVE INFORMATION

TRADE SECRETS

A trade secret is defined in the Restatements of the Law of torts as follows:

A trade secret may consist of any formula, pattern, device or compilation of information which is used in one's business and which gives him an opportunity to gain an advantage over competitors who do not know or use it. It may be a formula for a chemical compound, a process of manufacturing, treating or preserving materials, a pattern for a machine or other device or a list of customers.

A trade secret is a process or device for continuous use in the operation of the business.

Generally, a trade secret relates to the production of goods, for example, a machine or formula that is used to produce an article. It also may relate to operations in the business field, such as a code for determining discounts and rebates as well as a list of customers or method of bookkeeping.

The basic elements of a trade secret are as follows:

- It must be secret and not known to others.
- It must be used in the business of the owner of the secret to obtain an advantage.
- There must be continuous or consistent business application of the secret.

Some factors to be considered in determining whether a trade secret actually exists are as follows:

- To what extent are the data known to the outside world?
- To what extent are the data known by employees?
- What types of protective measures have been taken to safeguard the secrecy of your data?
- What is the value of the information to the company and competitors?
- How much effort or money has been expended in developing the data?
- How easily could these data be acquired legitimately by the competition?

The courts tend to find against those who have acted in bad faith where the use of confidential information is involved, but there must be a showing that the owner preserved the secrecy of the information to the maximum extent possible.

Some key points to remember with regard to confidential information and trade secrets are as follows:

- Trade secret information is entitled by law to more protection than other kinds of proprietary information.
- For trade secret protection, it will be necessary to prove all of the following elements:
  - Secrecy
  - Value
  - Use in the owner's business

- The measure of proof of the elements needed varies with the jurisdiction.
- For an established trade secret, the owner may get his or her protection through the fiduciary status of disclosee or through an agreement with the discloser.

A patent is a grant made by the government to an inventor, conveying and securing to him the exclusive right to make, use, and sell an invention for a term of years.

The primary distinctions between patents and trade secrets are as follows:

- Requirements for obtaining a patent are specific.
- To qualify for a patent, the invention must be more than novel and useful. It must represent a positive contribution beyond the skill of the average person.
- A much lower level of novelty is required of a trade secret.
- A trade secret remains secret as long as it continues to meet trade secret tests, but the exclusive right to patent protection expires after 17 years.
- Because anyone can purchase a patent, there are no industrial espionage targets in a patented invention.
- Trade secrets are targets.

The most serious internal threat to trade secrets is the employee.

If information is wrongfully obtained by one person and then disclosed by that person in such a fashion that others gain knowledge of it without being aware that it is or was the secret of someone else, the original wrongdoer is the only one against whom the original owner has recourse.

Once the information gets into the hands of innocent third persons without notice to them of its secret nature, it is generally lost.

Why is it important for employees to know whether confidential information is strictly defined as a trade secret or as merely another piece of confidential information? The answer is that if it is a trade secret, an employer can protect threatened disclosure by injunction.

Not all sensitive data are trade secrets. Some examples of data that are not trade secrets are as follows:

- Salary information
- Rank surveys
- Consumer usage evaluations
- Profitability margins

- Unit costs
- Personnel changes

Before instituting litigation with regard to trade secret cases involving former employees now working for a competitor, the following possible threats should be considered:

- The owner may have to expose the very secrets he or she is attempting to protect.
- The cost may be too high.
- The owner may lose the case.

Recognizing that the most serious internal threat to trade secrets is the employee, a measure of protection is often provided through the use of employee patent and secrecy agreements. These agreements restrict the employee's ability to disclose information without the authorization of the company.

US Government Classified Information

Official information or material that requires protection against unauthorized disclosure in the interest of the national defense of the United States is classified into one of three categories: top secret, secret, or confidential.

The test for assigning a top-secret security classification is whether its unauthorized disclosure could reasonably be expected to cause exceptionally grave damage to national security.

The test for assigning a secret security classification is whether its unauthorized disclosure could reasonably be expected to cause serious damage to national security.

The test for assigning a confidential security classification is whether its unauthorized disclosure could reasonably be expected to cause damage to national security.

Other than the categories of top secret, secret, and confidential, no other category is used to identify official information or material as requiring protection in the interest of national security, except as is otherwise expressly provided by statute.

Industrial Espionage

Industrial espionage is a major security problem in business today. This is especially true in the high-tech industries. The following are some of the basic concepts regarding industrial espionage.

The basis for any industrial espionage prevention program is protection of information. Any information that involves the following two elements is considered to be a valuable asset requiring protection:

1. Production of goods and services
2. Locating and retaining customers

Some of the types of information generally requiring protection in business and industrial firms are as follows:

- Basic manufacturing data
- Design manuals
- Plant operating instructions
- Plant test results
- Production reports
- Raw material specifications

In combating industrial espionage, the following external threats must be considered and addressed:

- The industrial spy
- An undercover operative
- Wiretaps
- Microphones and other listening devices
- Trespassers
- The collection of information from the company's trash
- Visitors
- Customers
- Subcontractors

A proprietary security program designed to prevent industrial espionage should consider the utilization of the following techniques:

- Preemployment screening
- Procedures to control the distribution of sensitive information
- Procedures to classify material
- Installation of adequate physical security measures
- The use of secrecy agreements
- Security education programs
- Supervised destruction of waste and trash
- Institution of electronic countermeasures, such as sweeps and debugging

- Investigation of selected personnel
- Controls to minimize access to sensitive information

The chief federal sanction that deals with an act of industrial espionage is the Federal Stolen Property Act—18USC 2314. The main features of this Act are as follows:

- Transporting the material or data by any means in the interest of interstate or foreign commerce.
- Goods in the value of $5000 or more.
- Knowing that the goods or data have been stolen, converted, or taken fraudulently.
- The individual convicted of violation of this act shall be fined not more than $1000 or imprisoned for more than 10 years, or both.

PROPRIETARY INFORMATION

Proprietary information is information involving a process or method of manufacture that may constitute an especially valuable trade secret, as when a process results in a product having a considerable market or in improving the competitive position of an existing product. An important point to remember is that all proprietary information is confidential, but not all confidential information is proprietary. It has been said that proprietary information can be grouped into two broad divisions: trade secrets and all other confidential information.

Common law uses two approaches in dealing with sensitive information:

1. The "property concept," which regards the information as having a considerable value if it amounts to a trade secret.
2. The imposition of duties on certain classes of people, other than the owner, not to use or to divulge information without the owner's consent. This approach treats these individuals as "fiduciaries" because they occupy special positions of trust or confidence.

Some of the rights provided by law to protect the property of proprietary information under common law are as follows:

- Right to sue for damages for loss or destruction
- Right to recover profits under the equity theory of "unjust enrichment"
- Right to restrain another from using the property
- Right to retain exclusive use of the property

There are three broad threats to proprietary information. They are the following:

1. It can be lost through inadvertent disclosure.
2. An outsider can deliberately steal it.
3. An insider can deliberately steal it.

In general, there are two forms of relief available under common law to a proprietor of confidential information:

1. Injunctive relief
2. Money damages

An effective proprietary information security program should include the following:

- Designation of appropriate data as sensitive
- Informing and notifying employees
- Full utilization of secrecy agreements with employees
- Providing physical means to protect sensitive data
- Treating sensitive information as proprietary

A total program of data protection should include all or most of the following:

- A clear policy and procedural statements by corporate management as to how sensitive information should be handled
- A comprehensive preemployment screening process
- Awareness and employee educational training programs
- The use of nondisclosure and secrecy agreements from the employer
- Appropriate physical security measures
- Continuous monitoring of routine activities in the field to detect appearances of sensitive data
- Implementation of a system of regular audits or internal inspections

A well-constructed applicant questionnaire is a key tool to assist in proprietary information control. The following items, at a minimum, should be found on all questionnaires:

- Name
- Age or date of birth
- Residence

- Educational information
- Employment history for 10 years or longer
- At least three references
- Criminal record (convictions)
- The appropriate authorization forms and signatures

EAVESDROPPING TACTICS AND EQUIPMENT

The term *eavesdropping* today should include both wiretapping and bugging. Wiretapping is the interception of communication over a wire without the consent of the participants and requires physical entry into the communication circuit. Bugging is the interception of communication without the consent of the participants by means of electronic devices and without penetration of a wire.

The first federal legislation that attempted to regulate electronic surveillance in the United States was enacted by Congress in 1934. It was included in Section 605 of the Federal Communications Act of 1934.

The most important federal statute that deals with electronic surveillance today is the Omnibus Crime Control and Safe Streets Act of 1968. Some of the key provisions of this Act are as follows:

- It prohibits wiretapping or bugging unless a party to the intercepted conversation gives approval.
- It provides for a uniform delineation of circumstances and conditions for authorized interception of oral and wire communications.
- It prohibits manufacture, distribution, possession, and advertising of wire or oral communication interception devices.
- Eavesdropping by private individuals is not allowed.
- A stated objective is to combat organized crime.
- Federal law enforcement officials may intercept both wire and oral communications but only under strict conditions.
- The criminal and civil penalties are severe.

As part of a robust security program, or if a company suspects that eavesdropping is occurring, technical countermeasure sweeps should be conducted. Technical countermeasure sweeps can be categorized into three categories—physical search, telephone search, and electronic search.

A physical search is detailed, time consuming, and expensive and should be conducted in specific areas only. Some of the key points of a physical search are as follows:

1. Walls are examined in detail for holes, mismatched paint, and new plaster or sheetrock.
2. All furniture is removed and examined.

3. Space above a dropped ceiling (plenum) is examined.
4. All wiring, including optical fibers, is traced and accounted for. Any wire that is not in use is to be removed.

A telephone search should be done by a technician who is familiar with the specific equipment. Some of the key points of a telephone search are as follows:

1. The telephone distribution room wiring is verified.
2. Examine all connections to the wiring closets and junction boxes and verify that they are properly connected and have not been modified.
3. Handsets are to be examined for drop-in transmitters or wiring alterations.
4. All cables are inspected for unusual attachments or bulges.

An electronic search is a search of the radio frequency spectrum to detect any unauthorized emanations from the area being examined.

A key point to remember is that no remote device or technique is guaranteed to find a well-installed device put in place by an experienced technician. Some of the key equipment and methods used for an electronic search are as follows:

1. A nonlinear junction detector is used to locate a semiconductor device that is dead by transmitting a microwave signal.
2. Time-domain reflectometry takes an electronic picture of a telecommunications line at a given time, which is compared to the same telecommunications line at a future time.
3. A countermeasure radio receiver searches the radio spectrum to isolate and identify a signal.

A "pen register" is a device used to monitor telephone calls by providing a record of all numbers dialed from a particular phone. It provides both the date and time a call was made.

The following are some basic facts concerning types of microphones used:

• A carbon microphone is commonly used in the mouthpiece of a standard telephone handset. A power source is required to supply the necessary voltage.
• A dynamic microphone is one that operates as a loudspeaker in reverse. It is popular as an eavesdropping device as it requires no power source to operate. It can be used in such items as cuff links, tie clasps, eyeglasses, etc.

- The contact microphone is usually a crystal microphone and is normally installed on a common wall adjoining a target area. There are, however, a number of disadvantages, such as the following:
  - Signals generated are weak.
  - The microphone receives other sounds.
  - It is affected by changes in temperature and humidity.

Sensitive or confidential information is extremely important to any business operation. The unauthorized dissemination of that information can have disastrous effects on a company.

Many companies have no moral scruples about stealing anything that would afford them an advantage in today's global business community. When the information is related to our national defense, you are faced not only by foreign companies but by foreign governments as well. Regardless of the location of the company, the best way to protect any type of data is to encrypt it. Encryption scrambles the information so that it is not usable unless there is knowledge of the code and how to translate the data.

The Certified Protection Professional (CPP) exam takes the information on this subject very seriously. The information and concepts outlined in this chapter will appear several times in the exam. Take notice of how other areas of the test relate to this subject, such as physical security measures and investigations. A well-rounded, competent security manager or director must be able to integrate all of these disciplines into daily routines.

5 Substance Abuse in the Workplace

Substance abuse is a scourge in all aspects of life. The toll in lives lost is very high; the enormous cost to fund police, corrections, federal agencies, and the courts drains billions of dollars from other much-needed areas. Families become ruined, and the billions of dollars pumped into the hands of criminal organizations to fund other crimes and public corruption is well documented.

Substance abuse also takes its toll on businesses everywhere. Areas in which businesses suffer most include the following:

- Absenteeism
- Workers' compensation claims
- Lost and damaged production
- Theft
- Losses due to accidents
- Needless lawsuits
- Additional security costs

Due to the negative impact that a substance abuser can have on an organization, it is extremely important to have a preemployment screening practice in place. If abusers or dealers do gain a foothold, it falls to the security department to identify and prosecute them.

To be successful in accomplishing the goal of a drug-free workplace, the security manager or director must master certain basic information about the various substances in use today.

The following is the basic information you will require.

CONTROLLED SUBSTANCES ACT (TITLE II, COMPREHENSIVE DRUG ABUSE PREVENTION AND CONTROL ACT OF 1970 [PUBLIC LAW 91-513])

CONTROL MECHANISM

The Drug Enforcement Administration (DEA) of the Department of Justice is responsible for enforcing the provisions of the Controlled Substances Act (CSA).

There are nine major control mechanisms imposed on the manufacturing, purchasing, and distributing of substances listed under the CSA. They are as follows:

1. Registration of handlers
2. Record-keeping requirements
3. Quotas on manufacturing
4. Restrictions on distribution
5. Restrictions on the dispensing of substances controlled under this act
6. Limitations on the import and export of drugs
7. Conditions for the safe storage of drugs
8. Reports of transactions to the government
9. Criminal, civil, and administrative penalties for illegal acts

Any person who handles or intends to handle controlled substances must obtain a registration issued by the DEA. A control mechanism applicable to all substances under control, regardless of the schedules they are listed under, is that full records must be kept of all quantities manufactured, purchased, sold, and inventoried for each substance by each handler. The DEA limits the quantity of controlled substances listed in schedules I and II that can be produced during any given calendar year. The dispensing of a controlled substance is the delivery of the controlled substance to the ultimate user, who may be a patient or research subject. Schedule I drugs are those that currently have no accepted medical use in the United States (Table 5.1). They may be used only in research situations.

For all schedule II, III, and IV medications, a prescription order is required under the Federal Food, Drug, and Cosmetic Act. Other major points are as follows:

- Schedule II prescription orders must be written and signed by a practitioner. They may not be telephoned in to the pharmacy except in an emergency. Such prescriptions cannot be refilled.
- For schedule III and IV drugs, prescription orders may be written or oral (telephoned). A patient may have the prescription refilled up to five times and at any time within 6 months from the date of the initial dispensing.
- Schedule V includes many over-the-counter narcotic prescriptions. However, the law imposes special restrictions, such as that the patient must be at least 18 years of age and his or her name must be entered into a special log maintained by the pharmacist.
- Note that the CSA distinguishes between trafficking offenses and use offenses, the latter being offenses by those possessing drugs solely for personal use.

TABLE 5.1

Federal Trafficking Penalties for Schedules I, II, III, IV, and V (except Marijuana)

Schedule	Substance/Quantity	Penalty	Substance/Quantity	Penalty
II	Cocaine 500–4999 g mixture	First offense: Not less than 5 years and not more than 40 years. If death or serious bodily injury, not less than 20 years or more than life. Fine of not more than $5 million if an individual, $25 million if not an individual.	Cocaine 5 kg or more mixture	First offense: Not less than 10 years and not more than life. If death or serious bodily injury, not less than 20 years or more than life. Fine of not more than $10 million if an individual, $50 million if not an individual.
II	Cocaine base 28–279 g mixture		Cocaine base 280 g or more mixture	
IV	Fentanyl 40–399 g mixture		Fentanyl 400 g or more mixture	
I	Fentanyl analog 10–99 g mixture		Fentanyl analog 100 g or more mixture	Second offense: Not less than 20 years and not more than life. If death or serious bodily injury, life imprisonment. Fine of not more than $20 million if an individual, $75 million if not an individual.
I	Heroin 100–999 g mixture	Second offense: Not less than 10 years and not more than life. If death or serious bodily injury, life imprisonment. Fine of not more than $8 million if an individual, $50 million if not an individual.	Heroin 1 kg or more mixture	
I	LSD 1–9 g mixture		LSD 10 g or more mixture	
II	Methamphetamine 5–49 g pure or 50–499 g mixture		Methamphetamine 50 g or more pure or 500 g or more mixture	Two or more prior offenses: Life imprisonment. Fine of not more than $20 million if an individual, $75 million if not an individual.
II	PCP 10–99 g pure or 100–999 g mixture		PCP 100 g or more pure or 1 kg or more mixture	

(Continued)

TABLE 5.1 (CONTINUED)
Federal Trafficking Penalties for Schedules I, II, III, IV, and V (except Marijuana)

Substance/Quantity	Penalty
Any amount of other schedule I and II substances	First offense: Not more that 20 years. If death or serious bodily injury, not less than 20 years or more than life. Fine of $1 million if an individual, $5 million if not an individual.
Any drug product containing gamma hydroxybutyric acid Flunitrazepam (schedule IV) 1 g	Second offense: Not more than 30 years. If death or serious bodily injury, life imprisonment. Fine of $2 million if an individual, $10 million if not an individual.
Any amount of other schedule III drugs	First offense: Not more than 10 years. If death or serious bodily injury, not more that 15 years. Fine of not more than $500,000 if an individual, $2.5 million if not an individual.
	Second offense: Not more than 20 years. If death or serious injury, not more than 30 years. Fine of not more than $1 million if an individual, $5 million if not an individual.
Any amount of all other schedule IV drugs (other than 1 g or more of flunitrazepam)	First offense: Not more than 5 years. Fine of not more than $250,000 if an individual, $1 million if not an individual.
	Second offense: Not more than 10 years. Fine of not more than $500,000 if an individual, $2 million if not an individual.
Any amount of all schedule V drugs	First offense: Not more than 1 year. Fine of not more than $100,000 if an individual, $250,000 if not an individual.
	Second offense: Not more than 4 years. Fine of not more than $200,000 if an individual, $500,000 if not an individual.

PROCEDURE FOR CONTROLLING SUBSTANCES

The procedures for controlling substances under the CSA are set forth in Section 201 of the Act.

Proceedings may be initiated by the following:

- Department of Health and Human Services
- DEA
- Petition from any interested person, such as
  - The manufacturer of a drug
  - A medical society or association
  - A pharmacy association
  - A public interest group
  - A state or local government agency
  - An individual citizen

CRITERIA BY WHICH DRUGS ARE SCHEDULED

The CSA sets forth the findings that must be made to put a substance in any of the five schedules. These requirements are listed as follows:

- Schedule I
  - The drug or other substance has a high potential for abuse.
  - It has no current acceptable medical use.
  - There is a lack of accepted safety for the use of the drug or other substance under medical supervision.
- Schedule II
  - The drug or other substance has a high potential for abuse.
  - The drug or other substance has no current acceptable medical use.
  - Abuse of the drug or other substance may lead to severe psychological or physical dependence.
- Schedule III
  - The drug or other substance has a potential for abuse less than the drugs in schedules I and II.
  - The drug or other substance has a current acceptable medical use.
  - Abuse of the drug or other substance may lead to moderate or low physical dependence or high psychological dependence.
- Schedule IV
  - The drug or other substance has a low potential for abuse relative to the substances in schedule III.
  - The drug or other substance has a current acceptable medical use.

- Abuse of the drug or other substance may lead to limited physical dependence or psychological dependence relative to the drugs or other substances in schedule III.
- Schedule V
  - The drug or other substance has a low potential for abuse relative to the drugs or other substances in schedule IV.
  - The drug or other substance has a current acceptable medical use.
  - Abuse of this drug or other substance may lead to limited physical dependence or psychological dependence relative to the drugs or other substances in schedule IV.

In making findings as to what schedule, if any, a drug or substance should be put in, the CSA requires that the following eight specific factors be considered:

1. The drug's or substance's actual or relative potential for abuse
2. Scientific evidence of its pharmacological effect, if known
3. The state of the current scientific knowledge regarding the drug or other substance
4. Its history and current pattern of abuse
5. The scope, duration, and significance of abuse
6. What, if any, risk there is to the public health
7. Its psychic or physiological dependence liability
8. Whether the substance is an immediate precursor of a substance already under control of the CSA

NARCOTICS

General Information

Narcotics refer to opium and its derivatives or synthetic substitutes. Heroin, morphine, codeine, hydrocodone, oxycodone, and the like are given under medical supervision. The drugs or substances are administered either orally or by intramuscular injection. As drugs of abuse, they may be used through sniffing, smoking, "skin popping" (self-administered subcutaneous injection), or "mainlining" (intravenous injection).

Possible characteristics of narcotic use include the following:

- Pinpoint pupils
  - Drowsiness
  - Inability to concentrate
  - Apathy

- Euphoria
- Reduced vision
- Respiratory depression
- Nausea and vomiting
- Dilation of blood vessels, causing flushing in the face and neck
- Slurred speech

As a general rule, there is no loss of motor coordination or slurred speech as in the use of depressants. Drug dependence can result from the use of narcotics. Drug dependence is defined as a condition that results from the repeated use of a drug that results in increasing tolerance, which thus requires the user to administer progressively larger doses to attain the desired effect. Physical dependence refers to an alteration of the normal functions of the body that necessitates the continued presence of a drug to prevent the withdrawal syndrome that is characteristic of addictive drugs.

Withdrawal characteristics of narcotics include the following:

- Watery eyes
- Runny nose
- Yawning
- Loss of appetite
- Irritability
- Tremors
- Panic attacks
- Chills and sweating
- Nausea

Overdose characteristics of narcotic use include the following:

- Slow and shallow breathing
- Clammy skin
- Convulsions
- Possible death

NARCOTICS OF NATURAL ORIGIN

The poppy is the main source of nonsynthetic narcotics. It is cultivated in countries around the world, including Hungary, Yugoslavia, Turkey, India, Burma, China, Mexico, Pakistan, and Afghanistan.

Opium

There are 25 alkaloids that can be extracted from opium. The alkaloids fall into two general categories:

1. The phenanthrene alkaloids represented by morphine and codeine that are used as analgesics and cough suppressants
2. The isoquinoline alkaloids represented by papaverine and noscapine

Virtually all the opium imported into the United States is broken down into its alkaloid constituents, principally morphine and codeine. Both physical and psychological dependence are rated high. Opium is usually administered orally or smoked.

Morphine

Morphine is one of the most effective drugs known for the relief of pain. Its legal use is restricted primarily to hospitals. It is odorless, tastes bitter, and darkens with age. Addicts usually administer it intravenously. It also is administered orally or through smoking. Both physical and psychological dependency are rated high.

Codeine

Most codeine is produced from morphine. When compared with morphine, codeine produces less analgesia, sedation, and respiratory depression. It is widely distributed in two forms:

1. Tablets or combined with other products such as aspirin
2. Liquids for the relief of coughs in such preparations as Robitussin cough syrup

It is by far the most widely used naturally occurring narcotic in medical treatment.

Thebaine

Thebaine is the principal alkaloid present in a species of poppy that has been grown experimentally in the United States. By itself, it is not used in this country for medical purposes, but it is converted into a variety of medically important compounds, including codeine.

Heroin

Heroin was first synthesized from morphine in 1874. The first comprehensive control of heroin in the United States was established with the Harrison Narcotic Act of 1914. Pure heroin is a white powder with a bitter taste. Pure heroin is rarely sold on the street. To increase the bulk of the material sold to the addict, diluents such as sugars, starch, powdered milk, and quinine are used.

The usual methods of administration of heroin are injecting, sniffing, or smoking it.

Both physical and psychological dependence are rated as high with the use of heroin.

Hydromorphine

Hydromorphine is most commonly known as Dilaudid. It is marketed in both tablet and injectable form. Because its potency is two to eight times as great as morphine, it is a highly marketable drug. Both physical and psychological dependence are rated as high.

Oxycodone

Oxycodone is synthesized from thebaine. It is similar to codeine but is more powerful and has a higher dependency potential. It is effective orally.

Etorphine and Diprenorphine

Both of these substances are made from thebaine. Etorphine is more than a thousand times as potent as morphine in its analgesic, sedative, and respiratory depressant effects. There is a great danger of overdose in the use of this drug. Diprenorphine is used to counteract the effects of etorphine.

SYNTHETIC NARCOTICS

Synthetic narcotics are produced entirely within a laboratory.

Meperidine

Meperidine is a synthetic narcotic also known as Demerol or pethidine. It is probably the most widely used drug for the relief of moderate to severe pain. It is administered either orally or by injection. Both physical and psychological dependence are rated as high.

Methadone and Related Drugs

Methadone was synthesized during World War II by German scientists because of the shortage of morphine. It became widely used in the 1960s in the treatment of narcotic addiction. Methadone is almost as effective when administered orally as it is by injection. Methadone was designed to control narcotic addiction. Methadone has been a major cause of overdose deaths.

A close relative of methadone is propoxyphine, under the brand name of Darvon, for the relief of mild to moderate pain. Both physical and psychological dependence of this drug are rated as high. The usual methods of administration of methadone are oral and injection.

NARCOTIC ANTAGONISTS

This term refers to a class of compounds developed to block and reverse the effects of narcotics.

DEPRESSANTS

GENERAL INFORMATION

These substances have been developed to produce central nervous system (CNS) depression and are prescribed by a physician for the relief of anxiety, irritability, tension, and sleep disorders, and for sedation. Depressant drugs or substances are known and referred to as downers, sedatives, hypnotics, minor tranquilizers, antianxiety medication, barbiturates, benzodiazepines, glutethimide, chloral hydrate, methaqualone, Quaalude, Valium, and Librium. If used in excessive amounts, they can induce a state of intoxication similar to that with heavy alcohol use.

Depressants have a high potential for abuse and can serve as a means for suicide. If these drugs are taken as prescribed by a physician, they may be beneficial for the relief of anxiety, tension, and irritability.

In contrast to the effects of narcotics, intoxicating doses of depressants result in the following:

- Intoxicating symptoms
- Impaired judgment
- Slurred speech
- Loss of motor coordination without the odor of alcohol
- Disorientation

Withdrawal characteristics of depressant use include the following:

- Anxiety
- Insomnia
- Tremors
- Delirium
- Convulsions
- Possible death

Overdose characteristics of depressant use include the following:

- Shallow respiration
- Cold and clammy skin
- Dilated pupils

- Weak and rapid pulse
- Coma
- Possible death

Chloral Hydrate

Chloral hydrate is the oldest of the sleep-inducing drugs. Its popularity declined after the introduction of barbiturates, but it is still widely used. It has a slightly acrid odor and a bitter, caustic taste. Withdrawal symptoms resemble delirium tremens. It is a liquid and is marketed under the names Noctec and Somnos. It is not a popular drug with youth. It is mainly used by older adults. Both physical and psychological dependence are rated as moderate.

Barbiturates

These are widely prescribed to induce sleep and sedation. Barbiturates are classified as follows:

- Ultrashort
- Short
- Intermediate
- Long acting

The ultrashort-acting barbiturates produce anesthesia within 1 minute after intravenous administration.

Three of the most used depressants are the following:

1. Nembutal
2. Seconal
3. Amytal

All barbiturates result in a buildup of tolerance, and dependence on them is widespread. Both physical and psychological dependence drug are rated as "high moderate."

Glutethimide

Glutethimide is known as Doriden. Because the effects of this drug are of long duration, it is difficult to reverse overdoses, which often result in death.

METHAQUALONE

Methaqualone is a synthetic sedative. It has been widely abused because it was once mistakenly thought to be nonaddictive and was effective as an aphrodisiac.

Methaqualone has been marketed in the United States under various brand names, such as the following:

- Quaalude
- Parest
- Optimil
- Somnafac
- Sopor

Both the physical and psychological dependence of this drug are rated as high.

MEPROBAMATE

Meprobamate was the first synthesized narcotic, in 1950, and introduced the era of mild tranquilizers. It was marketed in the United States under the following brand names:

- Miltown
- Equanil
- Kesso-Bamate
- SK-Bamate

It is a muscle relaxant and is prescribed primarily for the relief of anxiety, tension, and muscle spasms. Excessive use can result in psychological dependence.

BENZODIAZEPINES

This family of drugs, which are depressants, relieve anxiety, tension, and muscle spasms and also produce sedation. They are marketed in the United States under the following brand names:

- Librium
- Clonopin
- Tranxene
- Valium
- Dalmane

- Ativan
- Serax
- Verstran

The margin of safety of these drugs is greater than that of other depressants. Both physical and psychological dependence of this drug are rated low, but prolonged use of excessive doses may result in physical and psychological dependence.

STIMULANTS

GENERAL INFORMATION

Stimulants are the most powerfully reinforced of all the abused drugs and can lead to compulsive behavior. Two commonly used stimulants are nicotine and caffeine. These are not regulated by the CSA. However, the more potent and abused stimulants are under regulation. Stimulants are known and referred to as uppers, cocaine, amphetamines, methamphetamine, meth, crank, crystal meth, and speed. Stimulants used in moderation help to relieve fatigue and increase alertness. Stimulants are also used in the treatment of obesity, narcolepsy, and attention deficit disorders. Stimulants are commonly abused and highly addictive; abusers can sniff, smoke, or inject the drug or substance to produce a temporary sense of exhilaration, superabundant energy, enhanced self-esteem, extended hours of wakefulness, and appetite suppression, and to "get high." Use of stimulants may also induce irritability, insomnia, anxiety, and apprehension. The protracted use of stimulants is followed by a period of depression known as "crashing" that is described as unpleasant.

The possible effects generally associated with the use of stimulants are as follows:

- Increased pulse rate and blood pressure
- Euphoria
- Insomnia
- Increased alertness
- Loss of appetite

Withdrawal characteristics of stimulant use include the following:

- Apathy
- Long periods of sleep
- Irritability
- Depression
- Disorientation

Crashing symptoms of stimulants can include the following:

- Dizziness
- Tremors
- Excessive sweating
- Heart palpitations
- Hostility
- Aggression
- Paranoia
- Suicidal or homicidal tendency

Overdose characteristics of stimulant use include the following:

- Agitation
- Increase in body temperature
- Hallucinations
- Convulsions
- Possible death

COCAINE

Cocaine is the most potent stimulant of natural origin. It is extracted from the leaves of the coca plant. This plant has been cultivated in the Andean highlands of South America since prehistoric times. Cocaine has been used medically to act as an anesthetic in eye surgery and to relieve suffering associated with terminal illness.

Illicit cocaine is distributed as a white, crystalline powder. It is often diluted to about half its volume by such ingredients as sugars or local anesthetics such as lidocaine.

Cocaine can be snorted, smoked, or injected. It is most commonly administered by being snorted through the nasal passages. "Crack" is the chunk or "rock" form of cocaine that, when smoked, delivers large quantities of cocaine to the lungs, causing an immediate effect. This effect is very intense and quickly over, similar to intravenous injection. It is most popularly accepted as a recreational drug that facilitates social interaction. It has the potential for extraordinary psychic dependency especially in view of its pleasurable effects. Excessive doses of cocaine may cause seizures and death from respiratory failure. There is not a specific antidote for cocaine overdose.

AMPHETAMINES

Amphetamines were first used clinically in the mid-1930s to treat narcolepsy, a disorder resulting in an uncontrollable desire for sleep. Today, the medical use of amphetamines is limited to narcolepsy, hyperkinetic behavioral disorders in children, and in some cases, obesity.

The illicit use of these drugs closely parallels that of cocaine in both short-term and long-term effects. The physical dependence is rated as possible, and the psychological dependence is rated as high.

HALLUCINOGENS

GENERAL INFORMATION

Hallucinogens can come from either a natural or synthetic source and are used to distort the perception of reality. Hallucinogens are commonly known or referred to as LSD, mescaline, peyote, psilocybin, and PCP. Ecstasy, which is popular with young adults, is both a stimulant and a hallucinogen combined and is a schedule I drug. Hallucinogens induce an excitation of the CNS that can alter one's perceptions, thoughts, and moods. The effects of hallucinogens are unpredictable each time the drug or substance is used; usually, a euphoric mood is created, but one can also become severely depressed. Depression sometimes becomes so severe that suicide is possible. The use of hallucinogens can be very dangerous because of the distortion of perceptions and impaired judgment that often leads to rash decisions and accidents. Another side effect caused by hallucinogens is flashbacks. The user may experience fragmentary recurrence of the psychedelic effects without even actually taking the drug or substance. The occurrences of flashbacks or "acid flashbacks" are unpredictable and may arise during times of stress. Recurrent use produces tolerance that tends to encourage resorting to greater amounts. Abuse of these drugs reached a peak in the late 1960s but reemerged in the late 1970s.

Possible characteristics of hallucinogen use include the following:

- Illusions
- Hallucinations
- Poor perception of time and distance

Overdose characteristics of hallucinogen use include the following:

- Longer, more intense "trip" episodes
- Psychosis
- Possible death

PEYOTE AND MESCALINE

The primary active ingredient of the peyote cactus is mescaline, which comes from the fleshy parts or bottoms of the cactus plant. Mescaline can also be produced synthetically.

LSD

LSD is an abbreviation of the German expression for lysergic acid diethyl-amide. It is produced from lysergic acid, which, in turn, is derived from the ergot fungus that grows on rye. It is commonly known as acid and micro-dot. LSD is usually sold in the form of tablets, thin squares of gelatin, or impregnated paper. Tolerance develops rapidly.

CANNABIS

GENERAL INFORMATION

Cannabis is derived from the hemp plant and grows wild throughout most of the tropical and temperate regions of the world. Cannabis products are usually smoked in the form of loosely rolled cigarettes called "joints." The psychoactive component in cannabis is THC or tetrahydrocannabi-nol. Cannabis is known or referred to as marijuana, tetrahydrocannabinol, hashish, hashish oil, pot, Acapulco gold, grass, reefer, Thai sticks, sinse-milla, weed, and Mary Jane. Most wild cannabis is considered inferior because of the low concentration of tetrahydrocannabinol.

Possible characteristics of cannabis use include the following:

- Euphoria
- Relaxed inhibitions
- Increased appetite
- Red eyes
- Strong, sweet odor
- Disoriented behavior

Overdose characteristics of cannabis use include the following:

- Fatigue
- Paranoia
- Possible psychosis

HASHISH

The Middle East is the main source of hashish. Hashish consists of secre-tions of the cannabis plant that are collected, dried, and then compressed into forms such as balls, cakes, or cookie-like sheets.

MISCELLANEOUS POINTS

ALCOHOL

Alcohol is our most used and most abused recreational drug. Physical dependence can occur if alcohol is taken regularly in large quantities.

Some of the ways alcohol abuse can be noted include the following:

- Drunkenness on the job
- Absenteeism
- Accident-prone behavior
- Arrest for drunkenness
- Reports from coworkers

SUMMARY

Substance abuse is, in most people's opinion, the most devastating, pervasive, and insidious problem in our society today. The cost in lives lost and ruined is staggering. The cost to our business communities in lost production, theft, vandalism, accidents, and workers' compensation claims equals or exceeds the total gross national product of some of the world's smaller countries.

Add to that the enormous costs our law enforcement agencies (federal, state, and local), court systems, and corrections facilities incur to apprehend, prosecute, and incarcerate the offenders, and one can see how substance abuse drains our economy of billions of dollars annually. The goal of a security leader is to have a drug-free workplace. This will contribute greatly to a company's success in today's business world.

Hopefully, a better understanding of the various types of drugs and substances used—depressants, stimulants, or narcotics—their methods of use, and dependency rating was gained as a result of completing this chapter. In the upcoming chapters, the actual task of investigating and combating drugs in the workplace will be covered in the investigation and legal issues portions of this book. This is also how the Certified Protection Professional (CPP) exam will break down drug-related issues.

6 Physical Security

This is the longest of all of the chapters because of the sheer bulk of the information involved. The umbrella term *physical security* gauges the candidate's knowledge in the areas of closed-circuit television (CCTV), alarm systems, access controls, fencing, physical barriers, lighting, crime prevention through environmental design (CPTED), safes and vaults, locks and locking systems, key controls, and much more. The purpose of this chapter is to familiarize the reader with the various segments that compose the physical security portion of the test and to impart the knowledge required to pass the Certified Protection Professional (CPP) exam as it relates to physical security.

This can be one of the hardest chapters to master, not only because of the bulk and range of material involved but also because many security professionals may not have to, in their daily workday, deal with many of these areas. If a candidate does not have the expertise in a given discipline, it is strongly recommended that he or she confer with local experts and have them assist in the study program.

Billions of dollars are lost every year due to burglary, robberies, employee theft, etc. Many businesses without the proper security and protection can suffer tremendous losses and even possible failure. Even on the personal level, there is a need to provide security and protection for our assets and ourselves.

An asset is anything of value that is owned. For a business or enterprise to thrive, it must hold and conserve its assets. Loss or reduction in the value of assets can lead to failure. Physical security is needed to protect assets and address areas of vulnerability. Burglary and white-collar crimes have caused businesses irreversible losses, downtime, and even shutdowns. A qualified security professional can show what needs to be designed while being cost effective and meeting a company's needs. Crime is not always predictable because it is human nature, but we can reduce the window of opportunity by implementing effective security measures and countermeasures, depending on the immediate and future needs of the company.

Once risks or threats are identified, an effective security plan that implements good security practices and procedures can minimize the chances of loss or disaster of an undesirable event. A professionally designed, effective security plan will minimize the loss and damage that could occur. Ongoing assessments ensure that a company will have the ability to recover quickly from loss or disaster.

Physical security has been in a constant struggle to keep up with technology and what an industry needs. The American Society for Industrial Security (ASIS) is dedicated to providing an ongoing educational source to the industry. Although ASIS provides certification through the CPP program, there is also the Physical Security Professional (PSP) program, which is dedicated to the constant changing of today's technology and is available to certified, educated professionals.

Constant education, integrity, good business morals, and ethics are essential for the security professional. Corporations and private industries have recognized that security, especially when they hire or employ a skilled professional, has a greater value to them when providing security measures.

If someone wants to be successful and in control of his or her destiny, he or she must constantly seek out the best sources of information that are pertinent to the current and future needs of the security industry.

SECURITY FUNCTIONS

A comprehensive security plan can be thought of as a triangle consisting of information, physical, and personnel security on each side of the triangle. Information security is the protection of product information. Physical security is the countermeasures used to control access and prevent the disruption of the operation of the organization. Personnel security establishes rules for employees to reinforce that they are helpful in the operation of the organization. The physical security process is a functional subactivity within the total framework of the concept of security. The process is utilized to deny access and is a protective device against security hazards. Security hazards are conditions that may result in the loss of life, damage or destruction of property, the compromise of information, or the disruption of activities at the establishment's facilities. The role of loss prevention is to reduce the likelihood of accidents and injuries. Recognition of all risks is mandatory so that appropriate measures can be instituted to control or eliminate them. Some of the practices and procedures may include, but are not limited to, the following:

- Procedures: collective information systems involving what, who, when, where, and how
- Personnel: collective people to administer and implement the system
- Basic loss prevention: armored car and armed courier services, security guards at retail stores, etc.
- Protection: bodyguard protection
- Security management consulting

- Building and perimeter protection: fences, lighting, surveillance, etc.
- Intrusion and access control: locks and keys, safes, door and window security, visitor and employee identification procedures, and the like
- Alarm and surveillance systems: intrusion detection alarms, sensors, CCTV, etc.
- Annunciators: The recognition and verification of unusual activity that has been detected
- Communication subsystems: any transmission methods to convey the detection of unusual activity to its recognition
- Fire prevention and control: fire alarm systems, evacuation procedures, etc.
- Emergency management: disaster planning
- Personnel security: prescreening employees, background investigations, etc.
- Accident and safety procedures
- Bookkeeping: data of time records of detection, recognition, and use procedures

SECURITY VERSUS RISK

Risk can be defined in broad terms as a situation involving exposure to danger, the possibility that something unpleasant will happen, or a person or thing causing a risk that exposes others to danger or loss. In a business, it is essential to develop a risk management program. The goal is to determine an economic balance between the impact of risk on the company and the cost of implementing prevention and protective measures.

Every business is unique and operates differently from another. From a bank handling money to a factory making clothes, the impact of risks or threats varies from one to the next. Analyzing the risks, one can easily determine that some sort of security and protection system is needed.

Before any decisions can be made concerning the level of protection needed, an understanding of what is being protected and the surrounding environment must be analyzed. The cost of an overdesigned system can be enormous, or an inadequate protection plan can be disastrous.

Risk analysis or threat assessment should include the following:

- Identifying the asset in need of protection, such as money, jewelry, proprietary information, equipment, etc. This includes the impact and cost of any asset to the company should it be lost due to natural or man-made forces.

- Determining the existing state of security and locating the weaknesses in defenses.
- Identifying the risks, threats, and vulnerabilities (robbery, burglary, employee theft, fire, entry through ventilation ducts or windows, etc.).
- Gauging the risk assessment level: security survey to propose a plan of action.
- Estimating the probabilities of occurrence and losses that could occur, such as the probabilities of embezzlement or employee theft, and the chances of loss by fire or flood. Theft by a person is more likely than a loss by fire or flood damage.
- Figuring the cost/benefit ratio: efficiency versus cost.

Not every business loss will be a security loss. A loss due to legal competition from a competitor is not a security loss. That type of loss could have been a gain and would actually be related to profit and loss. Losses that do not have the probability of gains are considered direct losses and involve risks and threats that the average manager may never have had to analyze before.

The following is a list of common threats and vulnerabilities that are most often encountered in a business. A security program that considers these risks will have taken a major step in planning, and if the proper countermeasures are implemented, it will offer a high degree of reliability that what should have been done to prevent and control security losses has been done.

Some Common Security Risks

- War or insurrection
- Weapons of mass destruction: nuclear, biochemical, chemical attack
- Natural catastrophes
  - Tornadoes
  - Hurricanes
  - Earthquakes
  - Floods
- Industrial disasters
  - Explosions
  - Structural collapse
  - Major accidents
  - Fire
  - Radiation incidents

- Sabotage and malicious destruction
  - Arson
  - Incendiary fire
  - Labor violence
  - Vandalism
  - Product tampering
  - Bombs and bomb threats
  - Civil disturbance
  - Gang activity
  - Homicides
  - Terrorism
- Theft of assets
  - Pilferage
  - Fraud
  - Workers' compensation fraud
  - Records manipulation
  - Forgery
  - Car thefts
  - Embezzlement
  - Computer crimes
  - Industrial espionage
  - Proprietary information theft
  - Trade secret theft
  - Intellectual property theft
  - Shoplifting
  - Burglary
  - Robbery and hijacking
- Conflicts of interest
  - Employees with their own businesses
  - Employees working for competitors
  - Kickback situations
  - Extortion
  - Bribery
- Personnel problems
  - Gambling
  - Loan-sharking
  - Disaffection or discontent through having lost one's feeling of loyalty or commitment
  - Disgruntled employees
  - Disturbed persons
  - Workplace violence
  - Willful, malicious, or negligent personal conduct

- Absenteeism
- Misrepresentation
- Sexual harassment
- Narcotic and drug use
- Antisocial behavior
- Alcoholism
- Miscellaneous risks
  - Traffic accidents
  - Human error or lapses of judgment
  - Not following policy and procedures
  - Improper maintenance
  - Standard operating procedures not followed, creating crime or loss of opportunity
  - National security problems

This list of some of the common risks should be analyzed to determine how critically the measure of impact of a security loss would affect the company or business. How much will it really hurt if the loss event occurs? If crime is on the rise, such as robberies, embezzlement, etc. happening more frequently, the probability is higher. Serious though they are, the loss vulnerabilities from crime and violence are of less concern than those from catastrophes and disasters. Floods, fires, and major industrial and commercial accidents cause a tremendous impact from a single loss. Small businesses affected by a serious fire do not always reopen.

The dependence of almost all major businesses on the daily output of computers and electronic data processing has made such equipment a prime loss hazard, not only because of the value of the equipment but also because of the value of the larger related assets whose value cannot be realized without continuing computer output. Loss of computers through an accident or disaster can have a staggering cost consequence because of delay or termination of functions that were dependent on the computers' output.

Some risks are difficult to predict, while others are easy to identify by looking through the history of the company's records to estimate the probabilities. For example, how many instances of employee theft were investigated, and what was the rate of recovery of the company from that? Other risks may never occur or may only happen once. But a fire could shut down a business permanently. The ability to recognize real vulnerabilities is primary in the assessment of loss potential.

SECURITY SURVEY

A security survey is a basic instrument used to determine security vulnerability. A security survey is a checklist that determines existing security, identifies deficiencies, establishes the protection needed, and recommends measures to enhance overall security. A vulnerability or risk assessment survey is the identification of a wide variety of assets, threats, risk, as well as constraints. These include culture, cost, and operational issues, and the survey should be comprehensive and accurate so that it leads to the appropriate countermeasures. As circumstances and conditions change, risks must be reappraised. The risk assessment survey is not a task done once, but rather, it is a continuing effort on the business's general security program. A security survey can help a business save money by discovering what the most costly and out-of-date security conditions and procedures are. An ongoing security survey will also prevent crime by improving security, as well as ensuring that the business's security program complies with state and federal regulations, policies, and procedures. The implementation of better security measures can result in a safer environment and lower insurance premiums. The best way to effectively analyze the strengths and weaknesses of a business is to conduct a security survey, which is a critical on-site examination to determine the status of security, identify deficiencies, determine the needed protection level, and make qualified recommendations for improvement. A security survey is essentially a physical examination of the premises and a thorough inspection of all operational systems and procedures. No two businesses operate the same, and every survey is going to be different.

One of management's most valuable tools is the security survey. A risk management supervisor or security manager has the task of identifying and planning for control of all or certain classes of security vulnerabilities and risks. For businesses that do not have such security managers, consulting organizations that possess such skills and expertise are available. A security survey performed by persons who are not experts in the security risk assessment survey will almost certainly lead to improper countermeasure decisions.

Security surveys should be conducted by outside security consulting agencies with the cooperation of an inside source from the company. This prevents inside sources from being corrupted by their own influences.

A security survey should be conducted by a team of individuals, which includes at least one of the company's top executives and other personnel. The survey team should first conduct a presurvey to gather basic information about the facility to be inspected, such as basic geography, climate, social and political surroundings, local ordinances to be followed, the company's nature of business, etc. The survey team also needs to schedule a meeting with all of the top executives of the company to obtain information on prior surveys done; the layout and maps of the company; history of problems such as vandalism, thefts, and the like; employee handbook and policy and procedures; emergency disaster plans; employee work schedules; etc. The meeting should be able to establish the objectives of the survey, what areas of the company need to be reviewed, and which areas need special attention, and the personnel can be interviewed on the site. Throughout the inspection, the survey team will talk to employees and monitor their job activities. The survey team needs to be discreet and keep the details of the inspection vague so that the employees do not alter their behavior. The following is a sample of a security risk survey for appraisal of possible existing conditions that could occur. Every business has a different style and level of needs. A security professional will need to adjust the survey to fit that style and level of need to the business. The following are some guidelines that the survey team should consider before the actual survey is performed:

- Preliminary contacts are made with the appropriate personnel to arrange the time and other details.
- Look at prior surveys that were done, if any, and check for background information and action taken on noted deficiencies.
- Know the reason for the survey.
- The survey team is familiar with the mission and the history of the establishment, or intended use of the area.
- Know about any change in the mission or use since the previous surveys.
- Evaluate the installation and ground-floor plans of the establishment.
- Review the establishment's installation regulations and operating procedures.
- A checklist is prepared and used as a guide in making the survey.

Appendix B is an example of an actual, average security survey.

After the general assessment of risks has been completed and the dangers are identified, the identification of specific risks or threats needs to be addressed. A thorough examination of each department on procedures and policies should be analyzed. Each department and location within the company should be evaluated separately in terms of its potential for loss.

Security surveys should not just end there. An on-site follow-up survey should be performed at a later time to determine if the recommendations have been followed through properly. An informational report should be made and submitted to management. If it is determined that the recommendations were not followed properly at that time, another on-site evaluation and survey should be completed. Further evaluations and surveys may be necessary until such a time when all recommendations have been properly added or administered. Additional reviews help to guarantee the success of the security survey and, in the long run, could save the company from a detrimental loss.

Some important factors to consider when implementing a security survey are as follows:

- Physical environment: locations, composition, etc.
- Procedural aspects
- History: past losses, all data collected on crime incidents in the facility, etc.
- Criminal state of the art: new technology, capabilities, tools of the trade of the aggressor

MATRIX OR GRID TECHNIQUE

Risk assessment is the measurement of potential loss or the damage of an asset based on the probability of an undesired occurrence. A loss event profile identifies the type of risk, probability of frequency, and criticality of an event. The type of risk is the event that produces a measurable loss. The probability of frequency is simply as follows: The more ways an event can occur equals the likelihood that it will occur. Criticality is how the impact of the loss is measured; criticality is usually measured in assets and income. Risk can be assessed in terms of probability of occurrence, and a security system design can improve the ratio of favorable outcomes or reduce the ratio of unfavorable outcomes.

The use of a matrix can estimate the probability of loss. Each type of loss has its own circumstances and conditions that make its occurrence possible. This procedure is not without faults, mistakes, or incorrect outcomes, but if done by a professional, it can statistically show the probability of an event of loss. A practiced security professional should not have difficulty in distinguishing most risks and vulnerabilities if the matrix is adequate. However, sometimes, there are cases in which factors are not fully developed or historical information has not been collected that can ultimately reduce its reliability.

The use of a matrix can reflect the type of damage a natural disaster or a theft of assets can possibly cause. Any risk or threat can be used. For example, a typical matrix of cash theft vulnerability is shown in Tables 6.1 and 6.2.

With this example, by considering the gross sales of the company and its assets, the impact of loss can be statistically determined. Also, if one considers the history of loss and the security measures and devices that are in use at present, it is possible to determine the probability of loss.

CRITICALITY

Probability does not stand alone when determining the probability of loss. Although probability is important, it is not enough for the development

TABLE 6.1
Cash Theft Vulnerability Matrix (Original)

Building Location	Amount on Hand, Dollars		Accountability Records		Area Has Physical Bounds		Area Locked		Alarm Protection		Positive Control on Admittance		Surveillance Devices		Cash in Secured Containers		Bait Money Kept		History of Cash Loss	
	NBH	OT	NBH	OT	NBH	OT	NBH	OT	NBH	OT	NBH	OT	NBH	OT	NBH	OT	NBH	OT	NBH	OT
Supervisors/managers of offices	400,000	25,000	Y	Y	Y	Y	N	Y	Y	Y	N	Y	N	Y	Y	Y	Y	Y	N	Y
Accounting department	10,000	2000	Y	Y	N	N	N	Y	N	Y	N	N	N	N	Y	Y	N	N	Y	Y
Cafeteria	2000	0.00	N	N	Y	N	N	N	N	N	N	N	N	N	N	–	N	–	Y	N
Administration support	250.00	0.00	N	N	N	N	N	N	N	N	N	N	N	N	N	–	N	–	–	–

Note: N, no; NBH, normal business hours; OT, other times the business is open; Y, yes.

TABLE 6.2
Cash Theft Vulnerability Matrix (Alternate)

	Building Location	Supervisors/Managers of Offices	Accounting Department	Cafeteria	Administration Support
Amount on hand, dollars	NBH	400,000	10,000	20,000	250
	OT	25,000	2000	0	0
Accountability records	NBH	Y	Y	N	N
	OT	Y	Y	N	N
Area has physical bounds	NBH	Y	N	Y	N
	OT	Y	N	Y	N
Area locked	NBH	N	Y	N	N
	OT	Y	Y	N	N
Alarm protection	NBH	Y	N	N	N
	OT	Y	Y	N	N
Positive control on admittance	NBH	N	N	N	N
	OT	Y	N	N	N
Surveillance devices	NBH	N	N	N	N
	OT	Y	N	N	N
Cash in secured containers	NBH	Y	Y	–	N
	OT	Y	Y	N	N
Bait money kept	NBH	Y	N	–	–
	OT	Y	N	N	N
History of cash loss	NBH	N	Y	Y	–
	OT	Y	Y	N	–

Note: N, no; NBH, normal business hours; OT, other times the business is open; Y, yes.

of a cost-effective countermeasure. An event may be highly probable or even certain to occur but may be of small consequence in terms of impact. This is where the criticality is important. Security professionals must also evaluate the principle of criticality, which is the impact of loss measured in dollars. Many businesses will not be interested in a security plan if the cost of security is greater than the potential loss of money. Determining the criticality not only involves the direct cost of the item lost but also includes other factors, such as the following:

- Replacement costs: include purchase price, freight, labor material, other related costs, etc.
- Temporary replacement
- Downtime of the business
- Insurance rate changes
- Loss of product availability
- Discounted cash: cash diverted to pay for the above costs, instead of being reinvested into the company

PROBABILITY/CRITICALITY MATRIX

When all the costs have been totaled or approximated, a basis for assigning a criticality level can be implemented. This will assist in providing adequate safeguards in implementing the proper countermeasure that is most cost effective. By assigning levels of criticality to levels of probability, a priority can be established as to what countermeasures can be provided (Table 6.3).

By using the matrix technique and studying all the factors that are favorable to the occurrence of a security loss to the company, it would be possible to assign one of the first six levels of probability.

For instance, if a risk is determined to be at a level of 1A, it should be placed at the top of the list of priorities to be addressed. To help illustrate this, the level 1A would be an assessed value for the manager/supervisor

---

TABLE 6.3
Levels of Criticality to Levels of Probability

Risk Potential	Criticality Assessment
1: Virtually certain	A: Fatal
2: Highly probable	B: Very serious
3: Moderately probable	C: Moderately serious
4: Probable	D: Serious
5: Improbable	E: Relatively unimportant
6: Probability unknown	F: Seriousness unknown

---

office. This position would be given this level because it is of the utmost importance that the managers or supervisors are protected, as the loss of, for example, $400,000 during normal business hours due to intruders or natural disasters could put the company out of business. A risk rated as 3D or 4C may take a lower place in countermeasures. Countermeasure plans should be made for all losses with a risk of moderately probable or higher as well as any loss with a criticality of serious or higher.

Once the probability/criticality analysis has been completed, with the security problems identified and ranked in importance, a plan for countermeasures can be implemented. There are some alternatives to also consider when developing a countermeasure plan:

- Risk avoidance: Remove the problem by eliminating the vulnerability or risk.
- Risk reduction: After identifying the vulnerability or risk, implement countermeasures (alarms, CCTV, guards, etc.) to reduce the problem.
- Risk spreading: Spread the procedure or operation into different departments or locations. For example, the accounting department may have a high probability of embezzlement, so have that department be responsible for posting accounts payable and receivable and have a separate department process the checks.
- Risk transfer: Removing the vulnerability or risk to the company for the protection of an insurance policy and community.
- Self-assumption: Planning for an eventual loss without the protection of insurance.

COST-EFFECTIVENESS

Cost-effectiveness refers only to a countermeasure or technique that is designed and implemented into a system and that performs the needed job more effectively than the previous countermeasure or technique and at a lower cost. Costs are most often reduced by taking the large cost of manpower and replacing it with more reliable, practical, and updated procedures, hardware, and electronics that offer more effective countermeasures at less cost.

Benefits from risk prevention will outweigh the costs incurred to implement a means of protection. The means of protection must be tailored to the specific risk or threat in the real day-to-day working environment. The most important consideration when designing or upgrading a security protection system is to determine the threat level that the system will have to accommodate. This determination is essential to providing the best system possible and thereby creating the most cost-effective option to the company. This is an arena where the security survey results are of the utmost importance to help determine the appropriate direction for the company.

Risk prevention includes the following:

- Prevention: Attempt to stop loss before it can happen
- Control: Keep the incident from impacting assets or minimizing loss
- Recovery: Restore the company after the assets have been undesirably affected

Prevention is just the first part of dealing with a risk or threat. Prevention is not sufficiently met by just installing alarms, CCTVs, etc., but it is a constant effort to protect and reduce the potential threat or risk. Should a risk or threat come to fruition, controlling the incident once it happens then becomes the most important part of risk prevention. A proper and appropriate response and control of the incident allows for recovery. Insurance in addition to the above is very important to help recover from a fatal or very serious incident, such as a fire, kidnapping, etc.

A cost-effectiveness study should be done periodically to determine how much is being protected that could be damaged, stolen, or sabotaged. This would provide an indication as to whether the security design is performing effectively or not. Security surveys should be done continually and regularly to accommodate for change. Always collect incident reports and be aware of crime trends that happen at the company to help determine what the security needs of the company are.

LEVELS OF PHYSICAL SECURITY

Every day, technology advances through the creation of better designs and the continual development of new and improved methods of protection. The primary purpose of physical security planning is to deter and delay those with criminal intentions. Unfortunately, there are those with criminal intentions who want to deprive a person of what he or she is trying to protect. The criminal side can be just as sophisticated in technology. That is why no system can be 100% secured, and levels of security should be implemented to provide a robust security program. It is important to have security in depth, by placing progressively more difficult obstacles in the path of the aggressor using the four D's of loss prevention: deter, detect, delay, and deny. The following explains the levels of security with examples of how they should be used. When designing physical levels of security, it is important to layer them from minimum physical security levels to maximum physical security levels as the distance to the object, item, or material is decreased. For example, signage indicating private property should deter and advise that the area is not accessible to the public. If the area is breached, the subject should be detected by security via CCTV, alarm, observation, etc. If a subject breaches this layer of protection, delay systems should be in place, such as locks, swipe card access, checkpoints, etc. The types of items being protected usually dictate the level of physical security needed and what is done if security is breached. For example, if an area under maximum security is compromised, protocol and procedures should be in place to deny access but also to ensure that the asset is not removed from the premises. But with ongoing physical security surveys, education, and management using their resources to stay on top of new research and developments, a physical protection system can be designed to eliminate most threats depending on what is being protected. For example, the level of security at a nuclear power plant versus a storage unit full of furniture determines the level, style, and type of protection needed, depending on the value of the asset. The incorporation of security solutions in the design and construction has a human as well as a technological dimension that needs to be widely considered. The objective is to provide secure environments without hindering day-to-day operations and worker productivity. The basic reason countermeasures are implemented is to deter.

The following are the levels of security:

- Minimum security
- Low-level security
- Medium security
- High-level security
- Maximum security

There are two types of activity that one is concerned with when describing the levels of security. They are the following:

1. Internal activity: This ranges from simple theft to sabotage.
2. External activity: This originates from outside the security system and ranges from intrusion to armed attacks.

MINIMUM SECURITY

- Designed to delay or block access and detect intrusion from some unauthorized external activity
- Simple physical barriers, which can include locked doors and windows with ordinary locks
- Includes, for example, residential homes and the like

LOW-LEVEL SECURITY

- Upgraded form of minimum security level
- Designed to delay or block access and detect intrusion or some unauthorized external activity

- Physical barriers and locks upgraded with reinforced doors, window bars, and high-security locks
- Simple lighting system over doors and windows
- Basic alarm system that is monitored off site and provides detection and local annunciation
- For example, small businesses, retail stores, unsecured assets outside hardware stores, dealerships, etc.

MEDIUM SECURITY

- Upgraded from the above level
- Designed to delay or block access and detect intrusion on most unauthorized external activity and some unauthorized internal activity
- Advanced intrusion alarm that announces staff at a remote location
- Establishes a perimeter beyond the facility with high-security physical barriers, such as fences with barbed wire etc.
- Use of unarmed guards and guard dogs
- For example, bonded warehouses, larger retail stores, and storage units

HIGH-LEVEL SECURITY

- Upgraded from the above-mentioned levels
- Designed to delay, block, or restrict access, or detect intrusion to most unauthorized external and internal activities
- CCTV
- Perimeter alarm system that is remotely monitored at or near high-security physical barriers
- High-security lighting around the entire facility
- Trained armed guards
- Controls to restricted access only to authorized personnel
- Formal plans and coordination with local law enforcement agencies to deal with certain circumstances that could arise
- For example, pharmaceutical facilities, some prisons, jewelry outlets, and banks

MAXIMUM SECURITY

- Upgraded from the above-mentioned levels
- Designed to delay or block access, detect intrusion, assess, and neutralize all unauthorized external and internal activities

- Sophisticated alarm system that is remotely monitored in one or more protected areas; tamper indicators and backup source of power
- On-site, 24 h/day response force, with highly screened armed persons who are trained to neutralize and contain any threat until arrival of off-site assistance
- For example, nuclear power plants, some prisons, governmental research sites and related governmental locations, aerospace sites, and politically controversial establishments

PHYSICAL SECURITY DEFENSES

Physical security planning protects, at minimum, the basic elements:

- Grounds around the building
- Building perimeter
- Building interior
- All the facilities' contents
- Management of all of the above

PERIMETER BARRIERS

Perimeter barriers define the physical limits of a facility, activity, or area. A business's perimeter can be determined by the function and location of the establishment. An office building or retail store, for example, may only have the perimeter of its own walls. However, warehouses or other secured operations that have property may define their perimeter by the property boundary owned by them. In either case, protection begins at the perimeter, which most likely is the first place the intruder will penetrate.

The use of physical barriers is an effective method of providing security when they are designed correctly. Physical barriers make it hard for aggressors to approach in various types of circumstances, except through specific, controlled sectors. All barriers will need additional security.

The use of physical barriers also creates a psychological obstacle that deters most people from thinking of unauthorized entry and will also prevent or delay passage through the protected area, especially by vehicles for those who are still intent on entering the facility. Physical barriers have a direct impact on the number of security personnel that need to be posted at a facility so that it can operate safely. The primary objectives of perimeter security are to deter, detect, delay, and respond. Barriers can assist in delaying an intruder for a certain amount of time until a response group arrives to apprehend the suspect.

There are two main categories of barriers:

1. Natural barriers: Consisting of topographical features that assist in denying access
2. Structural barriers: Consisting of permanent or temporary devices that assist in preventing or denying access

The following list demonstrates some types of barriers:

- Structural or man-made barriers
  - Fences
  - Barbed wire
  - Electrified fences and barriers
  - Outer walls and openings of buildings
  - Inside walls and doors of buildings
  - Safes and vaults
  - Locking devices
  - Roofs
  - Grills
  - Ditches, trenches, moats, and similar deep hole systems
- Natural barriers
  - Mountains
  - Deserts and plains
  - Cliffs
  - Water-covered areas (for example, Alcatraz Prison)
  - Obstacles, such as trees, rocks, stones, etc.
  - Natural terrain
- Human barriers
  - Security guards
  - Bodyguards
  - Patrol units
  - Military troops
- Animal barriers
  - Guard dogs
- Vehicle barriers
- Energy barriers
  - Continuous
  - Standby
  - Movable
  - Emergency

Fence Barriers

Fences are used for the perimeter of an establishment more than all other types of barriers. The primary functions of fence barriers are to delay access, usually 3 to 5 s on average, and increase detection. There are three types of fencing that are authorized for use and should meet the federal specifications to be effective, and all three types can be used to increase security (Table 6.4):

1. Chain link
2. Barbed wire
3. Barbed tape or concertina

The typical, standard chain-link fences, which are the most popular and are used as perimeter barriers around industrial and commercial properties, are really not considered serious deterrents to intruders. However, chain-link fences do establish a legal boundary around an establishment and allow for the display of signs advising of trespassing violations or (for some establishments) the use of deadly force, both of which can provide a psychological deterrent to those thinking about entering. Increasing the security of the fence with barbed wire or concertina will not prevent intrusion 100% of the time, but it will increase one's capability in delaying intruders. Depending on city ordinances, another approach to consider rather than the traditional chain-link fence with barbed wire on top would be a fence with spikes on top of the fence pointing outward. A lesser option to a true perimeter fence would be to mark the boundary with a low wall or hedge. This barrier should be no more than 3 to 4 ft. in height to mark the property line, thus establishing territory and discouraging trespassers.

Top guards are an overhang of barbed wire, barbed tape, or concertina along the top of the fence facing outward and upward at about a 45° angle.

Permanently affixed to the top of the fence posts are supporting arms that will increase the height of the fence by at least 1 ft. The fence height, excluding the top guard, should be a minimum of 7 ft. It is recommended that a top guard be used on all perimeter fencing, and depending on the business, it may be added to interior enclosures for added protection. Concrete still may be cast at the bottom of the fence to protect against soil erosion. High-security fences should use bottom rails to prevent intruders from lifting the fence. All nuts and bolts holding hardware attachments on a fence should be welded.

TABLE 6.4
Fence Barriers

Chain-Link Fencing	Barbed-Wire Fencing	Barbed Tape or Concertina
Should be at least 7 ft., excluding top guard	Should be at least 7 ft., excluding top guard	Should be at least 7 ft., excluding top guard
9 gauge or heavier	Commonly 12 gauge or heavier; used with four-point barbs spaced equally apart	Commercially manufactured wire coil of high-strength steel barbed wire that is clipped together at intervals to form a cylinder
Vinyl or galvanized coated, with a mesh opening not larger than 2 in. per side (4 in.^{2})	Standard is twisted double strand	When opened, it forms a barrier 50 ft. long and 3 ft. in diameter
Twisted and barbed selvages at the top and bottom	Firmly affixed to metal posts no more than 6 ft. apart	Can be used in multiple coils, one on top of another, or in a pyramid arrangement with a minimum of three rolls
Wire must be taut and securely fastened to rigid metal or reinforced concrete posts set in concrete with additional bracing for corners and gate openings if necessary	Barbed strands should not be more than 6 in. (less is more effective) in vertical distance with at least one wire interlaced vertical and midway between posts	Can also be placed in stacked mounds of six rolls horizontally staked on the ground or against the fence fabric on the inside of a perimeter fence (approximately 6.5 ft. high and 9 ft. wide)
Fence must reach within 2 in. of hard ground or pavement		
On soft ground, it must reach below the surface deep enough to compensate for shifting soil and sand		

Barriers cannot be designed to prevent or protect a business or establishment from all situations that could occur, but they do accomplish the following:

- Defining a particular area.
- Weighing the cost-effectiveness of structural and natural barriers against alternative security devices, such as guard patrols, electronic surveillance, etc.

- Controlling pedestrian and vehicle traffic.
- Providing protection against suicide vehicle ramming.
- Providing access and entry-control points that require some means of identification for authorized personnel.
- Delaying forced entry.
- Allowing visibility on both sides of the perimeter to aid police and security personnel; other types provide a covering for seclusion to an area.
- Protecting assets.

Additional considerations must be given if the security level is at a maximum level, where the structure might need increased protection from such items as bullets, explosives, incendiaries, etc. Ballistic protection should be included in the design. The following are some examples of reinforcement of structural barriers:

- Armored steel, aluminum, and other metals
- Reinforced concrete with steel mesh bars in the casting
- Bricks, cinder blocks, etc.
- Ceramic tiles
- Bulletproof glass
- Ballistic fabrics, such as nylon, fiberglass, Kevlar, etc.
- Fire-resistant fabrics and materials

Structural barriers do not prevent against penetration. Fences can be climbed, walls can be scaled, and locked doors and barred windows can be broken into. The same holds true for natural barriers. Security measures need to be reinforced or strengthened by additional hardware. For barriers to be effective, they must be checked regularly for signs of weathering, rusting, or unusual marks that may indicate tampering or intrusion. Barrier structures can become weakened from erosion, while trees and other vegetative growth can damage a barrier and inhibit surveillance from CCTVs.

The time it takes to penetrate barriers depends on the attack mode and, of course, on the equipment used. The following are some examples of attack tools:

- Hand-tools: sledgehammers, axes, bolt cutters, wrecking bars, metal cutters, etc.
- Powered hand-tools: hydraulic bolt cutters, abrasive saws, electric drills, roto hammers, abrasive water jets, etc.
- Thermal cutting tools: oxyacetylene torches, oxygen lances, etc.
- Explosives: TNT, C4, etc.

- Vehicles: trucks, automobiles, trains, boats, planes, helicopters, motorcycles, and ATVs
- Miscellaneous: ladders, ropes, etc.

OTHER BARRIER ENTRY AND EXIT POINTS

Every effort should be made to reduce the number of open entrances and exits in the perimeter areas that could be potential security breaches but still allow the barrier to operate safely and effectively. The more gates and openings that are used, the more security personnel must be employed to monitor them. Some things to consider are as follows:

- If at all possible, secure and lock all other entrances into the perimeter and use one point of entry that allows entry and exit.
- Consider installing vehicle barriers at all entrances, either permanent or removable, subject to being rammed.
- Tire shredders or road-blocking security with lifting arm barriers can be used to control perimeter access.
- All emergency exits should have locking mechanisms that allow exit but not reentry. An alarm sensor should be installed to alert those who use the exit.
- Swinging and sliding gates are the most commonly used, and all gates should open out.
- The weak link in a gate is usually the hardware, such as hinges, latches, and locks. Gates often require additional hardening features.
- Lock all gates from the inside.
- Use company locks that are unique and a certain distinguishable color if at all possible. (Intruders cannot cut off the lock and replace it with their own as easily.)
- Locked gates should be checked frequently, especially if gates are outside the general traffic area and their locations are secluded.
- The gate in a security perimeter barrier should be as high as the adjoining perimeter fence.
- Gates can be fitted with anti-pass-over hardware.
- Warning signs should be posted on gates to warn drivers and pedestrians that the area is restricted, with no entry or unauthorized personnel allowed. This will also provide a deterrent.
- Directional signage should be located at all vehicle entrances to guide visitors, contractors, etc. to the appropriate areas. Visitor parking should be clearly designated.
- Place decals on authorized vehicles to monitor traffic.
- Parking of privately owned vehicles within the perimeter should not be allowed; have a designated parking area for employees

outside the perimeter to reduce employee theft. No parking spaces should be identified by employee name or position.

- Post a sign stating "no weapons allowed" on all normal building entrances.
- Install a high-sensitivity metal detection system to screen personnel when entering or exiting an area for safety reasons and to reduce theft.
- Packages brought into the establishment should be inspected or, in some cases, should be spot-checked.

ACCESS CONTROL SYSTEMS

Access control systems consist of doors, gates, or portals, operated by mechanical, pneumatic, hydraulic, or electromechanical hardware. Access control also includes the software to manage the databases or other records of those having authorized entry, as well as the physical means of restricting entry or exit.

The main objectives of implementing an access control system are as follows:

- To allow only authorized personnel to enter or exit
- To ensure that only personnel with proper cards can gain access
- To control which hours each card is authorized for entry
- To limit access to sensitive areas inside the facility to personnel who have clearance to do so
- To provide a complete record of all card usage and denials
- To allow for the immediate deactivation of an employee's card when he or she is terminated or when otherwise necessary
- To prevent and detect the entry or exit of contraband materials, such as drugs, explosives, weapons, etc.
- To alert security and provide information to security personnel for assessment and response

The portion of the access control system that determines authorized entry depends on the credentials used. There are many types of systems that can be used to gain entry:

- Credential based: something possessed
  - Keys
  - Photo identification badges
  - Tokens
  - Transmitters
  - Key card system or coded cards

- Magnetic-stripe encoding
- Wiegand effect sensors
- Proximity cards
- Hall effect sensors
- Barium ferrite
- Infrared (IR) optical
- Smart cards (integrated circuit cards containing specific user data)
- Hollerith machine
- Electrical circuit
- Active electronic
- Passive electronic
- Knowledge based: something known
  - Personal identification number (PIN)
  - Password
- Biometric based: unique, biological characteristics
  - Voiceprint
  - Fingerprint
  - Retinal scan
  - Hand geometry
  - Signature dynamics
  - Keystroke dynamics
  - Blood vessel patterns

The types of readers used to identify credentials include insertion, swipe, proximity, touch pad, key insertion, and IR transmitters.

With the exception of biometric devices, an unauthorized person seeking entry may use any of the above-mentioned credentials. Credentials only verify that a person requesting entry has a valid credential, whereas biometric devices match physical characteristics to verify the person's identity. Using a combination of credentials, such as a photo identification badge with a PIN or a coded key card, will make the access control system harder for an adversary to defeat.

Although both persons entering a site may be authorized to be in an area, it is necessary for security purposes for each person to gain access individually to deal with the pervasive problem of "piggybacking." Piggybacking is when two or more persons gain access on only one employee's credential. All personnel must use their own credentials to determine their access validity and to create a necessary record trail. Each person should be informed that there is a policy in place that strictly prohibits the practice and that he or she is responsible to prevent piggybacking behind him or her.

Other methods to control access of entry and exit include the following:

- Locked doors in tandem create a situation where after one person or group enters through one locked door, he or she must wait to enter the next set of locked doors until after he or she has been cleared by security or is permitted through.
- Manual, electrically operated doors, gates, etc. of access and entrance control.
- Push-button system: Announces the person before entry is allowed.
- Elevator access: Uses a key or electronic card access for only authorized personnel to gain entrance.
- Electronic door-opening system where authorized personnel use an electronically verifiable card that allows the door to open. There are other sophisticated systems that use, for example, voice or signature identification equipment, iris/retina examination, or palm print or fingerprint analysis for entry.
- The use of identification cards or badges to distinguish employees and visitors. The cards or badges should be tamper resistant and laminated, with a clear and recent photo in a 1 in. square. Identification cards and badges should be updated with a recent photo every 2 to 3 years or when an employee's appearance changes. Personal information regarding age, sex, height, weight, color of hair and eyes, and signature should be included on the badge. The identification cards or badges should be color coded to indicate what level of security or position they are in. Other anticounterfeiting measures that can be included on the card or badge are unique holograms, or ultraviolet (UV) fluorescent ink that is designed into the company's logo for quick identification. UV fluorescent ink is invisible to the naked eye but can be verified when placed under a black UV light.
- Entrances that use various locking mechanisms. These are generally only as good as their locks.
- Other openings, such as utility entrances, tunnels, manhole covers, air vents and ducts, unavoidable drainage ditches, culverts, and other openings, must also be protected from unauthorized use.
  - Any opening that is larger than 96 in.^{2} should have grills, bars, or a door with an adequate locking device.
  - Drainage ditches, culverts, etc. that are larger than 96 in.^{2} should have welded bar grills that will protect the perimeter and still allow drainage.
  - Manhole covers that are 10 in. or more in diameter must be secured and locked to prevent unauthorized entry.

SMART-CARD INTEGRATION

Today, technologies have improved and have provided many new uses for physical access control, identification, information technology (IT) security, banking, etc. The use of smart cards integrated with biometric technology has been on the rise, especially since 9/11. Combining the technologies has provided added security, both physical and IT security, that has prevented crime, while also protecting the privacy of the user. Smart cards with biometric data used in IT security help prevent unauthorized users from gaining access to confidential information while at the same time creating an audit trail. Built-in biometric scanners and desktop readers allow authorized users to be logged into the computer and confirm the information they have access to.

Smart cards are used to describe different types of cards ranging from those carrying data in memory to those carrying sophisticated data. They are fitted with microprocessor chips and are actually microcontrollers.

In the 1990s, the change began with the introduction of the Java card. This card allows multiple functions, which are protected by firewalls, to coexist on a single card, and it also allows for new functions to be added. In banking, for example, a command to deduct a certain amount of money off a bank card's balance would be sent to the card to store and keep track of your available balance, rather than having the transaction be sent to a bank, which would help to reduce or eliminate over-the-limit transactions or, more importantly, potential fraudulent transactions.

Similarly, the biometrics of matching a person's fingerprint to the one stored on the card can be carried on the card itself. Keeping the data on the card itself allows for additional security, and in addition, the establishment does not need to keep a large database of biometrics if all they want to do is verify that the person presenting the identification card is the person authorized to have the card. The Java cards work through applets, which are tiny programs that carry out individual applications. Each applet is isolated from others by a firewall that prevents applets from interacting with each other. Java cards can have many applets, which make them multifunctional: One applet can be used for biometric authentication, and another could allow access into the establishment.

Other trends with regard to smart cards include contactless, hybrid, and new smart-card readers that offer greater security and faster processing.

CONTACTLESS CARDS

With greater memory capabilities and faster processing, these cards can do more than just allow or deny access. They can hold employee data, medical information, encryption algorithms, and biometric identifiers. Contactless cards also offer better durability than the contact card due to insertion readers that can wear down the chip or wear them off so that they have to be replaced. Contactless readers do not have to be touched and are much faster. The number and types of applications are limited because they do not use the Java operating system.

HYBRID CARDS

These cards are multitechnology or combination cards that assist establishments in the transition from their old system to a higher level of reader technology without completely replacing the old system. The new system needs some level of compatibility to change from a magnetic-stripe card for physical access to a smart card with fingerprint biometric data. Instead of completely replacing an old system, which can be very costly, a company can take some of its existing technology, such as a magnetic-stripe card, and add a contact-smart module to it to provide more technologies. These technologies include magnetic stripes, proximity cards, bar codes, optical character recognition (OCR), etc., that do not share information or communicate with each other. Putting various technologies on a single card helps achieve compatibility and makes the transition to a smart-card/biometric environment smoother. The cards can also be contact or contactless. Another benefit of these cards is the built-in backup system that takes over: If one part of the card has a problem, it still allows the rest of the card to be accessible and usable. The hybrid card is much more stable because if, for example, a card possessed duel theologies that were on one chip and it also had both technologies of contact and contactless interfaces, then if the chip fails, it fails for everything.

The following are examples of different coded cards (Figure 6.1):

- Proximity card
- Contactless card
- Magnetic-stripe card
- Integrated smart-chip card

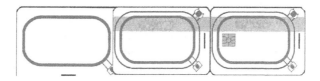

FIGURE 6.1 Coded cards.

READERS

Cards that are both contact and contactless are becoming more common. Card readers also have a dual interface reader that can read both contact and contactless cards.

Technological advances are also occurring in biometrics, which are closely aligned with smart cards, because smart cards are often the delivery mechanism for biometric technology. Biometrics are being incorporated in access control, using biometrically enabled access readers, safes, laptops, cell phones, etc., and they will continue to expand. Improvements in biometrics have allowed us to analyze odor, gait, vein structures, etc., but the most commonly used biometrics relating to the security industry are fingerprints, iris scans, face recognition, and hand geometry. The type of biometrics used depends largely on the application and the establishment for which it is best suited. Many biometric technologies use error rates as a performance indicator of the system:

- Type I, also referred to as false rejection rate (FRR), is the improper rejection of a valid user.
- Type II, also referred to as false acceptance rate (FAR), is the improper acceptance of an unauthorized user.

Selection of biometric devices depends on the establishment's security needs and where they will be used. A low FAR compromises security by allowing some unauthorized users entry. A high FAR will deny access to authorized users but maintain higher security.

The following are some of the biometric devices that are used to heighten security.

Fingerprints

Fingerprints have been used as personal identifiers for more than 100 years, and this is the biometric method of choice. Improvements have been made that are making identification more accurate and less expensive. In the past, fingerprint verification systems have had a high failure-to-enroll rate, due to the user being unable, for some reason, to generate a good-quality fingerprint. Some of the problems are related to dirty, greasy, or stained fingers. Technologies such as scanning more than one finger or using ultrasonic fingerprinting, which works like an ultrasound so the image is untainted by different environmental elements and is able to read the fingerprint peaks and valleys etched on the live layer below the outside layer of skin, allow for greater accuracy and acceptance rates.

Retinal Scans

Retinal scans were developed in the 1980s. This technology checks the blood vessels in the eye. Although it is one of the most well-known bio-metric technologies, it is also one of the least deployed. One reason for this is that usable image acquisition is difficult, and many attempts are often required to get to the point where a match can take place. In many cases, false rejection may occur.

Iris Scans

Iris scans are the most accurate of the biometric technologies. They have fewer false accepts and are most often used in high-security areas or as an added secondary security measure. Iris scans can work through vision wear. Improvements are being made so that the user does not have to stand as close to the scanner, thus making it more appropriate for high-volume situations.

Hand Geometry

Hand geometry has a higher FAR than fingerprints, but it has fewer false rejections. One of the problems encountered is that the user has difficulty putting the hand into the proper position. Hand geometry can also ana-lyze the webbing between the fingers, finger length, curvature, hand width, and amount of light transmitted through the skin. Another hand biometric measurement system is hand vascular pattern identification, which recog-nizes the unique vascular pattern on the back of the hand.

Face Recognition

Most systems capture images using a video camera, and some use an IR imager. This is the only biometric that can be confirmed quickly if a user is falsely rejected. A guard, or other security personnel, can visually con-firm the identification of the person. Face recognition is commonly used in surveillance measures and is an effective tool because the users are not aware of their faces being scanned and matched to a database. Even though they are less intrusive to the user, they are less accurate due to the camera's performance, facial position, expressions, and the possibility of users having changed their features by, for example, growing a beard or wearing sunglasses.

Face recognition works best with consistent lighting and cooperative users in a mug-shot-like position. Improvements are being made to over-come the differences in lighting conditions and by better camera perfor-mance using three-dimensional images that can be rotated through many angles. Scientists are also developing ways to analyze the dermal surface of the face by devising an algorithm called surface texture analysis, which allows the dermal surface of the skin to be analyzed for random features. The combination of surface texture analysis and three-dimensional images may improve the performance of facial recognition. Face technology does have the appeal of noncontact and the potential to provide face-in-the-crowd identification.

CLEAR ZONE

A clear zone is an area within the storage site perimeter and around the boundary of the storage site free of all obstacles, topographical features, and vegetation exceeding a specified height. The zone is designed to facilitate detection and observation of an intruder, deny protection and concealment to an intruder, maximize effectiveness of the security force, and reduce the possibility of a surprise attack. A clear zone of 20 ft. or more should be maintained on both sides of the perimeter barrier. A zone of 50 ft. or more should be maintained between the perimeter barrier and the structures within the property, except, of course, when a building's walls constitute part of the perimeter barrier. A clear zone can aid in the visualization of movement from outside and inside the barriers. Overgrowth of vegetation, weeds, trash, etc. that can conceal movement should be eliminated. In conditions where the clear zone is smaller than what is recommended, and it could reduce the effectiveness of the barrier, consideration to increasing the barrier's height or the installation of alarms or detection devices may prove to be more practical.

In high-security areas, such as nuclear plants, prisons, military bases, etc., a perimeter intrusion detection system works best in an isolated clear zone. An isolated clear zone is a restricted access area surrounding an establishment that has been cleared of any objects that could conceal vehicles or individuals and affords unobstructed observation or the use of other means for detection of entry into the area. No sensors should be placed on the outer fence and only associated security hardware, such as power lines, etc., should be in the clear zone. The purpose of a clear zone is to enhance visibility and, in conjunction with perimeter sensor systems, to increase security detection of intrusion and reduce the nuisance of false alarms.

LANDSCAPING

Trees, shrubs, or other vegetation used for landscaping should not be selected or planted where, in the future, they could interfere with lighting, block CCTV camera locations, or obstruct interior views of the facility or parking areas that would give an intruder a potential hiding place. The growth tendencies of all plant species should be taken into account when selecting items for landscaping. To eliminate any future climbing potential, trees should not be planted near buildings. Any existing tree foliage should be trimmed down to a 6 ft. level, and shrubs should be trimmed to approximately 2 ft. in height.

INNER BARRIERS

Inner barriers include inside walls and doors of buildings, blockaded or locked doors, skylights, window gates, and similar areas. Aside from just being locked or closed, they must also be designed with sufficient strength properties to resist actual forced entry. Although this is true for all types of physical barriers, movable barriers such as doors and windows, which are usually designed with intent and ease of mobility, require extra consideration to provide correct design with sufficient structural strength properties.

Windows, doors, or any openings greater than 96 in.^{2} should be protected by grills, bars, or heavy screens when they are less than 18 ft. from the ground or less than 14 ft. from trees, poles, fire escapes, or other structures. Windows with ledges that are 18 ft. or more above ground level are not as likely to be used by intruders. All windows should have strong window frames and be securely locked from the inside.

Many forced break-ins are accomplished by first breaking the glass that is installed in windows or doors. Depending on the type of business, whether it is a bank, retail store, or industrial facility, regular plate glass can be strengthened. The type of reinforcement used also depends on the visibility, ventilation, amount of sunlight, etc. that one wants to achieve.

WINDOWS

Normal windowpane glass is about 1/8 in. thick and is easily broken. Because windows are viewed as potential weak points in the building's defenses, intruders find them desirable to gain entry, and therefore, they must be protected. In securing windows, a good plan for emergency escape routes should also be considered because they provide a fast exit in case of a fire or other emergencies. The following are some examples of glasses and plastics that can be used to reinforce windows and have the appearance of regular windowpanes.

- Burglar-resistant glass: Windows can be measurably strengthened by burglar-resistant glass (safety glass) that has met the Underwriters Laboratories (UL) standards for resistance to heat, flame, cold, picks, rocks, etc. that an intruder may try to use. Burglar-resistant glass is a lamination of two sheets of flat glass and one or more interlayers of plasticized polyvinyl butyryl (PVB) varying in thickness that are permanently bonded together by heat and pressure. Applications of burglar-resistant glass include resistance to smash-and-grab burglaries, security, bullet resistance, etc.

- Plastic glazing: Sold under various trade names, in varying thicknesses thinner than burglar-resistant glass, this is used to reinforce windows, and it is shatter and blast resistant, providing protection from the danger of flying glass.
- Acrylic glazing: Also known as Plexiglas, this is cheaper and lighter in weight. One and a quarter inches thick meets the UL standards for a bullet-resistant barrier.
- Wired glass: This is used in fire doors and windows. The glass is manufactured with a layer of wire mesh approximately in the center of the sheet.
- Tempered glass: This is four times stronger than annealed glass but can still be broken. When broken, spalling occurs, and it usually breaks into small fragments, protecting against the hazards of flying glass. "Spalling is a property built into security glass that allows it to chip, fracture, and break into small harmless pieces."

See Appendix C for a list of common terms.

Doors

Once the function and the area, including the assets to be protected, are determined, the doors need to be evaluated with regard to the type of construction as well as the locking mechanism used. Doors should be made of a heavy and solid steel construction. If wood is used, the door should have a solid wood core. Hollow-core doors present a security risk because an intruder can easily penetrate them.

Reinforcing the doors will only prove efficient if the frames, hinges, bolts, locking mechanisms, etc. are also reinforced. Frames should be made of a heavy, solid steel construction to prevent being forced apart. Doors should be installed so that the hinges are located on the inside. Door hinges are another way to gain entry through a door. Door hinges exposed to the outside should be either spot welded or flanged (inserting a headless machine screw in a predrilled hole through a leaf of the hinge) to prevent removal. All external doors should be equipped with latch-guard protector plates. Doors should open toward the likely threat direction.

Door Latches and Bolts

Some other common ways intruders can defeat the locking mechanisms of doors are as follows (Figure 6.2):

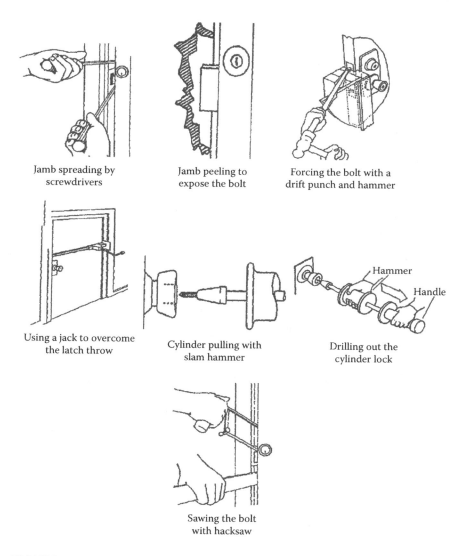

Jamb spreading by screwdrivers

Jamb peeling to expose the bolt

Forcing the bolt with a drift punch and hammer

Using a jack to overcome the latch throw

Cylinder pulling with slam hammer

Drilling out the cylinder lock

Sawing the bolt with hacksaw

FIGURE 6.2 Common attack methods on bolts.

- Breaking the doorknob with a pipe wrench
- Jimmying, prying, or sawing off bolts
- Forcing the bolt back into the body of the lock with a punch and a hammer
- Peeling back the thin sheet metal or aluminum of the doorjamb to expose the locking mechanism
- Using a fire axe for forced entry
- Prying open the door using a 15 lb. pry bar
- Spreading the doorjamb with screwdrivers

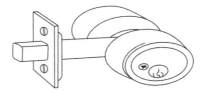

FIGURE 6.3   Dead bolt.

- Spreading the doorframe with a car jack
- Wedging a credit card in between the door and the jamb
- Ripping the lock cylinder from the door
- Pulling, wrenching, or prying the cylinder away from the door
- Drilling out the cylinder lock

The following are two common types of locking bolts that are found on doors:

1. Latch bolt: A latch bolt characteristic is a beveled head and a spring bolt that is designed to automatically retract when the beveled face contacts the lip of the strike and closes the door for privacy. Because the latch is spring loaded and functions primarily to keep the door closed, it can be easily opened with a plastic strip or credit card. There are antishim devices, or dead latches, that are added with the latch bolt that help protect from shimming or carding, but they can still be jimmied by a piece of thin metal or can be forced open by prying between the frame and the door.
2. Dead bolt: This is a square-faced solid bolt that is not spring loaded and is dead in the door whether it is opened or closed (Figure 6.3). The only way to open the door with a dead bolt is to use the key or other operating systems that are designed to open the door. Most dead bolts are 1/2 in. beyond the door edge to prevent carding; however, there are dead bolts that extend to 1 in. or longer (long-throw dead bolts), which provide reasonably adequate protection against doorjamb spreading or frame peeling, provided that the door and frame are constructed solidly. A dead bolt or dead latch is essential on all entry doors. A cylinder dead bolt with a 1 in. projecting bolt made of hardened steel can provide minimum protection against door spreading or jamb peeling.

Dead Bolts

Other types of dead bolts are available that increase security against jamb spreading, jimmying, etc. The most common are known as vertical interlocking dead bolt locks. The vertical dead bolt lock is attached to the inside surface of the door like the rim lock. The dead bolt mechanism uses two or more metal rings that are aligned vertically and extend out from a metal attaching plate. These rings mesh with similar rings on the edge of the lock when the door is closed. Each lock ring contains a bolt that is basically a vertical rod on the end of a lever. When the door is locked, the rods are moved vertically into the strike rings. This is an advantage because it restricts lateral movement and is thus resistant to jimmying and spreading.

Another type of dead bolt is the vertical pivoting dead bolt, which increases security on thin doors with small frames, such as glass storefront windows. Ordinary dead bolts are thrown horizontally, but on some narrow, glass-front doors, the space provided for the lock is too narrow to permit a long horizontal throw. This bolt is designed to pivot up from the lock, rather than to project horizontally, thus allowing the bolt to project at least 1 in. into the frame.

Types of Common Dead Bolt Door Locks Used

A lock's security is denoted by a grade given to it by the American National Standards Institute (ANSI). The ANSI grades are ratings of the minimum standard acceptable in regard to the different levels of security and quality performance.

Locksets

There are three grades given to locksets:

Grade I: Only the most secure dead bolts earn this rating; they incorporate features such as antipick pins, extra-long bolts in extra-tough alloys, and reinforced strike plates with extra-long screws. Locksets of this grade must pass a rigorous sequence of tests, which simulate physical attacks such as kicking and strikes with sledgehammers and wrenches. Be aware: Just because some locks boast grade I features does not mean they made ANSI grade I; they just may possess one or two high-security features. Grade I is used in most commercial applications and includes cylindrical key and lever locks, mortise locks, heavy-duty mortise locks, auxiliary dead bolts, and the locks used with electronic or other access control hardware.

Grade II: These are medium-security locks and will serve well in low-security applications, such as a handle set that contains a tubular lock and dead bolt in combination. They are the next strongest level of resistance and can resist numerous cycles of kick attacks, hammer hits, and prying assaults.

Grade III: These are the least secure, and this level indicates the standard level of performance and security testing against attacks.

The trim used with a lock should be built as strong as the rest of the lock.

Locks

Not all locks are created equal. They come in many types that are designed to perform a range of functions and provide different levels of security. Although the primary purpose is always security, locking needs will vary from locking a storage closet, to locking up assets, to securing a building entrance. The designations are based on the design of the lock, how and where it engages, and how it is mounted to the door.

Mortise

Mortise locks (Figure 6.4) are generally considered the heaviest-duty product for commercial usage where greater security is required. This lock is inserted into a cavity cut into the edge of a door or along the front of the door. The cylinder is screwed through the skin of the door directly into the metal lock case, with only the cylinder head and spin ring projecting from the face of the door. Some mortise locks have a single deadlocking latch bolt with push buttons on the edge of the door that are used to lock or unlock the exterior knob. Others have a dead bolt, separate from the latch bolt, that can be operated from the inside by turning a thumb turn. They are also available with double-cylinder dead bolts that must be key-operated from the inside or outside. A mortise lock should not be used in

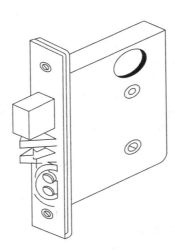

FIGURE 6.4   Typical mortise lock without the trim.

a wooden door, unless it is designed for such use, because the cavity cut in the door can severely weaken the door.

Rim Mounted

Rim locks are attached to the inside surface of the door with a cylinder installed on the outside surface in a hole bored through the door. They typically have either a spring-latch or dead bolt operation, engaging a strike mounted to the frame around the door. There are several types of dead bolt mechanisms found on rim locks. They are commonly used as supplementary, or auxiliary, locks where the primary lock is not considered enough protection against jimmying.

Figure 6.5 shows an example of a grade I rim lock. The interlocking dead bolt can be operated by a key on both sides.

Cylindrical Lockset

This is a very popular residential lock. This type of lock is installed in a door as part of the doorknob, rather than in a case or inside the door. The outside knob is locked against movement when a push button or thumb turn on the inside knob is operated and is then turned with a key. This type of lock should not be used as the only door lock unless it has a deadlocking latch bolt. With the cylinder mounted in the doorknob, they are vulnerable to just about any attack, such as hammering, twisting, wrenching, etc.

Padlocks

Padlocks feature a shackle instead of a bolt and are designed to secure areas with a detachable and portable lock. Padlocks can be opened for engagement through a hasp or a chain. Padlocks are vulnerable to attacks, such as the shackle being pried out of the lock by a crowbar, jimmied, or sawed off. The shackle should be close to the body to prevent prying, or better padlocks with positive heel-and-toe locking should be used. In the locked position, there should be no mounting screw or bolt accessible, and padlocks should be locked at all times, even when not securing an area. Heavy hardened steel cases and shackles are used to defeat cutting and prying. There are versatile padlocks that have a shackle-less "hockey puck" design when shackle protection is desirable.

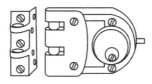

FIGURE 6.5 Grade I rim lock.

Emergency Exit Doors

Emergency exit doors (Figure 6.6) are required in public buildings for safety purposes and should be secured from unauthorized use. Emergency exit doors should be equipped with a panic bar allowing exit without the use of a key. Emergency exit doors consist of a massive lock and strike and a horizontal rod across the door. When the rod is pushed, the door is unlocked and opened at the same time. For added security measures, the door should be equipped with an audible alarm to alert security when opened. Posting signs that an alarm will sound if the door is opened will add another deterrent from the door being used for activities other than an emergency.

Exit Devices

There are three basic types: rim mounted, vertical rod, and mortise. Rim-mounted devices are the simplest ones. Vertical-rod devices (Figure 6.7) provide a means of securing a pair of doors by being attached to the top and bottom. Mortise devices are used to secure the active leaf of pairs of fire-rated doors, where each leaf is more than 3 ft. wide.

Not all locks function the same way. Commercial mortise and cylindrical locks may have several different functions for the combination of convenience and security requirements and are named for their most typical applications.

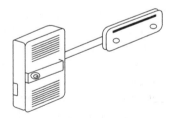

FIGURE 6.6   Example of an emergency exit device.

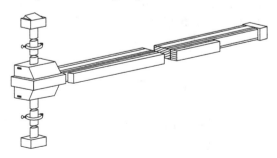

FIGURE 6.7   Example of a surface vertical rod device.

The most common include passage, privacy, communicating, office, entry, classroom, and storeroom locks.

Passage

Passage locks are not really locks but have a lever or knob on either side of the door and a latch to hold the door shut. The latch bolt can be operated by the knob or lever from either side at all times. There is no provision for a key, as no lock cylinder is installed.

Privacy

These locks are usually found in bathrooms or for inside applications. They usually have push buttons built into the knobs or levers but no key or cylinder mechanism. The latch bolt can be operated by the knob or lever from either side. The outside knob or lever is locked by a push button inside and can be unlocked by rotating the inside knob or closing the door. They also have a provision for emergency access from the outside, often by using a small screwdriver or wire to unlock the outside knob or lever through a hole in the trim. Some of the privacy locks have a dead bolt operated by a thumb turn on the inside that also has provisions for emergency release on the outside.

Communicating

Latch bolts are operated by the knob or lever on either side. They can also be installed with a push button on each side, deadlocking latch bolts, dead bolts, or split dead bolts operated independently by turns from both sides. These should not be used on doors in rooms that have no other entrance.

Office

These are locked from the inside by a push button or other locking mechanism placed in a locked position. The outside knob or lever remains locked until it is unlocked with a key from the outside. The inside knob or lever is always free for immediate exit.

Entry

These can be locked by pushing and turning a button and are unlocked by the key or by the inside button being manually unlocked. Closing the door does not release the push button or other locking device. The inside knob or lever is always free for immediate exit.

Classroom

These are always locked and unlocked from the outside with a key. The inside knob or lever is always free for immediate exit.

Storeroom

The outside knob or lever is always fixed. A key from the outside operates the latch bolt or deadlocking latch bolt. The inside knob or lever is free for immediate exit.

Cylinder Locks

Cylinder guards can help reinforce cylinder locks. Various types of physical attack can defeat any cylinder lock if the cylinder is unprotected. A cylinder guard prevents the cylinder from being wrenched or pried from the door. One type of guard is a steel plate that is fastened over the cylinder; another is a ring that is mounted around the cylinder that moves so that it is harder to wrench off.

- Single cylinder: This is a dead bolt controlled by a key-operated cylinder lock. The mechanism that projects the bolt may be a thumb-turn type or a blank plate on the inside. Cylinder dead bolts are also available with a loner bolt extending further into the locking area that provides greater security.
- Double-cylinder dead bolt: This uses a key-operated cylinder for both sides. This prevents the intruder from breaking the glass or punching a hole through the door and reaching inside to unlock the door. The problem with this is that rapid exit is difficult in case of an emergency without the key.

Key and Lock System

Locks are very important elements in physical security and are the most accepted and widely used security devices, especially because they secure the movable portions of barriers and protect our valuable assets. Regardless of quality or cost, no lock is completely invulnerable to attack. The sole purpose of using a lock is to delay an intruder, not to obstruct entry. Locks, cylinders, door and frame construction, and key control must be equally effective to delay an intruder. A good lock makes it much harder to gain entry and may be more trouble than it is worth to an intruder. By the same token, it is unwise to select a lock that is either stronger or weaker than the barriers around it. Criminals generally prefer either using an illicit key or forced entry for speed than risking exposure during the time it takes to pick a lock. A lock's effectiveness is determined by how long it will resist and the force of the best efforts of an intruder. Locks play a role in and defend against the following:

- Forced entry: Destructive application of force for quick entry, not caring about the property damage or evidence left behind

- Surreptitious entry: Obtaining a key or through the use of decoding or bypass tools designed to quickly and quietly defeat the locks to gain entry (espionage or law enforcement surveillance etc.)
- Safety of life and property
- Natural elements

Basic types of key-locking mechanisms are listed as follows.

Warded Locks

These are the longest in use, the least secure, and constructed by a simple arrangement of a bolt and an arm that moves the bolt. There are internal physical barriers that prevent the lock from operating unless aligned correctly. The key is used to align the internal barriers to operate the bolt or latching mechanism. The keyway is open and can be seen through, offering very little security, and can be easily picked, because once the locking tumbler is lifted, the bolt moves, and there is no need to keep lifting the locking tumbler. Figure 6.8 shows an example of a warded lock device.

Disc or Wafer Tumblers

These are constructed by having movable tumblers, which depend on the proper keys to arrange the tumblers into a straight line, permitting the lock to operate. There are flat, metal discs that are spring loaded, extending across the full height of the plug. Each wafer has a rectangular cutout through its middle and through which the key passes. When the proper key is inserted in the keyway, the disc tumbler aligns, and no disc is extended into the shell, allowing the plug to be turned. The disc tumbler serves as the lock barrier and will not operate with the improper key. Disc tumblers are commonly found on some automobiles, cabinets, files, and padlocks. They provide more security than warded locks but can be manipulated or picked easily without much skill involved.

Pin Tumbler

The conventional pin-tumbler lock (Figure 6.9) is the most widely used in security applications and common commercial and residential design

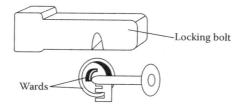

FIGURE 6.8 Warded lock device.

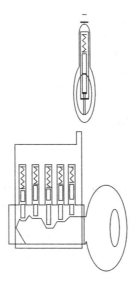

FIGURE 6.9   Example of a pin-tumbler device with the proper key inserted.

used in the United States. Some pin-tumbler locks have high-security features, including secondary locking mechanisms and features that are intended to frustrate picking, such as special elevating and rotating pin-tumbler designs, false slots on the bottom pins, mushroom-top pins, sidebar mechanisms, etc. The basic design consists of a rotatable cylinder tube, called the plug, linked to an underlying locking mechanism. Around the plug is a shell, or cylinder, that is fixed to the door or container. Rotation of the plug within the shell operates the locking mechanism.

The lock operates like a disc tumbler, but instead of using discs, the mechanism uses pins as the interior barrier. In the locked state, the plug is prevented from rotating by a set of pin stacks. With no key in the lock, all pin stack cuts rest within the plug. With a key properly cut and inserted into the keyway slot, or groove, at the front of the plug, the pin stacks are raised to align exactly at the shear point where the plug and shell meet. The plug can then rotate freely only if the key lifts every pin stack between the plug and the shell. The keyway is irregular in shape, and the key is grooved on both sides. Many high-security pin tumblers use mushroom, spool, or serrated security pins to make picking much harder, because they give a false impression that the pin has been picked. The pin is still preventing the cylinder from turning, but the recess of the spool pins allows the cylinder to turn slightly, and the lock picker thinks that that particular pin has been raised to the correct height. This type of locking mechanism is more secure than the warded lock or disc tumbler.

Tubular Pin-Tumbler Lock

Tubular cylinders typically have four to eight pin tumblers arranged in a circular pattern around the circumference of the plug. The basic principles are essentially the same as those of the pin-tumbler lock, except the tumblers are exposed at the front of the cylinder and a round tubular key is used. Locks of this type are seen on bicycle locks and vending machines.

Master-Keyed Pin-Tumbler Locks

Most pin-tumbler cylinders can be master keyed for a variety of applications with many different possible combinations that allow more than one key bitting to operate it. This involves using more than one cut in some or all of the pin stacks by adding driver pins known as spacer pins or master pins between the drivers and key pins. These spacer pins enable a second key to operate the same lock. The addition of more master pins will create more than one shear line in each pin chamber, giving more chances to lift a cut to the shear line for someone manipulating the lock.

Removable Core Cylinder

This is another variation of the pin tumbler. This type of cylinder uses a special key called the control key to remove the entire pin-tumbler mechanism, or core, from the shell. Then it can be quickly replaced with another core having a different combination and requiring a different key to operate it. This type is more vulnerable to manipulation because the added control pins increase the number of shear points in each chamber, giving more chances to lift a cut to the shear line.

Lever-Tumbler Mechanisms

Lever locks provide moderate to high security depending on the number of levers used. Lever locks employ a set of "lever" tumblers raised to a specific height by the key bit. Each lever has a cutout called a gate, through which part of the locking bolt (fence) must travel. Some mechanisms use a double set of levers, requiring a double-bitted key. This makes it very difficult to manipulate and pick the lock because the multiple plates must be lifted exactly to the right height before the bolt will move. Lever locks are used in safe boxes, strongboxes, post office boxes, etc. For practical purposes, lever locks are pickproof. Large lever locks are also used in prisons, mostly due to their massiveness and the strength of the springs on the levers, making them very resistant to picking.

Other locking mechanisms include the following:

- Combination locks: Not all locks use a physical key. Combination locks require the user to dial in a secret combination of numbers or a password to manually align the tumblers. Mechanical combination locks operate in much the same way as a lever tumbler mechanism and are commonly used on padlocks and safe locks and to control access to high-security safes and vaults. The typical combination lock design involves a set of three or four disc tumblers around a spindle connected to the external dial. Each disc has a notch cut in its edge. The lock mechanism can open when the notches on the disks are lined up at a particular rotation with the proper password. Combination locks that are used for securing highly valuable assets should have at least four or more tumblers. For example, 10-15-27-37 uses four tumblers.

- Card-operated locks: Electrical or electromagnetic cards are used to operate the locks.
- Code-operated locks: These are combination locks that are operated by pressing a series of numbered buttons in the proper sequence without the use of keys. The code of combination locks can be easily changed, and these locks are considered high-security locking devices. This type of lock should be monitored in case more than one person tries to enter an authorized opening, known as piggybacking.
- Electronic locks: These are inexpensive and low-power-embedded microcontrollers that, of course, do not require mechanical tumblers and therefore are not vulnerable to lock picking. They are activated by an electric current that releases the strike and permits entrance.
- Electromagnetic locking devices: These operate by holding the door closed by magnetism. These electrical units consist of an electromagnet and a metal holding plate.

Keying Systems

In larger establishments where a number of keys have been issued, loss, theft, or keys not being turned in can easily happen. Patent keys often prevent duplication, but of course, this does not solve the other issues of loss or keys not turned in. The cost to rekey the whole facility would be very expensive. Sometimes, it may be practical to install interchangeable cores that can be quickly replaced. These types of locks are easily removed with a core key, thus allowing a new pin tumbler or core to be inserted. The core is the lock, and this system has the concept of rekeying without changing the entire cylinder's locking device, which makes this type very popular in establishments where locks must be changed often.

Another variation that is in widespread use is master keying. Almost any pin tumbler can be master keyed. That allows an entire series of locks to be operated by the same master key.

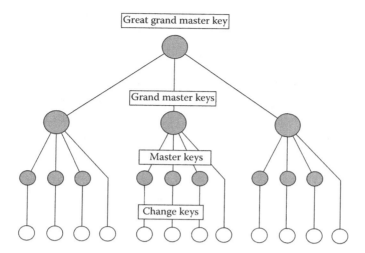

FIGURE 6.10   Example of a master-keying system.

The keys are divided into four types:

1. Control key: One key that will open all the locks within a master-keyed system.
2. Submaster key: Key designed to open locks within a particular area in the establishment. For example, a submaster key may open all the doors in the administration area, and another submaster key may be made to open only the doors to electronic areas.
3. Master key: The key will open all locks when two or more submaster key systems exist.
4. Grand master key (Figure 6.10): A key designed to open everything when two or more master key systems exist. This may be seen when an establishment has two or more locations that were each master keyed.
   - The top-level key, sometimes referred to as the great grand master key, can open all the doors of an establishment—avoid whenever possible.
   - The next level, the grand master key, can open only designated doors.
   - The next level, the master key, can open only designated doors.
   - The lowest level, the change key, represents the individual key, only opening one door or one group of doors.

Key Control

A key control system should be developed and strictly adhered to for positive control of all keys, and this must be constantly maintained. All keys need to be accounted for; this is easy to initiate if new locking devices were installed. If not, depending on whether critical keys are lost or not accounted for, the whole establishment may have to be rekeyed. Otherwise, it can be less expensive to install new locking devices in the critical areas and move the locks that were replaced to less sensitive areas. Reevaluation can be done later if rekeying is necessary. A good key control system that accounts for and secures the keys is critical and can prevent such problems from arising.

The following are some examples of initiating an effective key control system:

- Every effort should be made to have keys remain in the control of security or management. Keys should only be issued to those whose functions require them.
- All users should comply with all rules and regulations.
- A key record should be maintained when issuing keys, with the name of the person, his or her position, date of issuance, key number, etc.
- If an electronic key cabinet that requires a pass code, fingerprint, or handprint is not utilized, a key cabinet should be used to secure all keys. The key cabinet should be locked at all times, and only security or management should have access to the keys.
- Keys should not leave the facility.
- Inventories of all keys should be conducted annually at minimum.
- Master keys should be kept to a minimum because a lost master key can compromise the entire establishment and necessitate rekeying of the entire facility. Submasters should be used if at all possible and should only be issued to management or limited personnel.
- When a key is lost, the circumstances should be investigated and set forth in writing. If the key that is lost gives access to a highly sensitive area, the locks should be changed. If an employee who is suspended or discharged did not return a key, the locks should be changed.
- Combinations to safe locks and padlocks securing sensitive information should be changed annually, sooner if lost or if an employee who knew the combination has been discharged, suspended, or relocated. In some instances, frequent rotation of padlocks is necessary in very sensitive areas.
- Some locks are powered by electricity on mantraps and other sensitive areas. When these locks do not have a power supply, they will function in one of three modes.
  - Fail safe—unlocks for safety reasons, for example, fires
  - Fail secure—locks, for example, in prisons
  - Fail soft—limited mode of operability

- A successful key control system results from effective policies and procedures, documentation, and recovery procedures.

See Appendix C for a list of terms.

SAFES, FILE CABINETS, AND VAULTS

Valuable assets of the company, such as proprietary information, cash, records, plans, etc., will need to be stored in a high-security storage area. The company's own particular need for protecting assets will determine whether to select file cabinets, safes, or vaults. The decision is based upon value of the item and vulnerability. There are two categories of protection that one should assess: whether the file cabinets, safes, or vaults are burglar resistant and fire resistant. Even things that are not attractive to a burglar may still be lost and unrecoverable due to a fire. The more burglar resistant and fire resistant the security container, the more expensive it will be. Evaluating what is being protected will help to determine what type of security container to recommend.

There are two categories that describe the degree of protection security containers provide. UL has tested and provided specifications for the manufacturing of resistive containers. A UL label or rating means that the resistant containers have met the specifications. The ratings are mandated not by any federal or state law but through tests conducted by UL:

- Burglary resistant (money safe)
- Fire resistant (record safe)

In a fire-resistant safe, paper is destroyed at 350°F. Wet insulation between the steel walls creates moisture in the fire-resistant safe that dissipates the heat and protects the paper and documents. For example, a class 350 fire-resistant safe is rated to keep paper and documents safe for 4 h. Computer media storage temperature limits are 150°F for magnetic tape and microfilm and 125°F for diskettes. Humidity is a major computer media storage concern; the humidity limit is 80%. For more details, see Table 6.5. Remember, a burglary-resistant container does not protect against fire, and fire-resistant containers only provide a minimal deterrence to burglars.

Most file cabinet storage containers are used for protection of sensitive materials such as documents. They are designed to protect from destruction by fire and are usually reinforced with high-security locks, combination locks, hardened steel, etc. to provide some type of burglar resistance to a surreptitious attack.

TABLE 6.5
Underwriters Laboratories Listing Requirements

Burglary-Resistant Safes

Classification	Description	Tool Time Resistance	Construction
UL TL-15	Resistant to mechanical and electrical tools	15 min resistance on door and front-face attack	Must weigh at least 750 lb., or be anchored into concrete, with at least 1-in.-thick steel or equivalent
UL TL-15X6	Resistant to mechanical and electrical tools	15 min resistance equally on all six sides of safe	Must weigh at least 750 lb., or be anchored into concrete, with at least 1-in.-thick steel or equivalent
UL TL-30	Resistant to mechanical and electrical tools	30 min resistance on door and front-face attack	Must weigh at least 750 lb. with at least 1-in.-thick steel or equivalent
UL TRTL-30X6	Resistant to mechanical and electrical tools, oxy-fuel gas cutting or welding torches	30 min resistance equally on all six sides of safe	Must weigh at least 750 lb.
UL TRTL-60	Resistant to mechanical and electrical tools, oxy-fuel gas cutting or welding torches	60 min resistance	Must weigh at least 750 lb.
UL TXTL-60	Resistant to mechanical and electrical tools, oxy-fuel gas cutting or welding torches, and 8 oz. of nitroglycerine or equivalent	60 min resistance on door and entire-safe-body attack	Must weigh at least 1000 lb.

Burglary-Resistant Vaults

Classification	Description	Tool Time Resistance
UL M	Resistant to mechanical and electrical tools, cutting torches, portable electric drills, power saws, and hydraulic jacks and wedges	15 min resistance

(*Continued*)

TABLE 6.5 (CONTINUED)
Underwriters Laboratories Listing Requirements

Burglary-Resistant Vaults

Classification	Description	Tool Time Resistance
UL 1	Resistant to mechanical and electrical tools, cutting torches, portable electric drills, power saws, and hydraulic jacks and wedges	30 min resistance
UL 2	Resistant to mechanical and electrical tools, cutting torches, portable electric drills, power saws, and hydraulic jacks and wedges	1 h resistance
UL 3	Resistant to mechanical and electrical tools, cutting torches, portable electric drills, power saws, and hydraulic jacks and wedges	2 h resistance

Note: Common hand-tools include chisels, punches, wrenches, screwdrivers, pliers, hammers, and sledges not over 8 lb., and pry bars and other ripping tools not over 5 ft. in length.

Fire-Resistant Containers

Classification	Temperature	Time	Impact	Old Label
350-4	2000°F	4 h	Yes	A
350-2	1850°F	2 h	Yes	B
350-1	1700°F	1 h	Yes	C
350-1	1700°F	1 h	Yes	A
Insulated record container 350-1	1700°F	1 h	No	D

Computer Media Storage Classification

Classification	Temperature	Time	Impact
150-4	2000°F	4 h	Yes
150-2	1850°F	2 h	Yes
150-1	1700°F	1 h	Yes

Insulated Vault Door Classification

Classification	Temperature	Time	Impact
350-6	2150°F	6 h	No
350-4	2000°F	4 h	No
350-2	1850°F	2 h	No
350-1	1700°F	1 h	No

Vaults are like safes but are much larger, are part of the building's structure, and allow entrance and movement of one or more persons. Vaults are usually located at or below ground level because of their heavy weight. The vault's door should be made of at least 6 in. or more of steel or other torch-resistant and drill-resistant material, and it should be equipped with a manipulation-resistant combination lock, firelock, and lockable day gate. The vault's walls, floor, and ceiling should be reinforced with high-quality concrete at least 12 in. thick, or twice the thickness of the door.

Burglar-Resistant Safes and Vaults

No type of security container is impenetrable, and all will require additional security and frequent inspections. Safes should be anchored to prevent being carried or wheeled off and should possess manipulation-resistant combination locks. Small corridors should be designed around the safe, and there should not be any power outlets near the room where the safe is located. Relocking devices should be used on security containers. The security containers can be additionally supported by alarm systems: The two most commonly used are capacitance and vibration alarms. CCTV surveillance will also provide constant surveillance and inspection and, depending on what is being protected, would definitely be worth the investment. UL listing requirements are shown in Table 6.5.

LIGHTING

Security lighting serves as an essential element in the planning of a physical security program. Lighting is so important that NFPA 101 (National Fire Protection Association) requires that generated power systems provide illumination within 10 s. Protective security lighting, depending on the type and the needs of the establishment, will need to be designed to illuminate the perimeter barriers and approaches and the structures within the perimeter's general boundaries to provide practical and effective protective lighting during the hours of darkness. Adequate security lighting will not prevent unauthorized entry, but it will make detection more likely if entry is attempted and will also serve as a psychological deterrent, when used with other security measures. Security lighting also assists security personnel and outside law enforcement in being able to visually assist and intervene in the event an entry is made.

Effective lighting is the single most cost-effective deterrent to crime. It is relatively inexpensive to maintain and may reduce manpower, may relieve officers for other duties, and may protect officers. However, too much security lighting can actually be more detrimental because of the difficulty in seeing into the surrounding areas. The security lighting must be able to produce a high level of illumination while, at the same time, providing a low level of glare. Security lighting should never be used alone;

it should also be used in conjunction with alarms, CCTV, security posts, and guards.

Adequate protective lighting should be able to follow these principles:

- Protective lighting should allow security personnel to observe activities in and around the establishment without being seen, by providing object illumination enabling personnel to detect a breach of security.
- Adequate protective lighting should consist of even light on the bordering areas, glaring lights in the eyes of an intruder, and low light on security posts and patrol routes.
- Security personnel should be able to see long distances and be able to detect contrasts, such as indistinct outlines and silhouettes. This can be accomplished with higher levels of brightness.

Security lighting usually requires less intensity than working lights, except for visual inspection of identification and inspections, and in cases of emergency. Lighting at entrances and control points must be at an intensity to enable security personnel to see identification badges, perform inspections, etc. In designing and planning a lighting system, considerations should include the following:

- Descriptions, characteristics, and specifications of various lighting systems.
- Lighting patterns of various light sources.
- Layouts showing the most efficient height and spacing of equipment for the establishment.
- Minimum levels of lighting and intensity required for various applications. They should be positioned to prevent glare and avoid silhouetting security personnel.
- Cost of replacement and maintenance of lamps, as well as the equipment used to perform the maintenance (e.g., ladders, mechanical buckets, etc.).
- Weather conditions that are common to that area that may affect the lighting system.
- Fluctuating voltages in the main power source.
- Backup power supply in the event of a power failure or blackout. Diesel-operated generators, searchlights, portable lights, etc. should be available to security personnel in case of emergency.
- Automatic lighting control should be used to regulate the hours of operation, using timers that are switched on and off by an electric clock that is preset to a turn-on and turn-off cycle. They can be multiprogrammed to turn on and off many times in a 24 h period, depending on the needs of the establishment. Photoelectric cells

are widely used to control outside lighting systems. The amount of light falling on the photocell determines whether the light is on or off and will automatically compensate for the change in light due to sunrise and sunset. One photocell can be used to control a number of lights, or each light can be equipped with its own photocell. Manual override capability of all the systems should be available, especially during blackouts etc.

- Protective lights should be used so that the failure of one or more lights will not disable the operation of the remaining security lights.
- Use of lighting to support a CCTV surveillance system.
- Maintain a record of the life expectancy of the lamp, including type, wattage, area or utility pole used, date of insertion, and expected date of extraction, to maintain the lamp accordingly.
- Lighting in the perimeter and access control points should be in control of the security personnel and secured from attack. Utility poles should be within the perimeter, power lines buried, and light-switch boxes secured.
- The perimeter band of lighting must provide a minimum intensity of 0.2 foot-candle (fc), measured horizontally 6 in. above ground level, and at least 30 ft. outside the excluded area barrier. Lighting inside the excluded areas must be of sufficient intensity to enable detection of persons in the area or at entrances.

Common Types of Outside Security Lighting

There are four general types of security lighting used in applications of outside lighting. They are continuous lighting, standby lighting, movable lighting, and emergency lighting. No one type of lighting can be used in protective security lighting; sometimes, all of them are applicable, depending on the needs and security levels of the establishment. All exterior lighting fixtures should have vandal-resistant, weatherproof covers.

Continuous Lighting

Continuous lighting is the most common form of protective security lighting used. This type of security lighting consists of fixed or stationary luminaries arranged to flood a given area continuously during hours of darkness. They are effective in lighting the boundaries around an establishment and its entry points. There are two primary methods of employing continuous lighting, which achieve glare protection and controlled lighting.

Glare protection is a method of continuous lighting that illuminates the establishment without interfering with adjoining areas or properties. The direction of the lighting across the area causes difficulty seeing into the establishment by an intruder, producing a glare and allowing security personnel to observe the intruder at considerable distances without the glare. This produces a strong visual and psychological deterrent to those thinking of unauthorized entry.

The controlled lighting method, or surface method, is employed when the light must be directed to a more focused area, such as a wall, a roof, a strip inside or outside a fence, etc. The luminaries are directed at the source instead of away from it, providing an enhanced appearance at night. This method provides complete illumination of what the luminary is directed at.

Standby Lighting

Standby lighting also uses fixed or stationary luminaries, similar to continuous lighting in terms of placement. However, the luminaries are not continuously lit. Standby lighting is either automatically or manually turned on when suspicious activity is suspected or detected by alarms or security personnel.

Movable Lighting

Movable or portable lighting consists of manually operated searchlights that may be operated during the hours of darkness or used only as needed. They are normally used as a supplement to continuous or standby lighting.

Emergency Lighting

Emergency lighting may duplicate any one or all of the above lighting systems to provide backup in case the primary lighting system goes down. Emergency lighting operates on an alternative power source such as fixed or portable generators or batteries, so that in times of power failure or other emergencies that cause the normal system to be inoperative, protective lighting is still employed.

Types of General Lighting Sources

Light can be classified into two categories:

1. Natural light: sunlight, moonlight, stars, etc.
2. Artificial light: incandescent, mercury vapor, metal halide, fluorescent, and sodium vapor

There are different lamps that are used to provide protective lighting in indoor and outdoor applications. Each one listed here has different characteristics, degrees of illumination properties, life expectancies, and wattages. Light fixtures should be mounted well above surveillance camera height, so that the bright light does not intrude on the surveillance camera's field of view.

Note: Metal halide is generally considered to be the preferred external light source, followed by high-pressure sodium.

Incandescent Lighting

Incandescent lighting is, for example, used in the common light bulb found in most homes. It provides instant illumination and can be manufactured in a manner whereby light is reflected by interior coatings or with a built-in lens to focus and diffuse the light. The cost is relatively low, and it is the most commonly used protective lighting source and is typically used indoors with an instantaneous restrike time. The disadvantage of incandescent lamps is they have a short rated life ranging from about 500 to 4000 h.

Mercury Vapor Lamps

Mercury vapor lamps are a gaseous discharge type of lamp that emits a strong light with a bluish- or a purplish-white cast. They are more efficient than incandescent lamps because of a much longer rate of life, ranging from about 24,000 h or more. Mercury vapor lamps are commonly seen on bridges, highways, and most streets due to their long burning hours and lumen characteristics, and they can tolerate power dips of up to 50%. Some disadvantages are that they have a slow lighting time of 2 to 7 min when cold, and they take longer to relight when hot or after voltage interruptions.

Fluorescent Lamps

Fluorescent lamps have high lamp efficiency but cannot project light over long distances. They have long lives, ranging from about 9000 to 17,000 h or more, and are typically used indoors, with a near-instantaneous restrike time. Fluorescent lamps are usually temperature sensitive and are typically not used outdoors in colder climates. These types of lamps can also be a nuisance to some security personnel because of their common flickering effect and their occasional interference with radio reception.

Metal Halide Lamps

Metal halide lamps are physically similar to mercury vapor lamps and also have a long warm-up time. However, metal halide lamps have a better color rendition and a higher light source efficiency. Metal halide lamps also have shorter life spans than mercury vapor, ranging to about 6000 h, and have a long restrike time, up to approximately 15 min. These types of lamps are best suited for applications where color rendition is of importance.

High- and Low-Pressure Sodium Vapor Lamps

Sodium vapor lamps emit a soft yellow light and are more efficient than mercury vapor lamps. Sodium vapor lamps also have long life spans, about

24,000 h or more. The difference between the two types of sodium vapor lamps is the pressure at which the sodium vapor produces light. They are used especially in areas where fog is a problem because yellow light penetrates better than white light, and they are commonly found in exterior parking areas and on bridges and highways. Low-pressure sodium vapor lamps emit an almost monochromatic yellow light, which makes them unusable for color cameras, and have a long restrike time, ranging from about 7 to 15 min, while high-pressure sodium vapor lamps emit all visible frequencies and are more energy effective with color CCTV cameras, with a lower restrike start time.

Quartz Lamps

Quartz lamps are frequently used at very high wattage and produce a very bright light. They provide instant illumination and can be used along perimeters and in critical areas.

Light-Emitting Diodes

Light-emitting diode (LED) lamps are commonly seen on message displays.

Recommendations on Lighting

A lighting engineer should be consulted and prepare a photometric chart showing illumination readings at 10 ft. intervals. The illumination values listed in Table 6.6 are generally recommended.

The following is an equation that can be used to determine the illumination distribution:

$$\text{Illumination (fc)} = \frac{\text{Source intensity (in candles)}}{\text{Distance (in feet) squared}}$$

TABLE 6.6
Recommended Illumination (Foot-Candles)

Exterior entrances	5 fc: Out to a radius of 15 to 20 ft.
Covered parking lots	3 to 4 fc: Fixtures should be placed to illuminate between parked vehicles
Parking lots	1 to 2 fc
Trash receptacles	4 to 5 fc
Walkways	2 fc
Recreation areas	1 to 2 fc
Office areas	1 to 2 fc

For example, if the objective were to deliver 1 fc of illumination at a distance of 25 ft. from the source, then

$$1 \text{ fc} = \frac{\text{Unknown}}{25 \text{ feet(squared)}} = 625$$

Thus, 625 candles would be required for the distribution of illumination.

Types of Lighting Equipment

There are four basic types of equipment that are generally used in security applications.

Floodlights

Floodlights are lights that project light in a concentrated beam, ranging from a medium to wide beam, and are directed to specific areas for appropriate illumination of boundaries, buildings, fences, or critical areas. Floodlights can create a considerable amount of glare.

Streetlights

Streetlights are built either symmetrically or asymmetrically. Symmetrical units are centrally located and distribute light evenly where large areas need to be lighted, such as in parking lots, where they are used with high-pressure sodium vapor lamps. Asymmetric units direct the light by reflection in the direction where the light is needed and have to be placed away from the area that needs to be lighted.

Fresnel Lenses

Fresnel lenses are wide-beam units used to extend the illumination in long horizontal strips. Fresnel lenses are used in applications to light perimeters and approaches because little light is lost vertically. They project a narrow horizontal beam, approximately 180° in the horizontal plane and from 15° to 30° in the vertical plane. Because they do not project a focused beam and are used primarily to illuminate the perimeter and approaches, a glare is created to an intruder and to security personnel in the establishment.

Searchlights

Searchlights are highly focused incandescent lamps used to focus or pinpoint suspected problem areas. They can be permanently mounted or portable battery powered to supplement continuous light systems that can be directed to any area inside or outside the establishment. They are normally operated manually or can be set up to operate automatically to respond to potential trouble spots.

INTRUSION ALARM SYSTEMS

Intrusion alarm systems are composed of three major elements: detection, delay, and response. The level of protection depends on the security needs of the establishment, but the basic function of intrusion alarms is to alert the proper authorities or security personnel that an intruder is attempting to penetrate, or has penetrated, a protected area and to be able to respond in an adequate time period to allow interception and apprehension of the intruder. For this to be accomplished, there must be sufficient physical delay from the point of detection and the time for an intruder to achieve his or her objective for an adequate response force to arrive and intercept. Early detection of the outer perimeter and barriers allow the available response force to arrive earlier by several minutes.

An intrusion alarm system can either supplement or provide backup to security protection that is already established. Safes, locks, protective barriers, entry control, security personnel, guards, and CCTVs all working together, or an alarm system, can be used to replace costly guards or expensive protective barriers, largely depending on what the establishment needs. When considering an alarm system that will fit the company's needs, one should consider the following:

- Risk or vulnerability the alarm system is to protect against
- Review and evaluation of the facility's past history of burglary, robbery, or other crimes involving unauthorized entry
- Methods available for the proper protection needed, depending on what the establishment needs
- Weather conditions
- Type of sensors needed and their hardware design
- Method of alarm signal transmission, how it is to be sent, and who will respond to the alarm signal in the presence of an intruder
- Installation conditions
- Tamper resistance and tamper indicating. The hardware and system design should have features that prevent defeat by tampering
- Cost and effectiveness analysis of all the elements

ALARM SENSORS

The selection of an alarm sensor depends on the object, area, space, and perimeter to be protected. Other factors such as noise, motion, weather conditions, etc., must also be considered when selecting a sensor.

Intrusion detection alarms follow these basic principles of operation:

- Breaking of an electrical current
- Interruption of a light beam

- Detection of sound
- Detection of vibration
- Detecting a change in capacitance due to penetration of an electrostatic field

There are two types of alarm sensors:

1. Passive sensors: Detect some type of energy that is emitted by the intruder or detect some change in a field of energy caused by the intruder. Examples of passive sensors are vibration, heat, sound, and capacitance. Passive sensors are harder for an intruder to locate because no energy source is emitted, thus putting the intruder at a disadvantage.
2. Active sensors: Detect a change in the received energy created by the presence or motion of the intruder; includes a transmitter and receiver. Examples of active sensors are microwave, IR, and other radio-frequency (RF) devices. Active sensors do emit an energy source that makes stronger signals: This significantly reduces the amount of false or nuisance alarms.

There are two applications that detect intruders:

1. Volumetric sensor detectors: Detect intrusion in a volume of space or zone. The detection zone is usually not visible, and it is hard for an intruder to identify the volume of space that is being protected. Volumetric sensor detectors will detect an intruder moving in the detection zone, regardless of the point of entry.
2. Line sensor detectors: Detect activity at a specific location or within a narrow area. A line sensor detection zone is along a line or a series of lines that will detect activity at an entry point or area. Line sensors are easier for an intruder to identify.

EXTERIOR INTRUSION DETECTORS

Alarm sensors consist of exterior and interior intrusion sensors. An exterior perimeter intrusion detection system performs better when it is located in an isolated clear zone. This aids in the reduction of false alarms, increases detection abilities, and prevents defeat. When selecting exterior sensors, physical and environmental factors should be considered to allow for optimal performance in detection capability and the reduction of false alarms. The following are examples of exterior intrusion sensors.

Buried-Line Sensors

The sensor is in the form of a line buried in the ground. There are different types of buried-line sensors that operate differently from one another.

Pressure or Seismic

These types of buried-line sensors are passive line sensor detectors. They respond to the disturbances in the soil caused by an intruder walking, jumping, running, etc., on the ground. Pressure sensors are mostly sensitive to the lower-frequency pressure waves in the soil and consist of reinforced hoses that are filled with pressurized liquid and connected to a pressure transducer.

Seismic sensors are sensitive to higher-frequency vibrations of the soil and consist of a conducting coil and a permanent magnet. Either the coil or the magnet is in a fixed position, so that the one that is free can vibrate during a disturbance, generating an electrical current in the coil. False alarms may be caused by wind that is transmitted into the ground by poles, trees, etc.

Magnetic Field

These types of sensors are passive volumetric sensor detectors. They respond to changes in the local magnetic field caused by movement of nearby metallic materials. They consist of a series of wire loops or coils that, upon movement of metallic objects near the loop or coil buried in the ground, cause changes in the magnetic field and generate a current. Magnetic sensors are primarily used to detect vehicle traffic but can also detect intruders wearing or carrying metal objects. Of course, if intruders do not have any metal on them, they may be able to defeat the system.

Ported Coaxial Cables

These types of sensors are active volumetric sensor detectors. They respond to the motion of vehicles or intruders with a high conductivity near the cables. Some of the radiated signal leaks through the outer conductor, giving the radiated field above the ground surface approximately 3 ft., and about 3 to 6 ft. wider than the cable separation. Because of the ported shields, these cables are frequently referred to as leaky cables. Portable ported coaxial cables can be used for temporary perimeter protection that can be moved around. The cables are placed on the ground surface instead of being buried and are used for temporary protection for small areas or objects.

Fiber-Optic Cables

These types of sensors are very sensitive, passive line sensor detectors. Fiber optics are long, hairlike strands of transparent glass or plastic that allow light to be guided from one end of the strand to the other. Walking, running, crawling, etc., on top of the ground above the fiber-optic cable cause it to bend, changing the received signal and causing an alarm. Because the fiber-optic cable is buried only a few centimeters underground, it will sense the slightest change in the shape of the fiber-optic cable. To ensure that the intruder steps on the fiber-optic cable, it is woven into a mesh or grid and buried just beneath the surface. Anything stepping on the mesh or grid will bend the fiber-optic cable.

Buried-line sensors are susceptible to irregular terrain. The perimeter terrain should be flat because gullies and ditches crossing the perimeter can cause false alarms from running water. Large animals, such as deer or cows, can also cause false alarms; a dual chain-link fence with the sensors installed in between in the clear zone can minimize interference with animals.

Fence Sensors

These are intrusion sensors that are mounted or attached to a fence or use transducer material, such as switches, electromechanical transducers, electric cables, fiber-optic cables, strain-sensitive cables, etc., to form a fence. When two parallel fences bind clear zones, no sensors should be placed on the outer fence. This will reduce false alarms from small animals and blowing debris as well as reduce the chance of an intruder defeating the fence sensor without being seen. There are different types of fence sensors, which operate differently from one another.

Fence-Disturbance Sensors

These types of sensors are passive line sensor detectors that are attached to the fence using transducer material to detect motion or shock, primarily caused by an intruder climbing or cutting the fence. Because these types of sensors are sensitive to vibration, the fence must be maintained regularly by keeping tall grass, weeds, bushes, etc. from growing and rubbing on the fence and by keeping the fence poles rigid and the fence material tight to avoid false alarms caused by debris, rain, etc. blown into the fence by wind. Fence-disturbance sensors can be defeated by an intruder digging under the fence or by bridging over the fence without touching the fence itself. Pouring concrete under the fence can deter digging.

Taut-Wire Sensors

These types of sensors are passive line sensor detectors that use transducer material to form the fence itself. They are designed to detect intruders climbing, separating the wires, and cutting the fence. The fence wires, usually barbed wire, are connected under tension to the transducers at about the midpoint of the wire span. The transducers require approximately 25 lb. of pressure to cause an alarm and are not like fence-disturbance sensors that are sensitive to vibrations. However, these fences are also vulnerable to digging under the fence or bridging over the fence.

Electric Field Sensors

These types of sensors are passive volumetric sensor detectors that are designed to detect a change in capacitive, an electronic component that consists of two conductor plates separated by an electrical charge, coupling among a set of wires attached to but electrically isolated from a fence. Because the electric field sensors can be adjusted to extend beyond the fence plane, intruders have a harder time in digging under or bridging over the fence; however, small animals, rain, fence motion, etc., can cause false alarms due to the wider detection volume.

Freestanding Sensors

These types of sensors are mounted on a support in a clear zone and are not buried or associated with a fence for perimeter protection. These types of sensors are influenced by weather and climatic conditions, such as heavy rain, fog, dust, snow, etc., which can affect their performance or detection patterns.

Active Infrared Sensors

These are active, freestanding line sensor detectors. An IR beam is transmitted through a collimating lens to a photodetector receiver. A collimating lens is used to convert the radiating IR light into a parallel beam; otherwise, the light would disperse and provide a weaker signal to the photodetector. The sensor detects the loss of the received IR energy when an intruder blocks the beam. The IR beam is very difficult to see with the naked eye, and inexperienced intruders normally will not see the beam. Single-beam IR sensors can be defeated easily by stepping over the beam, sliding through, pole vaulting, digging under, etc., by skilled intruders. There are multiple-beam IR sensors available for high-level security establishments, which make it harder for intruders to bypass or spoof the beams with an alternative IR source.

Passive Infrared Sensors

These are passive, freestanding volumetric sensor detectors. They detect thermal energy emitted by an intruder and by vehicles well beyond the detection zone. They compare the difference between thermal energy from an intruder and that produced by changing weather conditions. If only one sensor detected thermal energy and the other did not, it would cause an alarm condition, whereas on a sunny day, the sensors would detect thermal energy equally.

Bistatic Microwave Sensors

These are active, freestanding line sensor detectors. Normally, two identical microwave antennas are installed at opposite ends of the protected area. One is connected to a transmitter and the other to a receiver sending and receiving RF energy. They will detect intruders crawling or rolling through the microwave beams.

Monostatic Microwave Sensors

These are active, freestanding line sensor detectors. This version of a microwave detector consists of the transmitter and receiver in the same transceiver or unit. RF energy is sent from the transmitter, and the receiver detects a change in the energy caused by the motion of an intruder. The sensors can have a range set so that motion can occur beyond that setting without causing an alarm.

Video Motion Detectors

These are passive, freestanding line sensor detectors that process a video signal from CCTVs. A video motion sensor generates an alarm when an intruder enters a selected portion of a CCTV camera's field of view. They can be used jointly for intrusion detection, surveillance, alarm assessment, etc., and they transmit a video signal when they detect movement. Adequate continuous lighting is required for cameras to operate 24 h/day.

Dual-Technology Sensors

These are a combination of active and passive freestanding volumetric sensor detectors. They are really popular in the security industry due to the combination of intrusion detection systems, which reduces the amount of false alarms, such as using a combination of a passive IR and a monostatic microwave sensor, which will not give an alarm until both sensors have been activated. This reduces the false alarms that are common with each and initiates an alarm when an actual intruder is present. An experienced intruder can defeat dual-technology sensors by defeating one of the combined sensors to bypass the other.

INTERIOR INTRUSION DETECTORS

Interior intrusion sensors that are also used in conjunction with administrative procedures, access controls, and material monitoring are highly effective against intruders in the event that the perimeter is bypassed. The following are examples of interior intrusion sensors.

Boundary Protection

These sensors protect openings into or out of the establishment, including doors, windows, vents, skylights, etc. Most of the time, the perimeter is the first place an intruder violates, and most alarm systems provide for this type of protection. But supplemental protection will still be needed in case the intruder tries to gain unauthorized entry by other ways, such as through utility openings, walls, ventilation systems, etc.

Electromechanical Switches

These devices are passive line sensor detectors that are normally found on doors and windows. The alarm is activated by the opening of the door and or window, causing a magnet to move away from the contact and break the circuit. The switch unit contains a magnetic reed switch that is mounted to the fixed part of the door or window. The movable part of the door or window contains a permanent magnet adjacent to the switch unit. When the door or window is closed, the magnetic field from the permanent magnet causes the switch to be in the closed or secure position. Opening the door or window, or removal of the magnet, causes a decrease in the magnetic field, and the switch opens, causing an alarm. Intruders can defeat the magnet switch by placing a strong magnet near the switch unit and forcing the switch to stay in the closed or secured position. Balanced magnetic switches (BMSs) for higher-security purposes help prevent defeat by placing a bigger magnet at the switch.

BMSs typically consist of a three-position reed switch and an additional magnet called a bias magnet located next to the switch. If the door is opened or an external magnet is brought near the sensor, the switch becomes unbalanced and generates an alarm.

Metallic Foil (Window Tape)

These devices are passive line sensor detectors that can be used on glass surfaces, show windows, transoms, etc. to detect glass breakage of any kind. Any action that breaks the foil also breaks the circuit and thereby activates the alarm.

Glass Break Detectors

These devices are passive line sensor detectors. The noise from the breaking of glass consists of frequencies in both the audible and ultrasonic range. These sensors use microphone transducers to detect the sound of breaking glass and are designed to respond only to those specific frequencies, thus minimizing false alarms from bumping, scraping, or banging on the glass. There are two types that can be used: One type can be directly attached to the glass to sense the breakage of glass by sound or shock, and the other type is located in the ceiling or in close proximity to the glass it is protecting to sense the sound or shock of breaking glass.

Area/Space Protection

These are highly sensitive devices that are used to provide invisible means of detection for interior spaces. Even if an intruder gained entry of the perimeter, the interior space is still protected. These devices should always be supplemented with boundary protection.

Photoelectric Sensor or Electric Eye

These sensors can be either passive or active line sensor detectors that transmit a photoelectric eye or beam across a protected area to a receiver. As long as the beam is directed into the receiver, the beam circuit is inactive. Once the beam is interrupted and contact with the receiver is broken, no matter how brief the interruption, the alarm is activated. Photoelectric sensors use UV or pulsed IR beams for the greatest security because these beams are invisible to the naked eye. The device must be installed properly and undetectable because if the beam is spotted, an intruder can either step over the beam or crawl underneath it. Mirrors can be installed to reflect the IR beam back and forth to form a fencelike pattern across an entrance or the like. The ranges of the devices differ: Some units can transmit up to 1000 ft. and can be used outdoors. They are useful as door openers or for driveways and may be used to activate CCTVs or other security devices.

Ultrasonic Motion Detection Devices

These devices are active volumetric sensors that consist of transceivers that transmit and receive energy in the acoustic spectrum, typically in the frequency range between 19 and 40 kHz, or ultrasonic waves. Ultrasonic detectors work on a change in frequency, also called the Doppler effect. The alarm is activated when there is any movement that causes a change in its reflected frequency. The unit can be used either as a stand-alone unit to cover a specific area or in multiple units to cover a broader area of protection. Ultrasonic waves do not penetrate most objects, such as walls, causing movement from the outside not to affect it. Other potential problems that can cause false alarms include air turbulence and drafts that may move the draperies etc., noise caused by air conditioners and telephones, and temperature or humidity.

Microwave Motion Detection Devices

These devices are active volumetric sensor detectors that detect intruders by a pattern of RF that is transmitted and reflected back to a receiving antenna. Interior microwave motion detectors are almost always the monostatic type of sensor. If the RF waves strike a moving object, they return at a different frequency or cause a Doppler frequency shift, which results in initiating the alarm. The Doppler frequency shift for a human intruder is usually between 20 and 120 Hz. The radio waves of microwave motion detectors can penetrate most objects except metal and can penetrate thin walls or glass and respond to outside activities. Moving people or vehicles outside the protected area can cause false alarms. Reflection of movement or patterns of metal objects from moving fan blades, overhead doors, etc., can also cause false alarms.

Passive Infrared Motion Detection Devices

These devices are passive volumetric sensors that do not transmit a signal that can be disturbed by an intruder. They operate by detecting moving IR radiation against the normal radiation environment of the area being protected. IR motion detectors detect radiation from a human body moving through the optical field view of the detector. False alarms can be triggered by rapidly changing temperatures; air turbulence and drafts causing movement of draperies; sunlight, heating, and air-conditioning units; etc. Design and installation are keys to avoiding sources of false alarms. To minimize false alarms caused by changes in temperatures, some of the devices use a dual-element sensor. The sensing element is split in half: One sensor produces a positive pulse, while the other produces a negative pulse when a change in temperature occurs, to create a balance. An intruder entering one of the sensors produces an imbalance between the two halves, causing an alarm. Quad-element sensors are also available that combine and compare two dual-element sensors:

- Pressure sensors: These types of devices are passive line sensor detectors that are basically mechanical switches that are activated when pressure is applied to them. In security applications, pressure sensors are usually in the form of mats and are used as a backup protection system to the perimeter. They can be placed in a strategic spot under carpeting or in other spots that the intruder would use.
- Dual-technology units (dual techs): The combination of two types of space protection sensors in one unit, which could be the combination of passive IR and microwave motion detection devices, or even passive IR and ultrasonic motion detection devices. The principle of dual techs is that by using a combination of two types of space protectors, both of the detectors must be tripped at the same time to cause an alarm condition, thus making it relatively difficult to defeat. This can cut down on the potential of false alarms that a single space protection device would have more problems with because of the environment or placement of the alarm system. When using more than one space detection device, be sure that there is adequate power supply to provide operational current and standby power.

Object Protection

Sensors are used to detect the activity or presence of an intruder at a single location, such as with safes, desks, protection of expensive objects, etc. The following are the types of alarm systems used to protect objects:

- Capacitance alarm systems: These devices are active line sensor detectors, also known as proximity alarms, that are used to protect metal containers of all kinds. They establish an electrical circuit between a protected metal object and a control unit, making them active sensors. One common example is the protection of a high-security storage building within a fenced enclosure. The object being protected becomes an antenna, electronically linked to the alarm control and creating an electromagnetic field. When an intruder approaches or touches the object being protected, the electromagnetic field becomes unbalanced, and the alarm is initiated. The electromagnetic field can be adjusted to project only a few inches from the object or several feet. Capacitance devices will activate the alarm when the intruder is close to the protected object, and only metal objects can be protected in this matter.
- Vibration detection systems: These types of detectors are passive line sensor detectors that provide a high level of protection in specific objects or places. They utilize a highly sensitive, specialized type of contact microphone or an electronic vibration detector. The detector is attached directly to the object that is to be protected, such as safes and file cabinets, or to surfaces like walls, floors, or ceilings. Any forced entry or movement of the objects or surfaces will cause vibration. The contact microphone picks up the vibration and, in turn, activates the alarms. The detectors will only activate the alarms if the object is moved or the surface is attacked.

All sensing devices are wired into an alarm control panel that receives and processes them. The type of control panel needed depends on the level and needs of the establishment. Included in the control panel is the backup or standby power in case of blackouts or some emergency that causes an interruption in power supply. Most of the time, batteries are used for backup, and some equipment uses rechargeable batteries, having a low-power charging unit that maintains the batteries in a fully charged condition.

Tampering protection can also be designed into the control panel with sensing devices, alarm monitoring systems, or all of the above. This feature provides protection for an alarm signal to be generated when the system is tampered with or compromised in any way.

DURESS ALARMS

Duress alarms may be fixed or portable devices and are used by personnel to signal a life-threatening emergency. Usually, these devices are manually operated in the event of an emergency, and once activated, an alarm is sent to the alarm monitoring station.

Fixed Duress Alarms

These are mechanical switches that are fixed permanently in an inconspicuous area, such as under a counter or desk. They are usually push-button switches activated by pushing with a finger or hand. If mounted to the floor, they can be activated by stepping on the switch.

Portable Duress Alarms

These are wireless units consisting of a transmitter and a receiver. The transmitter is carried on the person, and the receiver is mounted within the establishment. Either ultrasonic or RF energy can be used, and once activated, the transmitter sends an alarm signal to the receiver, which relays it to the alarm monitoring system.

ALARM MONITORING SYSTEMS

The purpose of an alarm monitoring system or station is to alert the proper authorities in stopping a crime in progress or to lead to the apprehension of the intruder in the shortest possible time. The type of alarm monitoring system employed depends on the operations of the establishment. The transmission of an alarm signal to a UL-listed central station is generally regarded as the most reliable method for reducing burglary losses. The grades of service dictate the requirements for the subscriber to operate their system as well as the requirements for the central alarm station to adhere to for opening, closing, and alerting the proper authorities.

All central-station UL-approved systems have one of the grades of service listed in Table 6.7.

In general, each subscriber and the central station have been given a scheduled time for opening, closing, and procedures that are strictly adhered to. If, for some reason, they are not followed, then the central station starts investigating either by responding to the premises or verifying as to why the scheduled time has not been adhered to.

There are three general types of alarm monitoring systems used to signal or transmit an alarm condition.

TABLE 6.7
Grades of Service

Grade A or AA	Service and security personnel response is 15 min after receipt of an alarm condition. (If a local sounding device is installed, this is considered a combination response, and this may be within 20 min.)
Grade B or BB	Service and security personnel response is 20 min after receipt of alarm condition.
Grade C or CC	Service and security personnel response is 30 min after receipt of an alarm condition.

LOCAL ALARM SYSTEM

The sensor activates the circuit that causes a bell, horn, siren, or a flashing light to be sounded or lit in the immediate vicinity of the protected area. The system either notifies security personnel or guards within the area who respond to the alarm condition, or alerts someone hearing or seeing the signal into contacting the proper authorities. The local alarm system can also deter intruders and, in some cases, scare them off. Such systems are also useful for fire alarm systems because they alert personnel to evacuate the premises during an emergency condition. Fire alarm systems are usually used in combination with a central station that is connected to the local fire department in signaling for assistance.

CENTRAL ALARM SYSTEM

Alarm signals are transmitted to a central station outside the establishment that is monitored 24 h/day, supervising, recording, and maintaining the alarms. Upon receipt of an alarm condition, the proper authorities are notified, such as the local police and fire departments.

There are different types of transmissions that a central station can employ depending on the risks and needs of the establishment.

- Direct wire systems: Single dedicated line connected from the protected establishment directly to the central station or the police station where a separate receiver monitors only that alarm. High-risk locations such as banks, jewelry stores, etc., are usually protected with this type of system. Some central stations use special methods that protect against shunting or "jumpering" the alarm signal by burglars. Alarm systems that are equipped with this security are classified as AA grade central station-approved systems.
- Circuit system (party line): Several subscribers share the same leased line or party line that transmits alarm signals to a single

receiving panel at the central station. Alarm signals are transmitted using a circuit transmission system, also known as a McCulloh circuit loop, on coded strips of paper to the central station. Each alarm has a distinct code to identify it from the others. By subdividing the cost of the telephone line among different subscribers, the telephone cost is reduced, making it more economically feasible for some when the telephone cost is a major factor.

- Multiplex system: The central station sends out a signal to different subscribers periodically to verify the alarm condition of the establishment. This is also known as alarm polling.
- Digital communicators: The alarm signal is transmitted in a series of coded electronic pulses through the regular telephone line system. A computer at the central station receives the alarm signal.
- Telephone dialer: When the alarm is activated, the alarm system is set to dial a predetermined telephone number. The telephone dialer transmits a prerecorded message that states that an intrusion is in progress at the location to any or all of the following: the central station, answering services, subscriber's home number, and police department. Because the system relies on the general phone lines, it could fail if the lines being used are busy or if the lines were cut.
- Radio signal: The alarm signal is transmitted via radio or cellular phone to the central station, police department, etc. The alarm signal can also be received in a patrol unit.
- Proprietary alarm system: This system is similar to the central alarm system, except it is owned by and located at the establishment. Responses made to the alarm are by the establishment's own security or fire personnel. Because the alarm system is operated locally, the response time to an alarm condition is considerably reduced.

See Appendix C for a glossary of terms.

FIRE ALARM SYSTEMS

Achieving a fire protection system for establishments is a fundamental requirement, a process that initially involves a risk assessment to identify the hazards and the potential consequences. The risk assessment is then reviewed to determine the level of protection that is appropriate and how this may be delivered. The goal in achieving fire protection is to preserve life safety, minimize equipment loss and damage, minimize data loss and damage, and ensure the continuity of the business. Fire has the potential to disrupt businesses, at the very least, and often deals a financial blow that many businesses may not be able to recover from. Fire protection systems play a vital role in preventing an outbreak of a fire, with integrated detection, alarm, control, and active fire-extinguishing elements working together to achieve the required level of protection.

Fire alarm systems must meet building codes, fire codes, and special Acts or bylaws. The choice of a particular type of equipment to be used in a fire alarm system depends on the nature of the establishment, the size of the building, the number of occupants, and the level of protection desired. To be the most effective, a fire alarm system must be tailored to the building and the types of fire that could develop, and it is important to understand the functions and limitations of the fire equipment chosen to obtain maximum efficiency and safety. The NFPA has the most impact on fire alarm system design and acceptability; therefore, most local authorities having jurisdiction have required that the NFPA guidelines be met. The NFPA requires that the power supply, initiating device and notification appliance circuits, installation conductors, and wiring connections of devices all be electronically supervised. All UL-listed fire alarm panels comply with these provisions.

The Americans with Disabilities Act (ADA) has made a significant impact on the fire alarm industry. Some of the changes must be implemented so that manual fire alarm systems are accessible to a person in a wheelchair, and the location of audiovisual devices must also be measured and standardized to accommodate the hearing- and seeing-impaired. The ADA has guidelines that one must also take in consideration when installing fire alarm equipment.

The primary function of a fire alarm system is to provide an early warning in the event of a fire, thus allowing the occupants to have sufficient time to reach safety. Fire alarm systems can also perform many other functions in the event of a fire. For example, the system can be designed to simultaneously alert the fire department by means of a direct or relayed signal where rapid response is essential, such as in certain industrial occupancies containing highly combustible or explosive materials, high buildings, establishments that need assistance in evacuation, etc. In other cases, depending on the nature of the business's occupancy, the alarm system may be designed to alert initially only the building staff before the general alarm is activated. Other examples can include the design of the fire alarm system to control the operation of the building service equipment to minimize the spread of fire and smoke. Alarm signals from the system can automatically engage equipment to pressurize stairwells and shut down recirculating air systems, thus confining smoke and assisting in minimizing the danger to life and property damage. They can also be

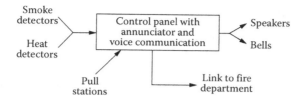

FIGURE 6.11   Basic fire alarm system.

designed to activate smoke exhaust systems to ventilate a fire and reduce heat buildup. Controls connected to the alarm system can recall elevators to the ground floor, removing them from public use. Fire alarm systems can also be designed to activate fire suppression systems, release hold-open devices on fire doors, and indicate the location of the fire inside the building. There are many design uses for alarm systems that can be implemented; it just depends on the establishment and what its needs are for proper fire protection.

Fire alarm systems are very complex—they are not just the pull boxes and alarm bells that are seen in buildings. They can also include fire detectors, annunciator panels, loudspeakers, telephones, control panels, and alarm and detection systems that also activate other safety measures in the building.

Figure 6.11 shows an example of a basic fire alarm system.

BASIC OPERATIONS OF FIRE ALARM SYSTEMS

- Manual fire alarm: Relies on an individual to operate it, such as a pull box that activates audiovisual devices. Audiovisual devices include horns, speakers, strobes, etc.
- Automatic fire detection: Activated by detectors, such as smoke and heat detectors that sense the fire and, in turn, trigger audiovisual devices.
- Intelligent or addressable analog fire detectors: Microprocessors and microcomputer-controlled panel and devices.
- Voice alarm and evacuation: A public address system that helps by providing a human voice in instructing to evacuate the building.
- Sprinklers and fire suppression systems: Interfaced with the fire alarm system to recall elevators, activate sprinklers, etc.
- Building controls: Designed to interface with the various systems that control electrical and mechanical systems within the building, such as fire and water pumps, electrical lights, backup power, air and vent control, etc.

BASIC COMPONENTS IN A FIRE ALARM SYSTEM

A fire alarm system is typically composed of a number of components, which include the following:

- Control panel: The brains of the system, which processes the inputs from the field devices, such as the smoke detectors, and triggers the audiovisual devices when it determines that an alarm condition is present. It also monitors and supervises the integrity of the power supply and the circuitry, including initiating and notification circuits.
- Standby power supply: Consists of a battery charger and a set of batteries, or an engine-driven generator. If the power went out, the batteries or the generator would keep the system operational for a predetermined amount of time.
- Annunciator status panel (Figure 6.12): Identifies the condition status of the alarm, the type of alarm, and where a trouble or fault condition has occurred. An indicator light flashes on the panel, identifying the location of the trouble zone. Emergency personnel can control the alarm system by using either reset switches or a code to either silence the alarm or reset the system.
- Field devices: They make up the initiating zone, such as heat detectors, smoke detectors, pull boxes, and audiovisual devices.

Fire alarm signals and communications can be transmitted over wire, fiber-optic cable, or RF wireless systems. Wire is the most commonly used, but fiber-optic cable is now being used for larger systems that are networked together. RF wireless systems are the new technology that will be in use for communicating fire alarm signals and other life safety applications.

CONVENTIONAL VERSUS ADDRESSABLE SYSTEMS

Fire alarm systems generally fall into one of two categories: conventional or addressable/intelligent systems.

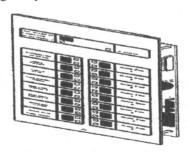

FIGURE 6.12   Annunciator status panel.

Conventional Systems

Conventional systems have been around for years, and few changes have been made in terms of technology, but design and reliability have improved. Conventional systems rely solely on the fire alarm control panel that receives a trigger signal from a detector or an initiating device, such as smoke, heat, flame, etc., which then signals the condition to the notification system, alarm, visual device, horns, etc. Conventional systems are set with a certain number of zones that are hardwired to the control panel or zone expander. There may be a dozen detectors in a single zone, and if one is faulty, the fire alarm technician has the responsibility of finding which one it is. For conventional systems, each circuit is a dedicated single zone or area of the building, and more cable is needed if multiple device types are used. A separate cable run for each type of device for a different zone is required because they are not wired into the same loop. Smoke detectors must be run in a separate zone from pull boxes, etc. In addition to that, the electronic transmission between the panel and the devices is either off or on, meaning that there is an increase or decrease in the total electric current, so the devices are usually normal, troubled, or in alarm.

A conventional system (Figure 6.13) communicates with the control panel by either a contact type of device or an automatic smoke detector. The contact type has an electrical contact switch that must change states before an alarm signal is sent to the panel, whereas an automatic smoke detector causes a change in the current, which is transmitted to the panel as an alarm. End-of-line resistors are used to supervise conventional circuits.

Unlike intelligent systems, conventional devices use set thresholds in a single sensor to determine alarm conditions and are rigidly designed to signal alarm conditions only after a specific level has been reached.

Addressable/Intelligent Systems

Addressable systems enable each and every initiating device, smoke and heat detector, pull box, etc. to have its own unique, individual address or zone identifier that is connected to the same loop (Figure 6.14). The system may contain one or more loops depending on the size of the system and design requirement. The fire alarm control panel communicates with each detector individually and receives a status report. As each detector has its

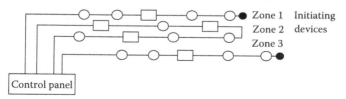

FIGURE 6.13 Conventional system.

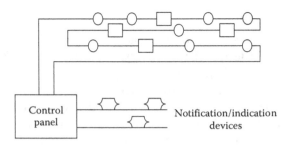

FIGURE 6.14 Intelligent addressable fire detection system.

own individual address, the fire alarm control panel is able to display or indicate the precise location of the device in question. This is very useful for servicing the system: If a detector is faulty, the fire alarm technician knows exactly which device is at fault. For this reason, zoning is not necessary, and of course, less cabling and installation time is required. All alarm systems, new or replacement, serving 50 or more alarm-initiating devices should be addressable fire detection systems.

Addressable systems were not always intelligent. Nowadays, intelligent systems, also thought of as analog-type detectors, can do a lot more than just provide a unique address for each detection device. They have also become more flexible, have a wider scope of control, and are more sophisticated on verification methods for an alarm signal. Although the capabilities of intelligent systems vary between manufacturers, intelligent systems incorporate detectors that use decision-making algorithms to determine alarm conditions. Some intelligent detection devices make all the alarm decisions; others report conditions to the alarm system control equipment, which then makes the alarm decision. Intelligent systems are designed to adjust to sensitivity according to preset conditions, such as automatic sensitivity compensation due to dust, dirt, humidity, age, and other environmental factors, and other features including setting of one or more prealarms. They also can store a variety of information, including the rate of environmental compensation, last maintenance date and analog signal for the last alarm, etc. Intelligent systems have a microprocessor or microcomputer chip that is capable of communicating with the panel during its normal and abnormal modes of operation, such as sending information concerning measurement of the environmental condition of the smoke measuring chamber, enabling maintenance to take place prior to the problem being experienced. Alarm systems serving more than 75 smoke detectors or more than 200 alarm-initiating devices should be analog intelligent addressable fire detection systems.

One is not better than the other at detecting a fire; they just use different technologies. Intelligent systems have higher equipment costs but save on labor and are ideal for larger premises and buildings with more complex system requirements. Smaller establishments with budget restraints, or a limited number of devices, may use the conventional system, which would suit the facility.

There are hybrid systems that mix conventional hardwired zones with addressable loops on the same control panel and that fit certain needs better than just one technology would.

It is important to note that all detectors, whether combination or intelligent, do require maintenance to be effective. Even with all of the new technologies that are available, maintenance of detectors and alarm systems should be viewed as one of the most important aspects of the fire alarm system.

System Types

The basic types of fire alarm systems currently used are single-stage and two-stage systems:

- Single-stage system: This system, when actuated, is designed to transmit an alarm signal immediately throughout the whole establishment to warn occupants that a fire emergency exists.
- Two-stage system: This system is designed to transmit a distinct alert signal to designated personnel. Usually, the signal is coded so that its meaning is apparent only to the proper personnel, and they are expected to immediately investigate the source of the alarm. If a fire condition exists, they actuate the alarm signal. There is a predetermined period of time in which an alarm signal is automatically set off if the proper personnel do not activate or reset the alarm system. In health care establishments, evacuation of the occupants is difficult and could be physically or psychologically harmful. Two-stage systems are used to reduce the possibility of false alarms, and it is essential that the designated personnel be instructed in the proper procedures to follow before silencing the alarm.

FIRE CHARACTERISTICS

Fire alarm signals can be initiated by several types of devices: manual systems, automatic fire detectors, intelligent systems, or extinguishing systems. Devices are activated, or preset conditions are reached or exceeded by heat, smoke, energy radiation, or other detectable by-products of fire that initiate a signal. Automatic fire detectors must differentiate between normal environmental fluctuations—that is, between nonfire conditions and prefire conditions. Deceptive phenomena can contribute or cause a false alarm or alarm malfunction. Initiating devices can be used in combination with a fire-extinguishing system that requires supervisory devices to detect abnormal conditions. Understanding how a fire progresses and how to protect an establishment and its occupants is critical in designing an effective fire detection system. From the moment of inception, fire produces a variety of changes in the surrounding environment. Any of these changes in the immediate surroundings is referred to as a fire signature and can be monitored by a fire detection system.

There are four basic stages to a fire:

1. During the first, incipient stage, which may last for seconds to days, there is no noticeable smoke, heat, or flame. IR and UV radiant energy is the earliest signature from a fire. The signature disadvantage is that this energy has a wide range of noise levels, which make it difficult to distinguish it from solar and man-made sources and thus can cause false alarms. During this stage, flammable gases or combustion products are emitted.

2. Next is the smoldering stage, in which there is still no substantial amount of flame or heat but the combustion increases enough to create visible smoke. Aerosol or smoke signatures are classified by size and the ability to scatter light. They are invisible when they are less than 0.3 μm and are visible at more than 0.3 μm. Low-energy smoldering fires produce larger particles than high-energy flaming fires, which produce smaller particles of combustion.

3. The flame stage usually involves less smoke, but flames break out and generate substantial heat. Convected thermal energy causes an increase in air temperature. A thermal signature disadvantage is convection of heat in the air, which, especially for small or beginning fires, takes a long time. In comparison to aerosol or energy signatures, thermal signatures often appear after life-threatening conditions have been reached.

4. The fourth stage of a fire is often referred to as the high-heat stage. At this point, the fire has spread rapidly, producing extensive flames, extreme heat, and many toxic gases. Many gases evolve during a fire, and most are fuel specific. The disadvantage of gas signatures is that they are not associated with a sufficiently large number of fuels to be used for general-purpose detection.

TYPES OF FIRE ALARM SYSTEMS

Fire alarm systems are required in many establishments as part of a fire protection plan In the event of fire emergencies, the alarm system warns the occupants of the establishment. Signal devices, such as sirens, gongs, bells, flashing lights, etc., are used to signal a fire condition. A signal indicating a fire condition may be sent directly to the fire department or may also be sent to an approved central monitoring station company. Aside from the regulations, it is important to remember that fire alarms save lives, and an understanding of the technology and limitations behind the various detectors is important. It is also important to know what technology is tested and rated for each fire device. Fire devices that are tested and rated have UL labels on them. Some of the different types of fire alarm systems available are listed as follows.

Manual Fire Alarm Stations or Pull Boxes

These types of fire alarms are activated manually, meaning that someone who notices a fire emergency must activate the alarm by hand. Manual fire alarm stations are not required for interior establishments having smoke detectors unless the building has a floor located more than 55 ft. above the lowest level of fire department access or it has more than three stories. These stations or pull boxes should be located on each floor of a building. Manual fire alarm stations can be either noncoded or coded. Noncoded stations operate normally on open or closed switches that transfer upon actuation a continuous signal, whereas coded stations operate with mechanical or electrical motors to produce a series of coded pulses that are transmitted to a central point.

There are two types of manual fire alarm stations. They are referred to as single-action or double-action stations:

- Single-action stations: Require only one step to activate the alarm, such as pulling down on a lever. Figure 6.15 shows an example of a single-action station.
- Double-action stations: Require two steps to activate the alarm. The person must first break glass, open a door, or lift a cover that allows him or her to gain access to a switch or lever that must then be operated to initiate an alarm. Figure 6.16 shows an example of a double-action station that must have the cover lifted before the lever is pulled.

FIGURE 6.15 Manual single-action station.

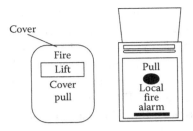

FIGURE 6.16   Manual double-action station.

Automatic Fire Alarms

Automatic fire alarm systems sound an alarm signal when a fire detection device indicates that there is a fire condition. Special sensors detect heat, smoke, flame, water flow, etc. These sensors are the initiating devices in automatic fire alarm systems. An automatic fire alarm system and a communication system are required in establishments that have floors located more than 55 ft. above the lowest level of fire department vehicle access. The following is a list of some of the different fire detector applications.

Heat Detectors

This type of detector has sensors that detect high temperature levels. Heat detectors offer protection in places where the environment is dirty or smoky, or where there is a high amount of airborne particles under normal conditions. They utilize the heat produced during the flame and high-heat stages of a fire to produce an alarm and are not as prone to false alarms. There are two types of heat detectors: fixed-temperature detectors and rate-of-rise detectors.

Fixed-Temperature Detectors   This type will signal an alarm when the heat of the surrounding air reaches a predetermined level. The air temperature at the time of the alarm is usually considerably higher than the rated temperature because it takes time for the air to raise the temperature of the operational element to its set point. This condition is known as thermal lag. The detector consists of two electrical contacts separated by a fusible link that will melt at a preset temperature, allowing the contacts to touch. When the contacts meet, the detector activates the alarm. Fixed-temperature detectors must be replaced after they have sounded an alarm. An example of this detector is shown in Figure 6.17. This kind is referred to as a line-type heat detector and uses a pair of wires in a small cable. The wires are held apart by heat-sensitive insulation. When the temperature limit is reached, the insulation melts, and the wires touch, initiating an alarm. Fixed-temperature detectors are available to cover a wide range of operating temperatures, from a selectable fixed temperature point of 135°F or higher.

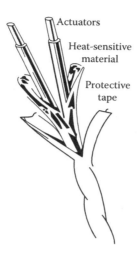

Actuators

Heat-sensitive
material

Protective
tape

FIGURE 6.17   One type of fixed-temperature heat detector.

Fixed-temperature heat detectors cannot be tested using heat. Using a heat source would melt whatever is used to separate the electrical contacts, and the detector would have to be replaced. Special testing methods are used, such as insulated wire alligator clips to connect to the electrical contacts inside the detector. The alarm will sound if the detector is working properly. Fixed-temperature detectors should be tested every 15 years.

Another type of heat detector that operates on the same principles as fixed-temperature detectors is the rate-compensation detector. It also responds when the heat of the surrounding air reaches a predetermined level. The device, by mechanical means, compensates for thermal lag. When heat builds up slowly, the detector will take longer to signal an alarm; if heat builds up quickly, the detector will signal an alarm sooner.

Heat detectors using expandable metals are self-restoring after the temperature drops to some point below the set point of the detector to reset. Two metals with different coefficients of thermal expansion are used; the heat causes the metal to bend or contract in such a way as to close an electrical contact that initiates a signal. Once cooled, the metals return to their original state automatically.

Rate-of-Rise Detectors   This type of detector activates an alarm when the room temperature increases at a certain rate, typically around 12°F to 15°F. This detector is more sensitive than the fixed-temperature detector. The rate-of-rise detector uses an air chamber with a small hole that allows a measurable amount of air to escape during expansion. A rapid increase in temperature will cause the pressure in the chamber to expand faster than the small hole will release, resulting in the expansion of the air chamber and activation of a switch. Rate-of-rise detectors do not have to be replaced

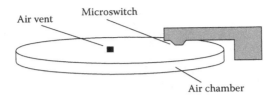

FIGURE 6.18 Rate-of-rise detector.

after they have activated the fire alarm. Figure 6.18 shows an example of a rate-of-rise detector.

Rate-of-rise detectors may be tested with a hair dryer or a heat lamp. The rate at which the temperature increases will be detected. The alarm will be activated once the rate of increase is higher than acceptable levels.

Combination Heat Detector

Combination detectors contain more than one element to respond to a fire condition. These detectors may be designed to respond to multiple types, with combined partial or complete responses from all. An example would be a heat detector that operates on the rate-of-rise and fixed-temperature principles. The advantage would be that the rate-of-rise detector would respond quickly to a rapidly developing fire, while the fixed-temperature detector will respond to a slowly developing fire when the detecting element reaches its set-point temperature.

Smoke Detectors

Smoke detectors sound an alarm when smoke is detected in a building. They have been shown to be very effective in saving lives and reducing fire damage, and they also respond faster than a heat detector. Smoke detectors can be installed on walls or ceilings. If installed on a wall, the detector should be located between 4 and 12 in. from the ceiling; if installed on a ceiling, it should be located at least 4 in. from the wall and at least 3 ft. from any ventilation ducts to prevent air coming from the vents from blowing the smoke away from the detector. In multistory buildings, smoke detectors should be installed on every floor or landing in the stairwell.

Smoke detectors can be installed in the return air ducts of heating, ventilating, and air-conditioning (HVAC) systems, to prevent circulation of smoke-contaminated air. The air duct detector is commonly used to initiate signals for the following functions:

- Shut down fans and close dampers, vents, etc., to prevent recirculation of dangerous quantities of smoke within the protected area
- Initiate operations of equipment to exhaust smoke within the protective area

- Initiate operation of equipment to pressurize smoke compartments
- Initiate operations of doors to close the openings in smoke compartments

Smoke detectors are defined by their operating principle—ionization or photoelectric:

- Ionization detectors have a high sensitivity to fires that produce small smoke particles from high-energy flaming fires that can burn for some time without generating a lot of combustion particles. The detectors' smoke chambers contain a radioactive source that emits radiation, resulting in a weak flow of electrical current. When smoke enters the smoke chamber, ionized air molecules attach to the smoke particles, thus reducing the ionizing current and triggering the alarm. These detectors are generally effective in detecting the products of combustion produced in the incipient stages of a fire. Ionization detectors have a higher false-alarm rate due to their sensitivity to minute smoke particles.
- Photoelectric detectors respond faster to the smoke generated by smoldering fires. Suspended smoke particles generated by a fire affect the passage of light in the air. Photoelectric detectors measure the passage of light by either obscuration or light scattering. Both types are effective; however, the obscuration-type detector requires more smoke to activate than the light-scattering type.
  - Obscuration involves the interruption of a beam of light. The light source is transmitted as a beam of light to a receiver. Smoke particles block the light beam, causing a reduction in light reaching the photocell. When a certain percentage of obscuration is measured, the detector responds and sends an alarm.
  - Light scattering utilizes the light diffusion properties of smoke to redirect a beam of light to a light sensor. The light is scattered by smoke particles onto a photocell that initiates an alarm. This type of detector has a T-shaped chamber fitted with an LED and a photocell. The LED transmits a beam of light in the horizontal bar of the chamber, while the photocell sits at the bottom of the vertical bar of the chamber. In normal smoke-free conditions, the LED transmits the beam of light in the chamber without striking the photocell. When smoke particles enter the chamber, the particles deflect some of the light rays and scatter them in all directions. When enough light rays hit the photocell, the detector responds and sends an alarm.

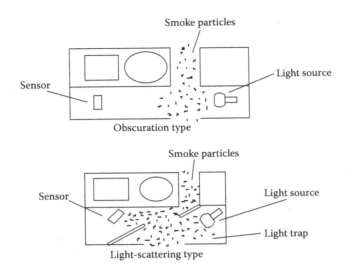

FIGURE 6.19   Photoelectric detectors.

Figure 6.19 shows examples of both types of photoelectric detectors.

Other Technologies Using Photoelectric Principles

These types of air-sampling smoke detectors are usually used in priceless or high-dollar establishments, such as museums and electronic data-processing areas, or where equipment survival is extremely important to operations:

- Cloud chamber smoke detector: An air pump draws a sample of air from the protected area into a high-humidity chamber that has a detector. After the air sample has been raised to a high humidity, the pressure is lowered slightly. If smoke particles are present, the moisture in the air condenses on them, forming a cloud in the chamber. The density of the cloud is then measured by the photoelectric principle. The detector responds when the density is greater than the predetermined level.
- Continuous-air-sampling smoke detector: The air is sampled continuously and actively from a protected space. The air-sampling system consists of sampling pipes that are spaced uniformly over the ceiling. The pipes monitor the air entering and exiting the monitored space. Each one of the pipes on the ceiling pipe drops are capped with a small hole drilled in it to draw in air, and the same is true for the pipes returning air. The piping is connected to an aspirator, or fan, that creates a flow of air in the piping network. The flow causes the pressure inside to be less than the atmospheric pressure. This creates a slight vacuum that allows

the piping network to continuously draw air. The sampled air is drawn through a filter to the detector. If there are smoke particles in the sampled air, an alarm condition is activated. This type of smoke detector can detect extremely low concentrations of smoke particles.

- Laser smoke detector: This technology operates on the photoelectric, light-scattering principle but with 100 times greater sensitivity. This way, it can detect a fast-flaming fire, like the ionization detector, and a slow, smoldering fire, like a photoelectric detector. The laser technology smoke detector also has algorithms to check for the presence of smoke before alarming. Its higher sensitivity can sense the earliest particles of combustion and can distinguish the transient signals caused by dust or smoke.
- Multisensor detector: This utilizes the photoelectric smoke detector and the heat detector to respond well to smoldering fires as well as fast-burning fires. Combining sensors enhances detection performance and can reduce phenomena that are likely to cause false alarms.

Flame Detectors

Flame detectors can respond to radiant energy that either is visible to the naked eye (about 4000 to 7700 Å) or is not visible to the naked eye. Their detection capability is defined by a viewing angle or cone of vision that is similar to that of the human eye. Sensitivity increases as the angle of incidence decreases. Flame detectors are sensitive to glowing embers, coals, or flames that radiate energy and activate the alarm. Flame detector systems are chosen for the type of fire that is more probable due to the different radiation characteristics of the types of fuel burned. Due to their fast detection capabilities, flame detectors are generally used only in high-hazard areas, such as oil refineries, power plants, or atmospheres where explosions and rapid fires may occur. Because flame detectors must be able to see the fire, objects should not block them.

There are two types of flame detectors that are designed to detect radiant energy emitted by a fire:

1. UV flame detector: Use either a solid-state device or a gas-filled tube as the sensing element. UV detectors are sensitive to most fires that emit in the 1850 to 2450 Å range. Those include fires with hydrogen, ammonia, metals, sulfur, and hydrazine.
2. IR flame detector: Basically composed of filters that screen out unwanted wavelengths and focus the incoming energy on a photoresistant or photovoltaic cell sensitive to IR radiation. They can

respond to the total IR component of flames alone or in combination with the flame flicker in the frequency range of 5 to 30 Hz. IR detectors can usually detect most hydrocarbon fires from liquids, gases, and solids, but fires from hydrogen, ammonia, etc. do not produce significant amounts of radiation in the 4.4 μm sensitivity range.

A combination UV and IR flame detector operates on the same principles and consists of a UV and single-frequency sensor paired together in one unit. A fire alarm is only actuated if both sensors detect a fire; this lowers the false-alarm rate compared to either detector by itself.

Carbon Monoxide Fire Detector

This type of detector does not detect smoke particles or heat, but it does sense the carbon monoxide (CO) given off by all carbon-based materials in the smoldering stage of a fire. These detectors are excellent for supplemental protection with smoke and heat detectors and, in some cases, will respond more rapidly to many types of fires compared to heat detectors. CO detectors are also more resistant to environmental conditions that cause false alarms, such as dust and small particles.

Gas-Sensing Fire Detector

Gas levels can be detected before heat levels are detected in a fire. This principle operates on semiconductor or catalytic elements.

- Semiconductor: This type of gas detector responds to either oxidizing or reducing gases by creating electrical changes in the semiconductor. The conductivity changes of the semiconductor cause the detector to signal an alarm.
- Catalytic element: The catalytic material in itself remains unchanged but accelerates the oxidation of combustible gases. The resulting temperature rise in the element causes the detector to send an alarm.

Noise Detector

This utilizes the environmental changes that occur during a fire. A fire produces characteristic noise depending on what is burning, such as the cracking a fire produces from a wood fire. Typical bands and sequences of acoustic waves can be analyzed by analog systems. For example, a plastics fire will emit different signals than a wood fire. This technology can only be used for solid fires.

OTHER FIRE DETECTION DEVICES

Water-Flow Indicators

These are designed to sense when water flows through the fire protection system, such as the water flow through the sprinkler system. There are methods that are used to detect water flow, usually known as vane-type indicators and check valves.

Vane-Type Indicators

These are installed inside the piping, and when water flows through the piping, the vane is moved, closing a switch and transmitting a signal to the alarm or central station.

Check Valves

These are installed close to the main control valve or at the location where the water supply enters the fire protection system. A clapper mechanism is located inside the valve, and under normal conditions, it is in a closed position. In the closed position, the clapper prevents water from entering the system, and the clapper will open when the sprinkler head opens to discharge water, initiating an alarm signal.

FIRE-EXTINGUISHING SYSTEMS

Fire containment by passive measures, such as using portable extinguishers, may be possible, but even if confined to one area, combustion is likely to cause direct fire and secondary heat and smoke damage of great magnitude. Oxygen, heat, and fuel are needed to produce fire. These basic elements, needed for a fire, are known as the fire triangle (see Figure 6.20). When oxygen, heat or fuel is removed, it will cause a side of the triangle to be broken, and the fire will die. Fire extinguishers and fire extinguisher systems are an important component in eliminating one or more sides of the fire triangle.

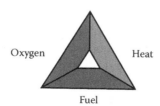

FIGURE 6.20 The fire triangle.

Active automatic fire-extinguishing systems are often a preferred solution, and sprinklers are usually the type considered. Initiating fire-detecting devices can be used in combination with a fire-extinguishing system. Extinguishing systems require supervisory devices to detect abnormal conditions.

The following are different types of fire-extinguishing systems:

- Wet-pipe automatic sprinkler: Water within all pipes is permanently under pressure. Sensing heat actuates the sprinklers.
- Preaction automatic sprinkler: Air is within the sprinkler pipes. Actuation of the fire alarm system transmits a signal to the sprinklers, causing them to open a valve to allow flow and discharge of water. This type of system is used if the threat of water standing in the piping is a concern.
- On–off automatic sprinkler: This system is similar to the preaction automatic sprinkler system, except that the water control valve will continue to open and close according to the temperature sensed by the heat detectors or by the restorable sprinkler heads.
- Dry-pipe automatic sprinkler: The sprinkler pipes have pressurized air inside them; when the sprinkler heads are actuated, the air is released, causing the valves to let out pressurized water. This type of system is often used in locations where the sprinkler pipes are subjected to freezing temperatures.
- Standpipe and hose system: A piping system for hose connection.

Other fire-extinguishing system agents include the following:

- Dry powder or a chemical extinguishing agent consists of a bicarbonate that supplies carbon dioxide and finely powdered salt metals that strongly absorb radiant heat, thus cooling the temperature.
- Foam extinguishing agents should be used on liquid fires. The foam forms a blanket over the liquid, preventing reignition while the liquid cools.

The potential for secondary fire damage from water itself leads to other considerations for alternative methods in using automatic fire-extinguishing systems that will not damage or destroy high-value assets. Prevalent in the 1960s, piping systems using halon gas were used that effectively extinguished a fire without damaging or destroying valuables. Because agents in the halon gas have an ozone depletion potential (ODP), the Montreal Protocol Treaty banned its use in 1994. In the mid-1990s, a number of new-generation gaseous systems emerged using zero-ODP agents. They are tested to be environmentally acceptable, emit clean gases at ambient temperatures, and offer fire suppression performance at concentrations below defined human toxicity levels.

The following are the different types of chemical gases and inert gases used in fire suppression systems:

- Inert agents
  - 100% argon
  - 100% nitrogen
  - 50% nitrogen, 50% argon (Argonite)
  - 50% nitrogen, 42% argon (Inergen)
  - 8% carbon dioxide
- Chemical agents
  - Trifluoromethane, CHF_3
  - Pentafluoroethane, CF_3CHF_2
  - Heptafluoropropane, CF_3CHFCF_3
  - Dodecafluoro-2-methylpentan-3-one, $CF_3CF_2C(O)CF(CF_3)_2$

The gases are noncorrosive and electrically nonconductive and do not cause any secondary damage due to the agent itself. This contrasts with sprinklers and other options such as dry powder and foam. Chemical gases are used well below the toxicity levels, and inert gases are safe based on resulting oxygen level consideration. Chemical gases are more space and weight effective and may be preferred where limited space is available; inert gases require a greater number of cylinders, but the ease of agent flow enables storage at a very remote location from the protected area.

CLASSIFICATION OF FIRES

The classification of fires (Table 6.8) is important when putting in a fire-extinguishing system because of the many kinds of burning materials encountered in a fire. The type used largely depends on what the business needs to protect. Certain fire-extinguishing systems will only work on certain types of fires, and some will actually aggravate a fire and cause more damage.

NOTIFICATION AND SIGNALING SYSTEMS

The signaling function of a fire alarm system notifies occupants and the central monitoring station that an alarm, supervisory, or trouble condition exists in a given establishment. This action may include any or all of the following:

- The sounding of audible alarm devices
- The illumination of visual alarm devices
- The announcement of the event locally or to a central monitoring system

TABLE 6.8
Classification of Fires

Class A	Fires involving wood, cloth, paper, rubber, or other carbonaceous solids where water is used to quench the fire and cool the material below its ignition temperature.
Class B	Fires involving flammable or combustible liquids, gases, and greases that include gasoline, oil, paint, etc., where smothering action is required. Dry powder, foam, carbon dioxide, or vaporizing liquid interrupts the fuel oxygen of heat triangles.
Class C	Usually involves a class A or B fire but also involves energized electrical equipment. A nonenergized agent is vital. When the agent melts, it forms an oxygen coating over the burning materials to suffocate them. Carbon dioxide, dry powder, or vaporizing liquid is effective. Water and foam should not be used, because they can be conductive.
Class D	Fires involving certain combustible metals, such as magnesium, sodium, potassium, and their alloys. A special dry powder that has a special smothering and coating agent should be used and is not suited for use on other classes of fires.

The system's signal notification may also occur at the same time emergency control measures are activated. Some of the emergency controls may include the following:

- Elevator recall
- Emergency lighting control
- Stairwell or elevator shaft pressurization
- Smoke control system, usually part of the HVAC system, including smoke damper closing and fan control
- Initiation of automatic fire-extinguishing equipment
- Unlocking of doors
- Announcement or communication to other systems or individuals
- Emergency shutdown of gas and fuel supplies

Evacuation Signals

Notification devices can be audible or visual. The most common means are the combination of audio and visual units. The following can produce a signal, tone, or message.

- Audible: Bells, chimes, horns, sirens, etc.
  - Speakers and a public address system can be used to warn and instruct building occupants in case of a fire emergency. Usually, a prerecorded message is played in the event of an

alam condition. The message informs occupants of the emergency situation and directs them to exit the establishment. Firefighters can use bullhorns and override the message to give occupants more specific information as needed.

- Visual: Strobe and flashing lights.
- Digital dialers: In addition to notifying occupants of an emergency situation, most fire alarm systems also activate a digital dialer to report the event to a UL-listed central monitoring station. The alarm receiver is actually a computer and tells the operator the alarm zone and all pertinent site information, so it can be relayed to the proper authorities. For example, if a trouble signal is reported, then management will be notified. If an alarm signal is received, then the fire department and local police will be notified. An alternative method is long-range RF that transmits the signal to various towers that are set up in a network to reach the central monitoring station.

System Design and False-Alarm Prevention

Proper system design and location of detectors will minimize the chances of false alarms. To be effective, fire alarm detectors should be located on or near the ceilings of protected areas because smoke or hot gases initially collect there.

The following are some suggestions and guidelines for detector and system placement:

- Detectors should not be placed in areas that have an abnormal amount of dust, moisture, insects, and high-powered or prolonged RF transmissions.
- Detectors should not be located near operable windows, supply duct outlets, or other ventilation sources that could interfere with natural air currents, or near any obstruction that would prevent smoke or heat from reaching the detector.
- Never place a spot detector or smoke detector in the corner of a room.

Maintenance and Testing

An ongoing proper maintenance and test program is the key factor in reducing false alarms and the proper and efficient operation of a fire alarm system. Many fire alarm systems will contain a combination of smoke detectors, heat detectors, and manual pull stations to help provide early warning and detection of a fire. These are usually regulated by building codes. Documented testing of the entire system should be completed after installation. This includes the control unit, each initiating device, the notification appliance, and its accessories.

The lights on the control and annunciator panels should be inspected a minimum of once a month. If an emergency power generator is installed, that should also be checked a minimum of once a month. Supervisory devices should be tested a minimum of once a year. The entire fire alarm system should be visually inspected a minimum of once a month. Defective equipment must be replaced immediately.

Smoke detectors should be tested at least once every 6 months and reset at least once a year to keep the detector in good working condition. When testing, follow the directions of the maker of the smoke detector. All detectors require periodic cleaning to remove dust, dirt, etc. The frequency of cleaning depends on the location of the detector and the ambient conditions. Care should be taken because detectors are extremely sensitive and easily damaged.

If break-glass fire alarms are installed, an extra supply of glass plates must be kept available on the premises. There should be a minimum of one extra pane of glass for each fire alarm station.

Fire alarm stations and related equipment must never be painted. Paint may prevent the equipment from working properly.

If a building is remodeled, the fire alarm system should be checked to make sure that it is functioning correctly.

Fire alarm drills should be conducted to ensure that occupants know what to do in case of a fire; this can also be done when testing the fire alarm system.

7 Personnel Security

This chapter is designed to make the candidate aware of the requirements, laws, and governmental regulations for, and importance of, the screening, interviewing, and hiring of the best possible employees. It is to everyone's benefit to screen out dishonest employees or employees who are in some way unstable or unsuited for the positions applied for. It is in the best interest of everyone to select those whose abilities and track records show them to be worthy of consideration.

PURPOSE AND FUNCTIONS

Personnel security's primary purpose is to ensure that a firm hires those employees who are best suited to assist the firm in achieving its goals and who, after being hired, assist in providing the necessary security to the employees while they are carrying out their functions. Screening the candidate should include the application of the "whole-man" rule being applied. This takes into consideration all relevant aspects of the candidate's background, which are weighed, thus including a totality of the person.

Personnel security is the most critical of the three major security processes utilized in providing the total protection of an organization. The other two components are the following:

- Information security
- Physical security

The key functions of the personnel security process are as follows:

- It serves as a screening device to assist the organization in hiring suitable employees.
- It is responsible for handling background investigations of prospective employees.
- It is responsible for the investigation of current employees suspected of violations of company rules and regulations.
- It assists employees in protecting themselves through security awareness and educational programs.
- It attempts to ensure the protection of employees from discriminatory hiring or terminating procedures as well as unfounded allegations of illegal or unethical activities and conduct.

A comprehensive personnel security program should include the following elements:

- Adequate job specifications and performance standards
- Appropriate recruitment and selection criteria
- Background applicant screening procedures and standards
- Background investigative standards
- Truth verification standards
- Criteria for employee conduct
- Investigations of questionable employee conduct
- Disciplinary procedures
- Termination procedures

EMPLOYEE SCREENING

The key to an effective personnel security program is to screen out employees who are bad risks before they are hired. Accordingly, the best place to start is the personnel office. A well-constructed application form serves as a prescreening device.

Rejection of bad risks should be on the basis of standards that have been carefully worked out with the personnel division. Such standards should be strictly adhered to and should be updated on a regular basis.

Federal law prohibits asking the prospective employee questions regarding the following:

- Marital status
- Number of children in the applicant's family, their ages, and information concerning their care
- Identity of person(s) living with the applicant
- Whether the applicant owns or rents his or her home
- If the applicant is a woman, her maiden name
- Religion and church affiliation
- Garnishment history, if any
- Whether applicant has been arrested (convictions may be subject to inquiry and questions if pertinent to the job)

Restrictions regarding screening are provided by a number of laws and regulations, such as the following:

- Civil Rights Act of 1964
- Privacy Act of 1974

- Fair Credit Reporting Act
- Consumer Protection Act of 1976
- Department of Justice Order 601-75

Under various provisions of the aforementioned Civil Rights Act, Privacy Act, and Consumer Protection Act, the following actions may *not* be taken:

- Ask the applicant to disclose his or her original name if a name change was made
- Inquire about the applicant's birthplace if it is outside the United States
- Require the applicant to produce military discharge papers before employment
- Inquire into foreign military experience
- Ask about age if it is not an occupational qualification or otherwise required by law
- Inquire about racial background
- Require a photo with the application
- Ask questions about organizational affiliations whereby race, religion, or national origin data can be obtained
- Ask a male applicant for data regarding the maiden name of his spouse or mother
- Ask about the place of residence of the applicant's spouse and relations
- Inquire regarding naturalization status or citizenship of the applicant's spouse or parents
- Inquire regarding the applicant's religion

The Consumer Protection Act, in addition, prohibits the following:

- Inquiries regarding records of arrests, indictments, or convictions of a crime where data is more than 7 years prior to the date of application
- Inquiries regarding any bankruptcies that took place more than 14 years before the application
- Inquiries regarding any paid tax liens, legal suits, or judgments that had a harmful effect

Department of Justice Order 601-75 prohibits a criminal justice agency from confirming or denying the existence of criminal history data for employment purposes.

On the positive side, however, there are still a number of things an employer can do in regard to the screening process, such as the following:

- Have the applicant write his or her name and address on the application form
- If the information is an occupational qualification, require an applicant to give his or her date of birth
- Inquire as to criminal indictments and convictions
- Explain duty hours required in the job
- Ask if the applicant is a US citizen
- Inquire about educational and training background
- Inquire about relevant work experience
- Make inquiries regarding the applicant's character and background
- Require a listing of persons to be notified in case of an emergency
- Inquire as to military experience (note, however, that discharge papers cannot be required until after hiring)
- Inquire as to membership in organizations that do not pertain to race, religion, or national origin
- Ask if the applicant belongs to any organization advocating the overthrow of the US government
- Inquire as to gender on those occasions when there is such a qualification for the job

Things to look for during the screening process include the following:

- Signs of instability in personal relations
- Indications of lack of job stability
- Indications of being clearly overqualified
- A declining salary history
- Unexplained gaps in employment history
- Inability to remember names of former supervisors
- Gaps in residences
- Inadequate references

PERSONNEL INVESTIGATIONS

These investigations usually involve four general techniques:

1. Backgrounding
2. Positive vetting
3. Polygraphing
4. Profiling

BACKGROUNDING

A complete background investigation usually covers four steps:

1. A personal history statement (PHS)
2. Evaluation of the PHS
3. A national agency check
4. A full field investigation

The PHS should cover at least the following topics when they are not in violation of local or federal laws:

- Personal history
- Marital history
- Residence history
- Citizenship history
- Availability
- Physical data
- Educational history
- References
- Employment history
- Military history
- Foreign travel history
- Court record
- Credit record
- Organizational memberships
- Family history

Some authorities estimate that 20% of any given workforce is responsible for 80% of the personnel problems that develop. A psychological deterrent sometimes utilized is to state on the application form that the applicant will be bonded, fingerprinted, or required to give permission for polygraphing. Those with criminal records may have second thoughts about the employment if faced with these possibilities.

Some tips in evaluating a PHS are as follows:

- Do not accept a post office box in lieu of a real address.
- Be alert to the fact that an address listed may merely be a mail drop and the applicant does not actually live there.
- Be alert to unverifiable listings on a PHS, such as firms that went out of business, military records lost or destroyed, courthouse records burned, etc.

The national agency check consists of a record check of at least the following agencies:

- Federal Bureau of Investigation (FBI)
- Department of Defense
- Departments of the Army, Navy, Coast Guard, Marine Corps, and Air Force
- Civil Service records
- Immigration and Naturalization Service
- Central Intelligence Agency
- Department of State
- Treasury Department

POSITIVE VETTING

Webster's dictionary defines *vetting* as the process of inspecting or examining with careful thoroughness. This process is rarely used in the United States; it is mostly used in England.

The essence of vetting is as follows:

- A personal interview is conducted under stress.
- The interview is based on answers previously given by the applicant.
- Other information is used during the interview that confirms or denies information given by the applicant.

The basic reasons for an interview during vetting are as follows:

- To impeach the applicant
- To observe the applicant's behavior under stress
- To open areas for exploration that were heretofore concealed
- To provide new investigative leads

POLYGRAPHING

The polygraph is *not* a lie detector; it is a stress detector. It measures stress indicators, such as the following:

- Quickened pulse
- Raised blood pressure
- Shallow respiration
- Lowered galvanic skin resistance

Devices attached to the body of the examinee are linked to a machine that makes a continuous record of changes in stress. The devices used are the following:

- A blood pressure cuff around the upper arm, forearm, or wrist
- An electrode attached to the fingertips
- One or two straps around the chest

The most important measure of stress is recorded by the heart. It is called cardiac stress and is shown in the subject's heartbeat and blood pressure. The least important measure is the galvanic skin response, which is shown by the amount of sweat on the skin. The majority of all polygraph tests are preemployment tests. They usually take about 1 h.

Before giving the polygraph test, the examiner conducts a pretest interview for the following reasons:

- To help the subject relax
- To help the examiner judge the subject's character

Also prior to the actual test, a control test is administered to give the examiner some indication of the subject's response pattern. One of the most common control tests involves the use of playing cards.

Many polygraph tests are inconclusive for the following reasons:

- The subject may not care whether he or she is found to be lying or not.
- The subject may be nervous because of a mental condition.
- The subject may suffer from a physical condition that does not let him or her sit still.
- The subject may exhibit feelings of guilt without any cause.
- The subject may be so angry so as to affect test results.
- The subject may suffer discomfort or pain.
- The subject may be suffering from shock.

A polygraph test cannot be given unless the subject agrees. Refusal to take a polygraph cannot be held against the employee.

Preemployment tests are limited to the following:

- National defense positions
- Law enforcement positions
- Positions with banks, savings and loans, or armored transports
- Federal positions involving law enforcement, national defense, and other relevant positions of trust

Specific-Issue Tests

The polygraph can be used as a tool for interrogation in certain circumstances (specific-issue tests). When investigating a crime or criminal activity, no one person may be singled out. For example, if cash is missing from the company safe, everyone who had access and opportunity must be tested. At least 48 h notice of the intent to test must be given in writing along with the reason for asking for the test. In the pretest, all questions to be asked must be presented in the order they will be asked. During the test, no additional questions may be asked. They must be presented in the same order as in the pretest. At least two tests must be run on each individual. After the test, any discrepancies or deceptive answers should be brought forth in a posttest interview, and the subject should be given an opportunity to explain his or her answers.

Some rights of the subject with regard to taking a polygraph test are as follows:

- As a general rule, an employee has the right to request and take a polygraph test.
- As a general rule, an employee or applicant has the right to limit the number of people allowed to see the test results.
- As a general rule, the employee may refuse to take the test without fear of losing his or her job. However, this does not apply if the employee signed a preemployment agreement authorizing polygraph testing.

Polygraphs in proprietary security are most often used in the following situations:

- Periodic tests of all employees to establish their conduct if they are a necessity of the job due to governmental regulations
- Specific questions to determine the causes of specific incidents
- Preemployment examinations if required or approved by law

PSYCHOLOGICAL STRESS EVALUATOR

The Psychological Stress Evaluator (PSE) detects, measures, and charts specific stress-related aspects of the human voice.

Voice recordings are used whereby the sound wave characteristics of subjects are reproduced. By running voice recordings through an instrument at different speeds, different aspects of the sound waves can be recorded on a graph for evaluation. Patterns produced by the involuntary nervous system indicate the truth or falsity of tested responses.

PROFILING

Profiling is a process whereby a subject's reaction to a future critical situation is predicted by observing his or her behavior, by interviewing him or her, or by analyzing his or her response to a questionnaire. An example of a test prepared for profiling purposes is the Reid Report developed by John E. Reid and Associates. Another example of a form of profiling is the personality questionnaire administered to young professional people who are applying for first-career jobs.

APPLICANT INVESTIGATION

If money is not a consideration, ideally, all information furnished by the applicant on the application form and given orally should be verified. This would constitute a full field investigation. A thorough investigation should include checks into the following areas:

- A national agency check
- Birth records
- Educational records (college attendance or, if no college, the last secondary school)
- Employment history (at least 5 consecutive years of employment and/or nonemployment immediately preceding application submission should be verified)
- Any gaps in employment more than 30 days should be explored and explained fully
- References
- Developed character references
- Neighborhood investigation
- Criminal records
- Military service
- Foreign travel
- Citizenship status
- Credit record

MISCELLANEOUS MATTERS

Personnel departments and security officers responsible for personnel clearance investigations should keep abreast of changes in the law through the status of court decisions. Note that the employee has the right to review his or her preemployment investigation file and to reasonably contest any findings. If academic background is verified by mail, be sure to include a photocopy of the applicant's authorization to obtain the information.

During an investigation, military records should be confirmed by having the applicant submit a copy of his or her service record (form DD-214).

Selective service numbers are generally coded in the following manner:

- First number—state issued
- Next two digits—local board
- Next two digits—year of birth
- Fourth group of digits—registration number

In most states, criminal convictions are matters of public record, with felonies being filed in superior court and misdemeanors in municipal court.

An exit interview is a valuable tool for the following reasons:

- It gives the employee an opportunity to list grievances.
- Management often learns of problems not previously known.
- It helps to reduce loss when a checklist is used to have company property returned.
- It is used to remind departing employees of a legal obligation to protect trade secrets or confidential records.

Bonding is used by some firms as a type of insurance in case the company controls prove ineffective. If loss involves a merchandise shortage, the prospects for recovery usually depend on being able to prove how the loss took place. Bonding should never be considered an alternative to an effective security program.

8 Crisis Management

Probably the most demanding of all of the duties the security professional is called on to accomplish is developing and directing the response of the company to emergency situations. These emergencies can be man-made, such as product tampering, arson, terrorist activities, robberies, large thefts, etc. Others are natural in origin, such as storm damage due to hurricanes, lightning strikes, tsunamis (tidal waves caused by underwater disturbances), earthquakes, etc. Some can be management-based or labor-based problems, as in the case of a labor dispute. Still others revolve around criminal activity and industrial espionage. Whatever the case may be, you are expected to foresee such occurrences, develop viable plans to respond to them, train the required personnel, and have the various outside resources available to quickly address these needs.

Preplanning and the ability to effectively respond can, many times, decide whether a company survives the emergency or folds up afterward. This chapter addresses those issues and helps to clarify the issues, needs, and solutions to those problems.

Emergency planning has always been an important part of every company's program to ensure its continuation. However, with the growth of terrorism, the importance of emergency planning has gained a much greater urgency in the business world. Any company that is complacent with regard to emergency planning is truly foolish. All one needs to do is consider the devastation of September 11 and its aftermath to realize how important proper emergency planning is.

Terrorism, however, is only a segment of a total program for emergency planning. Proper planning for emergencies must also include planning for the following:

- Natural disasters (i.e., tornadoes, hurricanes, and earthquakes)
- Fires/arson
- Major equipment breakdowns
- Water damage
- Criminal acts
- Sabotage
- Loss of key personnel
- Labor disputes/business interruptions

Today's security manager or director must have a comprehensive plan in place beforehand. After the emergency has occurred, it is too late to start preparing a plan. With this in mind, remember that there are three important parts of the plan. The plan should be directive in nature. Do not restrict the distribution of the plan only to senior management. Establish who can activate the plan; generally, it is activated by a person at a high level in the organization. The executives of the company will look to you to have in place and implement a comprehensive program. A company's very survival will probably rest on what you have done or failed to do.

The Professional Certification Board recognizes this fact and has made emergency planning an important part of the Certified Protection Professional (CPP) exam.

INTRODUCTION

There are four recognized segments in emergency management. They are the following:

1. Mitigations. In this context, mitigation refers to the pre-event efforts undertaken by the company to lessen the impact of the event. These efforts may run the gamut from the assessment of risks to equipment and personnel to the prevention of inadvertent damage to sensitive equipment.
2. Preparedness. This refers to the efforts exerted to prepare the staff for response and recovery requirements. These efforts may include planning, training, and obtaining the required equipment.
3. Response. This includes the activities necessary to address situations as they arise in the course of an emergency.
4. Recovery. After the emergency has occurred, what are the necessary actions to be taken to return the business to full, pre-event operation?

When contemplating what needs to be done to prepare your organization, always keep these four aspects of emergency management in mind.

There are five emergency management areas of focus that serve as a basis for preparedness, response, and recovery, namely congestion, communications, collection and distribution of resources, control, and coordination.

CONGESTION

This is the first area of the five to be considered. Congestion refers to learning to recognize early on the symptoms of congestion in any area of the facility. This recognition may save countless wasted man-hours and dollars.

Congestion does not necessarily refer to physical congestion but, rather, to the amount of work that flows through a given section. A failure to properly evaluate the congestion of work can bring on that operation an avalanche of work that can overwhelm the staff.

COMMUNICATIONS

This refers to understanding the limitations, expectations, and capabilities of the company's communications system before disaster strikes. This evaluation gives the emergency response team an opportunity to successfully respond to the incident. However, recognition of the need to talk to each other at every level is tantamount to success in understanding and responding to a disaster. The failure to communicate with each other is a significant issue, which could have severe consequences.

COLLECTION AND DISTRIBUTION OF RESOURCES

Knowing the who, when, where, what, and how about the available resources is not a task to be ascertained while under the stress of managing an emergency. Familiarization with operational data, emergency purchasing procedures, temporary credentialing policies, relocation criteria, and other similar activities are some of the subjects to broach during emergency management training.

CONTROL

This refers to regulating and coordinating all of the many responsibilities and tasks required to fulfill the emergency plan. This would require the ability to measure performance against the established policy or standard. You must be able to compare the actual performance with the policy or standard. Then compare the actual results with the policy or standard expectation. Finally, implement corrective actions to overcome deviations and bring the results back into line with the policy/standard expectations. Being prepared and able to accomplish the tasks set forth in the plan beforehand is essential.

COORDINATION

Recognizing when to employ corrective, preventive, regulatory, or promotive coordination will provide a distinct advantage in the cost-effective management of the response. Poor coordination leads to a waste of resources, erosion of staff morale, and replication of staff assignments.

OBJECTIVES

The overall objectives of emergency operations planning should be to do the following:

- Foster a systematic approach to emergency management.
- Support a capability for prompt coordinated response to emergencies and threats of all sizes simultaneously by all levels of the facility or corporate management.
- Provide an assured continuity of management and delivery of essential services for the duration of the emergency.
- Promote uniformity in principles, policies, concepts of operations, and compatible departmental standard operating procedures that facilitate a coordinated response.

Development and implementation of comprehensive plans to manage the necessary required activities to accomplish these emergency management objectives must address mitigation, preparedness, and response and recovery issues. Departmental efforts must also support the efforts of the entire organization. Flexibility and good judgment are the cornerstones of an effective planning effort. The outcome of the planning should be reduced to written form. It should be produced in a manner that makes it easy to read and understand. These written plans should never become so rigid in their formulation that they preclude the ability to address changing or unexpected situations.

DEVELOPING THE PLAN

A planning coordinator is recommended to oversee the process and to facilitate the development of the plan.

RESPONSE PRIORITIES

- Protect human life
- Prevent or minimize personal injury
- Reduce exposure of physical assets
- Maximize loss control for assets where exposure cannot be reduced
- Restore normal operations as soon as possible

FUNCTIONS TO CONSIDER WHEN DEVELOPING YOUR PLAN

There are 11 functions that occur in every emergency management situation *no matter what the event is!* All the tasks associated with the effective response effort to internal and external emergencies can be included in one of the following 11 functional categories.

Command—Managing Emergency Operations

Managing emergency operations provides for the overall management and coordination of the emergency response. This includes the management of the staff in the facility or coordination of the joint efforts of the departments in conjunction with governmental and private agencies supporting such operations:

- Emergency operations center organization
  - Will one location suffice, or are several locations required?
  - Is the location clearly communicated to the staff?
  - How often during the disaster will the staff be required to be there?
- Emergency management team composition
  - Is there training for the emergency management team?
- Public information officer (PIO) policy
  - Is the staff familiar with the PIO policy?
  - Does the staff understand the information release protocol?
  - Is there a system for notifying the media?
  - Is there a method for credentialing the media?
  - Is there a media center?
  - Are there provisions for rumor control?
  - Is there a distinction between emergency and nonemergency procedures?
  - Are there procedures for visitor control?
- Staff alerting recall
  - Who performs the recall? Do they know that?
  - Is there a coded message used for recall?
  - Are personnel expected to call in or not?
  - How long will the recall take?
  - Does the recall give priority to distance from the facility?
  - How does the recall get executed when the local telephone system is down?
  - When and how are on-duty employees notified?
  - Is there an opportunity for on-duty personnel to check on their families' welfare?
  - Is there a published order of succession?
  - Are there predetermined schedules?
  - Do you know what personnel resources are available at any time of the day?
  - How does the staff know when the response level has changed or ended?

- Communicating
  - Are you aware of the Radio Amateur Civil Emergency Services (RACES)?
  - How will information be transmitted within the facility?
- Appropriate level of response
  - Do you have different levels of response in the plan?
  - What determines changes in the response levels?
- Situation reporting
  - Is there accurate record keeping?
  - How often is the information updated?
  - Is there a system for situation reporting?
- Critique and evaluation
  - Is there an environment for honest critique?
  - Is there debriefing of the participants?

Fire Management/Facility Evacuation Operations

Fire management and facility evacuation operations limit the loss of life and property from the effects of fires and similar threats and provide for first aid at the scene and rescue of persons during emergencies. This function coordinates the activities of personnel engaged in fire and facility evacuation operations. These personnel interact with local fire department workers when they arrive on the scene. They are also tasked with evaluating status reports and make decisions regarding the commitment of resources. Mutual assistance and prior coordination with the fire department are critical. They must have the capability to quickly respond to, contain, and extinguish the fire with well-trained personnel:

- Liaison with local fire departments
  - Does the fire department have a copy of your fire and disaster plan?
  - Does the fire department participate in your exercises and training programs?
  - Does the facility participate in the fire department's training exercises?
- Rescue support personnel
  - Have you designated personnel to assist rescue units when necessary?
- Fire plan
  - Is the staff familiar with the company's *code red* policy?
  - Do evacuation maps show locations of fire suppression equipment?

Security/Traffic Control Operations

Security and traffic control operations provide for the protection of life and property. This function enforces the applicable orders, company policies, and traffic management on the facility grounds. This function also coordinates the activities of security and traffic control staff, interacts with community law enforcement agencies, maintains communications with mobile security forces, evaluates status reports, makes decisions regarding commitment of resources, and determines the need for additional resources:

- Mobilization and deployment of security resources
  - Has there been a review of the department communications system including the participants on a regular basis?
  - Has security defined and established a control center?
  - Has a priority post listing been developed by shift?
  - Are the emergency management plans consistent and in concert with the facility emergency management plan?
  - Is there enough management to achieve the plan's goals?
- Alerting and notifying on-duty staff (this is the most overlooked function in the planning process and one of the more often implemented when the emergency situation invalidates methods that are commonly used in day-to-day operations)
  - Has training been provided to officers to ensure they know how to alert personnel in the impacted areas of the facility in emergencies?
  - Is there a protocol available for on-duty officers that restates alerting notification procedures?
  - Has training for tactical search been conducted for the staff? Were holidays and weekends included?
  - Was the training conducted on off-shifts and weekends?
- Access control
  - What will be the accepted forms of identification for emergency response access?
  - Does the staff possess these forms and understand their use?
  - Is there an access control program, and are the security personnel familiar with the program?
  - Is there a method for identifying staff members who report without credentials?
  - How will volunteers (i.e., contractors, media, clergy, family, vendors, and city and government personnel) be identified?
  - Is there a policy that requires the employees to bear and display appropriate identification?

- Have the perimeter access points been identified and access addressed?
- Is there a designated staff recall reporting area?
- Have the controlled or restricted access areas been designated, and has the staff been notified about them?
- Is there special signage for these controlled areas?
- Damage assessment
  - Has appropriate training been provided that will allow security officers to assist facility management or engineering to assess damage, complete their reports, and make recommendations?
  - Is there a method to identify inspected and searched areas to avoid repetition of effort and expedite the process?
  - What will they be tasked with reporting initially?
  - Where will the information gathered be reported to, and to whom will the reports be disseminated?
  - Has the staff been trained to recognize the types of and motives for vandalism and sabotage?
- Traffic control
  - Is there a plan for managing the parking facilities?
  - Are officers aware of emergency access control procedures?
  - Is there adequate parking for all of the staff that will be recalled?
  - Is there adequate traffic control equipment and devices?
  - Is there an adequate number of officers to provide proper traffic control?
  - Are there supplemental personnel available?
  - Are there designated staging areas for cargo and supplies?
  - Are ambulance traffic patterns clear and posted?
  - Has consideration been given to removing injured personnel?
  - Has the safety officer been consulted for traffic safety considerations?
  - What considerations have been made for staging areas for mass casualties?
  - Are there provisions made for ancillary parking?
  - Are there provisions for the escorting and patrolling of parking areas?
- Specialized traffic control (air, marine, and large-vehicle traffic)
  - Is the facility accessible by specialized traffic?
  - Are there alternate areas available if the primary sites are impacted by the disaster?
  - Is the facility prepared to provide lighting for aircraft landing areas?
  - Are the personnel trained to communicate with watercraft, helicopters, etc.?

- Are officers trained to support loading and unloading operations?
- Has safety training been provided for these types of operations?
- Has training been provided to officers who must direct such traffic?
- Is there a special area designated for handling large-vehicle traffic?
- Is there signage available and ready for posting for traffic control?
- Crowd control
  - Is there a detailed protocol that states when to request law enforcement assistance?
  - What is the policy for managing looters?
  - What is the policy for managing unruly or combative persons?
  - Has a determination been made on how to use volunteers?
  - How will staging areas for cargo or equipment be protected?
  - How and where will cargo and equipment be stored for the short or long term?
- Other considerations
  - What provisions have been made for the preservation and protection of high-security items?
  - What provisions have been made to maintain sensitive company information?
  - Are there provisions to safeguard company funds and business office documents?
  - Does the facility participate in establishing and maintaining a liaison with the emergency disaster team and the appropriate law enforcement and emergency service agencies?
  - Does law enforcement participate in training and drills?
  - Has a detailed list of tasks that need to be performed been prepared, and is it in an easy-to-follow form and available to the officers?
  - Does this checklist have priorities?
  - Have packets of maps and instructions been prepared for use by officers and supplemental personnel?

Emergency Medical Operations

Emergency medical operations provide for the care and treatment of ill and injured personnel. This function coordinates the operation of the multiple-casualty emergency management plan. It also is tasked with the procurement and allocation of medical resources. It is further tasked with the location, collection, and transportation of the injured. They produce status reports and make decisions regarding the commitment of resources.

Additional assistance requests are evaluated, and decisions are made by the incident commander:

- First aid and casualty collection points
  - Are there predetermined casualty collection points?
  - Are there dedicated staff members for these collection points?
  - How many patients can each point handle safely?
  - When and how frequently are the first-aid teams trained?
  - What level of training is provided (i.e., doctor, nurse, paramedic, or EMT)?

Preventive Medicine and Safety Operations

Preventive medicine and safety operations provide for public health, environment, and sanitation/environment services. This function coordinates, evaluates, and commits resources that are involved in safeguarding public health and safety considerations. Personnel evaluate status reports and communicate public announcements with regard to radiological, biological, and hazardous chemical spills and emissions in the facility. They also determine what additional resources are required and coordinate all such requests:

- Hazard identification and management
  - Do you have protective clothing and equipment for first responders?
  - Is there a list of the facility's hazardous materials available?
  - Is there adequate record keeping?
  - If applicable, do you have a radiological emergency response team?
- Sanitation
  - Is there any water stored?
  - Are there natural reservoirs for water identified?
  - What is the volume of your sources?
  - Is there a source for chemical toilets?
  - Do you have a human waste disposal plan to implement?

Assistance to the Coroner Operations

Assistance to the coroner operations identifies and provides appropriate disposition of human remains. This function coordinates the efforts required to accomplish these tasks. Personnel evaluate status reports, make decisions regarding the commitment of resources, and determine the need for additional assistance:

- Identification of remains
  - Have you compiled a disaster worksheet to address this need?

- Disposition of personal effects
  - Is there adequate record keeping?
  - Are there provisions to safeguard these belongings?
- Storage of remains
  - How and where will human remains be stored?

Staff Care and Shelter Operations

Staff care and shelter operations provide for the basic human needs of the staff. This function coordinates the procurement and allocation of resources required to support the mass care operation, to provide appropriate lodging and feeding facilities, to coordinate the staffing of a child care facility (if needed), to evaluate status reports, to make decisions regarding the commitment of resources, and to determine if additional assistance is required:

- Food service
  - Do you have preplanned disaster menus?
  - Is there a charge for staff meals during a prolonged disaster response?
  - Is food service available on a 24 h basis?
- Staff care
  - Are shift supervisors familiar with the process to monitor staff fatigue and stress?
  - Is there a staff-only lounge area?
- Staff child care center
  - How are the children identified?
  - Is there adequate and properly trained staff?
  - Is the area properly safeguarded?

Facility Relocation Operations

Relocation operations provide for the internal evacuation and relocation of persons from the threatened or affected areas of the facility. This function coordinates the movement of victims in the emergency relocation program, the movement of victims through casualty collection points and treatment centers, the evacuation of the affected areas of the facility, the evaluation of status reports, and decision making regarding the commitment of resources. Personnel decide what further assistance may be required:

- Transportation
  - Do you have a system for transferring personnel to more distant job sites?
  - Is this system independent of the use of contractors?
  - Are there provisions for round-trip transportation?

- Facility relocation
  - Where do you go if you must relocate?
  - What will it take to accomplish the relocation?
  - Who will work at the new location?
  - When will you return?
  - Will the new location provide suitable phone and electric service?
  - Will special equipment or services be required?

Internal Rescue Operations

Internal rescue operations carry out the coordinated search and rescue operations for the location; provide immediate care; and safely remove endangered, entrapped, injured, or isolated individuals. This function evaluates status reports, makes decisions regarding the commitment of resources, and determines the need for additional resources:

- Location of victims
  - How will you locate and mark areas where there may be trapped persons?
- Safety zones
  - Who will establish safety zones when the facility is damaged?
- Other considerations
  - Are maps and floor plans available for the use of emergency responders and search teams?
  - Are there designated people to serve as guides for rescue teams?
  - Have you designated an area to manage rescues from?

Facility Management and Plant Operations

Facility management and plant operations provide for the procurement, distribution, and use of construction and engineering resources. This function provides for emergency debris removal, shelter construction, damage assessment, and other engineering operations. Personnel evaluate status reports, make decisions regarding the commitment of resources, and determine the need for additional assistance:

- Damage assessment
  - Is the staff prepared to assist in the engineering damage assessment survey?
  - Is the survey equipment prepacked and readily available?
  - Is there adequate record keeping?
- Emergency repairs
  - What are the priorities for emergency repairs?
  - Who will authorize emergency repairs?

- Serviceability
  - What are the guidelines for serviceability?
  - With what damage can we still function?
  - Can computers and other equipment operate if there is no public power for up to 3 weeks?
  - What communications are available, and are they sufficient for the facility's needs?
- Other considerations
  - Are there emergency supplies and equipment?
  - Do employees know how to operate emergency lights?
  - Do employees know how to operate the emergency power system?
  - Do employees know how to work emergency communications systems?

Resource and Support Operations

Resource and support operations provide for the procurement, distribution, and use of essential resources and services. This function evaluates status reports, makes decisions regarding the commitment of resources, and determines the need for additional services. The coordinator is aided by support assistants from the following:

- Supply/procurement
  - Human resources
  - Transportation
  - Utilities
  - Finances

Resource and Support Operation Considerations

- Supply/procurement
  - Do supply carts have color codes for ease of identification and distribution?
  - Do you have sufficient emergency supplies on hand?
  - Do you have a reliable source for procuring additional supplies?
  - How will you allocate essential supplies, such as food, fuel, and medicine?
- Human resources
  - During emergency response, can you readily identify directors and department heads?
  - Do incoming personnel report to the various centers? Do they get assigned to services and duties they perform on a daily basis?
  - Have you identified persons with special communication skills (i.e., foreign languages, sign language, etc.)?

- Have you predetermined staffing requirements?
- Have disaster work schedules been devised?
- Do you have a means of badging and clearance for temporary workers or workers reporting without identification?
- Transportation
  - Have you established contracts with realistic expectations?
  - Do you have the resources necessary to move people, equipment, and supplies?
- Utilities
  - Is your facility targeted for priority restoration of services?
  - Do you have emergency services and telephone numbers built into planning packages?
  - Are you familiar with the emergency sources of the utilities?
- Finances
  - Have you documented the cost and containment of financial expenditures?
- Operational data
  - Will data such as rosters, source lists, and suppliers be readily available?
  - Will these data be easy to use?
  - Is the information updated on a regular basis?
  - Are special agreements and contracts included?
- Other considerations
  - Have you planned to use all of your major resources?
  - Have you identified the resources you have on hand?
  - Are they suitable for emergency responses and uses?

TESTING THE PLAN: TYPES OF EXERCISES AND THEIR PURPOSES

- Orientation—The focus of this training is to familiarize you with the emergency response plan.
- Discussion—The focus of this training is to evaluate the plan, detect possible problems, and resolve issues beforehand.
- Functional—The focus of this portion is to evaluate the plan in depth by looking into specifics and addressing gaps in task assignment, management conflicts, and potential problems. Effective training requirements are also evaluated along with timetables for accomplishing both primary and follow-up training.
- Full scale—This is the ultimate test of the plan, which includes exercises, movement of personnel and equipment, and the incorporation of internal and external resources.

- Exercises—These should be as realistic as possible and should be constructed in such a way as to allow for note taking and evaluation of performance of personnel and equipment.

CORPORATE RECOVERY FUNCTIONS

Recovery may take days, weeks, or months. The facility may be the only site affected or may be in the middle of a widely affected area. Recovery may have to be undertaken with diminished resources on the part of the company and the government. The vital functions of the company must be coordinated to not waste time or resources. The main goal must be to reestablish the viability and functionality of the business. Developing and implementing a mutual aid program will assist in a return to normalcy as soon as possible. Mutual aid is a voluntary agreement of cooperative organizations of industrial firms, business firms, and similar organizations within an industrial community to assist each other during an emergency. To accomplish this, various functions must be coordinated:

- Damage assessment/impact evaluation
- Cleanup and salvage operations
- Business restoration
- Customer/client information
- Mutual aid
- Agreement activities
- Governmental relations

DAMAGE ASSESSMENT/IMPACT EVALUATION

This team's actions refine initial assessments made immediately preceding the event. Team members collect the data that allow for the setting of priorities and guide other functions in setting up their goals and work schedules.

Information will assist in the filing of insurance forms and applications for government disaster aid.

This function should include the following:

- A comprehensive survey of the facility in conjunction with insurance underwriters and government officials
- Itemized lists of structural and nonstructural damage, including photographic documentation
- Determining the need for temporary relocation and a time frame for return to the facility

- Identifying the need for contracted services, labor, material, and restoration of operations
- A written summary of damage, cost estimates, and recovery schedules

CLEANUP AND SALVAGE OPERATIONS

This team oversees cleanup, including decontamination if necessary. Temporary dump sites should be established on the premises for debris. Also, there should be secure contractor support in supplementing the crew in the repair of damaged utilities, fire protection systems, and production equipment.

BUSINESS RESTORATION

This team should obtain and provide engineering and architectural drawings to personnel. Also, team members should provide guidance, support, and technical assistance to in-house and contracted personnel; notify utility companies of the extent of damage to the facilities and of service disruption; request assistance from utility companies in establishing minimum service levels; secure a minimum operating level of transportation to and from the facility; and post alternative addresses and phone numbers.

CUSTOMER/CLIENT INFORMATION

There should only be one person or team responsible for the dissemination of information, coordinating with the news media to provide the public with accurate information about service hours, locations, and any changes in procedure. Team members should provide general information to the public about the best way to use the company's goods or services during the recovery phase and should advise the general public and specific customers and clients about the progress being made to restore services.

MUTUAL AID AND AGREEMENT ACTIVITIES

Mutual aid is a voluntary agreement of cooperative organizations of industrial firms, business firms, and similar organizations within an industrial community to assist each other during an emergency. This team reviews agreements that may be applicable to overcome deficiencies; analyzes requests from other companies to determine the extent and type of assistance that can be provided; and negotiates with other mutual partners to obtain specific terms of the joint use of facilities or equipment, the lending or borrowing of equipment or personnel, and the joint acquisition of temporary facilities.

GOVERNMENTAL RELATIONS

This team obtains information on the extent and magnitude of the damage in the area; gets information about government recovery efforts in the area; obtains information on recovery aid available; assists in inspection and demolition and *hazmat* management; and obtains special permits.

LONG-TERM RECOVERY

1. Evaluate options for recovery of function rather than the facility.
2. Participate in community planning and decision making.
3. Develop a long-term recovery plan, objectives, schedules, resources, priorities, and management.
4. Maintain coordination with the public sector (i.e., city, county, and state).

PREPARING FOR RECOVERY

1. Review personal and business insurance to ascertain if you have adequate coverage and the proper kind of coverage, including business interruption insurance, that is up to date.
2. Make duplicate sets of business records and photograph the facility and grounds. Keep these in a safe, yet separate, area.
3. Make a list of all essential supplies and equipment required for operation. Remove these items first.
4. Analyze your space needs (what you can and cannot store).
5. Develop joint plans with suppliers, contractors, service providers, and your neighbors.
6. Become involved in community preparedness.

9 Guard Force Management

The proper, effective, and economic use of security officers is of great importance to the security professional. The most expensive budget item is usually personnel costs. Also, the most litigious area of security usually involves acts or failures to act by security personnel.

This chapter deals with the proper utilization of these personnel and looks at some of the management theories involved in dealing with personnel and the various factors that motivate them. Understanding these concepts and mastering the abilities to deal effectively with and supervise these employees are of utmost importance to every security professional.

The cost of manpower is the most expensive line item in most security budgets. The utilization of uniformed security officers accounts for the largest portion of that line item cost in most instances. Some of the costs attendant with the utilization of security officers are as follows:

- The direct labor cost (pay) of the officer
- Applicable local, state, and federal payroll taxes
- Workers' compensation insurance
- Liability insurance
- Employee benefit packages (i.e., sick leave, vacation pay, medical/health insurance, retirement plans, profit-sharing programs, reimbursement for certain educational costs, etc.)
- Recruitment
- Background investigations
- Specialized state licensing (if applicable)
- Uniform costs
- Training costs (initial and refresher)
- Supervision costs
- Overtime and holiday pay

As you can see, manpower costs can escalate your security budget out of sight.

These costs are the main reason the use of technology has become more prevalent over the past 20 or 30 years. Technology is a workforce multiplier.

The use of closed-circuit televisions (CCTVs), access controls, alarm systems, and security hardware (gates, fences, locking systems, safes/vaults, and detection equipment) has been growing for quite a while. As technology expands and becomes increasingly more sophisticated, business and industry will depend more on these items. Some of the benefits that these items have over the use of manpower are as follows:

- They save money (return on investment [ROI]—although more expensive initially, over time, they offer substantial savings).
- They do not call in sick.
- They do not take vacations.
- They remove the problem of human error.
- They can document incidents more efficiently (via recording video, audio, etc.).

No matter how much is saved and how much more accurate these security hardware items are, a certain amount of manpower will always be needed to complete the well-rounded, effective security system.

Security managers and directors must therefore be adept at recruiting, screening, training, and supervising a guard force in the most efficient and effective manner.

You must decide, first, on the makeup of your force. The three choices are as follows:

1. An all-proprietary force, also known as an in-house force
2. An all-contract force
3. A mixture of both (the most common being that supervision is in-house and the line officers are contract workers)

SETTING UP A PROPRIETARY GUARD FORCE

To create an in-house force, there are certain steps that must be taken. The first step in creating an effective and efficient guard force is to recruit qualified applicants. The old axiom that says cheap security is not good and good security is not cheap does have a lot of credibility. Budgetary restrictions are a reality that must be considered. However, quality personnel come at a price. Recruiting, interviewing, screening, and training personnel is very expensive. Therefore, it is in the company's best interest to retain officers and eliminate these turnover costs.

Second, evaluate what duties the officers will perform. Will they be required to have specialized skills? Will jobs be physically strenuous? Will jobs require above-average written or verbal skills? Third, what hours of coverage by security personnel will be required? Fourth, how much manpower per shift will be required? Fifth, will coverage on holidays and weekends be required?

Once these decisions have been made, the minimum qualifications that the applicants need to possess must be finalized. Only then can the position be advertised for applicants.

Prescreen the persons calling or coming in. Require full and complete applications to be filled out. Request résumés and documentation of training and military service.

Interview only the persons you believe will best serve your needs. If necessary, do a second interview with the best candidates. Consider having someone else do the second interview to gain his or her insight.

Once initial decisions have been made, perform comprehensive background investigations that should include criminal history, work history, educational/professional credentials, and references.

For some types of industries and positions, financial histories, polygraph testing, drug screens, and psychological testing may not only be prudent but also be required by law. Make sure you familiarize yourself with any applicable laws or regulations with reference to performing these checks. Your company's human resources and legal departments can be most helpful in this area.

Formulate comprehensive job descriptions, and post orders and company rules and regulations. All personnel must have a complete understanding of their jobs and the rules and regulations they will work under as well as the ones they will enforce.

All personnel should be required to learn all of the duties that each position requires. This will make personnel more useful in emergencies and better able to fill in if needed.

Document all training in writing. Formulate tests that officers must take and pass to document their understanding of their responsibilities.

Besides job-specific training, other areas that should routinely be taught are as follows:

- Patrol methods
- Report writing/field notes
- The laws involved with the use of force and the company policy governing the use of force
- Legal terminology
- Testifying in court
- Courtroom demeanor
- Dress code/hygiene
- Basic search-and-seizure law
- Limitation of the officer's authority
- Public relations
- Interaction with law enforcement

- Basic interview techniques
- Crime scene preservation
- Handling emergency situations
- Basic fire suppression
- Radio and telephone communications
- Company rules and regulations

If an officer must be armed with a firearm or other weaponry, specialized training in the use of such items is a must. All such training must be supplied by a certified instructor, meet all state and federal requirements, and be documented. Refresher training should be given on a regular basis, and that too must be documented.

If officers are required to carry firearms, then the following should also be done:

- Establish a written firearms policy that outlines the company's position on the carrying and use of firearms, what types of weapons officers may carry, and what calibers of weapons and types of ammunition are acceptable for duty use.
- Establish training criteria and a written lesson plan.
- If there are state training requirements, make sure that the training, policies, and procedures conform to those legal requirements.
- When selecting an instructor, check his or her credentials carefully; speak to other companies that have used his or her services; and make sure not only that he or she has the right credentials but also that his or her credentials and license are up to date.
- Require periodic refresher training and requalification at the shooting range. Such requalification should be done at a minimum of one time per year.

OTHER CONSIDERATIONS

INSURANCE

Almost all companies carry liability insurance policies for their protection. However, once a decision has been made to form an in-house guard force, a specialized set of different kinds of coverage must be put into place. These specialized kinds of coverage should include the following:

- False-arrest insurance
- Defamation of character
- False detention
- Assault and battery

Coverage Limits

Strong consideration must be given to increasing your coverage limits. Check with the carrier to ascertain if defense costs, in the case of a claim, will be deducted from the policy limit. Many claims can cost many thousands of dollars to defend against, and if these costs are deducted from the policy limit, it could leave the company with an exposure, especially if your policy limit was marginal to start with.

Exclusions

Read the policy over and have it reviewed by your company's legal/insurance personnel. Pay particular attention to the policy exclusions. Much of the coverage you require can be gutted out of the policy by exclusionary wording. Once again, this can leave the company with an area of exposure.

Rating of the Insurance Carrier

Check on the carrier's "best rating." This is a service that rates companies' financial stability and their record of fulfilling contractual commitments.

Is the carrier registered and licensed to conduct business in the United States and the state your business is in? Is it an offshore company? If the latter, this could mean that should there be a large claim, they could disappear or simply refuse to cover the claim. Suing a carrier in a foreign country is a daunting task, if not an impossibility.

Once officers are armed, expect insurance costs to rise, sometimes a great deal. A decision must be made if the need for weapons is great enough to require this additional expenditure.

Uniforms

Some states have imposed restrictions on the types and color schemes of uniforms that private security officers may wear. They may also require certain wording to be used on shoulder patches or ban certain words entirely. Similar restrictions may apply to types of badges and wording used on badges. This is done to help the public not to confuse a private security officer with a law enforcement officer. Before committing to making a large expenditure on uniforms, state requirements must be checked.

Vehicles

As with uniforms, many states have established laws regulating signage on security vehicles. This is especially true in regard to the installation and use of lights and light bars. Blue and red lights are almost universally banned for private use (except private ambulances). Most states require amber lights to be used. Some states allow blue and red lights to be used solely on private property, such as a large private community. In these cases, however, any blue and red lights must be covered when the vehicle is taken onto public streets.

COMMUNICATIONS

Communicating is the most important management skill and should be both ways, up and down. Especially when you have multiple officers on duty at any one time, communication between the individual officers and the security base station is most important. If the security staff must cover extensive areas, a repeater system may be required. Research the types of radios and systems available before making a purchase. Many times, when it comes to communication equipment, a "good deal" can turn out not to be so good after all. When subscribing to a repeater supplier, have them set two of your radios to the frequency you will utilize. Test them out for areas of coverage, dead spots, and clarity of transmission. Listen to the sideband and see what level of sideband usage is on that frequency. Too many heavy users can make it difficult to get onto the air.

Develop and use a standard code for radios. This will assist you in keeping your transmissions confidential and short.

Familiarize yourself and your staff as to the Federal Communications Commission (FCC) rules that regulate the use of the airwaves. There can be harsh penalties for violation of these rules.

SCHEDULING OF MANPOWER

One of the most stressful and, at times frustrating, jobs in guard force management is scheduling manpower. This is especially true in the contract guard industry, where historically, a great deal of personnel are scheduled to work a variety of shifts to meet a myriad of specialized and ever-changing requirements of the client companies.

There are three basic needs that the scheduler must always keep in mind. They are as follows:

1. All of the hours of coverage must be covered.
2. The personnel posted to various locations and times must be fully qualified and capable of performing their responsibilities properly.
3. Overtime situations should be avoided. Overtime or premium pay can drain a security budget and thereby tax a company's ability to maintain a financially stable position.

Usually, when dealing with a proprietary situation, scheduling is an easier task. There are two concepts to keep in mind:

1. To provide coverage on a 168 h schedule, which is one standard week of 24 h coverage 7 days a week, 4.5 persons will be required to cover that shift utilizing a standard 8 h shift.
2. When determining the amount of supervision that is going to be required, consider "span of control," how many individuals one supervisor can effectively supervise. The optimum span of control is one supervisor to every five officers. As a practical matter, this optimum level is seldom maintained. Ideally, one supervisor effectively supervises three individuals. A good ratio is one supervisor to six individuals, and it is acceptable for one supervisor to supervise twelve individuals.

CONTRACTING WITH AN OUTSIDE GUARD AGENCY

Many companies choose to use a contract guard agency to provide their guard force. On the whole, the deciding factors in using a contract agency are finances and flexibility. Many companies choose to use a contract service because of the savings. Some of those savings are as follows:

- No recruitment or licensing costs.
- No standard training costs. Specialized training may be an added cost, however.
- No payroll taxes and insurance costs.
- No benefit package costs.
- No costs for providing uniforms.
- Many times, contract companies will not charge extra for communication equipment.
- No supervision costs.
- No costs for report forms or daily log forms.
- No bookkeeping or payroll preparation costs.

Some of the other benefits a company derives from using contract security are as follows:

- Total flexibility in changing out personnel and adding or reducing manpower for slow or peak periods.
- More flexibility in emergency situations.
- The ability to have professional management available without having to have a security professional on staff.

- Most agencies will offer a wide variety of ancillary services (i.e., investigations, undercover operatives, background investigations, etc.).

Some of the negatives about using contract security are as follows:

- The officers are not the company's employees, and they may not be as loyal to the company.
- Most people believe they are not as well trained as in-house personnel.
- Contract officers' pay and benefits are usually lower than those of in-house officers, and they are therefore considered less qualified.
- Turnover of personnel is usually higher.

Sadly, these perceptions are true in many cases. However, they can be overcome if there is an understanding between the client and the contract provider and the client is willing to provide to the contractor the finances necessary to combat these deficiencies.

NEGOTIATING WITH THE CONTRACT COMPANY

When a decision has been made to use a contract company to provide security service, the first step is to make a list of those companies to be contacted. Ask others in the industry for recommendations on contract services that they are using or have used in the past. Obtain references and check them out. The following are some questions that should be asked of the contract company:

- How long has the company been in business?
- Is the contract company properly licensed per state law to provide services?
- Is the company insured to provide the service needed?
- Are the insurance limits sufficient?
- What is the rating of the insurance company that provides the coverage?
- Does the company carry workers' compensation insurance?
- What does the company's screening process consist of?
- What does the training program consist of?
- Can you monitor one of these training classes?
- Is specialized training available?
- What is the professional background of their instructors?
- Does the company have past legal problems?

- Is the company listed with the Better Business Bureau, the state licensing entity, and civil court records?
- If the contract is a very large one, does the company have the financial resources to successfully meet the contract requirements?
- Does the company maintain supervision at all times?
- What does the company use for communications between their supervisors and their officers in the field?
- How often will your site be checked by supervisors? By management?
- What is the availability of additional officers in case of an emergency?
- What other ancillary services does the company provide?
- Is the company willing to name the company as an additionally insured party and hold it harmless in the service agreement?
- How long is the term of the service agreement?
- Is there a reasonable escape clause in the service agreement?
- Are unacceptable personnel allowed to be changed out ? How long does such a change take to accomplish?
- What type of benefit package does the company offer personnel? (This may impact the stability of their force.)
- What rate of pay will the company give to officers and supervisors (if applicable)?

The information needed from the contract agency is extensive. The time to ascertain this information is before the dotted line is signed, not afterward.

Obtain copies of all licenses and insurances required. *Trust, but verify.* Make sure copies of the additionally insured certificate name your company property and are reviewed by the company legal advisor. The legal advisor will advise you if any special wording is required.

Although price is always a consideration, it should be matched to what you are getting for your money. Too often, price is the sole determining factor and not the quality of the officers and the service.

BLENDING IN-HOUSE AND CONTRACT SERVICES

Many times, this is the best of both worlds. Some companies have in-house supervisors and blend them with contract line officers. This affords the savings that contract service provides and still allows for tighter, daily control by having in-house supervision there to watch over things.

Some problems may occur when the two forces are added together:

- Many times, the in-house officers will consider themselves better than the contract officers and will pass off less desirable tasks to the contract officers.

- In-house personnel can, at times, become paranoid about the contract officers, believing they are going to replace them.
- There can be a sizeable difference in pay and benefits between in-house and contract security.

If the security manager or director keeps these potential problems in mind and effectively handles them ahead of time, they can either be done away with or kept to a minimum.

NEED FOR EFFECTIVE COMMUNICATIONS IN SECURITY

There are a number of benefits that a company can gain from having a well-functioning security program. Some of these benefits include the following:

- Reduction of losses due to theft, both internal and external
- Reduction of losses due to vandalism
- Identification of safety and security hazards before they become losses
- Deterrence and prevention of unauthorized persons on the property
- The ability to quickly and more effectively respond to emergencies
- Investigation and elimination of losses due to frivolous lawsuits and phony workers' compensation claims
- Available information to management about potential problems, lazy and ineffective personnel, and other situations before they become major problems
- Prevention of crimes against persons on the property
- Identification and elimination of substance abuse on the property and the problems and losses that those activities produce

Even if an officer does an outstanding job, many times, the work done does not accomplish what it could have if it was reported to the appropriate authority. Management, if kept abreast of what the security department is truly accomplishing, will become much more amenable to providing the financing needed to keep the department properly funded and able to be much more proactive in preventing losses and problems.

There are three reporting mechanisms routinely used:

1. The daily activity report or log report. This is a chronological report that is written by each officer on each day in which he or she logs all of the duties performed, incidents that occurred, and observations made during assigned shifts.

2. Field notes. These are notes that the officer makes in his or her pocket notebook. These notes are very important in that they help avoid forgetting to put something into the log report or inadvertently giving incorrect information. Observations recorded in the officer's field notebook, although believed to be minor in importance at the time, can become extremely important later. For instance, a license plate number can become an important investigative lead for the police or security department investigators. Notes can also be saved and become useful later in preparing for various court, arbitration, and administrative hearings.
3. The incident report. This is written on a specific incident of importance. Usually, this is a form that is generic enough to be used for many types of reports. Some companies will construct specific forms for various kinds of incidents, such as on-site injuries, accidents, thefts, workers' compensation reports, incidents of vandalism to company or employee property, etc.

There should always be a clearly defined system for how information is conveyed throughout the organization. A report of maintenance deficiencies is of no real use if the maintenance department is not informed of the problems.

The security department should retain a copy of all incident reports. These will become important for two reasons:

1. If the officer who took the report must, at a later date, testify in court or another proceeding, he or she will have a copy of the report available to refresh his or her memory.
2. When the security manager or director has to produce a report to upper-level management about the efficiency and productivity of the department, the facts and figures he or she will require will be readily available.

INTERFACING WITH THE SECURITY CONTRACTOR

Communications between the client company and the security contractor are vital to the success of the operation. Communications must be held on a regular basis and must be honest and open.

Too many times, both the client and the security contractor will try to keep information from each other. This practice is to both of their detriments. Only through honest, open communication can trust be gained and problems solved. Both sides must endeavor to see situations from the other's perspective. Neither side should have unreal expectations of what can be accomplished. The goal of both should be to achieve the best possible security. If this goal can be obtained, both sides will benefit.

DISCIPLINARY PROCEDURES

Discipline is essential to the proper and orderly running of any organization. There will be times that disciplinary measures must be taken for violation of rules and policies. The security manager or director must be sure that all such measures meet the following criteria:

- Be legal and ethical
- Be in proportion to the offense
- Not single out one person and thereby create a situation where a discriminatory practice is created
- Be progressive
- Allow the employee a fair opportunity to state his or her side of the situation
- Not be capricious
- Be fully documented
- Allow for an officer to be rewarded in public and reprimanded in private

All rules of conduct should be in writing, should be given to the employee upon starting work, should outline all disciplinary actions that may be taken for each infraction, and should outline the employee grievance procedure available to the employee.

CONCLUSION

Guard force management is not difficult in concept but is, at times, difficult in practice. Certain skills must be mastered; rules, regulations, and laws must be learned and followed; and the interpersonal skills required must be honed. The successful security manager or director knows how to accomplish the technical portions of his or her job, how to communicate well with company management and his or her employees, and how to inspire all employees to do the best jobs they are capable of doing.

The Certified Protection Professional (CPP) exam, in the area of guard force management, is designed to measure your grasp of these concepts and skills. Many security managers and directors, at one time or another, are tasked with managing a guard force. Therefore, the concepts and skills that are tested throughout the CPP exam are extremely important to all management personnel in the security field.

10 Legal Aspects as They Relate to the Security Field

This topic, in some cases more than any other, reaches into and affects all of the other domains included in the Certified Protection Professional (CPP) exam. Even if the security professional does the right thing but in the wrong way, it can become a disaster for all involved. It can leave the security professional and the management of the company open to lawsuits and even criminal sanctions.

In taking the exam, one must guard against answering questions on the state level. The exam is set up not to reflect the laws of any specific state but as an overview of the federal laws and basic concepts of criminal and tort law as a whole. Those preparing for the test in Canada or the United Kingdom must look to their countries' laws for guidance in preparing for the exam.

The legal aspects portion of the CPP exam is one of the most important disciplines of the test. The legal aspects section impacts every other portion of the test. Whether the CPP is conducting an investigation, setting physical barriers, administering a guard force, or negotiating and administering a contract, the security manager or director must make sure that everything is completed and accomplished in a legal and ethical manner. The criminal and civil liability of the company and the individual employee can be great if their actions do not adhere to the legal restraints of the company.

The legal aspects portion of the CPP exam is designed to measure knowledge and understanding of the laws under which you must conduct your operations. One of the things you must guard against is answering the questions based on state, local, or provisional laws. The CPP exam is written in such a manner that these local laws should not be taken into account. The test looks to a broader, more national view of laws and concepts.

BASIC CONCEPTS OF CRIMINAL LAW

What is law? Some answers to that question would be as follows:

- That which must be obeyed
- A statute
- The body of principles, standards, and rules put out by a government
- A set of regulations governing the relationship between man and his fellow men and between man and the state

A crime can be defined as follows:

- Any violation of a government's penal law
- An illegal act or failure to act
- A public wrong
- An act or omission forbidden by law for which a state prescribes a punishment

Whether a wrong will be considered a crime or a civil tort is determined solely by the legislature or another governing body. There is often only a fine line distinguishing one from the other.

There are two main purposes of criminal law:

- It attempts to control the behavior of human beings.
- It punishes the violator.

Punishments for violations of criminal law can be one of the following:

- A fine
- Imprisonment
- Death

Common law is defined in a number of ways, such as the following:

- Judge-made law as opposed to statute
- Law that has its origin in England and grows from ever-changing customs and tradition
- Unwritten law from England

All criminal laws in the United States come from four basic sources:

- Old English common law
- Federal and state constitutions

- Laws passed by federal or state legislatures
- Court decisions

The legal principle of *stare decisis* goes hand in hand with the development of English common law. It is defined as follows:

"Let the decision stand"—it is a legal rule that holds that when a court has decided a case by applying a legal principle to a set of facts, courts should stick to that principle and apply it to all later cases with similar facts, unless there is a good strong reason not to.

It is also known as the law of precedence.

A number of states have abolished common-law offenses, but in the majority of the states common law survives in some manner.

The value of common law today is that states, known as common-law states, have the advantage of being able to look back into the common law to ascertain if an offense exists when no statute covers the alleged crime. Common-law states may look to common law for definitions and other meaningful explanatory information.

All criminal laws of the federal government are statutory: None are common-law crimes. The federal judiciary has no power to exercise common-law jurisdiction.

Crimes are classified in a number of ways:

- *Mala in se* crimes are crimes that are bad in and of themselves, such as murder and rape.
- *Mala prohibita* crimes are those crimes that are forbidden by statute.
- Treason is included as a separate category of crimes because it is considered to be the most serious of all crimes, as it threatens the existence of the state itself.

A felony is defined in many different ways:

- Under federal law, a felony is any crime for which the penalty is death or imprisonment for a period exceeding 1 year.
- Some jurisdictions define it merely as a serious crime.
- Each jurisdiction is able to label the crime as it sees fit. What is considered a felony in one state may not be a felony in another state.

A misdemeanor is any crime carrying a penalty of 1 year or less of imprisonment.

Ex post facto laws are prohibited by Article I, sections 9 and 10, of the US Constitution. These are laws that attempt to criminalize actions that were not crimes when they were committed. Violations of ordinances are often called quasi-criminal in nature. *Corpus delicti* is defined as the body of the crime. The combination of the elements that constitute the proof of a crime is the corpus delicti.

Jurisdiction is defined as the geographical area within which a court has the right and power to operate. It is the power of a court to handle a case. Trial courts are considered to be courts of original jurisdiction.

Extradition is defined in Article IV of the US Constitution as follows:

> A person charged in any state of Treason, felony or other serious crime who shall flee from justice and be found in another state, shall on demand of the Executive Authority of the state from which he has fled be delivered up to be removed to the state having jurisdiction of the crime.

Entrapment is when officers or agents of the government lead or induce a person to commit a crime not contemplated by the accused.

The venue is the place at which the crime was committed.

A bill of attainder is a legislative act directed against a particular person, pronouncing him or her guilty of a crime without allowing or providing a court trial. Section 9 of Article I of the US Constitution provides that "no bill of attainder" or *ex post facto* law shall be passed.

Double jeopardy is the situation that occurs when a person is prosecuted a second time for the same crime after having been found not guilty the first time. The US Constitution expressly forbids double jeopardy.

BASIC ELEMENTS OF A CRIME

In every case where a conviction is expected, the prosecution must prove the following:

- That a specific kind of legally forbidden harm or injury has occurred
- That the criminal act of some individual has caused this harm
- That the accused person on trial is the person who caused the harm

The *corpus delicti* of every true crime is made up of three basic parts:

- *Mens rea* (criminal intent)
- *Actus rea* (the criminal act)
- The coming together of the criminal intent and the criminal act

POSSESSION

As a general rule, someone who commits a crime must be conscious and knowing of the crime before it is punishable.

The following methods are used to commit an act, which is an element of a crime:

- By the offender's own hand
- Through an inanimate agency, such as sending a bomb through the mail
- Through an innocent human agent
- Through a nonhuman agency such as an animal

A crime may be committed by either doing an affirmative act or doing nothing. In either case, an evil state of mind must be proved.

For there to be a crime, there must be a direct causal connection between the criminal intent and the criminal act. This is known as the law of causations.

Several legal principles apply in cases involving the law of causations. A person is presumed to intend the natural and probable consequences of his or her act. For example, X hits Y, not intending to kill him. But Y has just had heart surgery and dies from the blow struck by X. X can be charged with homicide.

The prosecutor must prove that the defendant's act was the proximate cause of the harm suffered by the victim.

The methods of proving probable cause are as follows:

- Showing a direct cause
- Showing the defendant put in action a chain of events that led to the harm
- Showing the act of the accused placing the victim in a position that substantially increased the risk to the victim of being harmed by another cause

Another basic part of the crime is criminal intent, referred to as *mens rea*. As a general rule, most crimes require a combination of an act and intent, which must be simultaneous. The accused person cannot escape criminal responsibility by repenting after the act. Motive is not an essential element of the crime.

The legal principle of "transferred intent" is the term applied to a situation when an individual intends one criminal wrong but accomplishes another, and the law says the necessary criminal intent for the act is present by means of "transfer" from the original to the second act.

Intent is divided into two categories:

- General intent
- Specific intent

As a general rule, *mens rea* is all that is needed in most cases.

On the other hand, specific intent cannot be presumed but must be proved as any other element of the crime. Some examples are as follows:

- Burglary
- Robbery
- Larceny
- Illegal abortion

Recklessness is another wrongful state of mind of a lesser degree than intent, but nevertheless, it is still criminal.

Negligence is another mental element sometimes involved in criminal liability. There are generally considered to be four elements of negligence:

- A standard of care
- A breach of that standard
- Proximate cause
- Harm or injury produced

Criminal negligence is sometimes called gross or culpable negligence.

The test used in determining whether the person owing the duty met the required standard of care is the test of the "reasonable man." This test determines if the accused employed the same amount of care that a reasonable and prudent person who was exercising ordinary caution would have used under similar circumstances.

Negligence differs from recklessness in that recklessness is governed by the actual state of mind of the accused.

If conduct is grossly negligent, the same conduct can render a person both criminally and civilly liable.

Mala prohibita offenses, which are wrong only by statute, require no proof of intent. The mere accomplishment of the act is sufficient for criminal liability. Examples of *mala prohibita* offenses are as follows:

- Illegal sale of alcoholic beverages to a minor
- Sale of adulterated drugs
- Traffic violations

Mala prohibita crimes are sometimes called strict-liability crimes.

DEFENSES THAT OFTEN EXCUSE CRIMINAL RESPONSIBILITY

In legal terminology, the conditions that excuse individual responsibility for acts that the courts otherwise regard as criminal acts are called defenses.

Insanity is a legal defense in criminal cases. Note that insanity is a legal concept, not a medical one. A person is presumed to be sane at the time he or she commits a crime.

The major tests used in law to determine insanity are as follows:

- The M'Naughten rule, also known as the "right–wrong" test
- The irresistible impulse test
- The Durham rule
- The Model Penal Code of "substantial capacity"

Under the M'Naughten test, a person is excused for a criminal act if by reason of a diseased condition of the mind, the following exists: The person is unable to understand the nature of the act, or the person understood the nature of the act but still lacked the capacity to decide whether the act was right or wrong.

The irresistible impulse test for insanity is whether by reason of a mental disease, the accused had so far lost the power to choose between right and wrong that he or she was unable to avoid doing the act in question.

The Durham rule for insanity provides that the accused is not criminally liable if his or her unlawful act was the product of mental disease or mental defect.

The Model Penal Code states that the accused is legally insane if he or she "lacks substantial capacity either to appreciate the criminality of his conduct or to conform his conduct to the requirements of the law." Regardless of the test used to determine whether legal insanity exists, all tests operate on the premise that the accused is unable, due to mental illness, to form the intent necessary to commit a crime. The law does not recognize degrees of insanity. One is either insane or sane.

Another common defense is an alibi. In actuality, the alibi defense is one of physical impossibility. The testimony of an alibi witness must cover the entire time of the crime.

Another defense under certain circumstances is that of intoxication. Voluntary intoxication ordinarily is *not* a defense. Involuntary intoxication ordinarily is a defense.

Another defense is infancy. The key points of this defense are as follows:

- In common law, a child under 7 years of age is conclusively presumed incapable of formulating criminal intent.

- If a child is between the ages of 7 and 14, a rebuttable presumption goes into effect that the child is incapable of committing a crime.
- Children over 14 years of age are presumed capable of forming criminal intent.

The statute of limitations is another legal concept affecting criminal responsibility. The key points are as follows:

- In common law, there is no statute of limitations on prosecuting one guilty of a crime.
- Most jurisdictions today place no limitations on prosecuting for murder.
- In most states, statutes have been passed providing the state with only a certain amount of time to initiate the criminal process after a crime has been committed.
- A statute usually does not run out when the accused is a fugitive from justice.

Another defense sometimes used is "mistake of fact." The key points are as follows:

- The defense is used when one commits a violation of the law in good faith with a reasonable belief that certain facts existed that would make the act innocent.
- The mistake must be an honest one.
- There are three situations when mistake of fact will not operate as a defense:
  1. *Mala prohibita* misdemeanors not requiring intent
  2. Where the accused intended to commit a wrong but did not intend certain consequences of the act
  3. Where the culpable negligence of the accused brought about the crime

On the other hand, ignorance of the law is no excuse and is not allowable as a defense.

Another defense often used is entrapment. This could happen when government officials or their agents induce a person to commit a crime that the person would not have committed without the inducement. It does not extend to acts induced by a private person who is not an officer of the law.

Consent is also a defense under certain circumstances. There are four elements to the defense of consent. They are as follows:

1. The person giving consent must be capable of doing so.
2. The offense must be of the type for which consent can be given.
3. Consent cannot be obtained by fraud.
4. The person giving consent must have the authority to the commission of the crime.

Duress is another defense. The duress must involve a threat against the person. The threat must be a present one. As a general rule, the type of duress that will excuse a person who commits a crime must be the kind of threat that will induce a well-grounded apprehension of death or great bodily harm if the act is not done.

Necessity is also a defense. It is often confused with duress. Before this defense is allowed, the courts sometimes require two elements to be present:

1. The harm the accused was trying to prevent should be greater than the harm caused.
2. The accused must have exhausted all lawful alternatives or be able to show why the alternative could not be used.

In a criminal trial, guilt must be proven beyond a reasonable doubt, whereas in a civil action, proof only has to be a preponderance of the evidence. In the event that a defendant is convicted in a criminal trial, he or she could be placed on probation—released under certain conditions for a specific period of time; placed on parole—released from confinement under certain conditions after serving a period of confinement; or incarcerated.

Selective enforcement of the law can be used by the defense. To use this, the defendant must show two things:

1. A broader class of people than those prosecuted has violated the law.
2. The failure to prosecute was consistent and deliberate.

LAWS REGARDING ARREST

The law places severe limitations and restrictions on the exercise of the power of arrest by a law enforcement officer. The Fourth Amendment of the

US Constitution protects individuals from not only unreasonable searches but also illegal seizures of their persons, which means illegal arrests.

An arrest was defined by the state of Maine's Supreme Court in 1965 as "the apprehension or detention of the person of another in order that he or she may be forthcoming to answer for an alleged or supposed crime."

The basic elements necessary to constitute an arrest are as follows:

- A purpose of intention to make the arrest
- An actual or constructive seizure or detention of the person to be arrested
- A communication by the arresting officer to the arrestee of his or her intention to place the person under arrest
- An understanding by the person who is being arrested that he or she is being arrested

The following are examples of what are not technically arrests:

- Restraining a person who is behaving in a way possibly dangerous to himself or herself or others
- Services of a subpoena or summons
- Restraining an insane person to protect him or her or others from harm
- Asking a witness or suspect to appear at an office for questioning
- Stopping a vehicle to inspect a license, registration, or equipment
- The ordinary stop-and-frisk situation

The mere words of an officer, such as "you are under arrest," without anything else will not be sufficient to satisfy the seizure or detention element of the arrest.

Arrest Authority under a Warrant

The preferred authority for arrests is with a warrant as it places determination of probable cause in the hands of an impartial judicial authority. If a warrant is proper on its face and the officer acted within the scope of his or her authority in executing the arrest, the officer is protected against civil liability for false arrest.

Probable cause exists when the facts and circumstances within a person's knowledge of which he or she had reasonable trustworthy information are sufficient to warrant a person of reasonable caution and prudence to believe that an offense has been committed or is being committed.

Arrest warrants must conform to the following requirements:

- The warrant must bear the caption of the court from where it is issued.
- The person to be arrested must be named in the warrant, or if the name is not known, the warrant should contain enough identifying data by which he or she can be identified with reasonable certainty.
- It must describe the offense charged in the complaint.
- Time of issuance of the warrant should be stated.
- It should be directed to the proper officer for service.
- It must be signed by the issuing magistrate and must state his or her official title.

There is a difference between a warrant and a summons. The summons directs the defendant to appear before a court at a stated time and place, rather than ordering his or her arrest, which is done by a warrant.

ARREST AUTHORITY WITHOUT A WARRANT

As a general rule, a law enforcement officer may make an arrest without a warrant for a misdemeanor only when it is committed in his or her presence. If the offense was not committed in the officer's presence, he or she may not arrest the alleged offender without a warrant.

As a general rule, a law enforcement officer may make a warrantless public arrest for a felony if he or she has probable cause to believe that a felony has been committed by the person being arrested. If the officer making the arrest has probable cause to believe that the defendant has committed a felony, it makes no difference whether the officer was right or wrong in making the arrest. It was still a legal arrest.

Pertinent points with regard to effecting the arrest are as follows:

- Ordinarily, the officer should have a warrant in his or her possession when arresting someone.
- A law enforcement officer may request a private citizen to help in making an arrest. Some state laws require citizens to comply with these requests.
- When a private citizen aids a known law enforcement officer, he or she has the same rights and privileges the officer has. Thus, he or she is protected from liability.

CITIZEN'S ARREST AUTHORITY

A police officer operating out of his or her own jurisdiction is governed by the common law regarding citizen's arrests. As a private citizen, the officer has the same authority as any other private citizen to make an arrest without a warrant.

Under common-law rule in force in most states, a private citizen has the authority to arrest any person whom he or she has probable cause to believe has committed a felony. However, he or she can justify the arrest only by further showing that the felony was committed.

The private citizen acts at his or her own peril in making an arrest if no felony has been committed, whereas a police officer is protected if probable cause existed. A private citizen, under common law, has the right to make arrests for felonies and "breach of the peace" misdemeanors committed in his or her presence.

Use of Force in Making an Arrest

The general rule is that an officer who is making a lawful arrest may use only the amount of force that is reasonably necessary to secure and detain the offender, as well as the following:

- Overcome the offender's resistance to the lawful arrest
- Prevent his or her escape
- Retake him or her if he or she does escape
- Protect himself or herself from harm

Some of the facts and circumstances to be considered in determining the amount of force to be used are as follows:

- Nature of the offense
- Defendant's reputation, if known
- Availability of help
- Presence of any weapons
- Defendant's words or actions

The more serious the offense, the greater the latitude on the part of the officer in using force.

The common-law rule as to the amount of force that can be used to arrest for felonies is as follows. The officer is not required to retreat but must stand his or her ground in order to effect the arrest. Deadly force, however, is to be used only as a last resort when the officer is threatened with deadly force. There has been much criticism of the common-law rule with regard to the use of deadly force in felony cases.

The Model Penal Code adopted the following rule with regard to the use of deadly force. Deadly force is *not* justified unless under the following conditions:

- The arrest is for a felony.
- The persons effecting the arrest are authorized to act as peace officers or are assisting a person whom they believe to be authorized to act as a peace officer.
- The user of force believes that his or her use of force creates no risk to innocent parties.
- The person making the arrest believes or knows that the person being arrested has used deadly force or threatened to use it and, if he or she is not taken into custody, will use deadly force on someone.

It is important to remember that the law regarding the use of force is not clear-cut. Carefully study the statutes and laws in your jurisdiction as well as the rules and regulations of the department and company.

Self-Defense

One may use as much force as is reasonably necessary to defend one's self. Deadly force is justified only when death or serious injury is threatened and is imminent. Some states' laws require you to retreat before using deadly force; some do not. Study the laws in your individual state.

Resistance to Arrest

The most common cause for an officer to use force is the resistance to arrest by the person being arrested. Mere flight does not constitute resistance to arrest. Under the common-law rule, the offense of resisting arrest requires that the arrest be lawful. According to common law, a person faced with an illegal arrest has the right to resist and use reasonable force to prevent harm to himself or herself. Deadly force is rarely justified for resistance to an illegal arrest.

Use of Deadly Force to Prevent Escape

The use of deadly force to prevent an escape is almost never justified. The use of deadly force to prevent the escape of a prisoner must be considered carefully. The officer must believe there are great risks of death or great physical harm to himself or herself or innocent persons in the area.

Entering a Dwelling to Effect an Arrest

In common law, an officer has the right to enter any dwelling, with force if necessary, if he or she has the legal authority to arrest. The authority to enter a dwelling to arrest applies to misdemeanors as well as felonies. The trend today is to require a warrant to arrest within a dwelling unless exigent circumstances exist.

According to a 1970 District of Columbia Circuit Court of Appeals case, a warrantless entry of a dwelling to arrest could be justified if certain conditions exist:

- A grave offense was committed.
- The suspect is reasonably believed to be armed.
- The officer clearly has probable cause to arrest.
- There is strong reason to believe that the suspect is in the dwelling.
- The suspect is likely to escape if not swiftly apprehended.
- The officers can enter the premises peaceably.
- The officers can enter at a reasonable time of day.

The officer has the right to make a warrantless entry of a dwelling to arrest, but he or she must do the following:

- Knock
- Announce authority and purpose
- Demand admittance

In the following situations, failure to knock, announce, and demand admittance will be excused:

- When the officer's purpose is already known to the suspect
- When the officer's safety would be compromised by announcement
- When delay would permit escape
- When warning would allow for destruction of evidence

SEARCHES AND SEIZURES WITH A WARRANT

The basic legal requirements for a search come primarily from the Fourth Amendment. The definition of a search warrant is as follows:

A search warrant is an order in writing, by a Judge, in the name of the people, directed to a Law Enforcement Officer, commanding him or her to search for certain personal property and bring it before the judicial authority named in the warrant.

The preferable way of conducting a legal search is with a valid search warrant.

According to the US Constitution, the circumstances under which a search warrant may be issued are as follows:

- There must be probable cause.
- It must be supported by an oath or affirmation.

- The place to be searched must be particularly described.
- The things to be seized must be particularly described.

For a search warrant to be valid, the following requirements must be met:

- The proper official must issue the warrant.
- The proper official must have signed the warrant.
- A search warrant may be issued only for authorized objects. As a general rule, warrants may be issued for the fruits of the crime, instrumentalities of the crime, or contraband or property that might constitute evidence of the offense.
- A warrant must be issued on probable cause.
- A warrant must be supported by an oath or affirmation.
- The place and objects to be searched for and seized must be described.

In executing the warrant, the officer must follow these requirements:

- The warrant must be executed by the officer so commanded.
- The warrant must be executed within the time limits prescribed.
- Only necessary force may be used in executing the warrant.
- Prior notice and demand should usually be made before forcible entry is made.
- Only property described may be seized.
- The officer may only search where the property sought could reasonably be found.

If there is no provision in the statute concerning the execution of the search warrant, it must be executed in a reasonable time. It must require execution within 10 days. Some states require execution during the daytime. Others permit execution by night if special circumstances exist. As a general rule, the officer may take as much time as necessary to accomplish the search.

The US Code provides that in executing a search warrant, the officer has the authority to break both inner and outer doors if, after giving proper notice of authority, stating his or her purpose, and demanding entrance, he or she has been refused admittance.

In 1974, in the case of *U.S. v. Artier* (491 F. 2d 440 [2d Cir 1974]), the circuit court of appeals listed three exceptions to the requirement that the officer must knock and announce his or her authority and purpose and be refused before breaking in to execute the warrant. They are as follows:

1. When the person within already knows the officer's purpose and authority

2. When the officer is justified in the belief that people within are in imminent peril or bodily harm
3. When those within, aware of the officer's presence, are engaged in any activity that justifies the officer in the belief that an escape or destruction of the evidence is being effected

There are two main advantages of a search under a valid warrant:

1. The evidence obtained is more likely to be admitted.
2. The officer is protected when a search warrant is used.

There is no prohibition against executing a search warrant when the premises are unoccupied. The general rule is that the search warrant does not give the officer the right to search a person just for being on the premises. A search under a search warrant may extend to all parts of the premises described in the warrant, provided it is reasonable to assume items could be concealed therein.

The seizure of items not named in the warrant found during the lawful search will likely be held to be illegal if the following are true:

- Seizure was the product of an exploratory search.
- The items seized had no direct relation to the primary purpose of the search.
- The officer did not have probable cause to believe the items fell into one of the categories of the items subject to seizure.
- All of the requirements of the plain-sight doctrine had not been met.

The exclusionary rule is that evidence obtained illegally will not be admissible in court. There are four main exceptions to the application of the exclusionary rule:

1. It does not prevent the use of illegally seized items in the grand jury proceeding.
2. It does not prevent the use of these items for impeachment purposes in the trial.
3. It does not forbid the use of these items in civil proceedings in certain instances.
4. The evidence may be used if the defendant does not object.

PRIVATE SECURITY APPLICATIONS TO SEARCHES WITH A WARRANT

The provisions of the Fourth Amendment restrict only government agents. Therefore, where evidence is found and seized by a private person, without the knowledge or collusion of public law enforcement, the evidence will, most likely, be permitted to be used by the prosecution.

However, when a private person seizes evidence, he or she does so at great peril in some cases. Some of the hazards they face are civil liability, criminal liability, and personal danger.

If a private person seizes evidence to be used in a trial and is in any way connected to the police or acting as an agent of the police, the exclusionary rule would apply. In situations where private security is licensed under state law or deputized, there is a good chance that security will be held as public officials, and the exclusionary rule would apply.

SEARCHES AND SEIZURES WITHOUT A WARRANT

There are no provisions in the Fourth Amendment specifically authorizing a search without a warrant. The fact that we have legal searches without a warrant is due to court decisions.

The following searches and seizures may be made without a warrant:

- Incidental to the arrest
- Consent
- Movable vehicle
- By a private individual
- Under the plain-view doctrine
- Under the open-fields doctrine
- Under the no-standing doctrine
- Inventory searches of impounded vehicles
- Under stop-and-frisk situations

A search incidental to a legal arrest is permitted for two reasons:

1. To protect the arresting officer
2. To avoid destruction of evidence by arrested persons

Before an search incidental to an arrest can be made, the following requirements must be met:

- The arrest must be legal.
- Only certain articles can be seized, such as fruits of the crime, means by which the crime was committed, weapons to effect an escape, and evidence used in the commission of the crime.
- The search must be made at the same time as the arrest.
- The arrest must be made in good faith.

In making a search incidental to a lawful arrest, the following areas may be searched. As a general rule, a full search of the person may be made, and evidence may be seized even if it had no direct connection with the arrest. In 1974, the Supreme Court decision made in *U.S. v. Edwards* (415 U.S. 800) held that a search of an arrestee's clothes can be made after the arrest is made and he or she is placed in jail. In the case of *Chimel v. California* (395 U.S. 732 [1969]), the court ruled that when an arrest is made inside a building, a search of the immediate area is limited to where an arrestee could reach for a weapon or destroy evidence. If the arrest is made outside the residence, the search is limited to the person arrested and the immediate area where a reach could be made. In the case where the lawful arrest is made in a vehicle, the officer can search the person and his or her immediate area.

The burden of showing that the accused consented to a search is on the prosecution. To determine if rights have been waived, the courts have placed the following requirements:

- Consent must be voluntary.
- The extent of search is limited by the exact words of the one giving the consent.
- Consent may be withdrawn.
- The person giving consent must have the capacity to do so.

The plain-view doctrine holds that when an officer makes a legal arrest and can see, in plain view, contraband, instrumentalities of the crime, or other evidence, he or she may legally seize it.

The elements of the plain-view doctrine are as follows:

- The officer must be in a position in which he or she has a legal right to be.
- The officer must not unreasonably intrude on the person's reasonable right of privacy.
- The officer must actually see the item of evidence.
- The item must be in the open.
- It must be immediately apparent to the officer that the item is a piece of evidence to be seized.
- The discovery of the item must be inadvertent.

The open-fields doctrine is an exception to the rule that the officer must have a search warrant before making a search. In this regard, the courts have ruled that the Fourth Amendment does not apply to searches beyond the person's curtilage.

Evidence may be used, even if the search is proved to violate the Fourth Amendment, if it is used against someone who lacks the standing to challenge the search.

As a general rule, there is no legal prohibition concerning the use of evidence coming into the officer's possession as a result of an inventory search. If the search were ruled exploratory rather than inventory in nature, the evidence would be excluded.

The case of *Terry v. Ohio* (392 U.S. 1 [1968]) is known as the stop-and-frisk case. The court ruled that weapons are admissible when an officer frisks someone when detained for weapons.

As a general rule, the search of vehicles falls under the same legal principles as the search of fixed premises.

The Carroll doctrine, by which the courts allow warrantless searches of a vehicle when the officer knows or has probable cause to believe the vehicle contains items subject to seizure and exigent circumstances, does not permit a warrant to be obtained. The following requirements must be present before the Carroll doctrine may be invoked:

- It is impossible to obtain a warrant.
- There are no grounds for an arrest and, therefore, no grounds for a search incident to an arrest.
- Consent cannot be obtained.
- The officer must have probable cause.

PRIVATE SECURITY APPLICATIONS OF SEARCHES AND SEIZURES WITHOUT WARRANTS

There is very little law on the authority of a private person to make a search incidental to an arrest. The person cannot be a special police officer or commissioned. If so, the person is bound by existing case law. The prohibitions against unreasonable searches and seizures only apply to law enforcement officers or their agents.

Consent searches involving landlords and tenants hold that a landlord has no implied right to consent to search of the tenant's premises during the term of the tenancy.

Consent searches involving hotels and their guests and employees use the same rule as with landlord/tenant situations.

Consent searches involving hosts and guests have held that the host has the right to give consent for a legal search.

In consent searches involving employers and employees, the courts have ruled that all areas that the employee uses can be searched with the consent of the employer. In cases of lockers or locked desks, if the employer retained a master key, then he or she has the right to consent to the search.

With consent searches involving school officials and students, the courts have ruled that school officials have the right to consent to the search of students' lockers. However, with the issue of college students' dorm rooms, the courts have ruled the opposite.

The courts exercise a strong presumption against consent searches and place a heavy burden on the prosecution to show that consent was given voluntarily.

CONFESSIONS AND ADMISSIONS

No exception of the hearsay rule is better known than that of a confession. The Supreme Court has established strict rules pertaining to the admissibility of confessions. The definition of a confession is a statement or acknowledgment of guilt by a person accused of a crime.

A confession becomes hearsay when the person to whom it was made endeavors to repeat it on the witness stand. Prior to 1964, the principle test for the admissibility of a defendant's admission or confession in court was its voluntariness.

Under the totality-of-circumstances test for voluntariness, the following factors were considered:

- Promises made
- Threats made
- Brutality used
- The failure to bring the person before a magistrate
- Failure to warn the person of his or her right to keep silent

In June 1964, the Supreme Court decided a landmark case: *Escobedo v. Illinois* (378 U.S. 478 [1964]). The significance of this decision is that the Supreme Court did *not* follow the totality-of-circumstances approach. Instead, it took one circumstance that has come to be known as the Escobedo "focus-of-investigation" test. The court said, "When the process shifts from investigatory to accusatory when its focus is on the accused and its purpose is to elicit a confession... the accused must be permitted to consult with an attorney."

MIRANDA RIGHTS

In June 1966, *Miranda v. Arizona* (384 U.S. 436 [1966]) was decided by the US Supreme Court, which set forth the following requirements.

Whenever an individual is taken into custody or otherwise deprived of freedom of action by police authorities in any significant way, he or she must be given the following warnings before questioning takes place:

- He or she must be clearly and unequivocally informed of the right to remain silent.
- The warning of the right to remain silent must be accompanied by the explanation that anything he or she says can be used against him or her in a court of law.
- The individual must be informed of the right to consult an attorney and of the right to have the attorney present during any questioning.
- He or she must be told that if he or she cannot afford an attorney, one will be appointed by the court.

Under Miranda, a safe policy to follow is to give the warnings whenever there is any doubt whether or not they apply. To determine if the Miranda requirements are applicable, the officer needs to ask himself or herself the following:

- Is the defendant in custody?
- Are the statements a product of interrogation?
- Is the person asking the questions a law enforcement officer?
- Is the offense serious enough to require Miranda warnings?

If the answer to one of the above questions is in the affirmative, then the Miranda rule will usually apply.

Courts generally hold that questioning a suspect in his or her own home without arrest is not custodial interrogation unless coercion is used. Interrogation of a suspect in his or her place of business is usually held to be noncustodial.

The Miranda warnings apply only to custodial interrogations conducted by law enforcement personnel. Therefore, admission or confessions obtained by private individuals in response to interrogations are usually held to be admissible. However, the courts have universally held that law enforcement cannot use private persons to get around the Miranda warnings.

A confession that is obtained by the use of unlawfully obtained evidence or by an unlawful arrest is generally not admissible.

An admission is an act or declaration by the accused that is in some way incriminating to the accused.

Admission by silence, also sometimes referred to as an exception to the hearsay rule by the term "accusatory statements," may be introduced if the silence was in the presence of someone other than the law enforcement officer or other officers of the court.

DELAY-IN-ARRAIGNMENT RULE

If the officer "unnecessarily" delays taking the person apprehended before a judicial officer as required by state or federal law, a confession or statement made during the delay will not be admitted.

This rule is known as the McNabb–Mallory Rule because of the two primary cases that influenced it—*McNabb v. U.S.* (318 U.S. 332 [1943]) and *Mallory v. U.S.* (354 U.S. 449 [1957]).

The *corpus delicti* rule requires that the *corpus delicti* must be proved by independent proof, and a confession standing alone will not support a conviction.

Despite the court ruling, in recent years, confessions remain very important to law enforcement.

The following are instances where confessions may be admissible regardless of the technicalities of legal rulings:

- A confession, otherwise not admissible because of the Miranda decision, may be used to impeach the defendant if he or she takes the stand in his or her own defense.
- The Miranda warnings need not be given to a grand jury witness.
- If a private citizen obtains a confession, admission, or information without the encouragement or knowledge of a police officer, such voluntary information is admissible even if no Miranda warnings are given.
- Before a person can object to the use of a statement or confession on the constitutional grounds of failure to give the Miranda warnings, he or she must have *standing* to object. Therefore, if a person gives an otherwise illegally obtained confession in which he or she implicates a third person, that statement can be legally used against the third person.

Remember that the fundamental test with regard to the use of confessions or statements is the "free and voluntary" test.

PRETRIAL IDENTIFICATION PROCEDURES

Three terms are important with regard to pretrial identification procedures:

1. A *show-up* is the presentation of a suspect to a witness for the purpose of identifying the criminal.

2. A *lineup* is the presentation at one time of several persons, including the suspect, to a victim for the purpose of identifying the criminal.
3. A *confrontation* includes both show-ups and lineups and is considered to be any presentation of a suspect to a victim or witness for the purpose of identifying the perpetrator.

If a lineup or show-up is conducted before an indictment is returned on the suspect, he or she is not entitled to the presence or advice of counsel. At postindictment lineups or show-ups, the suspect is entitled to legal counsel. A criminal suspect is not entitled to the presence of counsel when a photographic identification procedure is held, no matter when it is done. No matter when the lineup or show-up or any other identification procedure is done, all efforts must be made to make sure the procedure is conducted in a fair manner and is not "suggestive." Fingerprinting and photographing a suspect for identification purposes does not violate the suspect's Fifth Amendment rights.

SPECIAL LEGAL ASPECTS OF PRIVATE SECURITY

CONSTITUTIONAL LAW APPLICATIONS

The Constitution says very little about the rights of private citizens in their relationships with other citizens. Most constitutional rights refer to the citizen's rights with regard to the government. But constitutional limitations do apply when the private security personnel act either in concert with or as agents of governmental law enforcement agencies. A security officer's authority is, most times, the same as any other private citizen. However, authority may be obtained through commissioning by a public law enforcement agency.

CRIMINAL LAW APPLICATIONS

Criminal law codes provide a source of power to the private security officer, as well as the requirement of restraint, especially in procedural matters.

Before a person can be convicted of a crime, all of the elements of the crime must be proved beyond a reasonable doubt. Therefore, each security officer must know and understand the elements of the crimes they will most likely encounter in his or her field of occupational responsibility.

The security officer must know two important concepts of criminal law:

1. Everyone is presumed to know the law.
2. A law must be so clear and understandable that an ordinary person will know what conduct is prohibited.

TORT LAW APPLICATIONS

A tort is a civil wrong done to another person. For an act to be a tort, there must be a legal duty owed by one person to another, a breach of that duty, and harm done as a direct result of that action. The primary source for the authority of private security officers and the restraints and limitations put upon them is tort law. Tort law varies from state to state.

Tort law defines certain limits for the conduct of private security personnel:

- An injured party may bring a lawsuit for damages caused by tortious conduct by a security officer.
- Tort law provides general parameters on reasonable conduct through case law precedents.

Negligence or absence of due diligence is the key to most cases involving a security officer. The standard used to ascertain if conduct constituted negligence is that of the reasonable man. However, the standard is higher when the conduct of certain professionals is involved and their special abilities or knowledge will be taken into consideration.

CONTRACT LAW

Doctrine of *Respondeat Superior*

This principle, which, in translation, means "let the master respond," is well established in common law.

In accordance with the principle of *respondeat superior*, the master is responsible for the actions of a servant while the servant acts on the master's behalf.

As a general rule, in-house security officers are servants, whereas contract security personnel are the employees of the supplying company and therefore may not be considered servants of the hiring company (client of the security agency).

The key to liability under contract law is whether the security officer is acting within the scope of his or her employment and commits a wrongful act. Some of the factors that determine if an employee is acting within the scope of employment are as follows:

- Was the offender hired to perform the act?
- Did it occur substantially within the authorized time and space limits of the employment?
- Was the offender motivated, at least in part, by a desire to serve his or her master?

In dealing with contract security companies, it would appear that if the hiring company engages in a total hands-off position with regard to the contract personnel, liability for their wrongful acts might be avoided in some jurisdictions. However, the legal concept of nondelegable duty must also be considered. This concept provides that there are certain duties and responsibilities that cannot be delegated to another, including a contract agency. Always consult your company attorney to keep abreast of all new legal developments.

ARREST AND DETENTION POWER OF PRIVATE SECURITY

As a general rule, the private security officer certainly does not have broad authority to detain or arrest.

Private security officers have three primary sources for their arrest authority:

1. Statutory and common-law provisions that authorize private citizens to make arrests
2. Statutes that grant shop owners and their agents power to detain and arrest
3. Statutes that grant private security officers arrest powers similar to public law enforcement, such as deputization

Today, as a general rule, a citizen may arrest without a warrant someone who commits a breach of the peace in the person's presence. The law regarding the authority of a private citizen to arrest for a felony varies from state to state.

State laws that authorize citizens to arrest in misdemeanor situations are even less uniform:

- The general rule is that a citizen may arrest for a misdemeanor committed in his or her presence.
- Some states do not allow a citizen to arrest for a misdemeanor under any circumstances.
- Some states allow a citizen to arrest for a misdemeanor if there are reasonable grounds to believe an offense other than an ordinance violation has been committed.

Special Laws Authorizing Merchants to Detain Shoplifters

Most states have enacted laws that authorize a merchant or employees to arrest or detain, upon probable cause, a person believed to have stolen merchandise.

Use of Force

There are three occasions where both public law enforcement and private security may legally use force against another: in self-defense, in defense of a third person, and to effect a legal arrest. In all of these cases, the amount of force used must be both reasonable and proportionate to the force used against the officer and, to some extent, to the severity of the crime committed. In all use-of-force situations, the amount of force used must meet the test of reasonableness under the prevailing circumstances.

As previously stated, more force can be used to effect a legal arrest on a felony charge than when making an arrest on a misdemeanor charge. Any force used in making an illegal arrest is illegal and would subject the law enforcement officer or security officer to both criminal and civil penalties. Their employers would also be civilly liable for their actions.

Therefore, great restraint and good judgment must always be exercised when considering the use of force.

In the case of an arrest for a misdemeanor, generally, the use of deadly force is forbidden except in self-defense situations. A public law enforcement officer has no requirement to retreat in such cases. Private security officers are, in most cases, required to retreat and resort to the use of deadly physical force if no other option is available. The retreat laws do vary from state to state.

Authority to Detain

The landmark case *Terry v. Ohio* (392 U.S. 1 [1968]) set forth the guidelines for the detainment of suspects by police. The Supreme Court upheld the authority of a peace officer to detain a person if unusual conduct is observed that leads an officer to reasonably conclude, in the light of his or her experience, that criminal activity may be afoot.

The decision of *Terry v. Ohio* does not apply to private security personnel, whose sole authority is that of private citizens. However, if the private security officer has been given the authority of a public law enforcement officer by statute, deputization, or license, then the authority of the police would accrue to the private officer.

Interrogation

A person who has been detained legally may be interrogated. However, he or she may exercise the constitutional right to remain silent. Any statements or confessions the detainee has made should be carefully scrutinized to make sure they were voluntarily given.

A private security officer who is not working under special authority of the state can interrogate a suspect without giving Miranda warnings.

Searches

Unless a security officer is working in concert with a police officer or has been given special authority by the state, he or she has no more right to search than any other citizen. The Fourth Amendment does not apply to searches by private persons. Evidence found in the course of a search by a private citizen is admissible and not subject to the exclusionary rule. The laws of search and seizure are not clearly defined for security officers. The search of employees' lockers, packages, or automobiles on the employer's premises is usually dictated by company policy and is part of the company employment contract.

LEGAL LIABILITIES OF PRIVATE SECURITY PERSONNEL

CRIMINAL LIABILITY

Because private security personnel, for the most part, act as private citizens, they have no more rights than average citizens. Actions taken in self-defense, if not justified, can lead to criminal charges for an officer.

As a general rule, only nondeadly force can be used to protect property. However, some states use a different standard when it comes to the defense of one's private dwelling. In some states, if a person has reason to believe that the suspect, if he or she gains entry, intends to commit a dangerous, violent felony, such as murder or rape, deadly force may be used.

CIVIL LIABILITY

Someone who commits a wrongful act against another is open to both criminal and civil penalties. The concept of tort liability operates basically on three principles:

- To compensate the victim for his or her loss
- To act as a deterrent for future conduct of the same kind
- To serve as evidence of society's disapproval of the wrong

The basic elements of intentional tort liability are as follows:

- A wrongful act
- By an action
- That brought about the intended result

Examples of intentional torts are as follows:

- Battery
- Assault

- False imprisonment
- Trespassing onto someone's land

Other torts are called "quasi-intentional" torts and include the following:

- Defamation
- Invasion of privacy
- Malicious prosecution

The basic concept in tort liability is negligence. Negligence is defined as the failure to exercise a reasonable or ordinary amount of care in a situation, which causes harm to someone or something.

As a general rule, in order for a person to recover damages from a negligence tort-feasor, the following elements must be proved:

- The tort-feasor acted negligently.
- The negligent act or reckless behavior was the cause of the loss suffered by the victim.

Gross negligence or reckless conduct shows a greater lack of concern for the rights of others than ordinary negligence. Where gross negligence is shown, punitive damages are available. This concept of negligence can have ramifications for companies that fail to investigate, train, and oversee their personnel.

Vicarious Liability for Torts

The pertinent points are as follow:

- Vicarious liability refers to indirect legal responsibility, as in an employer being responsible for the tortious acts of their employees.
- Under the doctrine of respondeat superior, any negligence of the agent is imputed to the principal, provided that the agent was acting within the scope of employment at the time the injury occurred.
- An employer may possibly avoid this liability if the employment contract is one of an independent contractor.

However, the employer can be held liable for the acts of an independent contractor if one of the following exists:

- The work contracted for is wrongful per se.
- The work contracted for is a public nuisance.
- The work contracted for is inherently dangerous.

- The act of the independent contractor violates a duty imposed on the employer by contract.
- The wrongful act by the independent contractor violates a statutory duty.

"Strict-Liability" Concept

In situations where the business being conducted is held to be "ultra-hazardous" or "abnormally dangerous," statutes have been passed that hold the employer responsible for all acts by their employees in their business.

The remedies provided by tort actions are as follows:

- An injunction to prohibit continuance of the wrongful conduct
- Special damages that are ascertainable as to an amount
- General damages that are not ascertainable as to the amount, such as pain and suffering
- Punitive damages to compensate for outrageous behavior

CONTRACT LIABILITY

A contract is defined as an agreement between two or more parties that creates an obligation to do or to not do a particular thing. Its essentials are competent parties, subject matter, a legal consideration, mutual agreement, and mutuality of obligation.

Contractual agreements are enforced by either a court action requiring a party to perform its obligation or assessment of money damages to compensate the injured party for the failure of the other party to perform its obligation under the contract.

Contractual liability is pertinent to private security in the following ways:

- The security company may be held liable for breach of contract.
- The private company that hires its own security employees will do so through employment contracts with its employees.

There are three primary types of contracts:

1. Express
2. Implied
3. Quasi

An express contract is an actual agreement of the parties, the terms of which are openly uttered or declared at the time of making it. An implied contract is one not created or evidenced by the explicit agreement of the parties but inferred by the law. A quasi contract is a legal fiction invented by common-law courts to permit recovery by contractual remedy in cases where, in fact, there is no contract but justice warrants a recovery.

Civil Liability for Violation of the Civil Rights Act of 1974 (42 USC [1983])

For private security personnel to be liable under this law, they must act under the color of law.

To state a valid claim under section 1983 of this act, the plaintiff must allege the following:

- The defendant deprived the plaintiff of a constitutional right or rights secured by the law of the United States.
- The deprivation was done under the color of law.

SELECTED CRIMINAL VIOLATIONS SIGNIFICANT TO THE SECURITY FUNCTION

- Larceny—The taking and carrying away of personal property of another with the intent to deprive the owner permanently of the property.
- Embezzlement—The conversion of personal property by a person to whom the property was entrusted.
- Uttering—When a person draws a check on an account knowing that there are insufficient funds to cover the check.
- Larceny by false pretense—Obtaining personal property of another with the intent of depriving them permanently by use of false pretenses in misrepresenting a past or present fact.
- Receiving stolen property—Receiving or concealing stolen property, knowing the property to be stolen.
- Robbery—The taking of something of value from a person through the use of force or fear of force.
- Extortion—The taking of something from a person through the fear of a future harm.
- Bribery—The attempt to influence a public officer in the discharge of his or her official duties by the offer of a reward or other consideration.
- Burglary—Breaking and entering or remaining in a building with the intent to commit a felony therein.
- Arson—The willful and deliberate burning of a dwelling or outbuildings of another. This also covers the burning of any building to defraud an insurer.

- False imprisonment—The unlawful restraint by a person of another.
- Kidnapping—The unlawful taking of a person against his or her will.
- Perjury—Deliberately and knowingly testifying falsely, under oath, to a material matter in a court proceeding. This also covers signing documents, under oath, which are known to contain falsehoods.
- Misprision of a felony—The active concealment and failure to report a federal felony in which the accused is not involved.
- Malicious mischief—The actual damage or destruction of property belonging to another and this being done voluntarily and knowingly.
- Trespass on real property—The unlawful violation of the person or property of another. Trespass is a tort as well as a crime.
- Homicide—The illegal and unjustified taking of a human being's life. Homicide can also be justified and legal, such as in self-defense or in wartime by armed forces. Lesser offenses include manslaughter and criminally negligent homicide.

BILL OF RIGHTS—PERTINENT POINTS AND CONCEPTS

The first 10 amendments of the US Constitution are known as the Bill of Rights. The key amendments from the security standpoint are as follows:

- The First Amendment provides for freedom of speech, religion, and press, and the right of peaceful assembly for redress of grievances.
- The Second Amendment prohibits the government from interfering with the right to keep and bear arms.
- The Fourth Amendment prohibits unreasonable search and seizure.
- The Fifth Amendment protects citizens against being compelled to testify against themselves; double jeopardy; being deprived of life, liberty, or property without due process; and being held for a serious crime without presentation to a grand jury for indictment.
- The Sixth Amendment provides for a speedy trial by an impartial jury, your right to be informed of charges against you, your right to present a defense, and your right to confront witnesses against you.
- The Seventh Amendment provides for a trial by jury.
- The Eighth Amendment prohibits excessive bail, excessive fines, and cruel and unusual punishment.

DUE PROCESS OF LAW

The Fifth and Fourteenth Amendments are considered the due-process amendments. Although the Supreme Court has not specifically defined due process, it has, in a number of cases, stated the following as fundamental rights coming within the purview of the due-process clauses:

- Freedom of speech and the press
- Unreasonable searches and seizures
- The right to have counsel
- The right against self-incrimination
- The right to have a jury trial
- Protection against double jeopardy

The legal aspects portion of the CPP exam, although not the largest as to the number of questions asked, is most likely the most important as to its impact on the security professional.

There is almost nothing that the security manager or director does that, in some way, is not impacted either directly or indirectly by the legal aspects we all work with every day. Therefore, as complete an understanding as possible should be the goal of every security person.

When taking the test, do not try to respond to the questions based on your state's laws and regulations. The test is *not* written in that fashion. The test relies on general, accepted legal concepts and terminology inherent to all legal matters.

11 Liaison

This chapter deals with the term *liaison*, which is the working relationship and interaction between the private-sector security industry and public-sector law enforcement agencies. Candidates need to know the proper and effective liaison between the public and private sectors and some of the concepts behind establishing such relationships. This chapter will provide information to pass this portion of the Certified Protection Professional (CPP) exam.

In today's world of tight public budgets, criminal activity that routinely operates on a global level, terrorist attacks, and more sophisticated criminals, the need for cooperation between the public and private sectors has increased exponentially.

Therefore, the CPP exam has, for quite a while, measured the knowledge the CPP candidate has about the subject. In taking the test, candidates must keep in mind not to attempt to answer the questions with the way they may personally conduct themselves in their local or state areas. A wider, national view must be maintained, and improper or illegal activity must be scrupulously avoided.

For many years, private security was not necessarily held in high esteem. The law enforcement community and the public in general had a negative perception of private security as being unprofessional. The attainment of the CPP certification and participation in professional organizations such as the American Society for Industrial Security (ASIS) demonstrates to all that persons who possess the CPP and are members of professional security organizations take their professions seriously and are indeed security professionals.

Private security has been around for centuries in one form or another. Even the guards who watched over the Caesars of Rome were private security hired and paid for by Caesar.

In the United States, the Wells Fargo stagecoach guard and the Pinkerton agents were forefathers of today's modern security officer.

In Great Britain, the original Bobbies were hired security and volunteers who walked the streets of London to curb the rampant street crime of the time.

Over the years, the industry has matured, grown, and evolved into a highly specialized and dedicated group of professionals. That is not to say that the industry does not have a long way to go. In many instances, selection standards, training, and pay are low. It is incumbent on all the security professionals of today to make sure the deficiencies that do still exist are done away with.

Over the past few years, not only has there been an ever-increasing need for security, but budgetary restrictions have also put a crunch on the law enforcement community. They are being forced to do more with significantly less resources.

If one event could ever have brought the need for and importance of security to the forefront, it was the tragedy of 9/11 and its aftermath. Today, the specter of terrorism hangs over everyone's head like the sword of Damocles. The need for security and law enforcement to communicate and learn how to work together is essential now more than ever.

CHANGING ROLE OF THE SECURITY PROFESSIONAL

Technology has had a tremendous effect on our whole society and the security industry in particular. New technologies have created whole new classes of criminals. Computers are being used to hack into company records and systems, commit fraud and identity theft, create counterfeit documents, distribute child pornography, and commit many other crimes.

Gone are the days when security meant only a guard who walked around a closed-up factory all night or checked a truck in or out. Today's security professional must be able to juggle many different tasks at once and to not drop the ball on any of them. The degree of professionalism and sophistication required has grown immensely. It has had to in order to keep up with the criminal whose sophistication has increased at a pace that is equal to or sometimes even greater than that of the security professional.

The security professional of today must be able to understand and deal with these complex problems. Computer literacy is essential. A complete working knowledge of the laws and court decisions that give us the parameters we can legally operate within must be known and taught to all security personnel. Into this complex arena steps the security professional who prepares himself or herself to compete and hopefully succeed.

SECURITY PROFESSIONAL AS A BUSINESS PERSON

Today, a security manager or director must be a business professional. He or she must know how and why business works as it does. He or she must be able to, in many instances, deal within the international community as well as nationally and locally.

Security, in many instances, has always been looked on as a necessary evil. We must have security, but it does not, in and of itself, make any profit. It is looked on as an overhead item in the company ledger. Of course, as we all know, security can pay for itself many times over through the savings it engenders by stopping thefts, sabotage, needless injuries, and lost production time. Security can also lower workers compensation costs, contain liability, and help in many, many other aspects of the corporate financial picture.

The security manager or director must be able to administer his or her department in a businesslike fashion while avoiding the pitfalls that come with that position. He or she must know how to establish a training program that not only prepares employees to perform their jobs but also can withstand scrutiny should something go wrong. He or she must be able to motivate others to perform to the best of their ability. He or she must deal with complex legal issues that could cut across state and national borders. He or she must be able to liaise effectively with corporate executives, law enforcement officials, and many other diverse groups. He or she must accomplish all of this while dealing with the budgetary restrictions that are the bane of all security departments.

INTERFACING WITH LAW ENFORCEMENT

As mentioned earlier in this chapter, *liaison* is used to describe the relationship between law enforcement and security. There are many similarities between the functions each does in many areas. However, security can never afford to forget that they are not the police. This is a double-edged sword in many ways. On one hand, security does not have the rights or powers vested in law enforcement, but neither are they hamstrung with the obligations of Miranda rights or many of the search-and-seizure rulings. That is not meant to imply that security should run rampant over the rights of their employees. However, the fact that confessions or admissions made to security during the course of their investigations are admissible in court does make putting a prosecution together much easier.

Many times, the technology that is available to security exceeds that which is available to many local and even state law enforcement agencies. Tight budgets restrict law enforcement from obtaining the newest and best resources. At the same time, however, law enforcement's ability to obtain information that private individuals are barred from obtaining as well as their ability to get search warrants are of much greater benefit in an investigation than the technical advantage enjoyed by private security. Another area in which security has an advantage, at times, over law enforcement is in the amount of manpower available. Depending on the gravity of the situation, private companies can elect to spend large sums of money and dedicate manpower resources as they choose. Private-sector investigators do not have to carry up to 50 or 60 open cases, all of which demand their time and resources.

Therefore, many times, the best of both worlds is to work together to accomplish a mutual goal. Each side using its abilities and strengths helps accomplish such goals. Security professionals must always be mindful that if they work directly with the police, they become agents of the police and are subject to the same restraints as the police.

In establishing a working relationship with law enforcement, some potential issues that may be encountered are as follows:

- Law enforcement officials must be careful not to reveal information that would be illegal for them to impart to private parties.
- The perception of many members of law enforcement that private security wants to work with them only to gain access to their information resources.
- The belief that they (members of law enforcement) are superior, in many ways, to private-sector security and therefore, it is of no benefit to work with security.
- The fear that if they are working in conjunction with security and security does something wrong, they will be held responsible for those mistakes.
- At times, law enforcement officials will not want the public to believe that they needed to seek the assistance of private security to accomplish their job.

Another roadblock that, at times, prevents or hampers the two entities from working together in a harmonious manner is that the desired outcome of each can be very different. While the goal of the police is to identify, arrest, and prosecute the offender, the businessperson may want to obtain restitution rather than prosecution.

Many times, the police will come into a situation after a crime has been committed, whereas security is there beforehand and is focused on preventing crime rather than apprehending the criminal.

In order to work well with one another, each side must work hard to earn the respect and trust of the other.

TRENDS IN SECURITY AND LAW ENFORCEMENT

Over the years, some very distinct trends have arisen in both law enforcement and security. These trends have, at times, blurred the lines between the two as they relate to the jobs they do.

Law enforcement has, as mentioned earlier, been forced to not only do more with less but also had to watch as some of their responsibilities have been privatized by security. Some examples of this are as follows:

- Many private communities have increased the size and roles of their security departments to the point that they virtually serve as a private police department. They patrol streets in patrol cars, respond to problem calls and alarms, take accident reports, and perform many other functions that were previously the bailiwick of the police.

- Many businesses have turned to private security consultants to provide a wide range of services. These services include advising clients on preventive measures to thwart criminal activity, crime prevention through environmental design (CPTED), crowd and traffic control, and the use of off-duty law enforcement officers for security responsibilities.
- The use of private investigators to investigate thefts and accidents or to screen prospective employees, as well as undercover investigators to ferret out dishonest employees and drug usage in their businesses.
- Fingerprinting services and other forensic-related services.
- The use of polygraphs to investigate various crimes.
- Providing various crime prevention and awareness training services for their employees.

In providing these services that, in the past, were supplied by the police through various programs—i.e., block watch programs, CPTED programs, burglary prevention surveys, personal protection programs, drug abuse resistance education (DARE) programs, and many others—security has effectively stepped in to fill the void left when the police could no longer provide such services.

There have been many communities that have contracted some of their investigative functions to private investigators in order to cut costs. Even the federal government contracts out background investigations of persons applying for positions with various governmental agencies to private individuals.

As security has become more and more involved in such activities, especially as they relate to criminal activity, the ability to interface or liaison with the public-sector law enforcement agencies has increased in importance.

BUILDING RAPPORT WITH LAW ENFORCEMENT

When trying to open a dialogue with law enforcement officials, keep in mind the potential problems mentioned earlier in this chapter. Any conversations will, at least at first, be guarded. Trust and rapport are earned slowly.

When approaching law enforcement with specific issues, do not ask for anything that is illegal—including information that would be illegal for the officer to impart. This could create resentment and call into question the ethics of the person or company making such requests.

Simply state the issue, concern, or need; solicit his or her opinion or advice; and then try to determine if anything can be done. See if you can be of service to the officer. Keep in mind that the officer has legal restraints that the private security sector does not have. Remember that these same restraints are placed on all operatives of security if they are deemed "agents of the police."

Never offer an officer any type of inducement to obtain information or cooperation. This would be considered illegal to start with and would be offensive to the officer.

Never violate the trust of the officer or the department. If you are assisted by the agency and given access to information (legally and out of necessity), never betray that confidence.

When the case or problem has been resolved, do not forget to thank the officer or department for the assistance. A note written to the head of the department offering thanks and praising the officer(s) who assisted you will go a long way toward cementing the working relationship between you and the department. Everyone likes to feel that his or her efforts are appreciated.

If you or your company is approached to assist the police or another agency with information, your facility, or the use of your personnel, every consideration should be made to cooperate. Remember, cooperation is always a two-way street. Depending on the help requested, consult management and the legal department to ensure that the help required is approved and the company is not put in legal jeopardy.

Over time, these ongoing efforts at establishing a working rapport with local, state, and even federal law enforcement agencies will pay a big dividend to both the business and the agency. Both are working toward a reduction in crime and losses. Although each has, to some extent, a different agenda, each can and will benefit from mutual cooperation.

CONCLUSIONS

This portion of the CPP exam was placed in the test in response to the ever-growing need for the private sector and the public sector to work together on problems of mutual concern. Despite the reluctance of the public sector to fully cooperate with the private sector, the growing capabilities of the private sector coupled with the shrinking budgets of the public sector have made cooperation more and more imperative.

The public sector has many conceptions of private security. Some are truly misconceptions of the truth; others are, at times, well placed. Only through professionalism can these misconceptions be alleviated.

The private sector must be very careful not to try to use the public sector in a way that is illegal or unethical. Any attempt to do so will destroy any effort at a mutually beneficial relationship between the two and could also put the private-sector employee and his or her company in legal jeopardy.

Mutual trust and respect are the key elements in establishing a professional working relationship, and these can only be built up slowly.

When bringing law enforcement into an investigation, make sure all of the information is accurate and can stand up to scrutiny and that the methods used were legal, ethical, and professional.

Look for areas of common interest or concern and use these areas as ways to establish rapport.

When taking the CPP exam, try to look at these liaison questions from the point of view of both sectors. If the basic thrust of the question is from the public sector, try to answer the question like someone from the public sector would perceive the answer to be. This should be vice versa if the question is written from the point of view of someone in the private sector.

Appendix A: Sample Test Questions

The following are not questions that appear on the actual examine, they convey the principles and concepts that the exam emphasizes, and are valuable in determining if you have mastered the required information. It is entirely by accident, if any question happens to be worded exactly the same as a question on the CPP examination.

CHAPTER 3: INVESTIGATIONS

1. Which of the following is not a legitimate purpose of an investigation for employee misconduct?
    a. To determine whether company rules have been violated
    b. To ascertain whether company policies have been violated
    c. To catalog information about employees that might be derogatory for future use
    d. To determine if state laws have been violated
    e. To determine if federal laws have been violated
2. The investigation's best approach to questioning relies on the following:
    a. Most suspects will lie or circumvent the truth.
    b. A suspect is innocent until proven guilty.
    c. A key suspect is guilty, and evidence must be found.
    d. A signed statement in the form of a confession must be obtained.
    e. None of the above.
3. Some facts about drug users that may assist in recognizing problem areas during a drug investigation are set forth as follows. Indicate the one that is erroneous.
    a. The only common characteristic is that drug abusers use drugs to a point where they feel they can no longer manage without its support.
    b. The adult abuser of drugs commonly has a history of social maladjustment.
    c. Drug abuse is concentrated in but not confined to "slum areas" of large cities.

    d. Those who can afford to buy drugs without resorting to crime are less likely to be arrested for drug violations.

    e. Chronic abuse of drugs is generally not considered a symptom of mental or emotional illness.

4. A craving for a drug is exhibited often by the following:
    a. Water running from nose or eyes
    b. Frequent yawning or sneezing
    c. Continual itching of arms and legs
    d. All of the above
    e. None of the above

5. A narcotic addict is sometimes called:
    a. A bingo
    b. A geezer
    c. A hophead
    d. A pop
    e. A bagman

6. One whose sexual desires are directed to both men and women is known as a:
    a. Lesbian
    b. Bisexual
    c. Homosexual
    d. Transvestite
    e. None of the above

7. When it is necessary to question a witness about sexual deviation, all of the following should be avoided except:
    a. Using street language
    b. Giving the impression of being avid to develop the facts
    c. Leaving the impression that you suspect subject of being a sex deviate
    d. Allowing the witness to frame the testimony in his or her own words
    e. None of the above

8. In conducting gambling investigations, the security officer should:
    a. Cooperate with local, county, state, or federal law enforcement
    b. Not use undercover operatives
    c. Wiretap the employee's home phone
    d. Search the lockers of all suspects
    e. None of the above

9. Which of the following investigative resources should not normally be used in a gambling investigation conducted by a proprietary investigative force?
    a. Closed-circuit TV cameras
    b. Undercover operatives

    c. Telephone surveillance

    d. Fluorescent powder

    e. Physical surveillances

10. In an investigation concerning regulations of common carriers in interstate commerce or investigation of railroad accidents, a good source of information would be the:

    a. Federal Bureau of Investigation

    b. Bureau of Customs

    c. Federal Trade Commission

    d. Interstate Commerce Commission

    e. General Accounting Office

11. In investigating homicide and suicide, the best source of information would probably be the:

    a. County coroner's office

    b. Health office

    c. State attorney general's office

    d. Federal Bureau of Investigation

    e. Sheriff's office

12. To obtain information concerning marriage licenses, an investigator would contact the:

    a. Appropriate health department

    b. Tax bureau

    c. Bureau of Vital Statistics

    d. Appropriate court

    e. Social Security Office

13. In conducting a "claim" investigation where the claim is a serious one and where there is cause for doubt in connection with the loss or claim, the type of investigation to be used is:

    a. Telephone

    b. Mail

    c. Personal contact

    d. Undercover

    e. Clandestine

14. One of the following is *not* one of the desired characteristics of a statement obtained during a claim investigation:

    a. It should be written in ink or indelible pencil, or typed.

    b. It must be dated.

    c. It should be in short paragraphs with two spaces between each paragraph.

    d. It may be signed or unsigned.

    e. It must contain the identification of the person making it.

15. A sudden, violent, and noisy eruption, outburst, or discharge by material acted upon with force, such as fire, shock, or electrical charge, which causes the material, either solid or liquid, to convert into gas and violently expand or burst is the definition of:
    a. A flash fire
    b. An explosion
    c. A detonation
    d. All of the above
    e. None of the above

16. A yellow-colored crystalline solid pertains to the following explosive:
    a. TNT
    b. Dynamite
    c. Nitroglycerin
    d. Mercury fulminate
    e. Picric acid

17. Which of the following is *not* a high explosive?
    a. Nitrocellulose
    b. Nitroglycerin
    c. Dynamite
    d. Nitro starch
    e. Picric acid

18. Which of the following could be considered a source of information?
    a. A record
    b. A custodian of record
    c. A public official
    d. All of the above
    e. None of the above

19. One of the following is *not* considered an element of the common-law crime of arson:
    a. Commercial building
    b. Maliciousness
    c. Burning
    d. Willfulness
    e. Of another

20. Which of the following is *not* usually applicable to a confession?
    a. It was voluntary.
    b. It was made subsequent to commission of a wrongful act.
    c. It is often applied to civil transactions.
    d. It gives no inference other than guilt.
    e. It is an admission of guilt.

21. Which of the following is *not* a requirement for a successful under-cover investigation?
    a. A qualified investigator
    b. A plausible cover story
    c. An effective control scheme
    d. Developing necessary evidence for prosecution
    e. A reliable method to discontinue or even suddenly abort the investigation
22. If it is necessary to terminate an undercover investigation, one of the following actions should *not* be done:
    a. Withdraw agent safely
    b. Withdraw agent immediately
    c. Salvage as much of the resultant data as possible
    d. Prepare explanations for those who demand them
    e. Reveal the agent's identity
23. The principal item of expense in an investigations budget will be:
    a. Communications
    b. Equipment
    c. Maintenance
    d. Personnel costs
    e. Training
24. The single most important administrative control in handling investigations is:
    a. Indexing
    b. Case assignment
    c. Case review
    d. Documentation of status
    e. Case "ticklers"
25. The frequency of a reinvestigation of the "financial lifestyle" inquiry should generally be:
    a. Never
    b. Every 6 months
    c. Every year
    d. Every 18 months
    e. Every 3 years
26. In conducting interviews during an investigation concerning "financial lifestyle," the investigator should more appropriately tell the person being interviewed that the employee is:
    a. Being considered for a position.
    b. Suspected of wrongdoing.
    c. Being interviewed in connection with a position of trust.
    d. Being considered for a promotion.
    e. None of the above: Tell the interviewee nothing.

27. One of the following is not prohibited by the Federal Civil Rights Act during an investigation:
    a. Asking questions about prior arrests
    b. Asking questions about prior convictions
    c. Directing inquiry into areas of race or color for discriminatory purposes
    d. Directing inquiry into areas of religion or sex for discriminatory purposes
    e. None of the above

28. Age discrimination in the Employment Act of 1967 bans discrimination against workers or applicants who are:
    a. At least 35 but less than 60
    b. At least 45 but less than 70
    c. At least 50 but less than 70
    d. At least 30 but less than 60
    e. At least 40 but less than 65

29. Questions on an application left blank or field investigative inquiries that deal with a union membership or affiliation should be avoided as they may lead to charges that constitute violations of:
    a. The National Labor Relations Act
    b. The Civil Rights Act of 1964
    c. The Civil Rights Act of 1976
    d. The Fair Credit Reporting Act
    e. The Federal Tort Claims Act

30. As a general rule, the number of consecutive years of employment or nonemployment to be verified preceding the date of investigation is:
    a. 5 years
    b. 7 years
    c. 3 years
    d. 2 years
    e. 10 years

31. Any investigation containing unfavorable information should be retained in a file for a period of not less than:
    a. 1 year
    b. 5 years
    c. 3 years
    d. 2 years
    e. 10 years

32. A question on an application form inquiring about prior arrests is illegal as a violation of:
    a. The National Labor Relations Act
    b. The Federal Tort Claim Act

    c. The Omnibus Crime Control Act

    d. The Civil Rights Act of 1964

    e. The Federal Full Employment Act

33. The rule that states that approximately 1 in 10 applications will have major omissions, which will require going back to the applicant, is called:

    a. The Rule of Ten

    b. The Rule of Nine

    c. The 1-10 Rule

    d. The Verification Rule

    e. Sullivan's Rule

34. Who of the following should be interviewed last or near the end of an investigation under usual circumstances?

    a. Those with extensive information

    b. Those preparing to take a trip out of the area

    c. Those likely to be hostile

    d. Those with less than extensive information

    e. Those only in the area temporarily

35. If the interviewee during an investigation is hostile, it is preferable to conduct the interview:

    a. At the security office

    b. In the home of the interviewee

    c. At a neutral spot

    d. In an automobile

    e. At the office of the interviewee's lawyer

36. Which of the following characterizations regarding investigative surveillance is *not* true?

    a. It is expensive.

    b. It is time consuming.

    c. It is often nonproductive.

    d. It is illegal in most jurisdictions.

    e. It can be fixed or mobile.

37. The process whereby communications are intercepted or recorded is known as:

    a. Physical surveillance

    b. Technical surveillance

    c. Surreptitious surveillance

    d. Black bag operations

    e. None of the above

38. Situations in which at least one party to a communication is aware and willing that the recording of his or her conversation with another person or persons is being made are:

    a. A violation of the Omnibus Crime Control Act

    b. A violation of the Federal Communications Act

    c. Not a violation

    d. Allowed by the Federal Anti-Racketeering Statute

    e. Allowed by 18 USC 2511

39. The specific emplacement of an agent or operative in an environ-ment or situation in which the agent's true role is unknown with the purpose of developing information to be used later in a crimi-nal investigation is known as:

    a. Closed investigation

    b. Secret investigation

    c. Technical investigation

    d. Concealed investigation

    e. Undercover investigation

40. It is becoming increasingly more difficult to do a good preemploy-ment background investigation because of:

    a. The expense

    b. The lack of skilled investigators

    c. Various rulings and court decisions that inhibit the use of tech-niques or instruments available

    d. The uncooperative attitudes of persons interviewed

    e. Such investigations being illegal in a number of states

41. Which of the following is an advantage of having investigations conducted by in-house security staff?

    a. It is cheaper as a general rule, depending on number of checks being done.

    b. In-house staff is better trained.

    c. In-house staff has a better grasp as to the objective of the investigation.

    d. In-house staff has better sources of information.

    e. None of the above.

42. The most widely recognized and best-known instrument designed to detect deception is:

    a. Fingerprint classifier

    b. Voice analyzer

    c. Polygraph

    d. Truth serum

    e. Stress analyzer

43. The most important factor in the use of a polygraph is:

    a. The examiner

    b. The make of the instrument

    c. Environmental factors

    d. The time of day

    e. The types of questions

44. Which of the following is *not* a good procedure with regard to the use of the polygraph by investigators?
    a. Pointing out its effectiveness
    b. Describing it as infallible
    c. Withholding detailed information from the examinee
    d. Telling the examinee how experienced the examiner is
    e. Working with the examiner as a team member

45. The US Army trains its polygraph operators as well as those from other US agencies at:
    a. West Point, New York
    b. Washington, DC
    c. Fort Gordon, Georgia
    d. Fort Leavenworth, Kansas
    e. Fort Meade, Maryland

46. A device used to detect deception through stress recorded by voice modulations is known as (a):
    a. Polygraph
    b. Lie detector
    c. Psychological stress analyzer
    d. Truth serum
    e. Hypnotism

47. Which of the following characteristics relate to the psychological stress analyzer?
    a. No physical connection with the body is required.
    b. The subject is not required to answer in a terse yes-or-no format.
    c. It can be used covertly.
    d. All of the above.
    e. None of the above.

48. The effectiveness of the voice analyzer in accurately detecting deception is:
    a. 100%
    b. 96%
    c. 94%
    d. 85%
    e. Not determined

49. Identify the act that basically prohibits discrimination, discharge, failure or refusal to hire, etc. on any of the grounds of race, color, religion, sex, or national origin:
    a. The Fair Credit Reporting Act
    b. The Civil Rights Act of 1964
    c. The First Amendment
    d. The Omnibus Crime Control Act
    e. None of the above

50. Under court interpretations of the Civil Rights Act of 1964, which of the following are *not* allowed during investigations?
    a. Questions regarding prior arrests
    b. Questions regarding prior convictions
    c. Questions regarding age
    d. Questions regarding residence
    e. Questions regarding prior employment
51. Interviews should be conducted:
    a. In the company of the suspect's attorney
    b. In an area where distractions are minimal
    c. In a comfortable room that is well furnished, like at home
    d. In an area where the light is focused on the suspect's face
    e. None of the above
52. The witness's idea of the suspect, described in words, is called:
    a. *Portrait parle*
    b. *Modus operandi*
    c. *Corpus delecti*
    d. All of the above
    e. None of the above
53. The most important qualification of a good undercover operator is:
    a. Resourcefulness
    b. Education
    c. Experience
    d. Good contacts
    e. None of the above
54. The main function of the private security agent is to:
    a. Locate stolen goods
    b. Ascertain and report illegal activities
    c. Receive well-rounded investigative experience
    d. Ascertain the state of morale
    e. None of the above
55. The person best suited for physical surveillance work is one who:
    a. Is tall enough to see over crowds
    b. Will blend into the area
    c. Has a college education
    d. Has a background of police work
    e. None of the above
56. In conducting a polygraph, it is important to note that the most important measure of stress is recorded by:
    a. Breathing
    b. Galvanic skin response
    c. Heartbeats

    d. Perspiration

    e. None of the above

57. The pretesting interview prior to the polygraph examination itself is for the purpose of:

    a. Helping the subject to relax

    b. Helping the examiner to get to know the subject

    c. Helping the examiner to judge the subject's character

    d. All of the above

    e. None of the above

58. On average, a polygraph examination takes:

    a. 10 h

    b. 1 h

    c. 15 min

    d. 5 h

    e. 4 h

59. Which of the following statements is *not* correct regarding the polygraph?

    a. The polygraph is not a lie detector.

    b. The polygraph does not automatically register truth or falsehood.

    c. A polygraph test is conclusive.

    d. Historically, polygraphs have more often been used to establish innocence rather than to prove guilt.

    e. None of the above.

60. Persons are protected from abuses of polygraph by:

    a. The courts through civil lawsuits

    b. State labor departments

    c. The National Labor Relations Board

    d. All of the above

    e. None of the above

61. The best way to verify an applicant's statements is:

    a. By judicious use of the telephone

    b. By a personal visit with the applicant

    c. By mail

    d. All of the above

    e. None of the above

62. Which of the following should *not* be included in the written investigative report of an applicant?

    a. Derogatory information

    b. Confidential sources of information

    c. Results of a lie detector examination

    d. Arrest records

    e. None of the above

63. Of all those with mental disorders, the most dangerous subject to handle is:
    a. One suffering hysteria
    b. A paranoid psychotic
    c. A neurotic
    d. One suffering phobia
    e. Schizophrenic

64. Mental disorders may be determined by symptoms. Which of the following is such a symptom?
    a. Sudden changes in behavior
    b. Behavior that is not harmonious with a situation
    c. Unduly prolonged depression
    d. All of the above
    e. None of the above

65. In handling a mentally disturbed person, one should:
    a. Take a strong position as the boss
    b. Assume a calm and friendly position
    c. Leave the impression he or she has control of the situation
    d. All of the above
    e. None of the above

66. Which of the following is true in handling persons with mental disorders?
    a. Don't deceive them.
    b. Don't become involved in their personal problems.
    c. Where physical restraint is required, use two officers.
    d. All of the above.
    e. None of the above.

67. There are several stages in an investigative process. Which of the following is not considered a stage?
    a. Whether to investigate
    b. Legal evaluation
    c. Gathering information
    d. Managerial decision making

68. Which of the following is not a requirement for a successful undercover investigation?
    a. A qualified investigator
    b. A plausible cover story
    c. An effective control scheme
    d. Developing necessary evidence for prosecution

69. The principal item of expense in an investigations budget will be:
    a. Office supplies
    b. Equipment

    c. Maintenance

    d. Personnel costs

70. The single most important administrative control in handling investigations is:

    a. Indexing

    b. Case assignment

    c. Case review

    d. Documentation of status

71. As a general rule, the number of consecutive years of employment or nonemployment that should be verified preceding the date of investigation is:

    a. 5 years

    b. 7 years

    c. 3 years

    d. 2 years

72. Any investigation containing unfavorable information should be retained in file for a period not less than:

    a. 1 year

    b. 5 years

    c. 3 years

    d. 2 years

73. The rule that states that approximately 1 in 10 applications will have major omissions, which will require going back to the applicant, is called:

    a. The Rule of Ten

    b. The Rule of Nine

    c. The 1-10 Rule

    d. The Verification Rule

74. Which of the following should be interviewed last or near the end of an investigation under usual circumstances:

    a. Those with extensive information

    b. Those preparing to take a trip out of the area

    c. Those likely to be hostile

    d. Those with less than extensive information

75. If interviewee during investigations is hostile, it is preferable to conduct the interview:

    a. At the security office

    b. In the home of the interviewee

    c. At a neutral location

    d. In an automobile

76. Which of the following characterization regarding investigative surveillance is not true?
    a. It is expensive
    b. It is time consuming
    c. It is often nonproductive
    d. It is illegal in most jurisdictions
77. The process whereby communications are intercepted or recorded is known as:
    a. Physical surveillance
    b. Technical surveillance
    c. Surreptitious surveillance
    d. Black bag operations
78. It is becoming increasingly more difficult to do a good preemployment background investigation because of:
    a. Expense
    b. Lack of skilled investigators
    c. Various laws and court decisions that inhibit the use of techniques and/or instruments available
    d. Uncooperative attitude of persons interviewed
79. An undercover operator should be:
    a. A member of the investigative staff of the organization
    b. A trusted employee in the department under investigation
    c. Unknown by anyone likely to be in the target population
    d. An off-duty law enforcement officer
80. One of the objectives of an undercover investigation is not to:
    a. Establish a method of diversion of goods
    b. Ascertain the level of organized labor activity in the work force
    c. Provide information for personnel action
    d. Obtain evidence of past or future crime
81. In an incident investigation, the general rule is to first interview persons who:
    a. Are not likely to be available for later interview
    b. Are likely to be hostile
    c. Have the most extensive information about the incident
    d. Are familiar with some part of the subject matter
82. Which of the following is not true regarding communications with an undercover agent:
    a. Normal contact is initiated by the agent.
    b. The contact telephone should be answered with the name of the company.
    c. An alternate contact telephone number should be established.
    d. The telephones should be reserved exclusively for investigations.

83. The basic rules of collecting, preserving, and maintaining evidence:
    a. Must be done by many untrained people
    b. Must be done in a quick manner
    c. Must follow the chain of custody to be used in court
    d. Must not be documented properly
    e. None of the above
84. Which of the following is *not* a kind of evidence:
    a. Physical evidence
    b. Scientific evidence
    c. Circumstantial evidence
    d. Testimonial evidence
    e. All of the above
85. Hearsay evidence is:
    a. Based on a witness's personal knowledge
    b. Usually admissible in court
    c. Information revealed to the witness by another person
    d. Never admissible in court
    e. None of the above
86. A pen register is:
    a. A device that records all numbers dialed on a telephone
    b. Used to keep track of those entering an event
    c. Signatures of those registering for an event
    d. A surveillance technique using a pen camera
    e. None of the above
87. Which of the following are the types of surveillance that can be used in an investigation?
    a. Fixed surveillance
    b. Proprietary surveillance
    c. Moving surveillance
    d. Relaxed surveillance
    e. Answers a and c
88. What are some common ways applicants falsify applications?
    a. Incomplete application
    b. Willful omission of facts or job references
    c. Misrepresentation of job history or education
    d. References that are nonexistent
    e. All of the above
89. Which act prohibits discrimination in hiring, firing, promoting, or giving raises or other benefits because of an employee's race, religion, sex, or national origin?
    a. Fair Credit Reporting Act
    b. Age Discrimination in Employment Act—1967
    c. Civil Rights Act—1964

   d. Americans with Disabilities Act (ADA)
   e. National Labor Relations Act (NLRA)
90. An explosion is defined as:
   a. An item that can cause fire damage
   b. A sudden, violent, noisy eruption, outburst, or discharge by material acted upon with force such as fire, shock, or electrical charge that causes the solid or liquid material to convert into gas and violently expand or burst
   c. Any chemical compound, mixture, or device that functions by explosion to release instantaneous gas and heat
   d. Objects that produce significant sound waves
   e. Materials that can cause injury to others
91. Which of the following are exceptions to the Omnibus Crime Control and Safe Street Act of 1968 (Title III)?
   a. Wiretapping takes place in a one-party consent state.
   b. The wiretap is obtained with a court order called an ex parte order.
   c. It is necessary for emergency cases involving national security.
   d. Answers a and b
   e. All of the above
92. Embezzlement is:
   a. Borrowing money from a company with the intent to pay it back
   b. The misappropriation of money and wrongful conversion of merchandise
   c. Taking money that does not belong to the taker
   d. Taking merchandise that does not belong to the taker
   e. None of the above
93. Bombs are defined as:
   a. Items that can cause fire damage
   b. Materials that can cause injury to others
   c. Objects that produce significant sound waves
   d. Any chemical compound, mixture, or device that functions by explosion to release instantaneous gas and heat
   e. A sudden, violent, noisy eruption, outburst or discharge by material acted upon with force such as fire, shock, or electrical charge that causes the solid or liquid material to convert into gas and violently expand or burst

CHAPTER 3 ANSWERS

   1. c. To catalog information about employees that might be derogatory
   2. b. A suspect is innocent until proven guilty.

3. e. Chronic abuse of drugs is generally not considered a symptom of mental or emotional illness.
4. d. All of the above
5. c. A hophead
6. b. Bisexual
7. d. Allowing the witness to frame the testimony in his or her own words
8. a. Cooperate with local, county, state, or federal law enforcement
9. c. Telephone surveillance
10. d. Interstate Commerce Commission
11. a. County coroner's office
12. c. Bureau of Vital Statistics
13. c. Personal contact
14. c. It should be in short paragraphs with two spaces between each paragraph.
15. d. All of the above
16. e. Picric acid
17. a. Nitrocellulose
18. d. All of the above
19. a. Commercial building
20. c. It is often applied to civil transactions.
21. d. Developing necessary evidence for prosecution
22. e. Reveal the agent's identity
23. d. Personnel costs
24. a. Indexing
25. d. Every 18 months
26. c. Being interviewed in connection with a position of trust.
27. b. Asking questions about prior convictions
28. e. At least 40 but less than 65
29. a. The National Labor Relations Act
30. b. 7 years
31. c. 3 years
32. d. The Civil Rights Act of 1964
33. a. The Rule of Ten
34. c. Those likely to be hostile
35. a. At the security office
36. d. It is illegal in most jurisdictions.
37. b. Technical surveillance
38. c. Not a violation
39. e. Undercover investigation
40. c. Various rulings and court decisions that inhibit the use of techniques or instruments available

41. c. In-house staff has a better grasp as to the objective of the investigator.
42. c. Polygraph
43. a. The examiner
44. b. Describing it as infallible
45. c. Fort Gordon, Georgia
46. c. Psychological stress analyzer
47. d. All of the above.
48. e. Not determined
49. b. The Civil Rights Act of 1964
50. a. Questions regarding prior arrests
51. b. In an area where distractions are minimal
52. a. *Portrait parle*
53. a. Resourcefulness
54. b. Ascertain and report illegal activities
55. b. Will blend into the area
56. c. Heartbeats
57. d. All of the above
58. b. 1 h
59. c. A polygraph test is conclusive.
60. d. All of the above
61. e. None of the above
62. b. Confidential sources of information
63. b. A paranoid psychotic
64. d. All of the above
65. b. Assume a calm and friendly position
66. d. All of the above.
67. b. Legal evaluation
68. d. Developing necessary evidence for prosecution
69. d. Personnel costs
70. a. Indexing
71. a. 5 years
72. c. 3 years
73. a. The Rule of Ten
74. c. Those likely to be hostile
75. a. At the security office
76. d. They are illegal in most jurisdictions.
77. b. Technical surveillance
78. c. Various law and court decisions that inhibit the use of techniques and/or instruments available
79. c. Unknown by anyone likely to be in the target population

80. b. Ascertain the level of organized labor activity in the work force
81. a. Are not likely to be available for later interview
82. b. The contact telephone should be answered with the name of the company.
83. c. Must follow the chain of custody to be used in court
84. e. All of the above
85. c. Information revealed to the witness by another person
86. a. A device that records all numbers dialed on a telephone
87. c. Moving surveillance
88. e. All of the above
89. c. Civil Rights Act—1964
90. b. A sudden, violent, noisy eruption, outburst, or discharge by material acted upon with force such as fire, shock, or electrical charge that causes the solid or liquid material to convert into gas and violently expand or burst
91. d. Answers a and b
92. b. The misappropriation of money and wrongful conversion of merchandise
93. d. Any chemical compound, mixture, or device that functions by explosion to release instantaneous gas and heat

CHAPTER 4: PROTECTION OF SENSITIVE INFORMATION

1. The purpose for employing an access control program includes:
   a. To protect persons, materials, or information
   b. To slow or speed up the rate of movement to, from, or within an establishment
   c. To permit or deny entrance
   d. Both a and c
   e. All of the above
2. Identification and access control systems have the widest application of:
   a. Manual identification systems
   b. Magnetic readers
   c. Biometric-based systems
   d. Dielectric readers
   e. None of the above
3. The performance requirements of any trustworthy system of identification include:
   a. Resistance to surreptitious substitution or counterfeiting
   b. Reliability

    c. Validity

    d. Both b and c

    e. All of the above

4. A general defect of manual identification systems is that:

    a. Many are made of plastic

    b. Many do not have biometric characteristics on them

    c. Once issued, they tend to remain valid indefinitely

    d. They lack identifying colors

    e. None of the above

5. Any formula, pattern, device, or compilation of information that is used in one's business and that gives you an opportunity to gain an advantage over competitors who do not use it or know about it is:

    a. A patent

    b. A trade secret

    c. A monopoly

    d. Copyrighted material

    e. None of the above

6. What is most likely the main reason for loss of sensitive information?

    a. Industrial espionage

    b. An employee's loose lips

    c. Inadvertent disclosure

    d. Deliberate theft by an outsider

    e. Both b and c

    f. None of the above

7. Which of the following should be part of an effective information security program?

    a. Preemployment screening

    b. Nondisclosure agreements from employees

    c. Employee awareness programs

    d. Policy and procedural statements on the recognition, classification, and handling of sensitive information

    e. All of the above

8. The primary tool of preemployment screening is the:

    a. Application form

    b. Interview

    c. Polygraph

    d. Investigator performing the interview

9. Which of the following is generally *not* allowed to be disclosed on an employment questionnaire?

    a. Current residence

    b. References

c. Prior employment
d. Prior arrests
e. None of the above

10. To be within the definition of a trade secret, sensitive information must meet which of the following criteria?
    a. Individuals to whom it is disclosed must know that it is secret.
    b. It must be identifiable.
    c. It must not be already available in public sources.
    d. There must be some obvious indication that the owner is attempting to prevent its unauthorized disclosure.
    d. a, c, and d.
    e. All of the above.

11. According to the "restatement of the law of torts," a trade secret is:
    a. All information about a company that the company desires to protect
    b. Any formula, pattern, device, or compilation of information that is used in one's business and that gives that business an opportunity to gain an advantage over competitors who do not know or use it
    c. Information about a company that is registered with the US Patent Office
    d. Both a and b
    e. All of the above

12. A trade secret may be:
    a. A formula for a chemical compound
    b. A process of manufacturing materials
    c. A pattern for a machine
    d. A list of customers
    e. All of the above

13. The characteristics of a trade secret as compared with other confidential information are:
    a. Those business secrets that have been duly registered pursuant to the requirements of law
    b. Continuous or consistent business applications of a secret not known to others, from the use of which some advantage is gained by the user
    c. Those business secrets that are fully protected in accordance with the Federal Privacy Act
    d. Both a and c
    e. All of the above

14. Which of the following is generally *not* true in regard to trade secrets?
    a. The more a business narrowly defines what it regards as a secret, the easier it is to protect that body of information.
    b. It is difficult to protect a trade secret that can be found in publicly accessible sources.
    c. Secret information does have to be specifically identifiable.
    d. Secret information must be effectively protected.
    e. None of the above.
15. In regard to a trade secret, it may be decided that its disclosure by another was innocent, rather than wrongful, even in the case where the person making the disclosure really was guilty of malice or wrong intent. This situation may occur when:
    a. The trade secret was not registered
    b. The trade secret did not involve national defense information
    c. The trade secret was not in current use
    d. There is absence of evidence that an owner has taken reasonable precautions to protect confidential information
    e. All of the above
16. Proprietary information is:
    a. Private information of a highly sensitive nature
    b. Information that must be classified according to executive order of the US government
    c. Sensitive information that is classified under federal regulations
    d. Anything that an enterprise considers relevant to its status or operations and does not want to disclose publicly
    e. None of the above
17. The class of person under a duty to safeguard a proprietary secret is known as:
    a. Agent
    b. Proprietary security employee
    c. Fiduciary
    d. Business associate
    e. None of the above
18. It is important for employees to know whether confidential information is a trade secret, or some other confidential material, because:
    a. If it is a trade secret, the employee may be prevented from disclosing it by injunction
    b. If it is not a trade secret and it is disclosed, the employer must take action after the disclosure and must be able to prove some actual damage in order to recover
    c. If it is not a trade secret, the information, once disclosed, is no longer defendable

    d. If it is not a trade secret, the information, once disclosed, cannot be further prevented from disclosure by an injunction

    e. All of the above

19. Which of the following is *not* a correct statement as a general rule involving the protection of proprietary information?

    a. As a class, employees are the largest group of persons bound to secrecy because of their status or relationship.

    b. By operation of common law, employees are presumed to be fiduciaries to the extent that they may not disclose secrets of their employers without authorization.

    c. Other than the employees, any other persons to be bound to secrecy must agree to be so bound.

    d. Any agreements to be bound must always be in writing and are not implied from acts.

20. To effectively involve the law for the protection of sensitive information, the owner of the proprietary information must be able to show "objective indications of attempts to protect secrecy." Which of the following has been recognized in the past as such an indication?

    a. Use of warning signs to alert employees to sensitive data and the places where it is stored

    b. Separately storing sensitive information in security containers with the appropriate security precautions

    c. Special instructions providing a "need-to-know" basis

    d. Restrictions to nonemployee access to places containing sensitive information

    e. All of the above

21. Which of the following should be made part of a proprietary information protection program?

    a. Preemployment screening

    b. Effective perimeter control system

    c. Execution of patent and secrecy agreement

    d. Paper and data control

    e. Both a and c

    f. All of the above

22. In designing a proprietary information protection program, the area of greatest vulnerability is:

    a. Personnel files

    b. Employees

    c. Computers

    d. Marketing data

    e. Perimeter boundaries

23. In devising proprietary information procedures, which of the following is considered to be a main area of paper or document vulnerability?
   a. Comprehensive paper controls
   b. A technical report system
   c. Control and issue of notebooks
   d. All of the above
   e. None of the above

24. When a loss of proprietary information is discovered, which of the following steps should be taken first?
   a. Attempt to recover the material
   b. Attempt to apprehend the perpetrators
   c. Assess economic damage
   d. Reevaluate the protection system
   e. All of the above

25. Which of the following would *not* be considered in the *trade secret* category?
   a. Salary data
   b. Market surveys
   c. Personnel matters
   d. Customer usage evaluations
   e. All of the above

26. Litigations concerning former employees involving trade secrets have some problems. Which of the following is considered to be such a problem?
   a. The cost of litigations is too high, and the owner of the trade secret may lose
   b. Litigation is a waste of time
   c. The owner of the trade secret may have to expose the information that is being protected
   d. Both a and c
   e. All of the above

27. A *trash cover* is:
   a. A sealed cover on a trash container
   b. The process of examining one's trash for information
   c. Placing the company's trash in a locked container
   d. Both a and c
   e. All of the above

28. Sound waves too high in frequency to be heard by the human ear, generally above 20 kHz, are known as:
   a. High-frequency sound waves
   b. Microwave waves

    c. Ultrasonic waves

    d. Short-frequency sound waves

    e. None of the above

29. The process of combining a number of transmissions into one composite signal to be sent over one link is called:

    a. Transmission integrity

    b. Communication integration

    c. A demultiplexer

    d. Multiplexing

    e. None of the above

30. Which of the following applies to the laser as a means of communication?

    a. Line-of-sight transmission is necessary.

    b. Poor weather conditions interfere with the beam.

    c. It is practically impossible to intercept the beam without detection.

    d. Both a and c.

    e. All of the above.

31. Which of the following is *not* correct in regard to microwave transmissions?

    a. Microwave signals penetrate fog and snow.

    b. Microwave signals are transmitted in short radio waves.

    c. A large number of microwave signals can be transmitted.

    d. Microwave signals travel in curved lines.

    e. Microwave signals are not affected by ordinary man-made noise.

    f. None of the above.

32. Electromagnetic radiation is detectable electromagnetic energy that is generated by electronic information processing devices. Which of the following is used to protect very sensitive equipment?

    a. A current carrier device

    b. Pneumatic cavity shielding

    c. Tempest shielding

    d. Pen register shielding

33. The practice of preventing unauthorized persons from gaining information by analyzing electromagnetic emanations from electronic equipment is often termed:

    a. Bugging

    b. Veiling

    c. Tempest

    d. All of the above

    e. None of the above

34. A term used to indicate a method of disguising information so that
    it is unintelligible to those who should not obtain it is:
    a. Interconnection decoy
    b. Multiplexing
    c. Scrambling
    d. Mixed signal
    e. None of the above
35. The most secure scrambler in common use is the:
    a. Frequency inverter
    b. Decoder
    c. Laser beam
    d. Vocoder
    e. None of the above
36. The method used to monitor telephone calls by providing a record
    of all numbers dialed from a particular phone is called:
    a. Electronic surveillance
    b. Phone bug
    c. Wiretap
    d. Pen register
    e. None of the above
37. A small hidden microphone and a radio transmitter are generally
    known as:
    a. A wiretap
    b. A bug
    c. A beeper
    d. Electronic surveillance
    e. All of the above
38. A specially constructed microphone attached directly to an object
    or surface to be protected, which responds only when the pro-
    tected object or surface is disturbed, is known as a:
    a. Parabolic microphone
    b. Special audio microphone
    c. Contact microphone
    d. Surreptitious microphone
    e. None of the above
39. A microphone with a disklike attachment that is used for listening
    to audio from great distances is known as a(n):
    a. Contact microphone
    b. Parabolic microphone
    c. Ultrasonic microphone
    d. Both a and c
    e. None of the above

40. A microphone that is installed on a common wall adjacent to the target area when it is impractical or impossible to enter the target area is known as a:
    a. Carbon microphone
    b. Parabolic microphone
    c. Contact microphone
    d. Dynamic microphone
    e. None of the above
41. Which method of protection against telephone line eavesdropping is most reliable?
    a. Don't discuss sensitive information
    b. Use a radio jammer
    c. Use encryption equipment
    d. Both a and c
    e. Use an audio jammer
42. The unauthorized acquisition or dissemination by an employee of confidential data critical to his or her employer is known as:
    a. Embezzlement
    b. Larceny
    c. Industrial espionage
    d. Burglary
    e. False pretenses
43. The term *eavesdropping* refers to:
    a. Wiretapping
    b. Bugging
    c. Trash cover
    d. Both a and b
    e. All of the above
44. Which of the following methods could be used as a form of eaves-dropping using a telephone instrument?
    a. Wiring can be altered so the handset or receiver will act as an open microphone.
    b. A radio transmitter can be concealed in the mouthpiece.
    c. The infinity transmitter can be used.
    d. Both b and c.
    e. All of the above.
45. A microphone that requires no power source, is very small, and is difficult to detect has the characteristics of a(n):
    a. Contact microphone
    b. Parabolic microphone
    c. Dynamic microphone
    d. Infinity microphone
    e. None of the above

46. Installation of a wireless radio eavesdropping device usually consists of the following:
    a. Transmitter and receiver
    b. Power supply
    c. Antenna
    d. Microphone
    e. Both a and d
    f. All of the above

47. The frequency range best suited for a wireless microphone because it provides better security and lower interference is:
    a. 25–50 mHz
    b. 88–104 mHz
    c. 88–120 mHz
    d. 150–174 mHz
    e. None of the above

48. The control software of a private board exchange (PBX) can be accessed and compromised by calling the telephone number of a device on the PBX from a computer and modem. The name of this PBX device is the:
    a. Internal and remote signal port
    b. Current carrier signaling port
    c. Time-domain reflectometer
    d. Remote maintenance access terminal
    e. None of the above

49. Which of the following is *not* true regarding electronic eavesdropping?
    a. An effective countermeasure to detect evidence of electronic eavesdropping in telephone equipment should be conducted by a person who is technically familiar with such equipment.
    b. An effective countermeasure would be to conduct a physical search as well as an electronic search.
    c. All wiring should be traced and accounted for.
    d. A listening device installed in a wire will cause a crackling sound, click, or other noise that can be heard on the line.
    e. None of the above.

50. The first federal legislation that attempted to regulate electronic surveillance in the United States was enacted by Congress in:
    a. 1910
    b. 1924
    c. 1934
    d. 1968
    e. 1971

51. The manufacture, distribution, possession, and advertising of wire or oral communication interception devices is prohibited by:
    a. The First Amendment
    b. The Fourth Amendment
    c. The Federal Communications Act of 1934
    d. The Omnibus Crime Control and Safe Streets Act of 1968
    e. The FBI

52. The criminal punishment for violation of the wiretapping phases of the Omnibus Crime Control and Safe Streets Act of 1968 is:
    a. A $10,000 fine
    b. 6 months in jail and/or a $5000 fine
    c. 1 year in jail and/or a $10,000 fine
    d. 5 years in prison and/or a $10,000 fine
    e. None of the above

53. Which of the following is *not* a requirement under the Omnibus Crime Control and Safe Streets Act of 1968 before a court may give permission for an electronic surveillance?
    a. The identity of the offender should be stated.
    b. The crime must be any felony under federal law.
    c. The place and location of the electronic surveillance must be stated.
    d. Initial approval must be granted by the attorney general of the United States or by a specially designated attorney general.
    e. All of the above.

54. Which of the following is provided for by the Omnibus Crime Control and Safe Streets Act of 1968?
    a. It prohibits wiretapping or bugging unless a party to the intercepted conversation gives consent.
    b. It prohibits the manufacture and distribution of oral communication interceptor devices.
    c. Nonfederal law enforcement representatives are denied the right to make use of electronic surveillance unless there is a state statute permitting it.
    d. Both a and b.
    e. All of the above.

55. Title III of the Omnibus Crime Control and Safe Streets Act of 1968 requires that an approval for electronic surveillance must be obtained from the:
    a. Chief justice of the Supreme Court
    b. Director of the FBI
    c. Attorney general of the United States or any specially designated assistant attorney general

    d. Director of the CIA

    e. All of the above

56. Criminal violations involving theft of trade secrets could be covered by:

    a. Statutes on theft of trade secrets

    b. Bribery statutes involving trade secrets

    c. Statutes on receipt of stolen property

    d. Statues on criminal conspiracy

    e. All of the above

57. The public statute passed to protect personal information in possession of federal agencies is:

    a. The Espionage Statute

    b. The Unauthorized Disclosure Act

    c. The Omnibus Crime Control Act

    d. The Privacy Act of 1974

    e. None of the above

58. The Privacy Act of 1974 provides which of the following safeguards?

    a. Permits individuals to gain access to certain information pertaining to themselves in federal agency records

    b. Permits individuals to determine what records pertaining to themselves are collected and maintained by federal agencies

    c. Permits individuals to prevent certain records pertaining to themselves from being used or made available for another purpose without their consent

    d. Requires federal agencies to be subject to civil suits for any damages that may occur as a result of willful or intentional action that violates an individual's rights under the Privacy Act of 1974

    e. All of the above

59. Which of the following would *not* be permitted to review a student's record according to the Family Educational Rights and the Privacy Act of 1974?

    a. Law enforcement officials

    b. Other school officials

    c. The school's registrar's office

    d. All of the above

    e. None of the above

60. Which of the following characteristics pertains to a good information management program?

    a. An employee education program for those who utilize the classification system

    b. Limited number of individuals who can initiate classification of information

    c. Limitation of the duration during which the classification will remain in effect

    d. All of the above

    e. None of the above

61. What are the three most common methods of information loss to be guarded against?

    a. Newspaper articles, magazine articles, television

    b. Employee payroll, personnel matters, market surveys

    c. Theft by an insider, inadvertent disclosure, industrial espionage

    d. Employee hirings, magazine articles, industrial espionage

    e. None of the above

62. The elements of an information security program include:

    a. Informing employees that the information is to be protected

    b. Establishing the use of patent or nondisclosure agreements

    c. Designation of certain information as sensitive

    d. Providing the means for employees to protect sensitive information

    e. All of the above

63. Which of the following statements is *not* true in regard to an information security program?

    a. The information security program is an attempt to make theft of sensitive information difficult, not necessarily to eliminate it.

    b. The protection afforded against losses by either internal or external sources is, at best, limited.

    c. A good information security program will provide total protection from industrial espionage.

    d. A trust relationship must be established and maintained with employees.

    e. The goodwill and compliance of employees is crucial for success.

64. Vital records normally constitute what percentage of the company's total records?

    a. 2%

    b. 5%

    c. 10%

    d. 15%

    e. 20%

65. Which of the following is considered to be an approved method of protecting vital records?

    a. On-site storage in vaults or safes

    b. Protection of original vital records

    c. Natural dispersal within an outside organization

    d. Planned dispersal of copies of vital records

    e. All of the above

66. The term *social engineering* is:
    a. A function of the personnel department in which like persons are teamed together in workshops or seminars for maximum productivity
    b. The subtle elicitation of information without revealing the true purpose of the call
    c. The specific design of a business structure to facilitate the interaction of the inhabitants
    d. Both a and c
    e. None of the above
67. Competitive intelligence gathering is a legitimate activity that is engaged in by many firms throughout the world. The most important function of competitive intelligence is to:
    a. Alert senior management to changes in protocol in foreign countries
    b. Alert senior management as to the personal habits of competitive senior management
    c. Alert government intelligence agencies to marketplace changes
    d. Alert senior management to marketplace changes in order to prevent surprise
    e. All of the above
68. The Secretary of Defense is *not* authorized to act on behalf of the following agency or department in rendering industrial security services:
    a. Department of Commerce
    b. Central Intelligence Agency
    c. Department of Justice
    d. Department of Labor
    e. None of the above
69. The overall policy guidance for the Defense Industrial Security Program is provided by:
    a. The Federal Bureau of Investigation
    b. The Deputy Undersecretary of Defense for Policy
    c. The Assistant Chief of Staff in Intelligence
    d. The Defense Intelligence Agency
    e. None of the above
70. The Defense Industrial Security Program on behalf of all user agencies is administered by the:
    a. Director, Defense Investigative Service
    b. Comptroller, Assistant Secretary of Defense
    c. Deputy Undersecretary of Defense for Policy
    d. Defense Industrial Security Clearance Office
    e. None of the above

71. The executive order that applies to classified information is:
    a. E.O. 1044
    b. E.O. 1066
    c. E.O. 12065
    d. E.O. 12523
    e. E.O. 14084
72. A controlled area established to safeguard classified material that, because of its size or nature, cannot be adequately protected by other prescribed safeguards is termed to be:
    a. A restricted area
    b. A classified area
    c. A closed area
    d. A limited area
    e. None of the above
73. The DIS regional office under the support of the director of industrial security that has jurisdiction over the geographical area in which a facility is located is called the:
    a. Regional Security Office
    b. Division Security Office
    c. Clearance Office
    d. Cognizant Security Office
    e. None of the above
74. Technical and intelligence information derived from foreign communications by other than the intended recipient is known as:
    a. Restricted data
    b. Communications intelligence
    c. Classified security matters
    d. Highly confidential
    e. None of the above
75. The designation that should be applied to information or material showing unauthorized disclosure that could reasonably be expected to cause damage to national security is:
    a. Restricted
    b. Top secret
    c. Confidential
    d. Unauthorized disclosure
    e. None of the above
76. Technical information used for training, maintenance, and inspection of classified military munitions of war would be classified as:
    a. Restricted
    b. Classified
    c. Top secret

    d. Confidential

    e. Cosmic

77. A designation or marking that identifies classified operational keying material and that indicates the material requiring special consideration with respect to access, storage, and handling is:

    a. Cosmic

    b. Special

    c. Crypto

    d. Communications intelligence

    e. Red flagged

78. The portion of internal security that is concerned with the protection of classified information in the hands of US industry is called:

    a. Information security

    b. Classified security

    c. National security

    d. Industrial security

    e. Communications security

79. The result of any system of administrative policies and procedures
for identifying, controlling, and protecting from unauthorized disclosure of information and is authorized by executive order or statute is called:

    a. Computer security

    b. Industrial security

    c. Personnel security

    d. Communications security

    e. Information security

80. An administrative determination that an individual is eligible for
access to classified information is:

    a. Personnel security clearance

    b. Industrial security clearance

    c. National security clearance

    d. Communications security clearance

    e. None of the above

81. The combinations to safes, containers, and vaults should be changed:

    a. Every 3 months

    b. Every 4 months

    c. Every 6 months

    d. Every 9 months

    e. Every year

82. The designation that shall be applied only to information or material
unauthorized disclosure of which could reasonably be expected to
cause serious damage to national security is:

    a. Restricted

    b. Secret

    c. Confidential

    d. Top secret

    e. Unauthorized disclosure

83. Information regarding the revelation of significant military plans or intelligence operations should be classified as:

    a. Restricted

    b. Secret

    c. Confidential

    d. Top secret

    e. Cosmic

84. The designation that should only be applied to information or material unauthorized disclosure of which could reasonably be expected to cause exceptionally grave damage to national security is:

    a. Restricted

    b. Secret

    c. Confidential

    d. Top secret

    e. Cosmic

85. Information that could lead to the compromise of vital national defense plans or complex cryptologic and communications intelligence systems should be classified:

    a. Restricted

    b. Secret

    c. Confidential

    d. Top secret

    e. Cosmic

86. Regulations of the Department of Defense require that the contractor shall establish such procedures as are necessary to ensure that any employee discovering the loss, compromise, or suspected compromise of classified information outside a facility promptly reports to:

    a. The Defense Intelligence Agency

    b. The Defense Industrial Security Clearance Office

    c. The nearest FBI office

    d. Comptroller, Assistant Secretary of Defense

    e. The Industrial Security Office

87. Defense Department regulations require the identification card of a defense contractor to include a:

    a. Distinctive color coding

    b. Thumbprint

    c. Photograph of the holder

    d. Symbol code

    e. All of the above

88. Which of the following should definitely *not* appear on the identification card of employees of defense contractors?

    a. Distinctive color coding

    b. Symbol code

    c. Top secret or secret

    d. Confidential

    e. Both c and d

    f. All of the above

89. No invitation, written or oral, shall be given to a foreign national or to a representative of a foreign interest to attend any session of a meeting sponsored by a Department of Defense activity until:

    a. A full field investigation has resulted in the necessary security clearance

    b. Approval for attendance has been received from the sponsoring activity

    c. The Department of the State has given approval

    d. The CIA has given approval

    e. None of the above

90. The basic document for conveying to the contractor the classification and declassification specifications for a classified contract is:

    a. Form DD-254

    b. Form DD-441

    c. Form DD-482

    d. Form DD-562

    e. Form DD-1541

91. A document that is classified "confidential" shall exhibit the marking at:

    a. The top of the page

    b. The bottom of the page

    c. The right-hand side of the page

    d. The left-hand side of the page

    e. Both the top and bottom of the page

92. Unclassified material should:

    a. Be marked "unclassified" at the top of the page

    b. Be marked "unclassified" at the bottom of the page

    c. Be marked "unclassified" at the top and bottom of the page

    d. Be marked "unclassified" anywhere on the page

    e. Have no marking

93. An unclassified document that is attached to a classified document should have a notation stating:
    a. "Classified same as enclosure"
    b. "Treat as classified"
    c. "Unclassified when separated from classified enclosure"
    d. No notation needed
    e. None of the above
94. Whenever classified information is downgraded, declassified, or upgraded, the material shall be promptly and conspicuously marked to indicate:
    a. What was changed
    b. The date it was changed
    c. The identity of the person taking the action
    d. All of the above
    e. None of the above
95. Foreign classified material should be marked in accordance with instructions received from:
    a. The Defense Intelligence Agency
    b. The foreign contracting authority
    c. The FBI
    d. The Industrial Security Office
    e. None of the above
96. Department of Defense regulations regarding the protection of classified information requires that defense contractors maintain accountability of top secret information for a minimum time of:
    a. 1 year
    b. 2 years
    c. 3 years
    d. 4 years
    e. 5 years
97. When not in use, top secret information should be stored in a:
    a. Class A vault
    b. Class B vault
    c. Class C vault
    d. Class D vault
    e. Class E vault
98. Which of the following is prohibited by the Department of Defense regulations regarding the method of transmitting top secret information outside a facility?
    a. Electronic means in a crypto system
    b. Armed Forces Courier Service

    c. Designated courier that has been cleared

    d. US Postal Service

    e. Specifically designated escort

99. Secret information can be transmitted by which of the following means according to Department of Defense regulations?

    a. Designated courier that has been cleared

    b. US Registered Mail

    c. Armed Forces Courier Service

    d. Both a and c

    e. All of the above

100. Department of Defense regulations indicate that destruction of classified information can be accomplished by:

    a. Melting

    b. Burning

    c. Mutilation

    d. Chemical decomposition

    e. All of the above

101. Which of the following has the appropriate security clearances in the destruction of top secret and secret information according to Department of Defense regulations?

    a. Two employees of the defense contractor

    b. Three employees of the defense contractor

    c. Four employees of the defense contractor

    d. One employee of the Department of Defense and two employees of the defense contractor

    e. None of the above

102. According to Department of Defense regulations, if classified material is removed from the facility for destruction, it should be destroyed:

    a. The same day it was removed

    b. Within 2 days

    c. Within 3 days

    d. Within 1 week

    e. Within 10 days

103. According to Department of Defense regulations, to be eligible for a personnel security clearance for confidential information, the following age must be attained:

    a. 16

    b. 18

    c. 20

    d. 21

    e. 25

104. According to Department of Defense regulations, the security clearance of a contractual employee shall be effective for:
    a. 6 months
    b. 1 year
    c. 2 years
    d. 5 years
    e. As long as he or she is employed by the contractor

105. According to Department of Defense regulations, the following are *not* eligible for a personnel security clearance:
    a. All foreign nationals
    b. All foreign nationals except those granted reciprocal clearances
    c. Only foreign nationals that are from a communist country
    d. Only foreign nationals that are under 16
    e. None of the above

106. A facility security clearance should not be granted to contractor activities:
    a. In Puerto Rico
    b. In facilities determined to be under foreign ownership, control, or influence
    c. In US trust territories
    d. Both a and c
    e. All of the above

107. For personnel security clearances required in connection with a facility security clearance, applications shall be submitted to the:
    a. Defense Intelligence Agency
    b. Industrial Clearance Office
    c. Contracting officer
    d. Cognizant Security Office
    e. Central Intelligence Agency

108. According to Department of Defense regulations, "interim" personnel security clearances must be approved by the:
    a. Defense Intelligence Agency
    b. Industrial Clearance Office
    c. Contracting officer
    d. Cognizant Security Office
    e. None of the above

109. Department of Defense regulations require initial approval in writing prior to processing any classified information in an ADP system by which of the following authorities?
    a. Head of the Industrial Security Clearance Office
    b. National Security Agency
    c. Cognizant Security Office

    d. Contracting officer

    e. Defense Intelligence Agency

110. An ADP system that operates in a manner where all users with access to the system have both a security clearance and a need-to-know status for all classified information that is in the system is known as:

    a. Classified security mode

    b. Restricted security mode

    c. Controlled security mode

    d. Dedicated security mode

    e. Limited security mode

111. An ADP system that operates in a manner in which all users with access to the system who have a security clearance for the highest classification and most restrictive types of information in the system is known as:

    a. Classified security mode

    b. Restricted security mode

    c. Controlled security mode

    d. System high-security mode

    e. Dedicated security mode

112. An ADP system that operates in a manner in which at least some of the users with access to the system have neither a security clearance nor a need-to-know status for all classified information that is in the system, but in a manner that the cognizant security officer or a higher authority has determined that the necessary degree of security has been achieved and maintained, is known as:

    a. Limited security mode

    b. Classified security mode

    c. Controlled security mode

    d. Restricted security mode

    e. Dedicated security mode

113. The ADP system security supervisor or designee should review the audit trail logs at least:

    a. Daily

    b. Weekly

    c. Monthly

    d. Bimonthly

    e. Quarterly

114. The Department of Defense Personnel Security Questionnaire (Industrial) Form is:

    a. DD-16

    b. DD-48

    c. DD-254

    d. DD-441

    e. DD-482

115. According to Department of Defense regulations, which of the following documents is *not* acceptable proof of US citizenship concerning the safeguarding of classified information?

    a. Birth certificate

    b. Certificate of naturalization

    c. Certificate of citizenship

    d. Uncertified copy of baptismal record

    e. All of the above

116. All proprietary information is sensitive, while not all sensitive information is proprietary. An example of information that is not proprietary even though the organization would treat it as sensitive is:

    a. The customer database of the organization

    b. Confidential personnel data in employee files

    c. Strategic marketing plans in which the use of outside marketing firms is contemplated

    d. Specifications for product components that are produced by a subcontractor

117. Trade secrets are generally afforded greater legal protection than other proprietary information. Which of the following in not an element of the test for a trade secret?

    a. Be identifiable

    b. Not already be available in public sources

    c. Be disclosed only to persons with a duty to protect it

    d. Be technical or product related

118. The major reason for the loss of sensitive information is:

    a. Espionage

    b. Intentional disclosure by an insider

    c. Inadvertent disclosure

    d. Disclosure through legal proceedings

119. Competitive intelligence gathering is a legitimate activity, which is engaged in by many firms throughout the world. The most important function of competitive intelligence is to:

    a. Alert senior management to marketplace changes in order to prevent surprises

    b. Alert senior management as to the personal habits of competitive senior management

    c. Alert government intelligence agencies to marketplace changes

    d. Alert senior management to changes in protocol in foreign countries

120. A microphone with a large disklike attachment used for listening to audio from great distances is known as a:
    a. Contact microphone
    b. Spike microphone
    c. Parabolic microphone
    d. Moving-coil microphone

121. Sound waves too high in frequency to be heard by the human ear, generally above 20 kHz, are known as:
    a. Microwaves
    b. Ultrasonic
    c. High frequency
    d. Short wave

122. Two methods of protection against telephone line eavesdropping are apparently reliable. The first method is "don't discuss sensitive information," and the other is:
    a. To a use wire tap detector
    b. To use a radio jammer
    c. To use an audio jammer
    d. To use encryption equipment

123. The unauthorized acquisition of sensitive information is known as:
    a. Industrial espionage
    b. Embezzlement
    c. Larceny
    d. False pretenses

124. Proprietary information is:
    a. Information that must be so classified under government order
    b. Private information of highly sensitive character
    c. Defense data that must be classified according to federal regulations
    d. Anything that an enterprise considers relevant to its status or operations and does not want to disclose publicly

125. A trade secret is:
    a. Any formula, pattern, device, or compilation of information that is used in one's business and that gives that business an opportunity to gain an advantage over competitors who do not know or use it
    b. All information about a company that the company desires to protect
    c. Information of a company that is registered as such with the US Patent Office
    d. Information so designed by the government

126. The control software of a Private Board Exchange (PBX) can be accessed and compromised by calling the telephone number of a device on the PBX from a computer and modem. What is this access device called?
    a. Time-domain reflectometer
    b. Remote maintenance access terminal
    c. Current carrier signaling port
    d. Internal and remote signal port

127. Which of the following is generally not true with regard to proprietary information?
    a. Secret information does not have to be specifically identifiable.
    b. Secret information must be such that it can be effectively protected.
    c. The more narrowly a business defines what it regards as secret, the easier it is to protect that body of information.
    d. It is difficult to protect as a trade secret that which can be found in publicly accessible sources.

128. With respect to trade secrets, it may be decided that its disclosure by another was innocent rather than wrongful, even in the case where the person making the disclosure really was guilty of malice or wrong intent. This situation may occur when:
    a. There is absence of evidence that an owner has taken reasonable precautions to protect confidential information
    b. The trade secret was not registered
    c. The trade secret did not involve national defense information
    d. The trade secret was not in current use

129. The class of person under duty to safeguard a proprietary secret is known as:
    a. Agents
    b. Principals
    c. Fiduciaries
    d. Business associates

130. Which of the following is not a correct statement, or a general rule, involving the protection of proprietary information?
    a. By operation of common law, employees are presumed to be fiduciaries to the extent that they may not disclose secrets of their employers without authorization.
    b. As a class, employees are the largest group of persons bound to secrecy because of their status or relationship.
    c. Other than employees, any other persons to be bound to secrecy must agree to be bound.
    d. Any agreements to be bound must always be in writing and are not implied from acts.

131. The term *eavesdropping* refers to:
    a. Wiretapping only
    b. Bugging only
    c. Both wiretapping and bugging
    d. Mail covers

132. A microphone that has the characteristics of requiring no power source to operate it and being quite small, relatively difficult to detect, and offered by equipment suppliers in such items as cuff links and hearing aids is known as a:
    a. Carbon microphone
    b. Dynamic microphone
    c. Contact microphone
    d. Parabolic microphone

133. A microphone that is normally installed on a common wall adjoining a target area when it is impractical or impossible to enter the area to make a microphone installation is a:
    a. Carbon microphone
    b. Dynamic microphone
    c. Contact microphone
    d. Parabolic microphone

134. Which of the following is not true with regard to electronic eavesdropping?
    a. A listening device installed in a wire will cause a crackling sound, click, or other noise that can be heard on the line.
    b. There should be an effective countermeasures survey to detect evidence of electronic eavesdropping.
    c. Equipment in telephones must be conducted by a person technically familiar with such equipment.
    d. All wiring should be traced out and accounted for in a countermeasures survey.
    e. In a countermeasures survey to detect electronic eavesdropping, a physical search should be utilized as well as an electronic search.

135. In designing a proprietary information protection program, the area of greatest vulnerability is:
    a. Personnel files
    b. Marketing data
    c. Employees
    d. Computers

136. A nonlinear junction detector is used to locate eavesdropping devices by:
    a. Detecting the semiconductor components that comprise their circuits
    b. Recording changes in the voltage on a telephone line

     c. Measuring the distance from a known point to the indicated location of a telephone line attachment

     d. Detecting infrared emissions

137. Which of the following statements is incorrect with regard to an information security program?

     a. A good information security program will provide absolute protection against an enemy spy.

     b. The information security program is an attempt to make theft of sensitive information difficult, not necessarily eliminate it.

     c. A trust relationship must be established and maintained with employees.

     d. The goodwill and compliance of employees is crucial for success.

138. A specially constructed microphone attached directly to an object or surface to be protected and that responds only when the protected object or surface is disturbed is known as a:

     a. Parabolic microphone

     b. Special audio device

     c. Contact microphone

     d. Surreptitious microphone

139. *Social engineering* is:

     a. The conversation involved in the beginning of a romantic relationship

     b. A function of the personnel department in which like persons are teamed together in workshops or seminars for maximum productivity

     c. The subtle elicitation of information without revealing the true purpose of the call

     d. The specific design of a business structure to facilitate the interaction of the inhabitants

140. A former employee, who had access to your trade secret information, is now employed by a competitor and is apparently using the trade secret information to gain market share. There are several serious factors you should consider before you institute litigation in the matter. Which of the following is not a serious factor to be considered?

     a. You may have to expose the very secrets you are attempting to protect.

     b. The cost of litigation may exceed the value of the secret information.

     c. You may lose a law case.

     d. Other employees may leave the company and attempt to use the trade secret information in the business of a new employer.

141. Electromagnetic radiation is detectable electromagnetic energy generated by electronic information processing devices. Which of the following is used to protect very sensitive equipment?
    a. A current carrier device
    b. Pneumatic cavity shielding
    c. Tempest shielding
    d. Pen register shielding
142. Piracy refers to the illegal duplication and distribution of recordings. Which form is not considered piracy?
    a. Pirating
    b. Downloading
    c. Bootlegging
    d. Counterfeiting
143. To prevent cyber crime, it is not a good strategy to:
    a. Install a fire protection system
    b. Assign passwords or codes
    c. Disable unused computer services
    d. Update software for improving security
144. Which federal statute does not protect information and communication systems?
    a. USA PATRIOT Act
    b. Economic Espionage Act
    c. Civil Rights Act
    d. Sarbanes–Oxley Act
145. A trade secret consists of which of the following?
    a. Any formula, pattern, device, or compilation of information that is used in one's business and that gives him or her an opportunity to gain an advantage over competitors who do not use it
    b. Answers a and c
    c. It may be a formula for a chemical compound; a process of manufacturing, treating, or preserving materials; or a pattern for a machine or other device.
    d. A list of customers
    e. Answers a, c, and d.
146. Which of the following are basic elements of trade secrets?
    a. It must be secret and not known to others.
    b. It must be used in the business of the owner of the secret to obtain an advantage.
    c. There must be continuous or consistent business applications of the secret.

    d. Answers a and b
    e. All of the above
147. Which of the following is *not* a primary distinction between patents and trade secrets?
    a. Requirements for obtaining a patent are not specific.
    b. A much lower level of novelty is required of a trade secret.
    c. Trade secrets are targets.
    d. To qualify for a patent, the invention must be more than novel and useful.
    e. It must represent a positive contribution beyond the skill of the average person.
    f. Because anyone can purchase a patent, there are no industrial espionage targets in a patented invention.
148. Which of the following statements is correct involving proprietary information?
    a. All confidential information is proprietary, but not all proprietary information is confidential.
    b. All proprietary information is not confidential.
    c. All proprietary information is confidential, but not all confidential information is proprietary.
    d. All confidential information is proprietary.
    e. Answers b and d
149. Which of the following are broad threats to proprietary information?
    a. It can be lost through inadvertent disclosure.
    b. An outsider can deliberately steal it.
    c. An insider can deliberately steal it.
    d. Answers b and c
    e. Answers a, b, and c
150. Which of the following should *not* be included in an effective proprietary information security program?
    a. Designation of appropriate data as insensitive
    b. Informing and notifying employees
    c. Full utilization of secret agreements with employees
    d. Providing physical means to protect sensitive data
    e. Treating sensitive information as proprietary
151. The contact microphone is usually a crystal microphone and is normally installed on a common wall adjoining a target area. Which of the following is a disadvantage of the contact microphone?
    a. Signals generated are weak.
    b. Microphones receive other sounds.
    c. It is affected by changes in temperature and humidity.

     d. Answers b and c

     e. All of the above

152. What is the best way to protect any type of data?

     a. Encrypt it

     b. Patent it

     c. Apply for a trademark

     d. None of the above

     e. All of the above

153. Any information containing which of the following elements is considered to be a valuable asset requiring protection?

     a. Production of goods

     b. Locating and retaining customers

     c. Production of services

     d. Answers a and b

     e. All of the above

154. Which of the following is the most serious threat to trade secrets?

     a. Companies

     b. Media

     c. Employees

     d. Customers

     e. None of the above

CHAPTER 4 ANSWERS

1. e. All of the above

2. a. Manual identification systems

3. e. All of the above

4. c. Once issued, they tend to remain valid indefinitely

5. b. A trade secret

6. e. Both b and c

7. e. All of the above

8. a. The application form

9. d. Prior arrests

10. e. All of the above.

11. b. Any formula, pattern, device, or compilation of information that is used in one's business and that gives that business an opportunity to gain an advantage over competitors who do not know or use it

12. e. All of the above

13. b. Continuous or consistent business applications of a secret not known to others, from the use of which some advantage is gained by the user

14. e. None of the above.

15. d. There is absence of evidence that an owner has taken reasonable precautions to protect confidential information
16. d. Anything that an enterprise considers relevant to its status or operations and does not want to disclose publicly
17. c. Fiduciary
18. e. All of the above
19. d. Any agreements to be bound must always be in writing and are not implied from acts.
20. e. All of the above
21. f. All of the above
22. b. Employees
23. d. All of the above
24. e. All of the above.
25. e. All of the above
26. d. Both a and c.
27. b. The process of examining one's trash for information
28. c. Ultrasonic waves
29. d. Multiplexing
30. e. All of the above.
31. d. Microwave signals travel in curved lines.
32. c. Tempest shielding
33. c. Tempest
34. c. Scrambling
35. d. Vocoder
36. d. Pen register
37. b. A bug
38. c. Contact microphone
39. b. Parabolic microphone
40. c. Contact microphone
41. d. Both a and c.
42. c. Industrial espionage
43. d. Both a and b
44. e. All of the above.
45. c. Dynamic microphone
46. f. All of the above
47. e. None of the above
48. d. Remote maintenance access terminal
49. d. A listening device installed in a wire will cause a crackling sound, click, or other noise that can be heard on the line.
50. c. 1934
51. d. The Omnibus Crime Control and Safe Streets Act of 1968
52. d. 5 years in prison and/or a $10,000 fine
53. b. The crime must be any felony under federal law.

54. e. All of the above.
55. c. Attorney general of the United States or any specially designated assistant attorney general
56. e. All of the above.
57. d. The Privacy Act of 1974
58. e. All of the above
59. a. Law enforcement officials
60. d. All of the above
61. c. Theft by an insider, inadvertent disclosure, industrial espionage
62. e. All of the above
63. c. A good information security program will provide total protection from industrial espionage.
64. a. 2%
65. e. All of the above
66. b. The subtle elicitation of information without revealing the true purpose of the call
67. d. Alert senior management to marketplace changes in order to prevent surprise
68. b. Central Intelligence Agency
69. b. Deputy Undersecretary of Defense for Policy
70. a. Director, Defense Investigative Services
71. c. E.O. 12065
72. c. A closed area
73. d. Cognizant Security Office
74. b. Communications intelligence
75. c. Confidential
76. d. Confidential
77. c. Crypto
78. d. Industrial security
79. e. Information security
80. a. Personnel security clearance
81. e. Every year
82. b. Secret
83. b. Secret
84. d. Top secret
85. d. Top secret
86. c. The nearest FBI office
87. c. Photograph of the holder
88. e. Both c and d
89. b. Approval for their attendance has been received from the sponsoring activity
90. a. Form DD-254

91. e. Both the top and bottom of the page
92. e. Have no marking
93. c. "Unclassified when separated from classified enclosure"
94. d. All of the above
95. b. The foreign contracting authority
96. c. 3 years
97. a. Class A vault
98. d. US Postal Service
99. e. All of the above
100. e. All of the above
101. a. Two employees of the defense contractor
102. a. The same day it was removed
103. a. 16
104. e. As long as he or she is employed by the contractor
105. b. All foreign nationals except those granted reciprocal clearances
106. b. In facilities determined to be under foreign ownership, control, or influence
107. d. Cognizant Security Office
108. c. Contracting officer
109. c. Cognizant Security Office
110. d. Dedicated security mode
111. d. System high-security mode
112. c. Controlled security mode
113. b. Weekly
114. b. DD-48
115. d. Uncertified copy of baptismal record
116. b. Confidential personnel data in employee files
117. d. Be technical or product related
118. c. Inadvertent disclosure
119. a. Alert senior management to marketplace changes in order to prevent surprise
120. c. Parabolic microphone
121. b. Ultrasonic
122. d. To use encryption equipment
123. a. Industrial espionage
124. d. Anything that an enterprise considers relevant to its status or operation and does not want to disclose publicly
125. a. Any formula, pattern, device, or compilation of information that is used in one's business and that gives that business an opportunity to gain an advantage over competitors who do not know or use it
126. b. Remote Maintenance Access Terminal
127. a. Secret information does not have to be specifically identifiable.

128. a. There is absence of evidence that an owner has taken reasonable precautions to protect confidential information
129. c. Fiduciaries
130. d. Any agreements to be bound must always be in writing and are not implied from acts.
131. c. Both wiretapping and bugging
132. b. Dynamic microphone
133. c. Contact microphone
134. a. A listening device installed in a wire will cause a crackling sound, click, or other noise that can be heard on the line.
135. c. Employees
136. a. Detecting the semiconductor components that comprise their circuits
137. a. A good information security program will provide absolute protection against an enemy spy.
138. c. Contact microphone
139. c. The subtle elicitation of information without revealing the true purpose of the call
140. d. Other employees may leave the company and attempt to use trade secret information in the business of a new employer.
141. c. Tempest shielding
142. b. Downloading
143. a. Install a fire protection system
144. c. Civil Rights Act
145. e. Answers a, c, and d.
146. d. Answers a and b
147. a. Requirements for obtaining a patent are not specific.
148. c. All proprietary information is confidential, but not all confidential information is proprietary.
149. e. Answers a, b, and c
150. a. Designation of appropriate data as insensitive
151. e. All of the above
152. a. Encrypt it.
153. e. All of the above
154. c. Employees

CHAPTER 5: SUBSTANCE ABUSE

1. Of the following substance schedules, which has no current accepted medical use?
   a. Schedule I
   b. Schedule II

    c. Schedule III

    d. Schedule IV

    e. Schedule V

2. Of the following substance schedules, which one has an accepted medical use in treatment and a high potential for abuse that could lead to severe psychological and physical dependence?

    a. Schedule I

    b. Schedule II

    c. Schedule III

    d. Schedule IV

    e. Schedule V

3. Of the following substance schedules, which one has an accepted medical use in treatment and a low potential for abuse with limited psychological and physical dependence when compared to other substances and drugs?

    a. Schedule I

    b. Schedule II

    c. Schedule III

    d. Schedule IV

    e. Schedule V

4. The Controlled Substances Act has imposed certain record-keeping requirements on those involved in the manufacturing, purchasing, and distribution of substances under the act. Which of the following is *not* one of the specific requirements?

    a. Record-keeping requirements apply to all substances under control, regardless of schedule.

    b. Record-keeping requirements state that full records be kept of all quantities that are manufactured, purchased, sold, and inventoried of the substance by each handler.

    c. Records for schedule I and schedule II drugs must be kept separate from all other records of the handler.

    d. Records for schedule III, IV, and V drugs must be kept in a form defined as "readily available."

    e. Record-keeping requirements only apply to schedule I, II, and III substances.

5. The primary federal law that provides the legal foundation for the current federal strategy of reducing the consumption of illicit drugs is:

    a. The Harrison Narcotics Act

    b. The Volstead Act

    c. Title II, Comprehensive Drug Abuse Prevention and Control Act of 1970

    d. The Drug Enforcement Administration Act of 1982

    e. None of the above

6. Which of the following is correct in the regulatory requirements of schedule V substances under the Controlled Substances Act?
   a. Keeping readily retrievable records.
   b. Registration by those who handle or intend to handle the substance.
   c. Use of a regulated storage area.
   d. No written prescription is required.
   e. International transactions must be made with prior notice to the DEA.
   f. All of the above.
7. The Federal Act mandates that for simple possession of any controlled substance, the first offense is:
   a. Up to 1 year in jail/prison and/or a $5000 fine
   b. Up to 2 years in prison and/or a $5,000 fine
   c. Up to 3 years in prison and/or a $10,000 fine
   d. Up to 5 years in prison and/or a $15,000 fine
   e. Up to 15 years in prison and/or a $25,000 fine
8. The federal trafficking penalty for a schedule I narcotic that is the first offense is:
   a. 5 years in prison and/or a $10,000 fine
   b. 10 years in prison and/or a $20,000 fine
   c. 15 years in prison and/or a $25,000 fine
   d. 20 years in prison and/or a $30,000 fine
   e. 30 years in prison and/or a $50,000 fine
9. Which of the following is *not* correct regarding narcotics?
   a. They have been used for a long period of time as a remedy for diarrhea.
   b. The term *narcotic* in its medical meaning refers to opium and opium derivatives or a synthetic substitute.
   c. They tend to intensify vision and increase alertness.
   d. They are the most effective agents known for the relief of intense pain.
   e. They can cause respiratory depression in some cases.
10. Which of the following is *not* designated as a narcotic?
    a. Codeine
    b. Morphine
    c. Heroin
    d. Cocaine
    e. Librium
11. The main source of nonsynthetic narcotics is:
    a. The laboratory
    b. Poppy, *Papaver somniferus*
    c. The coca plant

    d. Peyote

    e. None of the above

12. Narcotics are known by a number of trade names. One of the trade names is:

    a. Quaalude

    b. Azene

    c. Valium

    d. Paregoric

    e. Butisol

13. Which of the following is a characteristic of morphine?

    a. It is the principal constituent of opium.

    b. Its legal use is restricted primarily to hospitals.

    c. It is odorless and bitter tasting, and darkens with age.

    d. Only a small part of the morphine obtained from opium is used medically.

    e. Both a and d.

    f. All of the above.

14. Which naturally occurring narcotic is by far the most widely used and is often combined with other products such as aspirin or Tylenol?

    a. Methadone

    b. Codeine

    c. Barbiturates

    d. Chloral hydrate

    e. None of the above

15. Watery eyes, runny nose, yawning, loss of appetite, irritability, tremors, panic, chills and sweating, cramps, and nausea would indicate withdrawal symptoms of:

    a. Barbiturates

    b. Stimulants

    c. Heroin

    d. Cocaine

    e. LSD

16. Which of the following is a correct statement pertaining to heroin?

    a. The first comprehensive control of heroin in the United States was established with the Harrison Narcotics Act of 1914.

    b. Pure heroin is rarely sold on the street.

    c. The Bayer company in Germany first started commercial production of heroin as a pain remedy in the latter part of the nineteenth century.

    d. Pure heroin is a white powder and is also known as "horse."

    e. Both b and d.

    f. All of the above.

17. Which of the following does *not* apply to synthetic narcotics?
    a. Two of the most widely available synthetic narcotics are meperidine and methadone.
    b. Synthetic narcotics are produced entirely within the laboratory.
    c. Synthetic narcotics are also covered by the Controlled Substances Act.
    d. Meperidine can be administered by injection or taken orally.
    e. Large doses can result in convulsions.
    f. None of the above.
18. Which of the following is *not* a correct statement regarding methadone?
    a. Methadone was synthesized in Germany during World War II because of a shortage of morphine.
    b. Methadone was introduced to the United States in 1947 and was distributed under such names as amidone, dolophine, and methadone.
    c. Methadone is chemically like morphine and heroin.
    d. Methadone was widely used in the 1960s in the treatment of narcotic addicts.
    e. Methadone is only effective when administered by injection.
    f. Both c and e.
19. Which of the following drugs is classified as a depressant under the Controlled Substances Act?
    a. Morphine
    b. Cocaine
    c. Phenmetrazine
    d. Methaqualone
    e. None of the above
20. Cold and clammy skin, dilated pupils, shallow breathing, and a weak and rapid pulse are overdose symptoms resulting from which of the following substances?
    a. Cocaine
    b. Barbiturates
    c. Methylphenidate
    d. Heroin
    e. LSD
21. Which of the following is *not* correct pertaining to the use of depressants?
    a. Excessive use results in drunken behavior similar to that with alcohol.
    b. Taken as prescribed, they are beneficial for relief of tension and anxiety.

    c. Taken in low doses, they will produce mild sedation.

    d. The intoxicating effects of depressants are the same as those of narcotics.

    e. Depressants can be used as a means of suicide.

22. Which of the following substances would be classified as a depressant under the Controlled Substances Act?

    a. Preludin

    b. Darvon

    c. Miltown

    d. Dilaudid

    e. Pethadol

    f. All of the above

23. Depressants of various types are included in schedules II, III, and IV of the Controlled Substances Act. Which of the following does *not* apply to the use of depressants?

    a. Depressants have a high potential for abuse.

    b. Some drug abusers often resort to the use of depressants to soothe their nerves after the use of stimulants.

    c. The use of depressants compounded with alcohol can cause death.

    d. Moderate depressant poisoning closely resembles intoxication from alcohol.

    e. One of the recognized features of the use of depressants is that tolerance will not develop.

24. Which of the following withdrawal characteristics can result from the abrupt cessation or reduction of high-dose depressant usage?

    a. The withdrawal symptoms associated with depressants are more serious than those of any other drugs of abuse.

    b. Convulsions can be experienced that are indistinguishable from those occurring in grand mal epilepsy.

    c. Detoxification and treatment must be carried out under close medical supervision.

    d. Both a and c.

    e. All of the above.

25. Which of the following is *not* a correct statement regarding chloral hydrate?

    a. It is the oldest of the sleep-inducing drugs, also known as hypnotic drugs.

    b. It is a liquid marketed in the form of syrups and soft gelatin capsules.

    c. Its popularity decreased after the introduction of barbiturates.

    d. Its main abuse is by young adults.

    e. It has a bitter caustic taste and a slightly acrid odor.

26. Which of the following characteristics describes barbiturates?
    a. They are used by both physicians and veterinarians to induce sedation and sleep.
    b. Larger doses cause sleep 20 to 60 min after oral administration.
    c. Some individuals may experience a sense of excitement before sedation takes effect.
    d. Barbiturates are classified as ultrashort, short, intermediate, and long-acting.
    e. All of the above.
    f. None of the above.
27. Barbiturates have about 2500 derivatives of barbituric acid and are known by a variety of names. Which of the following is another name for a barbiturate?
    a. Demerol
    b. Pethadol
    c. Leritine
    d. Butisol
    e. Talwin
    f. All of the above
28. Which of the following is *not* another name for a barbiturate?
    a. Tuinal
    b. Butisol
    c. Phenobarbital
    d. Amobarbital
    e. Dilaudid
    f. None of the above
29. Which of the following identifies the depressant methaqualone?
    a. It was once mistakenly thought to be effective as an aphrodisiac.
    b. It is administered orally.
    c. It is a schedule I drug in the Controlled Substances Act.
    d. It is chemically unrelated to the barbiturates.
    e. It is also known as Quaalude.
    f. All of the above.
30. Which of the following is *not* another name for methaqualone?
    a. Optimil
    b. Darvon
    c. Parest
    d. Sopor
    e. Voranil
    f. Both b and e
31. Which of the following describes meprobamate?
    a. It was first synthesized in 1950.

  b. It is primarily prescribed for the relief of anxiety and tension as well as muscle spasms.

  c. It does not produce sleep at therapeutic doses.

  d. Excessive use can result in physical and psychological dependence.

  e. All of the above.

  f. None of the above.

32. Which of the following is *not* a brand name of meprobamate?

  a. Miltown

  b. Equanil

  c. Preludin

  d. SK-Bamate

  e. Kesso-Bamate

33. Which of the following is *not* correct with regard to benzodiazepine?

  a. This family of depressants is used to relieve anxiety and tension.

  b. This depressant relieves muscle spasms and prevents convulsions.

  c. When used to induce a "high," this depressant is taken in combination with other substances such as alcohol or marijuana.

  d. This depressant is safer to use than other depressants.

  e. Excessive use may result in physical and psychological dependence.

  f. None of the above.

34. Which of the following is a member of the benzodiazepine group known in the United States?

  a. Librium

  b. Klonopin

  c. Valium

  d. Serax

  e. All of the above

35. Excitation, increased alertness, euphoria, increased pulse rate and blood pressure, insomnia, and loss of appetite are symptoms of:

  a. Hallucinogens

  b. Depressants

  c. Stimulants

  d. Benzodiazepines

  e. Marijuana

36. All of the following are controlled substances grouped as stimulants except:

  a. Cocaine

  b. Methyphenidate

  c. Mescaline

  d. Amphetamines
  e. Phenmetrazine
37. Which of the following characteristics describes stimulants as a controlled substance?
  a. Younger individuals who use stimulants for a euphoric effect often go on to experiment with other drugs of abuse.
  b. Users tend to rely on stimulants to feel stronger, more decisive, and self-possessed.
  c. Stimulants are usually administered by injection or taken orally.
  d. Heavy use could result in psychological dependence.
  e. Tolerance develops from heavy use.
  f. All of the above.
38. Which of the following is *not* known as a stimulant?
  a. Cocaine
  b. Doriden
  c. Ritalin
  d. Bacarate
  e. Preludin
39. Cocaine is derived from which of the following?
  a. Cactus plant
  b. Poppy plant
  c. Coffee bean
  d. Coca plant
  e. Mushrooms
40. Which of the following is a correct statement regarding illicit cocaine?
  a. It is very popular as a recreational drug.
  b. It has the potential for extraordinary psychic dependency due to its pleasurable effect.
  c. It is distributed as a white crystalline powder and is also known as snow.
  d. It is often adulterated to about half its volume by a variety of other ingredients.
  e. It is commonly administered by snorting through the nasal passages.
  f. All of the above.
41. Cocaine is placed in which of the following controlled-substance schedules?
  a. Schedule I
  b. Schedule II
  c. Schedule III

    d. Schedule IV

    e. Schedule V

42. Which of the following is *not* known as an amphetamine?

    a. Biphetamine

    b. Delcobese

    c. Desoxyn

    d. Dexedrine

    e. None of the above

43. Which of the following substances would induce poor perception of time and distance?

    a. Stimulants

    b. Depressants

    c. Hallucinogens

    d. Cannabis

    e. Narcotics

44. Which of the following does *not* describe hallucinogens?

    a. Pupils are dilated, with a rise in body temperature and blood pressure.

    b. They induce a state of excitation of the central nervous system.

    c. They are schedule III substances.

    d. Long after hallucinogens are eliminated from the body, users may experience "flashbacks."

    e. Suicide can sometimes result from severe depression after use.

45. Which one of the following substances is *not* an hallucinogen?

    a. Lysergic acid diethylamide

    b. Mescaline

    c. Phencyclidine

    d. Phencyclidine analogs

    e. None of the above

46. The hallucinogen mescaline is derived from:

    a. The coca plant

    b. The sage bush

    c. The peyote cactus

    d. Mushrooms

    e. Dandelions

47. Which of the following statements is correct regarding LSD?

    a. It is produced from lysergic acid, which is a substance derived from the ergot fungus that grows on rye.

    b. Its psychotomimetic effects were discovered accidentally.

    c. Its popularity declined after the 1960s.

    d. Tolerance develops rapidly.

    e. All of the above.

48. According to a consensus of drug treatment professionals, the drug that now poses a greater risk to the user than any other drug of abuse is:
    a. Heroin
    b. Cocaine
    c. Phencyclidine
    d. Chloral hydrate
    e. Marijuana

49. Which of the following is *not* a true statement in regard to phencyclidine?
    a. It is also known as angel dust and PCP.
    b. It is unique among popular drugs of abuse in its power to produce psychoses that are indistinguishable from schizophrenia.
    c. Most phencyclidine is produced in clandestine laboratories.
    d. It is a schedule I substance.
    e. None of the above.

50. Marijuana comes from:
    a. The peyote cactus
    b. The cannabis plant
    c. The poppy plant
    d. The coca plant
    e. Mushrooms

51. Marijuana and other cannabis products are usually administered by:
    a. Sniffing
    b. Injection
    c. Rubbing into the skin
    d. Smoking
    e. "Mainstreaming"

52. Marijuana is known by which of the following names?
    a. Reefer
    b. Acapulco Gold
    c. Grass
    d. Pot
    e. Thai sticks
    f. All of the above

53. Hashish mainly comes from:
    a. Peru
    b. Chile
    c. Colombia
    d. South Africa
    e. The Middle East

54. The physiological adaptation of the body to the presence of a drug whereby the body develops a continuing need for the drug is known as:
    a. Tolerance
    b. Addiction
    c. Psychological dependence
    d. Physical dependence
    e. Habituation

55. The condition whereby a user must keep increasing the dosage to maintain the same effect is known as:
    a. Tolerance
    b. Addiction
    c. Psychological dependence
    d. Physical dependence
    e. Habituation

56. The condition whereby the user of a substance develops an attachment to the drug because of the substance's ability to satisfy some emotional or personality need of the user is known as:
    a. Tolerance
    b. Addiction
    c. Psychological dependence
    d. Physical dependence
    e. Psychosis

57. The state of periodic or chronic intoxication produced by the repeated consumption of a substance is known as:
    a. Tolerance
    b. Addiction
    c. Drug dependence
    d. Habituation
    e. Psychosis

58. Which of the following is not a correct statement with regard to narcotics?
    a. The term *narcotic* in its medical meaning refers to opium and opium derivatives of synthetic substitutes.
    b. They are the most effective agents known for the relief of intense pain.
    c. They have been used for a long period of time as a remedy for diarrhea.
    d. They tend to intensify vision and increase alertness.

59. Which of the following characteristics does not pertain to morphine?
    a. It is the principal constituent of opium.
    b. Its legal use is restricted primarily to hospitals.

c. It tastes sweet and is marketed in the form of yellow crystals.

d. Tolerance and dependence develop rapidly.

60. Most of this substance is produced from morphine, but it is often combined with other products such as aspirin or Tylenol. It is often used for relief of coughs, and it is by far the most widely used naturally occurring narcotic in medical treatment. It is:

a. Barbiturates

b. Mescaline

c. Chloral hydrate

d. Codeine

61. German scientists synthesized methadone during World War II because of a shortage of morphine. Which of the following is not characteristic of methadone and its usage?

a. Although chemically unlike morphine and heroin, it produces many of the same effects.

b. It was distributed under such names as amidone, dolophine, and methadone.

c. It was widely used in the 1960s in the treatment of narcotic addicts.

d. It is only effective when administered by injection.

62. Which of the following characteristics do not pertain to the use or effects of depressants generally?

a. The usual methods of administration are oral or injection.

b. Excessive use results in drunken behavior similar to that with alcohol.

c. There is no danger of tolerance developing.

d. Taken as prescribed, they may be beneficial for the relief of anxiety and tension.

63. Another widely abused depressant is methaqualone. All of the following are factually descriptive of methaqualone except one. Identify this exception.

a. It is chemically unrelated to the barbiturates.

b. It was once mistakenly thought to be effective as an aphrodisiac.

c. It is administered orally.

d. It is one of the depressants that does not lead to tolerance and dependence.

64. All of the following are controlled substances grouped as stimulants except one. Identify the exception.

a. Cocaine

b. Amphetamines

c. Phenmetrazine

d. Mescaline

65. All of the following are factual statements descriptive of illicit cocaine except one, which is that:
    a. It is distributed on the street as a white to dark brown powder
    b. It is often adulterated to about half its volume by a variety of other ingredients
    c. This substance is only used through the process of injection
    d. It is popularly accepted as a recreational drug
66. Which of the following is another name for cocaine?
    a. Adipex
    b. Bacarate
    c. Piegine
    d. Snow
67. Which of the following statements does not pertain to cocaine?
    a. It has a medical use as a sedative.
    b. There is a possibility that sustained use could result in physical dependence.
    c. There is a high possibility that sustained use could result in psychological dependence.
    d. Tolerance is a distinct possibility.
68. The effects of illusions and hallucinations with poor perception of time and distance possibly indicate the use of which of the following substances?
    a. Cannabis
    b. Hallucinogens
    c. Stimulants
    d. Depressants
69. All of the following are hallucinogens except:
    a. LSD
    b. Marijuana
    c. Mescaline
    d. Phencyclidine
70. The source of marijuana is the:
    a. Peyote cactus
    b. Mushrooms
    c. Coca plant
    d. Cannabis plant
71. Cannabis products are usually taken:
    a. Through sniffing
    b. By Injection
    c. By smoking
    d. By rubbing into the skin

72. The condition whereby a user develops an attachment to the use of a substance due to its ability to satisfy some emotional or personality need of the person is known as:
    a. Tolerance
    b. Physical dependence
    c. Addiction
    d. Psychological dependence
73. The state of periodic or chronic intoxication produced by the repeated consumption of a substance is known as:
    a. Tolerance
    b. Addiction
    c. Habituation
    d. Drug dependence
74. Which of the following is a characteristic of a schedule I drug?
    a. Has high potential for abuse
    b. Has no acceptable medical use
    c. Can be purchased at a drugstore without a prescription
    d. Answers a and b
    e. None of the above
75. Which of the following is *not* a characteristic of narcotic use?
    a. Pinpoint pupils
    b. Apathy
    c. Drowsiness
    d. Insomnia
    e. Respiratory depression
76. Which of the following is *not* a characteristic of a schedule II drug?
    a. Has a high potential for abuse
    b. Has no acceptable medical use
    c. Abuse may lead to severe psychological dependence.
    d. Abuse may lead to severe physical dependence.
    e. Has low potential for abuse
77. Which of the following is *not* a characteristic of use?
    a. Pinpoint pupils
    b. Apathy
    c. Drowsiness
    d. Insomnia
    e. Respiratory depression
78. Which of the following is *not* a characteristic of a schedule III drug?
    a. Has a potential for abuse less than schedule I or II drugs
    b. Has no acceptable medical use

    c. Abuse may lead to low psychological dependence.

    d. Abuse may lead to low physical dependence.

    e. Has a current acceptable medical use

79. Which of the following is *not* an overdose characteristic of narcotic use?

    a. Agitation

    b. Clammy skin

    c. Convulsions

    d. Possible death

    e. Slow and shallow breathing

80. Which of the following is *not* a characteristic of a schedule IV drug?

    a. Has low potential for abuse relative to the substances in schedules I, II, and III

    b. Has a current acceptable medical use

    c. Abuse may lead to limited physical dependence.

    d. Abuse may lead to low psychological dependence.

    e. None of the above

81. The possible effects generally associated with the use of stimulants include all of the following *except*:

    a. Euphoria

    b. Insomnia

    c. Decreased pulse rate and blood pressure

    d. Increased alertness

    e. Loss of appetite

82. Which of the following is *not* a characteristic of a schedule V drug?

    a. Has low potential for abuse relative to the substances in schedules I, II, III, and IV

    b. Has a current acceptable medical use

    c. Abuse may lead to limited physical dependence.

    d. Abuse may lead to limited psychological dependence.

    e. None of the above

83. The overdose characteristics of stimulants include all of the following *except*:

    a. Agitation

    b. Increase in body temperature

    c. Hallucinations

    d. Yawning

    e. Convulsions

CHAPTER 5 ANSWERS

1. a. Schedule I
2. b. Schedule II
3. d. Schedule IV
4. e. Record-keeping requirements only apply to schedule I, II, and III substances.
5. c. Title II, Comprehensive Drug Abuse Prevention and Control Act of 1970
6. f. All of the above.
7. a. Up to 1 year in jail/prison and/or a $5000 fine
8. c. 15 years in prison and/or a $25,000 fine
9. c. They tend to intensify vision and increase alertness.
10. e. Librium
11. b. Poppy, *Papaver somniferus*
12. d. Paregoric
13. f. All of the above.
14. b. Codeine
15. c. Heroin
16. f. All of the above.
17. f. None of the above.
18. f. Both c and e.
19. d. Methaqualone
20. b. Barbiturates
21. d. The intoxicating effects of depressants are the same as those of narcotics.
22. c. Miltown
23. e. One of the recognized features of the use of depressants is that tolerance will not develop.
24. e. All of the above.
25. d. Its main abuse is by young adults.
26. e. All of the above.
27. d. Butisol
28. e. Dilaudid
29. f. All of the above.
30. f. Both b and e
31. e. All of the above.
32. c. Preludin
33. f. None of the above.
34. e. All of the above
35. c. Stimulants
36. c. Mescaline
37. f. All of the above.

38. e. Preludin
39. d. Coca plant
40. f. All of the above
41. b. Schedule II
42. e. None of the above
43. c. Hallucinogens
44. c. They are schedule III substances.
45. e. None of the above
46. c. The peyote cactus
47. e. All of the above.
48. c. Phencyclidine
49. d. It is a schedule I substance.
50. b. The cannabis plant
51. d. Smoking
52. f. All of the above
53. e. The Middle East
54. d. Physical dependence
55. a. Tolerance
56. c. Psychological dependence
57. b. Addiction
58. d. They tend to intensify vision and increase alertness.
59. c. It tastes sweet and is marketed in the form of yellow crystals.
60. d. Codeine
61. d. It is only effective when administered by injection.
62. c. There is no danger of tolerance developing.
63. d. It is one of the depressants that does not lead to tolerance and dependence.
64. d. Mescaline
65. c. This substance is only used through the process of injection
66. d. Snow
67. a. It has a medical use as a sedative.
68. b. Hallucinogen
69. b. Marijuana
70. d. Cannabis plant
71. c. By smoking
72. d. Psychological dependence
73. b. Addiction
74. d. Answers a and b
75. d. Insomnia
76. e. Has low potential for abuse
77. d. Insomnia
78. b. Has no acceptable medical use
79. a. Agitation

80. d. Abuse may lead to low psychological dependence.
81. c. Decreased pulse rate and blood pressure
82. e. None of the above
83. d. Yawning

CHAPTER 6: PHYSICAL SECURITY

1. What process does a security manager use in establishing priorities in the protection of assets?
   a. Audit survey
   b. Security survey
   c. Risk analysis or assessment
   d. Inspection review
   e. Both b and c
   f. All of the above
2. The degree of protection desired in any installation is predicated on an analysis of which of the following?
   a. Cost and vulnerability
   b. Cost and criticality
   c. Criticality and vulnerability
   d. Vulnerability and environmental conditions
   e. None of the above
3. A critical on-site examination *and* analysis of a facility to ascertain the present security status and to identify deficiencies or excesses in determining the protection needed to make recommendations to improve overall security is the definition of a(n):
   a. Full-field inspection
   b. Inspection review
   c. Audit survey
   d. Security survey
   e. None of the above
4. What is a key consideration in a risk analysis or risk assessment process?
   a. Vulnerability to attack
   b. Probability of attack
   c. Cost
   d. Impact to the business if loss occurs
   e. Both a and b
   f. All of the above
5. From a security perspective, what is the first factor to be considered in facility construction?
   a. The identity of experienced consultants
   b. An effective security plan

c. The building site itself

d. An architect with knowledge of physical security

e. None of the above

6. Which of the following is *not* correct regarding a security education program?

a. Many people are naive and trusting.

b. All installation personnel must be made aware of the constant threat of breaches of security.

c. Structural aids to security are valueless without active support of all personnel.

d. Security consciousness is an inherent state of mind.

e. None of the above.

7. The most vulnerable link in any identification system is:

a. Poor quality of identification badges

b. Educational background of security officers

c. Not enough security officers assigned to control posts

d. Identification cards being too small

e. Perfunctory performance of duty

f. None of the above

8. Which of the following is *not* true in regard to establishing and identifying personnel to control movement?

a. The identification card should be designed as simply as possible.

b. Detailed instructions should be disseminated as to where, when, and how badges should be worn.

c. Procedures should be designed to show employees what to do when an identification card or badge is lost.

d. The identification card or badge should be designed in a relatively complicated manner to avoid duplication.

e. Prerequisites for reissue should be devised and disseminated.

9. The use of a simple code word or phrase during a normal conversation to alert other security personnel that an authorized person has been forced to vouch for an unauthorized individual is termed:

a. Code one

b. SOS

c. Security alert

d. Duress code

e. Basic alert

10. The practice of having at least two authorized persons, each capable of detecting incorrect or unauthorized procedures with respect to the task being performed, present during any operation that affords access to a sensitive area is referred to as the:

a. Two-man access procedure

    b. Two-man control rule

    c. Two-man rule

    d. Controlled access rule

    e. Information security rule

    f. None of the above

11. The designation and establishment of "restricted areas" according to army regulations is performed by the:

    a. Joint Chiefs of Staff

    b. National Security Agency

    c. Secretary of Defense

    d. Secretary of the Army

    e. Military commander of the installation or facility

12. Which of the following is *not* a known advantage of the establishment of restricted areas?

    a. They provide an increase in security without slowdown in operation.

    b. They provide increased security through buffer zones.

    c. They allow for varying degrees of security as required.

    d. They improve overall security.

    e. They make it possible to have security compatible with operational requirements.

13. A restricted area containing a security interest or other sensitive matter, in which uncontrolled movement can permit access to the security interest or sensitive matter but within which access may be prevented by security escort and other internal restrictions and controls, is called a(n):

    a. Exclusion area

    b. Controlled area

    c. Limited area

    d. Sensitized area

    e. None of the above

14. What type of fencing is generally used for protection of limited and exclusion areas?

    a. Concertina

    b. Barbed tape

    c. Barbed wire

    d. Chain link

    e. Wood

15. Excluding the top guard, a chain-link fence for general security purposes should be:

    a. 6 gauge

    b. 7 gauge

    c. 8 gauge

   d. 9 gauge

   e. 10 gauge

16. In a chain-link fence with mesh openings for general security purposes, the openings should be no larger than:

   a. 1⅛ in.

   b. 2 in.

   c. 2½ in.

   d. 4 in.

   e. 4½ in.

17. Excluding the top guard, standard barbed-wire fencing that is
intended to prevent human trespassing should not be less than:

   a. 6 ft. high

   b. 7 ft. high

   c. 8 ft. high

   d. 9 ft. high

   e. 10 ft. high

18. The federal specification regarding standard barbed-wire fencing
that is twisted and double-strand is that it should be:

   a. 8 gauge

   b. 10 gauge

   c. 12 gauge

   d. 14 gauge

   e. None of the above

19. A standard barbed-wire, twisted, double-strand fence has how
many point barbs spaced an equal distance apart.

   a. 1

   b. 2

   c. 3

   d. 4

   e. 5

20. The distance between barbed strands in a barbed-wire fence
should not exceed:

   a. 2 in.

   b. 3 in.

   c. 4 in.

   d. 5 in.

   e. 6 in.

21. Top-guard supporting arms should be permanently affixed to the
top of the fence posts to increase the overall height of the fence by
at least:

   a. 1 ft.

   b. 1½ ft.

   c. 2 ft.

   d. 2½ ft.

   e. 3 ft.

22. A top guard must consist of:

   a. Two strands of barbed wire or tape

   b. Three strands of barbed wire or tape

   c. Four strands of barbed wire or tape

   d. Five strands of barbed wire or tape

   e. Six strands of barbed wire or tape

23. How many inches apart should strands of barbed wire or tape used as a top guard on a fence be spaced?

   a. 2

   b. 3

   c. 4

   d. 5

   e. 6

24. Unavoidable drainage ditches, culverts, vents, ducts, and other openings should be protected by securely fastened welded-bar grills when they have a cross-sectional area greater than:

   a. 10 in.^{2}

   b. 48 in.^{2}

   c. 64 in.^{2}

   d. 96 in.^{2}

   e. 104 in.^{2}

25. Between the perimeter barrier and exterior structures should be a clear zone covering:

   a. 10 ft.

   b. 15 ft.

   c. 20 ft.

   d. 30 ft.

   e. 40 ft.

26. As a general rule, between the perimeter barrier and structures within the protected area, except when a building is a part of the perimeter barrier, there should be a clear zone of at least:

   a. 10 ft.

   b. 20 ft.

   c. 30 ft.

   d. 40 ft.

   e. 50 ft.

27. Manhole covers _____ in. or more in diameter should be secured to prevent unauthorized openings.

   a. 10

   b. 20

   c. 30

d. 40
e. 50

28. Which of the following characteristics of protective lighting is *incorrect*?
    a. It may be unnecessary where the perimeter fence is protected by a central alarm system.
    b. It usually requires less intensity than working light.
    c. It may also provide personal protection by reducing advantages of concealment.
    d. It should only be used as a psychological deterrent.
    e. Such lighting is expensive to maintain.

29. Measured horizontally 6 in. above ground level and at least 30 ft. outside the exclusion area to barrier, the perimeter band of lighting must provide a minimum intensity of:
    a. 0.2 foot-candle
    b. 0.3 foot-candle
    c. 0.4 foot-candle
    d. 0.6 foot-candle
    e. 0.10 foot-candle

30. Which of the following principles of protective lighting is *not* correct?
    a. Lighting should be used with other measures, such as fixed security posts, fences, etc., and not used alone.
    b. A large amount of light should be focused on security patrol routes.
    c. Adequate, even light should be used on bordering areas.
    d. There should be a high brightness contrast between an intruder and the background.
    e. Glaring lights should be directed at the eyes of an intruder.

31. Lighting units of four general types are used for protective lighting. Which of the following is *not* used?
    a. Emergency
    b. Movable
    c. Standby
    d. Intermittent
    e. Continuous

32. What is the most common protective lighting system, which consists of a series of fixed luminaries arranged to flood a given area during the hours of darkness with overlapping cones of light?
    a. Emergency lighting
    b. Movable lighting
    c. Standby lighting
    d. Intermittent lighting
    e. Continuous lighting

33. Piers and docks located on an installation should be safeguarded by illuminating both water approaches and the pier area. Decks on open piers should be illuminated to at least:
   a. 0.5 foot-candle
   b. 1.0 foot-candle
   c. 1.5 foot-candles
   d. 2.0 foot-candles
   e. 3.0 foot-candles

34. Water approaches that extend to 100 ft. from the pier should be illuminated to at least:
   a. 0.5 foot-candle
   b. 1.0 foot-candle
   c. 1.5 foot-candles
   d. 2.0 foot-candles
   e. 3.0 foot-candles

35. The US Army illumination intensity minimums for lighting the perimeter of a restricted area is:
   a. 0.15 foot-candle
   b. 0.40 foot-candle
   c. 1.00 foot-candle
   d. 2.00 foot-candles
   e. 2.15 foot-candles

36. What agency should be consulted before installing protective lighting adjacent to navigable waters?
   a. Local law enforcement agencies
   b. The Department of Transportation
   c. The Bureau of Customs
   d. The US Coast Guard
   e. Both a and b

37. The intrusion detection system in which a pattern of radio waves is transmitted and partially reflected back to the antenna is known as a(n):
   a. Capacitance detection system
   b. Ultrasonic detection system
   c. Vibration detection system
   d. Electromechanical detection system
   e. Microwave detection system

38. The intrusion detection system that is used on safes, walls, and openings in an effort to establish an electrostatic field around an object to be protected is known as a(n):
   a. Capacitance detection system
   b. Ultrasonic detection system
   c. Contact microphone detection system

    d. Microwave detection system

    e. Radio-frequency detection system

39. An alarm system in which the installation-owned system is a direct extension of the police or fire alarm system is known as a(n):

    a. Central station system

    b. Local alarm system

    c. Proprietary system

    d. Auxiliary system

    e. Bell-sound system

40. An alarm system that is monitored by an outside company to provide electric protective services in which they provide the appropriate actions is known as a(n):

    a. Central station system

    b. Local alarm system

    c. Proprietary system

    d. Auxiliary system

    e. Bell-sound system

41. An alarm system whereby the central station is owned by and located within the installation being protected is known as a(n):

    a. Central station system

    b. Local alarm system

    c. Proprietary system

    d. Auxiliary system

    e. Bell-sound system

42. The principle of the pin-tumbler lock can be traced back historically to:

    a. Egyptians more than 4000 years ago

    b. The Civil War period

    c. The late eighteenth century

    d. 1905

    e. World War I

43. Which of the following is *not* true with regard to lock-and-key systems?

    a. The locking system should be supplemented with other security devices.

    b. Most key locks can be picked by an expert in a few minutes.

    c. A high-quality pickproof lock is considered a positive bar to entry.

    d. The lock is the most accepted and widely used security device of the basic safeguards in protecting installations.

    e. Locks, regardless of quality or cost, should be considered as delay devices only.

44. Of the following locks, which type is generally considered to have the poorest security value?
    a. An interchangeable core system
    b. Conventional combination locks
    c. Key locks
    d. Manipulation-resistant combination locks
    e. Both a and d
    f. None of the above
45. The number of combinations possible with a lock that has 40 numbers and a 3-number combination is:
    a. 12,000
    b. 16,000
    c. 32,000
    d. 64,000
    e. 86,000
46. Which lock is generally used on automobiles, desks, and cabinets?
    a. Wafer
    b. Ward
    c. Pin tumbler
    d. Combination
    e. Cypher
47. Which of the following is *not* true with regard to door latches?
    a. A dead-bolt latch is easy to install and can be used on almost any door.
    b. Chain latches are highly recommended as effective security measures.
    c. A dead-bolt latch is very expensive.
    d. A dead-bolt latch increases the security posture of the facility.
    e. Both b and c.
    f. Both a and d.
48. An inventory of key systems should be conducted at least:
    a. Weekly
    b. Monthly
    c. Quarterly
    d. Semiannually
    e. Annually
49. A sentry dog normally does not perform as well at:
    a. Radar sites
    b. Warehouses
    c. Gasoline storage areas
    d. Ammunition storage areas
    e. Offices containing classified materials

50. Which of the following is more of a probable disadvantage in the use of sentry dogs?
   a. A dog is more effective than a human during inclement weather.
   b. A dog has a keen sense of smell.
   c. A dog provides a strong psychological deterrent.
   d. The type of dog best suited for security work is naturally dangerous.
   e. A dog can detect and apprehend intruders.
51. In meeting federal specifications, insulated units must have the following fire-resistant minimum ratings:
   a. Class 150: 2 h
   b. Class 150: 4 h
   c. Class 350: 1 h
   d. Class 350: 3 h
   e. Class 350: 4 h
52. In meeting minimal federal specifications, noninsulated security containers must satisfactorily pass a drop test of:
   a. 15 ft.
   b. 20 ft.
   c. 22 ft.
   d. 25 ft.
   e. 30 ft.
53. In meeting minimal federal specifications, government security containers must be equipped with a combination lock capable of resisting manipulation and radiological attack for:
   a. 10 man-hours
   b. 20 man-hours
   c. 30 man-hours
   d. 40 man-hours
   e. 45 man-hours
54. Which of the following is *not* an approved UL safe classification?
   a. 350-1
   b. 350-2
   c. 350-3
   d. 350-4
   e. None of the above
55. Underwriters Laboratories does independent testing on security containers that simulate a major fire where the heat builds up gradually to:
   a. 750°F
   b. 1000°F
   c. 2000°F
   d. 2500°F
   e. 3000°F

56. The acceptable vault construction of insulated doors has a minimum reinforced concrete wall, floor, and ceiling of:
    a. 4 ft.
    b. 6 ft.
    c. 8 ft.
    d. 10 ft.
    e. 12 ft.

57. Which of the following would be a UL computer media storage classification?
    a. 100-4
    b. 150-4
    c. 250-4
    d. 350-4
    e. 450-4

58. Safes that are UL classified must be anchored to the floor or must weigh at least:
    a. 750 lb.
    b. 1000 lb.
    c. 1500 lb.
    d. 2000 lb.
    e. 3000 lb.

59. Which of the following is *not* generally true regarding money safes?
    a. Those manufactured prior to 1960 have round doors.
    b. They provide good protection against fire.
    c. They always have wheels.
    d. Today, money safes have square doors.
    e. Both b and c.
    f. All of the above.

60. A "relock" on a vault door will automatically prevent the bolt mechanism from operating when:
    a. A timer is used
    b. A switch is flipped
    c. There is an attack on the door or the combination lock
    d. It is locked by remote control
    e. All of the above

61. Money safes are classified by both Underwriters Laboratories and:
    a. The Bureau of Standards
    b. The American Society for Industrial Security
    c. The Federal Deposit Insurance Corporation
    d. The Insurance Services Office

62. Security vaults differ from safes in that:
    a. They do not have both fire- and burglary-resistant properties
    b. Steel is used

    c. They are tested by UL for burglary resistance

    d. They are permanently affixed to the building

    e. None of the above

63. Most theft is committed by:

    a. Professionals

    b. Organized crime

    c. Amateurs

    d. Maladjusted criminals

    e. Semiprofessionals

64. An experienced safecracker will ordinarily use which of the following methods?

    a. Trying the maintenance standard combination

    b. Trying the day combination

    c. Trying the handle

    d. All of the above

    e. None of the above

65. Which of the following methods has not been used in recent years to crack open record and money safes?

    a. Punching

    b. Core drilling

    c. Using a fluoroscope

    d. Torching

    e. Using a laser beam

66. The weakness of the burning bar as a burglary tool is that:

    a. It will not burn through concrete

    b. Its actual heat is not intense enough

    c. It requires hydrogen tanks

    d. It produces a large volume of smoke

    e. All of the above

67. A 50% insurance discount is generally allowed to protect a safe if:

    a. The premises are guarded by security guards

    b. The premises are open 24 h/day

    c. Multiple coverage is purchased

    d. The safe is UL tested

    e. The safe has wheels

68. Which of the following is *not* correct with regard to safes?

    a. Money safes do not have accredited fire resistance.

    b. UL classification labels are removed from all safes exposed to fires.

    c. Record safes are designed to resist fires only.

    d. Quality equipment should be purchased only from reputable dealers.

    e. Insulation in record safes more than 30 years old may negate fire-resistant qualities.

    f. None of the above.

69. The UL symbol "TRTL" indicates:
    a. The type of locking devices used
    b. That the safe is resistant to both torches and tools
    c. That the safe is resistant to torches
    d. That the safe is resistant to tools
    e. None of the above

70. Vaults are designed to meet most fire protection standards that are specified by the:
    a. Local fire department
    b. American Society for Industrial Security
    c. National Fire Protection Association
    d. All of the above
    e. None of the above

71. Fire-resistant safes must pass which of the following tests?
    a. Explosion
    b. Impact
    c. Fire exposure
    d. All of the above
    e. None of the above

72. Which of the following methods of attacking newer-model safes is considered to be impractical?
    a. Peel
    b. Punch
    c. Burn
    d. Manipulation
    e. Explosion

73. The temperature that paper may be destroyed at is:
    a. 200°F
    b. 250°F
    c. 300°F
    d. 350°F
    e. 400°F

74. Electronic data and material can begin to deteriorate at:
    a. 100°F
    b. 125°F
    c. 150°F
    d. 200°F
    e. 300°F

75. The maximum safe period of fire-resistant vaults is:
    a. 2 h
    b. 4 h
    c. 6 h
    d. 7 h
    e. 8 h

76. The interior height of a vault should not exceed:
    a. 8 ft.
    b. 9 ft.
    c. 10 ft.
    d. 11 ft.
    e. 12 ft.

77. The roof of a vault should be at least:
    a. 3 in. thick
    b. 4 in. thick
    c. 5 in. thick
    d. 6 in. thick
    e. 8 in. thick

78. The control of traffic through entrances and exits of a protected area is referred to as:
    a. Access control
    b. Patrol management
    c. Traffic stops
    d. Traffic management
    e. None of the above

79. A system whereby the alarm signal is heard only in the immediate vicinity of the protected area is known as a:
    a. Local alarm system
    b. Proprietary system
    c. Central alarm system
    d. Portable alarm system
    e. None of the above

80. A system using inaudible sound waves to detect the presence of an intruder or other disturbance is known as a(n):
    a. Motion detection system
    b. Ultrasonic motion detection system
    c. Sonic motion detection system
    d. Vibration detection system
    e. None of the above

81. Which one of the following is true regarding structural barriers?
    a. Structural barriers serve as psychological deterrents.
    b. The objective of barriers is to cause as much delay as possible.

    c. A series of barriers is usually used in any effective physical protection plan.

    d. A series of concentric barriers should separate the area to be protected.

    e. Even with good planning, most structural barriers do not prevent penetration by humans.

    f. All of the above.

82. Which of the following is *not* true regarding the use of security doors as barriers?

    a. Locking hardware is an important aspect of door security.

    b. The doorframe may be a weak point if not properly installed.

    c. Door hinges may add to the weakness of a door if not properly installed.

    d. The door is usually stronger than the surface into which it is set.

    e. All of the above.

83. The weakest area in a window is usually:

    a. The frame

    b. The glass

    c. The sash

    d. Caulking

    e. Both a and d

    f. All of the above

84. Which of the following is considered to be the most resistant to a blast explosion?

    a. Steel-frame building walls

    b. Thick brick or concrete walls

    c. Thick earthen barricades

    d. Thick reinforced concrete walls

    e. Wire-reinforced glass windows

85. Two sheets of ordinary glass bonded to an intervening layer of plastic material that is used in street-level windows and displays that need extra security is known as:

    a. Tempered glass

    b. Plastic-coated glass

    c. Vinyl-coated glass

    d. Laminated glass

    e. Plate glass

86. Bullet-resistant glass is made of:

    a. Reflected glass

    b. Plate glass

    c. Insulated glass

    d. Laminated glass

    e. None of the above

87. What type of glass would be better for a storefront in terms of resistance to breakage, resistance to heat or extreme cold, and resistance to overall deterioration?
    a. Laminated glass
    b. Wired glass
    c. Plate glass
    d. Bullet-resistant glass
    e. Acrylic material
88. The type of glass that is often used for both safety and security purposes because it is three to five times stronger than regular glass and five times as resistant to heat is:
    a. Reflective glass
    b. Coated glass
    c. Wired glass
    d. Tempered glass
    e. None of the above
89. The most widely used security device is:
    a. An alarm system
    b. A lock-and-key device
    c. Protective lighting
    d. CCTV
    e. A fence
90. Which of the following locks has been in use the longest and has no security value?
    a. The disk-tumbler lock
    b. The warded lock
    c. The wafer lock
    d. The pin-tumbler lock
    e. The lever lock
91. The lock that is mostly used today for cabinets, lockers, and safe-deposit boxes is:
    a. The wafer lock
    b. The disk-tumbler lock
    c. The pin-tumbler lock
    d. The lever lock
    e. Any locking device
92. The most widely used lock in the United States today for exterior building doors and interior room doors is:
    a. The disk-tumbler lock
    b. The pin-tumbler lock
    c. The lever lock
    d. The wafer lock
    e. None of the above

93. The best-known performance standard for guidance on the criteria of effective locking systems is published by:
    a. Medeco
    b. The Bureau of Standards
    c. Underwriters Laboratories
    d. Best Access Systems
    e. None of the above

94. UL standards for the resistance to picking to align tumblers should be at least:
    a. 3 min
    b. 5 min
    c. 10 min
    d. 20 min
    e. 30 min

95. The sensor that is used when air turbulence is present in the room being protected and when there are no potential false-alarm sources outside the room and in the field of the detector is a(n):
    a. Vibration detector
    b. Microwave motion detector
    c. Ultrasonic motion detector
    d. Acoustic detector
    e. None of the above

96. The sensor that is used when light air turbulence, vibration, or motion is present outside the room is a(n):
    a. Vibration detector
    b. Microwave motion detector
    c. Ultrasonic motion detector
    d. Acoustic detector
    e. None of the above

97. Foil used as a detector on a glass window to signal a surreptitious or forcible entry is an example of a(n):
    a. Vibration sensor
    b. Microwave sensor
    c. Capacitance sensor
    d. Acoustic sensor
    e. Electromechanical sensor

98. The type of sensor that is designed to place a current-carrying conductor between an intruder and an area to be protected is known as a(n):
    a. Vibration sensor
    b. Microwave sensor
    c. Capacitance sensor

    d. Acoustic sensor

    e. Electromechanical sensor

99. Which of the following does *not* pertain to the foil-type sensor?

    a. The cost of installation is cheap.

    b. The cost of the sensor is cheap.

    c. It acts as a psychological deterrent.

    d. It is subject to false alarms because of breaks.

    e. Small cracks in the tape, or foil, will disable it.

    f. All of the above.

100. The kind of sensor that is based on the Doppler principle, named after the Austrian scientist who originated the concept, is a(n):

    a. Capacitance sensor

    b. Electromechanical sensor

    c. Microwave sensor

    d. Acoustic sensor

    e. Photo sensor

101. The sound wave sensor is commonly referred to as a(n):

    a. Radar detector

    b. Proximity detector

    c. Vibration detector

    d. Ultrasonic detector

    e. Electromechanical sensor

102. The type of sensor that is not influenced by exterior noise, reacts only to movement within a protected area, and can also be adjusted to the movement of air caused by a fire to activate the alarm is known as a(n):

    a. Proximity sensor

    b. Radar sensor

    c. Vibration sensor

    d. Ultrasonic sensor

    e. Microwave sensor

103. An alarm system that uses a sound- or light-generating device, such as a bell or strobe lights, located on the exterior wall of the protective area to call attention to a violation is known as a(n):

    a. Intruder alarm

    b. Local alarm

    c. Direct alarm

    d. Proprietary alarm

    e. Central station alarm

104. An alarm system that is monitored by security personnel under the control of the owner of the establishment being protected is known as a(n):

     a. Intruder alarm
     b. Local alarm
     c. Direct alarm
     d. Proprietary alarm
     e. Central station alarm

105. A visual indicator that displays several zones or buildings from which an alarm signal has originated is called a(n):
     a. Zone alarm panel
     b. Contact alarm panel
     c. Break alarm panel
     d. Annunciator
     e. Trouble signal

106. Which of the following is true regarding CCTV?
     a. CCTVs reduce the amount of security personnel assigned to monitor entrances and exits.
     b. CCTVs are effective for control of personnel at entrances.
     c. CCTVs can be used as a psychological deterrent.
     d. CCTVs are equipped with pan/tilt/zoom and digital recording features.
     e. Both a and b.
     f. All of the above.

107. The degree of protection desired in any installation is predicated upon an analysis of the following two factors:
     a. Cost and environmental conditions
     b. Criticality and vulnerability
     c. Cost and vulnerability
     d. Cost and criticality

108. The process used by the security manager in establishing priorities of protection of assets is known as:
     a. Security survey
     b. Vulnerability study
     c. Risk analysis
     d. Inspection review

109. Lighting units of four general types are used for protective lighting systems. Which of the following is not used:
     a. Continuous
     b. Intermittent
     c. Standby
     d. Moveable

110. Which of the following is not an authentic characteristic of the guard operation?
     a. Guards are costly.

b. Guards are generally recognized as an essential element in the protection of assets and personnel.

c. Guards are the only element of protection that can be depended upon to give complete security.

d. Guards can also perform as a public relations representative when properly trained.

111. Each guard post that is manned 24 h/day, 7 days a week requires:
   a. Three guards
   b. Six guards
   c. Two guards
   d. Four and a half guards

112. Usually, in facilities where visitors are to be escorted, this is done by:
   a. Guards
   b. Individuals being visited
   c. Special escort service
   d. Supervisor of unit visited

113. One of the main reasons for not arming private security guards is:
   a. The cost of extra equipment
   b. The extra salary costs
   c. Very few are qualified to handle them
   d. The typical business or government facility is not customarily a place where violent crime occurs

114. The argument usually used by contract guard representatives as a selling point in their service is:
   a. That they are better trained
   b. That they are nonunion
   c. That they entail no administrative problems
   d. The reduction in cost

115. The most important written instructions for the guard force are known as:
   a. Memoranda
   b. Post orders
   c. High policy
   d. Operational orders

116. Which of the following should be a required criterion of post orders?
   a. Each order should deal with multiple subjects.
   b. The order should be detailed.
   c. The order should be written at the lowest level possible.
   d. Orders should be indexed sparingly.

117. The guard's primary record of significant events affecting facility protection is called the:
   a. Guard log

   b. Ingress log
   c. Egress log
   d. Daily record manual
118. A personal identification method based on the length of each finger of one hand from base to tip and the width of the hand inside the thumb is called the:
   a. Henry fingerprint system
   b. Hand geometry identification
   c. Bertillion method
   d. Bausch–Lomb method
119. A visual indicator that shows from which of several zones or buildings an alarm signal has originated is called a(n):
   a. Annunciator
   b. Contact device
   c. Break alarm
   d. Cross alarm
120. A specially constructed microphone attached directly to an object or surface to be protected and that responds only when the protected object or surface is disturbed is known as a:
   a. Parabolic microphone
   b. Special audio device
   c. Contact microphone
   d. Surreptitious microphone
121. One of management's most valuable tools is:
   a. Matrix
   b. Grid technique
   c. Security survey
   d. Questionnaire
   e. None of the above
122. Risk can be defined as:
   a. A situation involving exposure to danger
   b. The possibility that something unpleasant will happen
   c. A person or thing causing a risk that exposes others to danger or loss
   d. Answers a and c
   e. Answers a, b, and c
123. Which of the following are *not* human barriers?
   a. Security guards
   b. Patrol units
   c. Guard dogs
   d. Body guards
   e. Military troops

124. The type of fire involving flammable or combustible liquids, gases, and greases, including gasoline, oil, paint, etc., where smothering action is required that interrupts the fuel oxygen of the heat triangle is classified as which of the following?
    a. Class A
    b. Class B
    c. Class C
    d. Class D
    e. Class E
125. Risk avoidance is:
    a. After identifying vulnerability or risk, implementing countermeasures to reduce the problem
    b. Removing the problem by eliminating the vulnerability or risk
    c. Spreading the procedure or operation into different departments or locations
    d. Removing the vulnerability or risk to the company for the protection of an insurance policy
    e. Planning for an eventual loss without the protection of insurance
126. Which of the following are *not* natural barriers?
    a. Mountains
    b. Deserts and plains
    c. Moats
    d. Cliffs
    e. Water-covered areas (for example, around Alcatraz prison)
127. This type of fire usually involves a class A or B fire but also involves energized electrical equipment. A nonenergized agent is vital. When the agent melts, it forms an oxygen coating over the burning materials to suffocate them. Water and foam should not be used, because they can be conductive.
    a. Class A
    b. Class B
    c. Class C
    d. Class D
    e. Class E
128. Risk spreading is:
    a. After identifying vulnerability or risk, implementing countermeasures to reduce the problem
    b. Removing the problem by eliminating the vulnerability or risk
    c. Spreading the procedure or operation into different departments or locations
    d. Removing the vulnerability or risk to the company for the protection of an insurance policy
    e. Planning for an eventual loss without the protection of insurance

129. Which of the following is *not* an energy barrier?
    a. Continuous
    b. Standby
    c. Moveable
    d. Immoveable
    e. Emergency
130. Self-assumption is:
    a. After identifying vulnerability or risk, implementing counter-measures to reduce the problem
    b. Removing the problem by eliminating the vulnerability or risk
    c. Spreading the procedure or operation into different departments or locations
    d. Removing the vulnerability or risk to the company for the protection of an insurance policy
    e. Planning for an eventual loss without the protection of insurance
131. This type of fire involves certain combustible metal, such as magnesium, sodium, potassium, and their alloys. A special dry powder that has a special smothering and coating agent should be used and is not suited for use on other classes of fires.
    a. Class A
    b. Class B
    c. Class C
    d. Class D
    e. Class E
132. Risk reduction is:
    a. After identifying vulnerability or risk, implementing counter-measures to reduce the problem
    b. Removing the problem by eliminating the vulnerability or risk
    c. Spreading the procedure or operation into different departments or locations
    d. Removing the vulnerability or risk to the company for the protection of an insurance policy
    e. Planning for an eventual loss without the protection of insurance
133. Risk transfer is:
    a. After identifying vulnerability or risk, implementing counter-measures to reduce the problem
    b. Removing the problem by eliminating the vulnerability or risk
    c. Spreading the procedure or operation into different departments or locations
    d. Removing the vulnerability or risk to the company for the protection of an insurance policy
    e. Planning for an eventual loss without the protection of insurance

134. When using biometric devices, which of the following is the improper acceptance of an unauthorized user?
    a. Type II
    b. False acceptance rate (FAR)
    c. Type I
    d. False rejection rate (FRR)
    e. Answers a and b

135. Which of the following is not a level of security:
    a. Minimum security
    b. Low-level security
    c. High-level security
    d. Lack of security
    e. Maximum security

136. Which of the following are *not* structural or man-made barriers?
    a. Fences
    b. Barbed wire
    c. Safes and vaults
    d. Cliffs
    e. Locking devices

137. When using biometric devices, which of the following is the improper rejection of a valid user?
    a. Type II
    b. False acceptance rate (FAR)
    c. Type I
    d. False rejection rate (FRR)
    e. Answers c and d

138. Fires involving wood, cloth, paper, or rubber where water is used to quench the fire and cool the material below its ignition temperature are classified as which of the following?
    a. Class A
    b. Class B
    c. Class C
    d. Class D
    e. Class E

139. Which of the following is the weakest point in a personnel identification system:
    a. Hardware
    b. Software
    c. People
    d. Structure
    e. Environment

140. Which of the following is checked on a retina scan?
    a. Pupil
    b. Eye
    c. Fingerprints
    d. Blood vessels
    e. DNA

CHAPTER 6 ANSWERS

1. e. Both b and c
2. c. Criticality and vulnerability
3. d. Security survey
4. f. All of the above
5. c. The building site itself
6. d. Security consciousness is an inherent state of mind.
7. e. Perfunctory performance of duty
8. d. The identification card or badge should be designed in a relatively complicated manner to avoid duplication.
9. d. Duress code
10. c. Two-man rule
11. e. Military commander of the installation or facility
12. a. They provide an increase in security without slowdown in operation.
13. c. Limited area
14. d. Chain link
15. d. 9 gauge
16. b. 2 in.
17. b. 7 ft. high
18. c. 12 gauge
19. d. 4
20. e. 6 in.
21. a. 1 ft.
22. b. Three strands of barbed wire or tape
23. e. 6
24. d. 96 in.^{2}
25. c. 20 ft.
26. e. 50 ft.
27. a. 10
28. e. Such lighting is expensive to maintain.
29. a. 0.2 foot-candle
30. b. A large amount of light should be focused on security patrol routes.
31. d. Intermittent
32. e. Continuous lighting
33. b. 1.0 foot-candle

34. a. 0.5 foot-candle
35. b. 0.40 foot-candle
36. d. The US Coast Guard
37. e. Microwave detection system
38. a. Capacitance detection system
39. d. Auxiliary system
40. a. Central station system
41. c. Proprietary system
42. a. Egyptians more than 4000 years ago
43. c. A high-quality pickproof lock is considered a positive bar to entry.
44. c. Key locks
45. d. 64,000
46. a. Wafer
47. e. Both b and c.
48. e. Annually
49. c. Gasoline storage areas
50. d. The type of dog best suited for security work is naturally dangerous.
51. c. Class 350: 1 h
52. e. 30 ft.
53. b. 20 man-hours
54. c. 350-3
55. c. 2000°F
56. b. 6 ft.
57. b. 150-4
58. a. 750 lb.
59. e. Both b and c.
60. c. There is an attack on the door or the combination lock
61. d. The Insurance Services Office
62. d. They are permanently affixed to the building
63. c. Amateurs
64. d. All of the above
65. e. Using a laser beam
66. d. It produces a large volume of smoke
67. b. The premises are open 24 h/day
68. f. None of the above.
69. b. That the safe is resistant to both torches and tools
70. c. National Fire Protection Association
71. d. All of the above
72. d. Manipulation
73. d. 350°F
74. c. 150°F
75. c. 6 h

76. e. 12 ft.
77. d. 6 in. thick
78. a. Access control
79. a. Local alarm system
80. b. Ultrasonic motion detection system
81. f. All of the above.
82. d. The door is usually stronger than the surface into which it is set.
83. c. The sash
84. d. Thick reinforced concrete walls
85. d. Laminated glass
86. d. Laminated glass
87. e. Acrylic material
88. d. Tempered glass
89. b. A lock-and-key device
90. b. The warded lock
91. d. The lever lock
92. b. The pin-tumbler lock
93. c. Underwriters Laboratories
94. c. 10 min
95. b. Microwave motion detector
96. d. Acoustic detector
97. e. Electromechanical sensor
98. e. Electromechanical sensor
99. a. The cost of installation is cheap.
100. c. Microwave sensor
101. d. Ultrasonic detector
102. d. Ultrasonic sensor
103. b. Local alarm
104. d. Proprietary alarm
105. d. Annunciator
106. f. All of the above.
107. b. Criticality and vulnerability
108. b. Vulnerability study
109. b. Intermittent
110. c. Guards are the only element of protection that can be depended upon to give complete security.
111. d. Four and a half guards
112. b. Individual being visited
113. d. The typical business or government facility is not customarily a place where violent crime occurs
114. d. Thee reduction in cost
115. b. Post orders
116. c. The order should be written at the lowest level.

117. a. Guard log
118. b. Hand geometry identification
119. a. Annunciator
120. c. Contact microphone
121. c. Security survey
122. e. Answers a, b, and c
123. c. Guard dogs
124. b. Class B
125. b. Removing the problem by eliminating the vulnerability or risk
126. c. Moats
127. c. Class C
128. c. Spreading the procedure or operation into different departments or locations
129. d. Immoveable
130. e. Planning for an eventual loss without the protection of insurance
131. d. Class D
132. a. After identifying vulnerability or risk, implementing counter-measures to reduce the problem
133. d. Removing the vulnerability or risk to the company for the protection of an insurance policy
134. e. Answers a and b
135. d. Lack of security
136. d. Cliffs
137. e. Answers c and d
138. a. Class A
139. c. People
140. d. Blood vessels

CHAPTER 7: PERSONNEL SECURITY

1. The most critical component of all security processes is:
   a. Information
   b. Personnel
   c. Physical location
   d. Perimeter
   e. Intrusion control
2. A comprehensive personnel security program should include:
   a. Adequate job specifications and performance standards
   b. Truth verification standards
   c. Appropriate selection and recruitment criteria
   d. Both a and b
   e. All of the above
   f. None of the above

3. The standard of employment of military and government personnel was established by which executive order?
   a. 11596
   b. 12300
   c. 9450
   d. 1099
   e. 1045
4. The real meaning of the governmental policy in personnel security is:
   a. To hire only those who have high IQ test scores
   b. To keep those considered to be "risky" from obtaining jobs
      that are considered sensitive
   c. To detect and fire those found disloyal
   d. Both a and c
   e. All of the above
   f. None of the above
5. When an individual is eligible to have access to classified information, this is called:
   a. A security clearance
   b. A Q clearance
   c. An FBI clearance
   d. A VIP clearance
   e. A field operative clearance
6. Which of the following security clearances is *not* used by the
   government?
   a. Top secret
   b. Secret
   c. Confidential
   d. Restricted
   e. Q clearance
7. What agency is responsible for processing requests for security
   clearances?
   a. The Federal Bureau of Investigation
   b. The Department of Justice
   c. The Central Intelligence Agency
   d. The National Security Council
   e. The Department of Defense
8. Individuals who are not US citizens, or are immigrants, are not
   eligible for security clearances except under reciprocal clearance
   involving:
   a. Israel and Canada
   b. NATO countries
   c. Canada and the United Kingdom

    d. Canada and NATO countries

    e. Both c and d

    f. None of the above

9. Which is a type of personnel security investigation?

    a. National Agency Check

    b. Preemployment

    c. Background investigation

    d. Department of Defense investigation

    e. Both a and c

    f. Both c and d

10. An investigation that consists of checking the records of appropriate federal agencies for information bearing on the loyalty and suitability of a person under investigation is known as a(n):

    a. FBI investigation

    b. National Agency Check

    c. Loyalty investigation

    d. Background investigation

    e. Full field investigation

11. A National Agency Check consists of:

    a. CIA records

    b. Civil Service records

    c. Coast Guard records

    d. Both a and b

    e. All of the above

12. A background investigation for a security clearance consists of:

    a. Checking college attendance, if attended

    b. Verifying service in the armed forces

    c. Interviewing character references

    d. Both b and c

    e. All of the above

13. During a security clearance background investigation, verification of naturalization will primarily be done by:

    a. Checking State Department records

    b. Checking FBI records

    c. Checking records of appropriate US district courts

    d. Checking records of the Bureau of Vital Statistics

    e. All of the above

14. The Act passed to require that consumer reporting agencies adopt reasonable procedures for meeting the needs of commerce for consumer credit is commonly known as:

    a. The Uniform Credit Act

    b. The Fair Credit Reporting Act

    c. The Consumer Relief Act

    d. The Consumer Reporting Act

    e. The Commercial Credit Act

15. During a security clearance background investigation, when travel outside the United States is detected, which of the following should be checked?

    a. FBI records

    b. CIA records

    c. Immigration records

    d. Customs records

    e. All of the above

    f. None of the above

16. The attitude or state of mind through which individuals are conscious of the existence of the security program and are persuaded that it is relevant to their own behavior is a concept known as:

    a. Security motivation

    b. Security awareness

    c. Security consciousness

    d. None of the above

17. The theory that the human organism is motivated by an ascending series of needs and that once the lower needs have been satisfied, they will be supplanted by the higher needs as motives for behavior is known as:

    a. Maslow's "hierarchy of prepotency"

    b. McGregor's Theory X

    c. McGregor's Theory Y

    d. Herzberg's Two Factor Theory

    e. Both b and c

    f. None of the above

18. Security awareness is motivated by what technique?

    a. Integration into line operations

    b. Formal security briefings

    c. Use of written material

    d. Both b and c

    e. All of the above

    f. None of the above

19. Which of the following is *not* an example of an intelligence test?

    a. Manual placement test

    b. Stanford-Binet IQ test

    c. Armed Forces General Classification Test

    d. Henman-Nelson IQ test

    e. None of the above

20. An example of an honesty test given by firms to determine dishonest employees is:
    a. The Stanford-Binet test
    b. The Reid survey
    c. The Minnesota Multiphase Personality Inventory (MMPI)
    d. Both b and c
    e. All of the above
21. A personality test that uses the MMPI evaluation and states that it is specially designed for police and security applicants is:
    a. The Caldwell Report
    b. The Reid survey
    c. The Stanford-Binet test
    d. The Stanton Survey
    e. None of the above
22. The main hurdle to overcome for personality tests is the requirement of the Civil Rights Act of 1964 that such a test not be discriminatory against protected minorities. This rule used as a test is known as the:
    a. 30% rule
    b. 40% rule
    c. 60% rule
    d. 80% rule
    e. None of the above
23. According to a 1979 survey by the American Society for Industrial Security, the number of organizations in the United States offering security courses is greater than:
    a. 50
    b. 75
    c. 150
    d. 180
    e. 250
24. What are the advantages of having an outside organization perform background screening on your employees?
    a. Company personnel are spared potential embarrassments as well as liability claims.
    b. Depending on the number of checks, the costs will be lower.
    c. Screening will be done by trained staff with extensive sources of information.
    d. Screenings will be unbiased with no corrupt motivation.
    e. All of the above.

25. Background investigations of an applicant should:
    a. Be based on the application and an interview record form
    b. Be done by a carefully screened investigator
    c. Be conducted without any prior contact from the applicant by the investigator
    d. All of the above
    e. None of the above

26. Which of the following is *not* a requirement for handling preemployment interviews?
    a. Interviews must be voluntary.
    b. Interviews must be unbiased.
    c. For an interview to be effective, it should be conducted with a witness or a friend of the applicant present.
    d. The interviewer should not give out information.
    e. Complete and accurate notes should be taken.

27. The quality of service rendered by security personnel is determined by which of the following?
    a. Personnel selection process
    b. Training
    c. Wages
    d. Supervision
    e. All of the above

28. A Burns security survey covering 847 banks found that the most important single step toward improved crime prevention was:
    a. Adding more guards or public police
    b. Training of bank employees
    c. Better security equipment
    d. Both b and c
    e. None of the above

29. The basic principle of personnel security is:
    a. That education is the key to loss prevention
    b. That attitudes and honesty of rank-and-file employees are key to minimizing losses through theft
    c. To weed out bad apples among employees after they are located
    d. Both a and c
    e. All of the above

30. Of the following questions, what cannot be asked of an applicant because of federal laws?
    a. Whether an applicant is married, divorced, separated, widowed, or single
    b. Whether an applicant owns or rents a residence
    c. Whether an applicant has ever been arrested
    d. Whether an applicant's wages have ever been garnished

     e. All of the above, except a

     f. All of the above

31. Inquiring about an applicant's age and date of birth on a preemployment form may be prohibited by:
     a. The Civil Service Act of 1970
     b. Title VII of the Civil Rights Act of 1964
     c. The Age Discrimination in Employment Act
     d. All of the above

32. Which of the following may be a clue on the employment form for considering refusal to hire?
     a. Gaps in employment history
     b. Long list of jobs over a relatively short period
     c. A significant reduction in salary at a recent job
     d. 3 to 6 months spent in the military
     e. All of the above

33. Which of the following should *not* be a policy in considering applicants for hire?
     a. Similar problems in numerous areas, such as bad credit, absenteeism, and numerous short-term jobs.
     b. A problem in one area of interest should be enough to disqualify an applicant for hire.
     c. If obviously overqualified, find out why applicant is willing to accept the current job.
     d. Both a and c.
     e. All of the above.

34. Dishonest employees cost employers _____ as much as all the nations' burglaries, car thefts, and bank holdups combined.
     a. A quarter
     b. Half
     c. Just
     d. Twice
     e. Thrice

35. According to estimates, about one-third of all business failures are caused by:
     a. Theft from employees
     b. Bad management
     c. Theft from outsiders
     d. Poor quality of product or service
     e. None of the above

36. Store inventory shortages are mainly caused by:
     a. Shoplifting losses
     b. Employee theft
     c. Poor inventory control

      d. Paperwork errors

      e. a, b, and d

      f. All of the above

37. The single most important safeguard for preventing internal theft is probably:

      a. The personal interview

      b. Interviewing an applicant's references

      c. Use of the polygraph

      d. An extensive personal history search

      e. Upgrading the screening of new employees

38. An employer may reject an applicant on the basis of:

      a. Incomplete data on the personal history search

      b. Unexplained gaps in employment history

      c. Unsatisfactory interview

      d. An arrest for a crime against property

      e. A conviction for a crime against property

39. An employer may not question an applicant about:

      a. An unsatisfactory interview

      b. Unexplained gaps in employment history

      c. An arrest for a crime against property

      d. A conviction for a crime against property

40. A study by scientists at Yale University (1939) found that theft resulted from:

      a. Lack of religious and moral values

      b. Aggression, frustration, and need

      c. Aggression, frustration, and lack of moral values

      d. Aggression, low morale, and low anticipation of being caught

      e. Aggression, frustration, and low anticipation of being caught

41. Scientists at Yale University (1939) concluded that frustration almost always results in some aggressive reaction, the most important point being:

      a. Open aggression against the supervisor

      b. Aggression against the person who the employee feels is responsible

      c. Unrelieved aggression building up until relief from inner pressures becomes imperative

      d. A substitute satisfaction, in which the employee "gets even" by stealing from the company

42. The theft triangle consists of the following components:

      a. Motivation, skill, and opportunity

      b. Opportunity, desire, and skill

      c. Motivation, opportunity, and rationalization (desire)

      d. Rationalization, skill, and opportunity

      e. None of the above

43. Of those acquitted or dismissed by the courts for theft, over
    _____% were rearrested within 30 months.
    a. 50
    b. 60
    c. 70
    d. 80
    e. 90

44. Individuals who find integrity tests offensive are:
    a. Usually found to have a violent criminal past
    b. Sensitive individuals who do not like to take tests
    c. Twice as likely to be involved in some type of drug abuse
        behavior
    d. Twice as likely to admit to criminal activity or drug abuse
    e. None of the above

45. A psychopath can often pass a polygraph test with a clean record
    because of the following characteristic:
    a. Uncooperative attitude
    b. Unstable personality
    c. An inferiority complex
    d. An abnormal lack of fear
    e. Both b and c
    f. All of the above

46. Many experts agree that the most important deterrent to internal
    theft is:
    a. The chance of being fired
    b. Fear of discovery
    c. Threat of prosecution
    d. Guilt
    e. Lawsuits

47. An employee should be questioned:
    a. With the door open
    b. With coworkers present
    c. Behind a closed door
    d. Behind a closed and locked door

48. Frustration and aggression may be caused by:
    a. Increasing debts
    b. Personal problems
    c. Lack of recognition by superiors
    d. Dishonest supervisors
    e. The supervisor's lack of consideration in dealing with his or
        her employees or by unrealistic company policies
    f. All of the above

49. An impelling type of leadership tends to reduce employee dishonesty because:
    a. It improves morale
    b. It increases discipline
    c. It sets a good example
    d. It reduces employee frustration
    e. All of the above
50. Stores that rely on stapling packages shut with the register tape folded over the top of the bag do this:
    a. To keep the customer from adding more items to the bag
    b. To show that the customer paid for the package
    c. To help the loss prevention officer
    d. For the psychological effect
    e. On the assumption that employees will not help each other
    f. All of the above
51. Which of the following should the manager or supervisor immediately approve by signature:
    a. All voids and overrings
    b. All overrings and underrings
    c. All underrings and no sales
    d. All voids and overrings over a certain amount
    e. All of the above
52. Overrings should not be corrected by undercharging on other items because this:
    a. Upsets the customer
    b. Confuses inventory controls
    c. Eliminates interaction by a manager or supervisor
    d. Is probably the easiest method of theft by employees
    e. All of the above
    f. None of the above
53. The most effective deterrent to shoplifting is:
    a. Covert CCTVs
    b. Highly trained and educated loss prevention officers
    c. Well-trained personnel
    d. Sensor devices at the doors
    e. None of the above
54. Employee complaints often arise from:
    a. Poor management
    b. Dissatisfaction
    c. Management having operating problems
    d. Employees airing their grievances

    e. A form of substitution for expressing their fears and frustrations concerning their personal lives

    f. All of the above

55. Directional counseling of upset employees:

    a. Means giving advice

    b. May dominate the role of the manager or supervisor

    c. May be the wrong advice

    d. May be disturbing to the personnel director

    e. Is not usually desirable

56. Nondirectional counseling of upset employees:

    a. Does not directly advise, criticize, or try to help

    b. Does not carry the danger inherent in giving advice

    c. Involves primarily being a good listener

    d. Should not be used because it is not effective

    e. None of the above

57. The first skill the manager or supervisor must learn is:

    a. How to supervise or manage

    b. How to give orders

    c. How to check up on procedures

    d. The ability to listen

    e. How to maintain authority

58. In the United States, employee thefts are:

    a. Fewer than thefts by shoplifters

    b. Fewer than the nation's burglaries

    c. Fewer than the nation's car thefts

    d. Equal to the nation's burglaries

    e. Greater than the problem of crime in the streets

59. One thousand shopping tests across the nation showed that in a 10-year period, cash register thefts had increased by what percentage?

    a. 46

    b. 56

    c. 66

    d. 76

    e. 86

60. Personnel security problems are caused by:

    a. Dishonesty

    b. Disloyalty

    c. Disinterest of employees

    d. Low morale

    e. Both a and b

    f. All of the above

61. Employees, for the most part, are:
    a. Honest
    b. Dishonest
    c. Disinterested
    d. Disloyal
    e. Conscientious, honest individuals who have the company's best interests at heart

62. Employees' attitudes are directly affected by:
    a. The supervisor's attitude and actions
    b. Lack of recognition
    c. Personal problems that originate within and outside the company
    d. Fellow employees
    e. None of the above

63. A major concern of a company, above all else, should be:
    a. Internal theft
    b. External theft
    c. Policies and procedures
    d. Reduction of shrinkage
    e. The care and well-being of its employees

64. Of all security processes, the most critical is:
    a. Information
    b. Personnel
    c. Physical
    d. Perimeter

65. The concept that an individual should be aware of the security program and persuaded that the program is relevant to his or her own behavior is known as:
    a. Security consciousness
    b. Security awareness
    c. Security motivation
    d. Motivation analysis

66. An important task that faces every organization is the hiring of personnel. The purpose of applicant screening is:
    a. Workplace diversity
    b. Prohibiting discrimination in the hiring process
    c. Testing candidates on their honesty
    d. To identify the most appropriate person

67. Which of the following laws would not serve as a legal guide in the hiring of personnel?
    a. Civil Rights Act
    b. Age Discrimination in Employment Act
    c. Lanham Act
    d. Americans with Disabilities Act

68. Which is not a strategy for managing violence in the workplace?
    a. Establish a committee to plan violence prevention.
    b. Consider OSHA guidelines to curb workplace violence.
    c. Have professionally trained and armed security officers.
    d. Establish policies and procedures and communicate the problems of threats and violence to all employees.
69. When interviewing an applicant for employment, the interviewer may ask which questions:
    a. Have you ever been arrested?
    b. How old are you?
    c. Are you married?
    d. Can you meet the attendance requirements of this job?
70. Under federal law, the use of the polygraph for preemployment is permissible, except in which industry?
    a. Drug manufacturing
    b. Nuclear power
    c. Banking
    d. Alcohol manufacturing
71. When conducting an interview during a background investigation, the investigator should advise the party being interviewed that the applicant/employee is:
    a. Being considered for a promotion
    b. Suspected of wrongdoing
    c. Being investigated in connection with a position of trust
    d. Tell the interviewee nothing
72. The frequency of a reinvestigation of the "financial lifestyle" inquiry should generally be:
    a. Never
    b. Every 6 months
    c. Every year
    d. Every 18 months
73. Any investigation that includes unfavorable information or results in an adverse employment decision should be:
    a. Retained in file for a minimum of 3 years
    b. Retained in file for a minimum of 5 years
    c. Retained in file for 1 year
    d. Destroyed when the employment decision is made
74. Which of the following is not true with regard to a résumé?
    a. It does not provide the information that the company requires.
    b. It is never accepted in lieu of a completed application form.
    c. It is always accepted and is reviewed as part of the investigation.
    d. It is an acceptable form of information for a professional position.

75. The persons who find integrity tests offensive are:
    a. Twice as likely to admit to criminal or drug abuse behavior
    b. No more likely than anyone else to admit to criminal or drug abuse behavior
    c. Sensitive persons who should not be required to take the test
    d. Usually found to have a violent criminal past
76. Personnel investigations usually involve which of the following techniques?
    a. Backgrounding
    b. Positive vetting
    c. Polygraphing
    d. Profiling
    e. All of the above
77. Which of the following is *not* permitted by an employer in regard to the screening process?
    a. Ask if the applicant is a US citizen.
    b. Have the applicant write his or her name and address on the application form.
    c. Require a photo with the application.
    d. Explain duty hours required in job.
    e. Inquire about educational and training background.
78. A complete background investigation usually covers which of the following steps?
    a. A personal history statement (PHS)
    b. Evaluation of the PHS
    c. A national agency check
    d. A full field investigation
    e. All of the above
79. Which of the following is permitted by an employer in regard to the screening process?
    a. Ask if the applicant is a US citizen.
    b. Inquire about racial background.
    c. Require a photo with the application.
    d. Inquire regarding the applicant's religion.
    e. Ask questions about organizational affiliations whereby race, religion, or national origin data can be obtained.
80. Preemployment polygraph tests are limited to which of the following?
    a. National defense positions
    b. Law enforcement positions
    c. Positions with banks, savings, loans, or armored transportation
    d. Federal positions involving law enforcement, national defense, and other relevant positions of trust
    e. All of the above

81. The polygraph measures the following stress indicators *except*:
    a. Quickened pulse
    b. Raised blood pressure
    c. Rate of speech
    d. Shallow respiration
    e. Lowered galvanic skin resistance

82. An exit interview is a valuable tool for which of the following reasons?
    a. It gives the employee an opportunity to list grievances
    b. Management often learns of problems not previously known.
    c. It helps to reduce loss when a checklist is used to have company property returned.
    d. It is used to remind departing employees of a legal obligation to protect trade secrets or confidential records.
    e. All of the above

83. In which of the following situations in proprietary security are polygraphs most often used?
    a. Periodic tests of all employees to establish their conduct if they are a necessity of the job due to government regulations
    b. Specific questions to determine the causes of specific incidents
    c. Preemployment examinations if required or approved by law
    d. Answers b and c
    e. All of the above

84. For persons in responsible and sensitive positions, financial and lifestyle reinvestigations should be conducted every:
    a. 6 months
    b. 12 months
    c. 18 months
    d. 24 months
    e. 30 months

CHAPTER 7 ANSWERS

1. b. Personnel
2. e. All of the above
3. e. 1045
4. b. To keep those considered to be "risky" from obtaining jobs that are considered sensitive
5. a. A security clearance
6. d. Restricted
7. e. The Department of Defense
8. c. Canada and the United Kingdom

9. e. Both a and c

10. b. National Agency Check

11. e. All of the above

12. e. All of the above

13. c. Checking records of appropriate US district courts

14. b. The Fair Credit Reporting Act

15. f. None of the above

16. b. Security awareness

17. a. Maslow's "hierarchy of prepotency"

18. e. All of the above

19. a. Manual placement test

20. b. The Reid survey

21. a. The Caldwell Report

22. d. 80% rule

23. d. 180

24. e. All of the above.

25. d. All of the above

26. c. For an interview to be effective, it should be conducted with a witness or a friend of the applicant present.

27. e. All of the above

28. b. Training of bank employees

29. b. That attitudes and honesty of rank-and-file employees are key to minimizing losses through theft

30. f. All of the above

31. c. The Age Discrimination in Employment Act

32. e. All of the above

33. b. A problem in one area of interest should be enough to disqualify an applicant for hire.

34. d. Twice

35. a. Theft from employees

36. e. a, b, and d

37. e. Upgrading the screening of new employees

38. e. A conviction for a crime against property

39. c. An arrest for a crime against property

40. e. Aggression, frustration, and low anticipation of being caught

41. d. A substitute satisfaction, in which the employee "gets even" by stealing from the company

42. c. Motivation, opportunity, and rationalization (desire)

43. d. 80

44. d. Twice as likely to admit to criminal activity or drug abuse

45. d. An abnormal lack of fear

46. b. Fear of discovery

47. c. Behind a closed door

48. e. The supervisor's lack of consideration in dealing with his or her employees or by unrealistic company policies
49. d. It reduces employee frustration
50. e. On the assumption that employees will not help each other
51. d. All voids and overrings over a certain amount
52. d. Is probably the easiest method of theft by employees
53. c. Well-trained personnel
54. e. A form of substitution for expressing their fears and frustrations concerning their personal lives
55. e. Is not usually desirable
56. c. Involves primarily being a good listener
57. d. The ability to listen
58. e. Greater than the problem of crime in the streets
59. e. 86
60. f. All of the above
61. e. Conscientious, honest individuals who have the company's best interests at heart
62. c. Personal problems that originate within and outside the company
63. e. The care and well-being of its employees
64. b. Personnel
65. b. Security awareness
66. d. To identify the most appropriate person
67. c. Lanham
68. c. Have professional trained and armed security officers
69. d. Can you meet the attendance requirement of this job?
70. d. Alcohol manufacturing
71. c. Being investigated in connection with a position of trust
72. d. Every 18 months
73. a. Retained in file for a minimum of 3 years.
74. d. It is an acceptable form of information for a professional position.
75. a. Twice as likely to admit to criminal or drug abuse behavior
76. e. All of the above
77. c. Require a photo with the application.
78. e. All of the above
79. a. Ask if the applicant is a US citizen.
80. e. All of the above
81. c. Rate of speech
82. e. All of the above
83. e. All of the above
84. c. 18 months

CHAPTER 8: CRISIS MANAGEMENT

1. Searches made during work hours as a result of a bomb threat call should be made by:
   a. The fire department
   b. The local police department
   c. The Department of Army personnel
   d. The Federal Bureau of Investigation
   e. Employees familiar with the work area where the bomb is reportedly located

2. The usual reaction of a corporation victimized by the kidnapping of an employee or extortion involving threat to lives of employees has been:
   a. To meet the negotiated demands of the terrorists
   b. To absolutely refuse to negotiate
   c. To negotiate but refuse to put up money
   d. To refer the terrorist to the police
   e. None of the above

3. A cooperative organization of industrial firms, business firms, and similar organizations within an industrial community that are united by a voluntary agreement to assist each other by providing materials, equipment, and personnel needed to ensure effective industrial disaster control during emergencies is called a(n):
   a. Emergency squad
   b. Mutual aid association
   c. Community emergency cooperative
   d. Disaster control squad
   e. None of the above

4. Which of the following procedures should *not* be advocated as part of emergency planning?
   a. The emergency plan should be in writing.
   b. The emergency plan should be revised as needed.
   c. Distribution of the plan must be made down to the lowest echelons.
   d. Distribution should be limited to senior management.
   e. The plan should be tested through practice.

5. The federal agency in charge of disaster planning is the:
   a. Federal Emergency Management Agency
   b. Office of Civil Defense
   c. Department of the Army
   d. Department of the Interior
   e. Government Accounting Office

6. The greatest single destroyer of property is/are:
   a. Bombs
   b. Sabotage
   c. Fire
   d. Earthquakes
   e. Floods
7. Responsibility for shutdown of a plant as a result of a disaster should be assigned to:
   a. The security office
   b. The board of directors
   c. The plant engineering service
   d. The accounting office
   e. The plant manager
8. In the event the media makes contact as a result of a crisis situation, they should:
   a. Be given "no comment"
   b. Be put in touch with the person designated in the emergency plan for orderly release of information
   c. Be put in contact with the president of the company
   d. Be put in contact with the plant manager
   e. Be told to get in touch with the police
9. First-aid training in regard to emergency planning can be obtained at no cost from:
   a. The local police
   b. The American Red Cross
   c. The fire department
   d. The local hospital
   e. The local high school
10. Which of the following does not fit into good emergency planning?
   a. An individual should be appointed as coordinator.
   b. The plan should be in writing.
   c. The plan should be simple.
   d. A new organization should be developed to handle emergency situations.
   e. Key departments within the plant should be represented.
11. In an emergency, planning records placed in storage should be in the form of:
   a. Microfilm
   b. Microfiche
   c. Computer tapes
   d. Any of the above
   e. None of the above

12. The amount of combustible materials in the building is called:
    a. Fire loading
    b. The combustion quotient
    c. The fire hazard level
    d. All of the above
    e. None of the above

13. Which of the following is *not* an element in the classic fire triangle?
    a. Oxygen
    b. Heat
    c. CO_2
    d. Fuel
    e. None of the above

14. Most deaths from fire are caused by:
    a. Visible fire
    b. Panic
    c. Smoke or heat
    d. Inexperienced firefighters
    e. Inadequate equipment

15. A fire involving ordinary combustible materials such as waste-paper and rags would be classified as:
    a. Class A
    b. Class B
    c. Class C
    d. Class D
    e. Class E

16. Fires involving certain combustible metals would be classified as:
    a. Class A
    b. Class B
    c. Class C
    d. Class D
    e. Class E

17. Fires involving live electrical equipment such as transformers would be classified as:
    a. Class A
    b. Class B
    c. Class C
    d. Class D
    e. Class E

18. Fires fueled by such substances as gasoline, oil, grease, etc. would be classified as:
    a. Class A
    b. Class B
    c. Class C

    d. Class D

    e. Class E

19. Soda and acid water-based extinguishers are effective on:

    a. Class A fires

    b. Class B fires

    c. Class C fires

    d. Class D fires

    e. Class E fires

20. Dry powder as a fire extinguisher is used on:

    a. Class A fires

    b. Class B fires

    c. Class C fires

    d. Class D fires

    e. Class E fires

21. A carbon tetrachloride extinguisher would *not* be used on the following type of fire:

    a. Fire involving gasoline

    b. Fire involving grease

    c. Fire in a live transformer

    d. Fire in closed spaces

    e. All of the above

22. The most effective extinguishing device known for dealing with class A and B fires is:

    a. CO_2

    b. Soda and acid

    c. Dry powder

    d. Water fog

    e. None of the above

23. The ionization fire detector warns of fire by responding to:

    a. Invisible products of combustion emitted by a fire at its earliest stages

    b. Infrared emissions from flames

    c. Light changes

    d. Smoke

    e. Heat

24. The fire detector that responds to a predetermined temperature or to an increase in temperature is known as a(n):

    a. Ionization detector

    b. Photoelectric smoke detector

    c. Infrared flame detector

    d. Thermal detector

    e. None of the above

25. The fire detector that responds to an interruption in the light source is known as a(n):
    a. Ionization detector
    b. Photoelectric smoke detector
    c. Infrared flame detector
    d. Thermal detector
    e. None of the above

26. After a bomb threat has been received, the bomb search should be conducted by:
    a. The police
    b. The military
    c. The FBI
    d. The Bureau of Alcohol, Tobacco, and Firearms (ATF)
    e. Employees familiar with threatened areas

27. One of the two most important items of information to be learned at the time of the bomb threat is the expected time of the explosion; the other is the:
    a. Gender of the caller
    b. Location of the bomb
    c. Voice peculiarities of the caller
    d. Motive of the caller
    e. None of the above

28. After a bomb threat is made, if a suspicious object is found during search, it should be:
    a. Handled with great care
    b. Disarmed immediately
    c. Reported immediately to the designated authorities
    d. Placed in a bucket of water
    e. None of the above

29. The decision whether to evacuate a building as a result of a bomb threat will be made by the:
    a. FBI
    b. Police
    c. Management
    d. Military
    e. Employees' union

30. If a bomb threat is an obvious hoax, the following action should be taken:
    a. Do nothing.
    b. Report the call immediately to the local police for investigation.
    c. Wait at least 2 h to find out if the threat is actually a hoax.
    d. Contact the telephone company and report the call.
    e. Notify the Secret Service.

31. The removal of any suspected bomb should be by:
    a. A proprietary guard force
    b. Office employees
    c. Professional bomb-disposal personnel
    d. The patrol office of the police department
    e. None of the above

32. Which of the following fire losses is excluded from the widely used standard policy form?
    a. Military action
    b. Invasion
    c. Insurrection
    d. Civil war
    e. All of the above

33. In order for an insurance policy to cover a burglary, there must be:
    a. Evidence of forcible entry
    b. A police report
    c. A police investigation
    d. Photos of the stolen property
    e. All of the above

34. Which of the following is a requirement regarding kidnapping insurance?
    a. A kidnapping demand must occur during the policy period.
    b. Kidnap ransom is specifically made against the named insured.
    c. No disclosure of insurance is made outside corporate headquarters.
    d. All of the above.
    e. None of the above.

35. Which of the following is *not* suggested behavior for the victim of a kidnapping?
    a. Stay calm.
    b. Do not cooperate with captors.
    c. Do not try to escape unless there is a good chance of success.
    d. Try to remember the events.
    e. Do not discuss possible rescues.

36. In setting up a plan to cope with kidnapping, the first contact should be with:
    a. Law enforcement
    b. The organization's executive committee
    c. Banking authorities
    d. The Federal Emergency Management Agency
    e. None of the above

37. In connection with corporate kidnapping by terrorists, the decision as to whether ransom is to be paid should be made by:
    a. Local police
    b. The spouse or blood relative of the victim
    c. The FBI
    d. An employee at the highest corporate level
    e. None of the above

38. A specific objective of the political kidnapper is:
    a. Publicity for cause
    b. Cash
    c. Penetration of a bank or other facility
    d. All of the above
    e. None of the above

39. Responsibility for emergency shutdown should be assigned by the disaster plan to:
    a. The plant manager
    b. The plant security chief
    c. The plant engineering service
    d. The chairman of the board
    e. None of the above

40. Which of the following should be part of a disaster recovery plan?
    a. Make one person responsible for health and sanitary conditions.
    b. Provide a plan for emergency headquarters.
    c. Provide a briefing for employees returning to work.
    d. All of the above.
    e. None of the above.

41. The advantage of a mutual aid association in disaster planning is that it:
    a. Establishes a workable disaster control organization to minimize damage
    b. Helps ensure continued operation of the damaged facility
    c. Helps in restoring a damaged facility
    d. All of the above
    e. None of the above

42. Which of the following should *not* be applicable to the development of an effective emergency disaster plan?
    a. The plan should be written.
    b. It should involve the minimum number of people possible in the preparation of the plan.
    c. It should contain an inventory of available resources.
    d. It should list preventative measures.
    e. None of the above.

43. Once published, an emergency plan for disaster control should be distributed:
    a. On a need-to-know basis
    b. Only to the highest echelon
    c. Only to division heads
    d. Down to the lowest echelons assigned responsibility
    e. To none of the above

44. The executive responsible for the development of the written emergency plan of an organization should be one who possesses which of the following qualifications?
    a. Technical aptitude
    b. Employment as a member of middle or senior management
    c. Complete familiarity with the company's organization
    d. All of the above
    e. None of the above

45. A study in 1976 by the Institute for Disaster Preparedness at the University of Southern California revealed that the actual behavior of people during a postdisaster period was:
    a. Widespread panic
    b. Calmness
    c. Docile and "zombielike"
    d. Antisocial
    e. All of the above

46. Voluntary participation in disaster control activities may be motivated by:
    a. An interesting training program
    b. Training in fire fighting
    c. Training in bomb threat searches and related matters
    d. Instruction in safety and fire hazard control
    e. All of the above

47. The correct procedure with respect to a bomb threat is that:
    a. Searches should be performed only when the call appears to be valid
    b. Searches should always be conducted by the police
    c. Personnel in work areas should not participate in searches
    d. All of the above
    e. None of the above

48. In emergency plans concerning a bomb threat, such a plan should require:
    a. Training for employees involved in searches
    b. A listing of telephone numbers of explosive disposal teams
    c. That, in evacuation, employees should ordinarily use exits other than main entrances

    d. All of the above

    e. None of the above

49. Earthquake emergency plans should stress that the safest place during a quake is:

    a. Within a work area under preselected cover

    b. In open spaces away from a building

    c. At home

    d. In a building made of concrete

    e. None of the above

50. In a strike, the refusal by management to allow members of the bargaining unit on the premises is called a:

    a. Lockout

    b. Shutout

    c. Lock-in

    d. All of the above

    e. None of the above

51. The most important single relationship of a security organization with outside agencies during a strike is with:

    a. The fire department

    b. The hospital

    c. The police

    d. A prosecuting attorney

    e. None of the above

52. At the time of a strike, if no guard force is available, the following action should be taken as a general rule:

    a. Immediately hire one.

    b. Mobilize supervisory personnel into a patrol group.

    c. Have police come on the property to act as a security force.

    d. All of the above.

    e. None of the above.

53. During a strike, the professional position of the police should be:

    a. To prevent violence

    b. To enforce laws firmly and fairly

    c. To suppress criminal conduct whenever it occurs

    d. All of the above

    e. None of the above

54. Which of the following officers or employees will always be placed on a staff to develop an emergency evaluation and disaster plan?

    a. The finance office

    b. The personnel office

    c. The medical office

    d. The facility's security director

    e. The corporation's president

55. Which of the following should *not* generally be incorporated in a company's emergency evacuation and disaster plan?
    a. Shutdown procedures
    b. Evacuation procedures
    c. Communications procedures
    d. Public information procedures
    e. A specific plan to deal with civil disturbances if conditions dictate

56. The emergency evacuation and disaster plan should be:
    a. Detailed
    b. Tested initially
    c. Updated as required
    d. All of the above
    e. None of the above

57. The activation of the company's emergency plan generally will be done by the:
    a. Security officer
    b. Plant manager
    c. Chairman of the board
    d. President of the company
    e. Personnel manager

58. The National Bomb Data Center is operated by the:
    a. CIA
    b. FBI
    c. ATF
    d. LEAA
    e. Census Bureau

59. The purpose of formulating a civil disorder plan is to:
    a. Ensure the safety and well-being of all personnel
    b. Ensure full protection of company property
    c. Ensure the continued operation of the facility
    d. Help bring about a peaceful solution of the community problem
    e. All of the above

60. The civil disorder plan should be:
    a. Disseminated widely
    b. Restricted only to those responsible for formulating policy in connection with the plan and implementing it
    c. Posted on appropriate bulletin boards
    d. Disseminated only to security personnel
    e. None of the above

61. A civil disorder planning committee should be staffed by which of the following?
    a. Director of security
    b. Personnel manager
    c. Facility manager
    d. All of the above
    e. None of the above

62. With regard to civil disorder planning, the responsibility for maintaining law and order rests with:
    a. The FBI
    b. The Army Department
    c. Local authorities
    d. The proprietary security authority
    e. None of the above

63. In connection with monitoring labor disputes, which of the following measures is *not* advisable?
    a. Change all perimeter-gate padlocks.
    b. Issue special passes to nonstriking employees.
    c. Notify employees who go to work to keep windows rolled up.
    d. Provide armed guards.
    e. All of the above.

64. Additional security personnel required to augment the regular security force during an emergency is usually accomplished by:
    a. Using the National Guard
    b. Using US Army personnel
    c. Using uniformed guards from a private security company
    d. Using the facility's supervisory force
    e. None of the above

65. Which of the following is generally used by saboteurs to disrupt industrial operations?
    a. Chemical means
    b. Electronic methods
    c. Fire
    d. All of the above
    e. None of the above

66. Sabotage can effectively be combated by:
    a. Reducing target accessibility and vulnerability
    b. An effective training program
    c. A close liaison with FBI and other agencies
    d. All of the above
    e. None of the above

67. The least-often used method of sabotage is:
    a. Mechanical
    b. Fire
    c. Explosive
    d. Electronic
    e. Psychological

68. In any strike procedure plan, all security personnel should be briefed by company management regarding:
    a. Company policy regarding the strike
    b. Property lines
    c. The importance of taking detailed notes on illegal activities
    d. All of the above
    e. None of the above

69. Usually, the most difficult part of an executive protection plan is:
    a. To secure trained personnel
    b. To initiate liaison with federal agencies
    c. To initiate liaison with local authorities
    d. To convince the executive being protected of the need for such protection
    e. None of the above

70. Which of the following precautionary actions to provide executive protection is *not* advisable?
    a. Maintain a low profile
    b. Do not use commercial airlines
    c. Do not publicly announce travel
    d. Consider the use of armor-plated autos
    e. None of the above

71. In a government-sponsored study of civil defense problems, the National Academy of Sciences and the National Research Council predict that the strategic warning before a general nuclear war would be:
    a. Days to months
    b. Hours
    c. Minutes
    d. None
    e. Approximately 30 days

72. Defense Readiness Condition (DEFCON) ratings—a numerical indication of world tension—are established by the:
    a. FBI
    b. NSA
    c. CIA
    d. NORAD
    e. State

73. In emergency planning, vital records should be maintained at:
    a. The Emergency Operating Center (EOC) Record Center
    b. The National Archives in Washington, DC
    c. The company headquarters
    d. The local police department
    e. The Federal Emergency Management Agency
74. Which of the following is a characteristic of a mail bomb?
    a. It was mailed from a foreign country.
    b. It is addressed to an individual by name or title.
    c. Its bulk and weight are greater than a normal airmail letter.
    d. All of the above.
    e. None of the above.
75. Which of the following is an abnormal reaction to stress?
    a. Individual panic
    b. Depression
    c. Overactivity
    d. Bodily disability
    e. All of the above
76. A type of bodily disability wherein a person unconsciously converts his or her anxiety into a strong belief that some part of his or her body has ceased to function is:
    a. Malingering
    b. Hysterics
    c. Conversion hysteria
    d. Depression
    e. Phobia
77. Which of the following is *not* recommended as a preventive measure to prevent panic?
    a. Give people a routine to keep down anxieties.
    b. Don't emphasize discipline.
    c. Provide full and appropriate information to combat ignorance.
    d. Control rumors.
    e. None of the above.
78. Which of the following is *not* a recommended action in planning for continuity of management during an emergency?
    a. Avoid assigning as alternatives for the same key positions people who reside in the same neighborhood.
    b. Keep top management from traveling together in the same vehicle.
    c. Tell only top executives of the plan.
    d. Require at least yearly medical exams for key people.
    e. Prepare a job classifications file showing interrelated skills.

79. Which of the following methods of duplication of records for emergency planning purposes is the least desirable?
   a. Handwritten notations
   b. Carbon copies
   c. Photocopying
   d. Microfilming
   e. None of the above

80. The storage of records in vaults, safes, or storerooms on the premises rather than in dispersed storage is called:
   a. Dispersion
   b. Vaulting
   c. Restricted storage
   d. Physical protection
   e. None of the above

81. Which of the following steps should be taken to provide viable emergency financial procedures?
   a. Provide for duplicate billing daily and proper record storage
   b. Arrange vital files in readily portable units
   c. Avoid hazardous areas for record storage
   d. Have an adequate supply of actual cash on hand
   e. All of the above

82. With regard to a nuclear attack, studies have shown that the number of persons who would survive the initial effects of blast and heat would be:
   a. Tens of millions
   b. Less than 5%
   c. Less than 10%
   d. Less than 3%
   e. None of the above

83. With regard to nuclear attack, depending on one's location and other circumstances, the following action should be considered for survival:
   a. Seek private shelter at home.
   b. Seek public shelter in your own community.
   c. Leave your community for shelter in a less dangerous area.
   d. All of the above.
   e. None of the above.

84. A unit for measuring the amount of radiation exposure is called a(n):
   a. Gamma ray
   b. Roentgen
   c. Isotope
   d. Gamma meter

85. With regard to a possible nuclear attack, the attack warning signal is a:
    a. 30-s-long alarm
    b. 2-min-long alarm
    c. 3 to 5 min wavering sound on sirens, a series of short blasts, whistle, etc.
    d. 30 s wavering sound
    e. None of the above

86. With regard to a potential nuclear attack, the attention or alert signal is usually a:
    a. 30 s wavering sound on sirens
    b. 30 s steady blast
    c. 2 min wavering sound
    d. 4 min wavering sound
    e. 3 to 5 min steady blast on sirens

87. Which action should *not* be taken if one hears a standard warning signal for a potential nuclear attack?
    a. Go to a public fallout shelter.
    b. Go to a home fallout shelter.
    c. Turn on the radio.
    d. Telephone the nearest civil defense office for more information.
    e. None of the above.

88. Which of the following is *not* a recommended treatment for a person who may be in shock?
    a. Keep the person lying down.
    b. Keep the person from chilling.
    c. Keep the person's head a little lower than his or her hips.
    d. Encourage the person to drink.
    e. Give the person alcohol to drink.

89. A symptom of radiation sickness is:
    a. Lack of appetite
    b. Nausea
    c. Vomiting
    d. Fatigue
    e. All of the above

90. Flood forecasts and warnings are issued by the:
    a. Federal Emergency Management Agency
    b. National Weather Service
    c. Department of the Interior
    d. National Oceanic and Atmospheric Administration
    e. Agriculture Department

91. Which of the following is *not* a recommended action with regard to survival of earthquakes?
    a. If outside, immediately go inside.
    b. Keep calm.
    c. Douse all fires.
    d. Keep away from utility wires.
    e. Don't run through buildings.
92. The firing train of a bomb generally consists of a:
    a. Detonator
    b. Booster
    c. Main charge
    d. All of the above
    e. None of the above
93. Of all reported bomb threats, it is estimated that the percentage of real threats is:
    a. 2%
    b. 10%
    c. 15%
    d. 20%
    e. 22%
94. A full evacuation of a building should be ordered upon receipt of a bomb threat when:
    a. There is a reasonable suspicion that a bomb is present
    b. Any threat is received
    c. The threat is received during working hours
    d. The caller has a foreign accent
    e. None of the above
95. Which of the following may be an indication of a planted bomb?
    a. Loose electrical fittings
    b. Tinfoil
    c. Fresh plaster or cement
    d. All of the above
    e. None of the above
96. If a kidnapper warns the family of the victim not to notify police, the best course of action is to:
    a. Do nothing
    b. Contact a reliable detective agency
    c. Notify the police anyway
    d. Notify the telephone company
    e. None of the above

97. The ZYX Corporation is in the process of relocating its facilities after several years of planning. The president, who is well aware of the necessity for emergency planning, directs you as the security manager to draw up necessary plans to cope with natural disasters. Which of the following is *not* a valid assumption to be considered?
    a. Some plants or facilities just are not vulnerable to natural disasters and therefore should not be involved in the planning.
    b. Most disasters considered likely will arrive with very little warning.
    c. Each plant and facility must be evaluated in terms of disasters most likely to occur as well as the facility's capacity to cope with and minimize the effects of the disaster.
    d. In assessing the vulnerability of individual plants and other facilities, environmental, indigenous, and economic factors must be considered.
    e. Most disasters considered likely will have a rapid development and have a potential for substantial destruction.

98. A natural hazard that poses a threat to many areas of this country is a hurricane. As soon as the weather forecaster determines the a particular section of the coast will feel the full effects of a hurricane, he or she issues a hurricane warning. Such a warning specifies which of the following?
    a. Coastal areas where the eye of the storm will pass
    b. Coastal areas where winds of 74 mph or higher are expected
    c. Coastal areas where inhabitants should listen closely for further advisories and be ready to take precautionary actions
    d. The fact that there are definite indications that a hurricane is forming and the name given to the storm
    e. Coastal areas where winds are 100 mph or higher are expected

99. One natural disaster that seems to occur with increasing frequency is the tornado. It is necessary for the security manager to be knowledgeable regarding all aspects of tornados so that adequate disaster plans can be formulated. Which of the following statements is incorrect?
    a. Tornados are violent local storms with whirling winds of tremendous speed that can reach 200–400 mph.
    b. The individual tornado appears as a rotating, funnel-shaped cloud that extends toward the ground from the base of a thundercloud.
    c. The tornado spins like a top, may sound like the roaring of an airplane or locomotive, and varies from gray to black in color.

    d. Tornados only occur in the middle plains, southeastern states, and some Middle Atlantic States.

    e. The width of a tornado path ranges generally from 200 yd. to 1 mi.

100. You are the security manager of the ZYW Corporation, located in Phoenix, Arizona. A report is received from the national weather service that a tornado warning has been issued. Which of the following would be the correct action to take?

    a. Institute appropriate emergency notification procedures as this means that a tornado has actually been sighted in the area or is indicated by radar.

    b. Alert top management as this indicates tornados are expected to develop.

    c. Request the weather service to keep you advised on a 15 min basis.

    d. Have all windows in the facility closed and be alert to additional weather reports.

    e. Do nothing because tornados are usually not spotted in Arizona and the report is probably in error.

101. As the security manager of a large corporation located in Southern California, you are charged with formulating a disaster plan to handle emergencies that arise as a result of earthquakes. Which of the following warnings to be issued to employees should *not* be included in the plan?

    a. If employees are outside, proceed to the nearest building and head for the basement promptly.

    b. If employees are indoors at the time of shaking, they should stay there.

    c. If inside, take cover under sturdy furniture.

    d. If inside, stay near the center of the building.

    e. If inside, stay away from glass windows and doors.

102. Earthquakes constitute a definite concern to the emergency management responsibilities of security managers in certain areas of our country. Accordingly, it is incumbent upon security professionals to have a clear understanding of the basic facts concerning earthquakes. Which of the following is an incorrect statement?

    a. Earthquakes are unpredictable and strike without warning.

    b. Earthquakes may last from a few seconds to as long as 5 min.

    c. The actual movement of the ground in an earthquake is usually the direct cause of injury or death.

    d. Earthquakes may also trigger landslides and generate tidal waves.

    e. Most casualties during an earthquake result from falling material.

103. Potential man-made disasters should be included when developing an emergency plan. One of the most common man-made disasters is the plant fire. Which of the following is considered to be the most important aspect of plans for coping with major plant fires?

    a. To make certain that the plant's fire response team is adequately manned

    b. To make certain that the plant's fire-fighting equipment is adequate and in good operating condition

    c. To make certain plant personnel are well trained in fire-fighting techniques

    d. To make certain that there is a command center with excellent communications

    e. To make certain that mutual assistance agreements have been developed with local governments, other plants, and nearby installations

104. Another area of potential concern from a disaster-planning standpoint is the handling, movement, and disposition of hazardous chemicals. Which of the following agencies is responsible for regulating the movement of hazardous chemicals?

    a. The Federal Bureau of Investigation

    b. The Interstate Commerce Commission

    c. The US Department of Transportation

    d. The Department of Health and Human Resources

    e. The US Department of Commerce

105. Security managers must know all aspects of hazardous chemicals used in the plant, especially pertinent data concerning their locations, hazardous properties, characteristics, and potential hazardous reactions to each other. Which of the following is not a primary source of technical information on chemical hazards?

    a. The National Fire Protection Association, Boston, Massachusetts

    b. The Manufacturing Chemists Association, Washington, DC

    c. The National Agricultural Chemists Association, Washington, DC

    d. The Association of American Railroads

    e. The US Department of Commerce

106. Compared with other plant emergencies, bomb threats present a highly complex problem for plant management and emergency service personnel. Which of the following actions should *not* be in the bomb threat emergency plan, as it is incorrect?

    a. Prior planning to meet the threat should include contact with a nearby military explosive ordnance disposal detachment (EODD).

    b. Prior planning should include contact with the local police department.

    c. Training programs for plant specialists in handling improvised explosive devices should be utilized when available from the military explosive ordinance disposal control center.

    d. The chief of police must make the decision whether or not to evacuate the building after a bomb threat has been received.

107. One of the most difficult emergency decisions to be made involves the evacuation of a building because of a bomb threat, especially because statistics show that over 95% of such threats are hoaxes. Suppose your firm's switchboard operator receives such a threat, wherein the caller identifies himself as a member of a recognized terrorist group and gives the location of the bomb as to floor as well as the time of detonation. Which of the following actions should receive priority as to evacuation?

    a. Promptly consider evacuation.

    b. Call the FBI to have a subversive check made on the terrorist group.

    c. Secure advice from the FBI as to evacuation.

    d. Conduct a detailed search of the area involved and make a decision relative to evacuation after the search is completed.

    e. Do not evacuate, as odds are 95% in your favor that it is a hoax.

108. An emergency plan with regard to bombs and bomb threats should include the steps to be taken if a bomb is located as a result of a search. Which of the following would be a proper procedure if the local police cannot dispose of an object that was located and thought to be a bomb?

    a. The FBI should be requested to dispose of the object.

    b. Volunteers in the plant should be utilized and instructed to handle the object carefully.

    c. The services of a bomb-disposal unit should be requested.

    d. The US Secret Service should be requested to handle the object.

    e. The object should be thoroughly isolated and defused by a robot.

109. Complete and effective disaster planning should certainly include plans to deal with sabotage, as no plant is immune to sabotage. Which of the following is generally considered to be incorrect?

    a. Types of targets for sabotage, as a rule, cannot be predicted with any degree of accuracy.

    b. The saboteur will generally look for a target that is critical, vulnerable, and accessible.

    c. In general, saboteurs are enemy agents, disgruntled employees who commit sabotage for revenge, or individuals who are mentally unbalanced.

d. The prevention of sabotage may be accomplished by reducing target accessibility.

e. The methods of sabotage are varied and include psychological sabotage to cause slowdowns or work stoppage.

110. The widespread and increasing industrial and commercial use and transportation of radioactive materials has increased the possibility of radiological hazards resulting from accidents involving these materials. Which of the following is not a valid observation?

a. If plant and local emergency services are not adequate to cope with the situation, federal assistance can be requested.

b. Accidents may occur in facilities where radioactive materials are used or processed.

c. In accordance with an interagency radiological assistance plan, the radiological emergency response capabilities of federal agencies can be used to protect public health and safety.

d. Special emergency response capabilities have been established by the Environmental Protection Agency for coping with accidents involving nuclear weapons.

e. When a radiological incident occurs in a plant, some degree of immediate response by state and local public safety personnel usually will be required.

111. All security managers must have a disaster plan to deal with nuclear attacks and must be well informed regarding the disaster propensities of such an explosion. The effects of nuclear weapons differ from those of conventional weapons in all of the following ways *except* what?

a. An experimental device exploded in the Aleutian Islands in November 1971 had an estimated yield of more than 5 megatons (MT), which means it released more energy than the explosion of 50 million tons of TNT.

b. A fairly large amount of the energy in a nuclear explosion is referred to as *thermal radiation.*

c. *Thermal radiation* is capable of causing skin burns and of starting fires at considerable distances.

d. A nuclear detonation also produces an electromagnetic pulse (EMP) sometimes called "radio flash."

e. If a nuclear explosion occurs at or near the ground, great quantities of radioactive earth and other materials are drawn upward to high altitudes. When the radioactive particles fall back to earth, the phenomenon is known as "fallout."

112. One of the greatest hazards that would result from a nuclear attack is radioactive fallout. A security manager should be well informed concerning the full potential of damage associated with this type of disaster. Which of the following is an incorrect statement?
   a. Gamma radiation most concerns civil preparedness planners as it cannot be detected by any of the human senses.
   b. Gamma radiation is measured in units called roentgens.
   c. In an all-out nuclear attack against US military, industrial, and population centers, it is estimated that severe to moderate damage from the blasts and heat effects would occur in about 50% of the nation's area.
   d. Gamma radiation can be detected only with special instruments.
   e. It is estimated that millions of Americans could survive the radiation effects of a large-scale nuclear attack by seeking protection in fallout shelters.

113. The federal effort in preparing for a nuclear attack includes providing state and local governments with necessary advice and assistance. All of the following are valid observations regarding federal assistance *except* for what?
   a. The federal government has conducted a nationwide survey to identify fallout shelter space as part of the national shelter program.
   b. As a result of the national fallout shelter survey, it was determined that very few existing buildings contain usable shelter space.
   c. Nationwide radiological monitoring capability consists of several thousand federal, state, and local monitoring stations.
   d. The National Warning System (NAWAS) has warning points strategically located throughout the continental United States.
   e. The Emergency Broadcast System (EBS) is composed of nongovernmental radio and television stations.

114. In emergency planning, nothing is more important than making sure that employees of your plant are thoroughly familiar with the National Attack Warning Signal. Which of the following is the correct signal?
   a. A 10 min wavering sound on sirens
   b. A 3 to 5 min steady sound on sirens
   c. A series of 1 min steady sounds on sirens
   d. A 3- to 5-min wavering sound on sirens or a series of short blasts on whistles, horns, or other devices as necessary
   e. A ringing of all church bells for 5 min

115. At 1500 hours, you, as well as other employees of the ZYX firm, hear a 3 to 5 min wavering sound on sirens. There has been no previous notification of an impending test of the siren system. If you have adequately done your job as security manager, the employees should recognize that the following action should be taken.
    a. Ignore it as there has been no confirmation that it is for real.
    b. Because this signal means that an actual enemy attack against the United States has been detected, protective action should be taken immediately.
    c. Because this is merely an alert signal, proceed with normal activities until you are advised to take other action.
    d. Do nothing until the Federal Emergency Management Agency verifies the status of an emergency.
    e. Ignore it because most situations such as this have proven to be equipment malfunctions.

116. The continuity of business and industrial leadership and direction are essential parts of all industrial emergency plans. The following specific measures should be included in the development of a plan for continuity of leadership *except*:
    a. Ensuring a functioning board of directors
    b. Establishing lines of succession for key officers and operating personnel
    c. Establishing alternate company headquarters
    d. Providing for a special stockholder meeting immediately after the attack to provide for methods of operation
    e. Ensuring record preservation

117. In reviewing the emergency plans of the ZYX Corporation, the legal counsel of the firm notes that under nuclear disaster conditions, there is a definite possibility that a quorum of the board of directors cannot be readily assembled, which will not allow action in accordance with law. Which of the following methods generally would *not* be acceptable to remedy this legal problem?
    a. Reduce the quorum number if allowed by state law.
    b. Fill board vacancies if allowed by state law.
    c. Establish an emergency management committee, if allowed by state law.
    d. Appoint alternate directors, if allowed by state law.
    e. Utilize a chain of command and execute proper power-of-attorney papers for the top three officials so the most senior could execute legal affairs if the board is not functioning.

118. Provisions for the establishment of emergency lines of executive succession should be included in a company's emergency plans. Which of the following cannot be relied on as being valid in making decisions in this regard?
    a. The board of directors sets general policy.
    b. The board of directors is the entity legally responsible for corporate activity.
    c. The board of directors usually meets at stated times such as monthly or perhaps even only quarterly.
    d. Responsibility for day-to-day operations is vested in the officers.
    e. Generally speaking, state statutes usually vest specified functions in particular officers and usually set out in detail the duties of officers.

119. As security manager of the ZYX Corporation, you have been instructed to devise company plans to protect vital records in the event of a disaster. You immediately realize the serious nature of such plans and begin to make appropriate plans. Approximately what percentage of the company's records would normally constitute a company's vital records to be safeguarded during an emergency?
    a. 2%
    b. 5%
    c. 8%
    d. 10%
    e. 20%

120. In devising plans to protect vital records during an emergency, a prime decision to make would be the identification of vital records. Whether such records are vital depends, to a large extent, on the type of business conducted. However, as a general rule, all of the following would be considered vital to any corporate organization *except*:
    a. The incorporation certification
    b. Personal identification fingerprints of employees
    c. The bylaws of the corporation
    d. The stock record books
    e. Board of directors' minutes

121. The selection of records to be protected under an emergency vital-records protection program is a difficult operation. Which of the following statements is considered to be incorrect in making such a selection?
    a. Management should protect vital records by systematically determining what information is vital.

    b. The vital-records protection program is an administrative device for preserving existing records.

    c. If a particular record does not contain vital information, it has no place in the company's vital-records protection program—even though it may have other value for the company.

    d. Decision making in determining individual vital records should be rapid. A record either contains vital information or does not.

    e. Vital information is not necessarily on paper.

122. Some of the vital company information that management seeks to protect is processed by a computer and captured on distinctive media associated with electronic data processing. Effective protection of this vital information is complicated for a number of reasons. Which of the following is incorrect in this regard?

    a. A nuclear detonation produces an electromagnetic pulse (EMP) that could cause considerable damage. However, well-tested EMP-protective devices are available.

    b. Formerly dispersed information is consolidated, which intensifies its exposure to possible destruction or compromise.

    c. The data-processing medium is extremely vulnerable to a wide variety of perils such as fire, water, dirt, and hazardous chemical gases.

    d. Both the computer and the area in which it is located must be protected along with the vital information.

    e. Information transmitted over a distance for remote computer processing is out of the company's direct control for an extended period of time.

123. As the security manager of the ZYX Corporation, you have been given the responsibility of improving the security of the computer facility. Which of the following would least improve the security?

    a. Make the facility as inconspicuous as possible.

    b. Provide 24 h security guard surveillance of the area.

    c. Strengthen controls over access to the facility.

    d. Make sure all unused wiring, including telephone cables, is neatly stored in the computer room.

    e. Wherever local fire codes permit, remove water sprinkler fire extinguisher systems and replace with carbon dioxide or halon 1301 systems.

124. The vital-records protection program is designed to protect and provide the information needed by the company for survival in a disaster or emergency. Periodic vital-records protection program tests must be provided for to determine the adequacy of the protection program. Which of the following observations is incorrect?

a. The company security officer, records manager, and internal auditor should test or evaluate the program at least once a year.
b. Every effort should be made to make test conditions as realistic as feasible.
c. Specifically, the test should determine that the company's various vital information needs can be satisfied in a typical emergency situation.
d. The test period should not be limited in time but should be extended as long as needed.
e. The test should be located off of company premises, if possible.

125. The president of the ZYX Corporation expresses concern relative to the company's ability to act in an emergency to protect life and property. He instructs that you undertake the necessary action to establish the desired emergency capability within the facility. Which of the following should be the first step in initiating this action?
    a. Contact established guard companies to make bids to oversee the operations.
    b. Do nothing until funds have been appropriated.
    c. Appoint an emergency coordinator at the corporate level.
    d. Make a physical survey of the plant.
    e. Form a committee of key executives to operate out of the command level.

126. Providing for proper succession of management in the event of a disaster is a key part of any disaster plan. Your prime responsibility in the development of a management successor list would be to select:
    a. Key personnel who have engineering degrees
    b. Those individuals who have been with the company in excess of 10 years
    c. Enough names so as to make sure that at least one person on the list would always be available during an emergency
    d. Those who hold an executive position of president, vice president, treasurer, or secretary
    e. Either the plant manager or security director to head the corporate emergency planning activities

127. In establishing a disaster plan, provision should be incorporated that would permit you to be prepared for a variety of emergency situations. Which of the following probably would *not* have a key role in such plans?
    a. Employee welfare service
    b. Rescue teams
    c. The recreational coordinator

    d. The Radiological Defense Service

    e. The engineering service

128. In any well-designed disaster plan, you, as security manager, have as a primary goal the achievement of "emergency readiness." Which of the following explanations most adequately defines the term *emergency readiness*?

    a. It means that you are prepared to react promptly to save lives and protect property if your plant is threatened or hit by a major emergency or disaster of any type.

    b. It means that the Federal Emergency Management Agency has inspected and approved the company's disaster plans.

    c. It means that all security personnel have met minimum training standards of the state in which the plant is located.

    d. It means that all officials of the security department have successfully passed the Certified Protection Professional® (CPP) examination.

    e. It means that the security staff is 100% manned.

129. Perhaps one of the most difficult tasks in planning for disasters and emergencies is the actual formulation of a basic disaster plan. Which of the following is an incorrect procedure in developing such a plan?

    a. The basic plan should provide for coordination of government and company actions before and during a disaster.

    b. A glossary of terms used should be included.

    c. There should be a listing of types of emergencies limited to those experienced by the company in the past.

    d. The plan should utilize appendices as needed, such as maps, call-up lists, and mutual aid agreements.

    e. The plan should specifically provide for coordination of government and company action before and during a disaster.

130. Although protection of people is, without a doubt, the first priority in planning for emergencies, shutdown procedures must be thorough and done by those who are trained to do so. Your disaster plan should have such shutdown procedures assigned to:

    a. The security force

    b. The plant manager

    c. Maintenance employees on each shift who handle these procedures on a regular basis

    d. The fire brigade

    e. Supervisors of the plant

131. Emergency shutdown procedures are of great importance because orderly shutdown measures may help avert damage and loss. Your emergency preparedness planning should provide for the following actions *except* what?
    a. Such plans should be developed and tested by the department managers concerned.
    b. Time should not be wasted in attempting to move critical or valuable items inside.
    c. Personnel on each shift should be designated to close doors and windows.
    d. Section heads must complete shutdown check-off lists and supervise shutdown procedures in their particular areas.
    e. Precious metals and original drawings should be in locked storage or be moved to safer locations.
132. After the disaster plan has been fully prepared and tested, you, as the security manager, must make certain that the employees thoroughly understand it and actually take an active interest in it. Which of the following should *not* be done in your program of informing and educating the employees as to the plan?
    a. Information disseminated to management should be prepared no differently from that contained in a general employee announcement.
    b. Safety committees play a very important role in the development of the emergency plan.
    c. Daily newsletters, bulletins, postings, and sales magazines should be closely evaluated as possible channels for the dissemination of disaster information.
    d. New employees should be made aware of the existence of the disaster plan as soon as they come on duty.
    e. Supervisory personnel are considered spokesmen for the company, and employees naturally turn to these individuals for information.
133. In order to adequately plan for emergencies, the security manager must make certain that the corporation has access to all necessary resources that will save lives, minimize damage, and ensure the continued operation of rapid restoration of damaged member plants. Most plants ensure access to such resources by:
    a. Providing for a budget that will supply all the resources needed to cope with a major emergency
    b. Establishing appropriate liaison with the police, fire, rescue, and medical forces of the community to provide services as needed

c. Relying on their own self-help organization and equipment and joining hands with other plants in the community for mutual aid

d. Establishing appropriate contact with the nearest military base

e. Contracting with local security companies to provide necessary resources, if needed during an emergency

134. In forming an industrial mutual aid association, a number of definitive plans must be made. Which of the following is *not* true and should *not* be relied on in formulating these plans?

a. Each member firm must be willing to defray industrial mutual aid association expenses.

b. Capital outlay and operating costs are usually modest.

c. The basic operating element of a mutual aid association is an operating board.

d. Any industrial mutual aid association should be established in advance of emergencies, not afterwards.

e. A small operating headquarters should be established where appropriate files and records can be maintained.

135. A key role in any emergency will be played by the plant manager or, in his or her place, an authorized official, such as the emergency coordinator or security chief. Which of the following should *not* be done personally by this official?

a. Take personal charge of all operations at the disaster scene.

b. Activate the plant control center.

c. Alert and inform the local government emergency coordinator.

d. Brief plant control center staff on the emergency situation.

e. Mobilize employees and other resources to the extent required.

136. No document associated with disaster planning is more important than the disaster plan manual. In preparing this manual, all of the following are applicable *except* what?

a. Do not clutter this manual with such minor items as the geographic location of the plant, site plans, floor plans, and utilities layouts.

b. All plant emergency operations plans should be put in writing.

c. Prepare and test the emergency plan before it is needed.

d. Make the disaster plan manual distinctive by using a special color for the cover.

e. Each plan should contain statements of company policy regarding emergency planning.

137. The keys to the success of any emergency organization and plan are training and testing. In designing effective testing procedures, the following are all valid observations *except* what?

a. Records should be maintained so deficiencies can be corrected following the test.

b. The testing exercise should be as realistic as possible.
c. Plenty of advance notice should be given so all possible preparations can be made.
d. One of the best times to test the plant emergency plan is in coordination with your local government periodic test exercises.
e. Testing of the emergency plan should require the actual operation or simulation of every element of the plan in all possible emergency conditions.

138. Comprehensive emergency management (CEM) is the term for a four-pronged process used by the emergency management community throughout the United States. The four elements of CEM are:
a. Mitigation, preparedness, response, and recovery
b. Mitigation, containment, response, and recovery
c. Mitigation, preparedness, containment, and recovery
d. Preparedness, containment, response, and recovery

139. Which of the following is the purpose of a discussion exercise?
a. The focus of this training is to become familiar with the emergency response plan.
b. The focus of this training is to evaluate the plan, detect possible problems, and resolve issues beforehand.
c. The focus of this portion is to evaluate the plan in depth by looking into specifics, addressing gaps, and establishing timetables for accomplishing both primary and follow-up training.
d. This is the ultimate test of the plan that includes exercises, movement of personnel, equipment, and the incorporation of internal and external resources.
e. These should be as realistic as possible and should be constructed in such a way as to allow for note-taking and evaluation of performance of personnel and equipment.

140. What role does mitigation play in emergency management?
a. The pre-event efforts undertaken by the company to lessen the impact of the event
b. The efforts exerted to prepare the staff for response and recovery requirements
c. The activities necessary to address situations as they arise in the course of an emergency
d. After the emergency has occurred, the actions to be taken to return the business to full, pre-event operations
e. None of the above

141. In emergency planning, which of the following is the purpose of exercises?
a. The focus of this training is to become familiar with the emergency response plan.

    b. The focus of this training is to evaluate the plan, detect possible problems, and resolve issues beforehand.

    c. The focus of this portion is to evaluate the plan in depth by looking into specifics, addressing gaps, and establishing timetables for accomplishing both primary and follow-up training.

    d. This is the ultimate test of the plan that includes exercises, movement of personnel, equipment, and the incorporation of internal and external resources.

    e. These should be as realistic as possible and should be constructed in such a way as to allow for note-taking and evaluation of performance of personnel and equipment.

142. In emergency planning, which of the following is a response priority?

    a. Protect human life and prevent or minimize personal injury

    b. Reduce exposure of physical assets

    c. Maximize loss control for assets where exposure cannot be reduced

    d. Restore normal operations as soon as possible

    e. All of the above

143. In emergency planning, which of the following is the purpose of a functional exercise?

    a. The focus of this training is to become familiar with the emergency response plan.

    b. The focus of this training is to evaluate the plan, detect possible problems, and resolve issues beforehand.

    c. The focus of this portion is to evaluate the plan in depth by looking into specifics, addressing gaps, and establishing timetables for accomplishing both primary and follow-up training.

    d. This is the ultimate test of the plan that includes exercises, movement of personnel, equipment, and the incorporation of internal and external resources.

    e. These should be as realistic as possible and should be constructed in such a way as to allow for note-taking and evaluation of performance of personnel and equipment.

144. What role does preparedness play in emergency management?

    a. The pre-event efforts undertaken by the company to lessen the impact of the event

    b. The efforts exerted to prepare the staff for response and recovery requirements

    c. The activities necessary to address situations as they arise in the course of an emergency

    d. After the emergency has occurred, the actions to be taken to return the business to full, pre-event operations

    e. None of the above

145. In emergency planning, which of the following is the purpose of a full-scale exercise?
   a. The focus of this training is to become familiar with the emergency response plan.
   b. The focus of this training is to evaluate the plan, detect possible problems, and resolve issues beforehand.
   c. The focus of this portion is to evaluate the plan in depth by looking into specifics, addressing gaps, and establishing timetables for accomplishing both primary and follow-up training.
   d. This is the ultimate test of the plan that includes exercises, movement of personnel, equipment, and the incorporation of internal and external resources.
   e. These should be as realistic as possible and should be constructed in such a way as to allow for note-taking and evaluation of performance of personnel and equipment.

146. What role does response play in emergency management?
   a. The pre-event efforts undertaken by the company to lessen the impact of the event
   b. The efforts exerted to prepare the staff for response and recovery requirements
   c. The activities necessary to address situations as they arise in the course of an emergency
   d. After the emergency has occurred, the actions to be taken to return the business to full, pre-event operations
   e. None of the above

147. What role does recovery play in emergency management?
   a. The pre-event efforts undertaken by the company to lessen the impact of the event
   b. The efforts exerted to prepare the staff for response and recovery requirements
   c. The activities necessary to address situations as they arise in the course of an emergency
   d. After the emergency has occurred, the actions to be taken to return the business to full, pre-event operations
   e. None of the above

148. In emergency planning, which of the following is the purpose of an orientation exercise?
   a. The focus of this training is to become familiar with the emergency response plan.
   b. The focus of this training is to evaluate the plan, detect possible problems, and resolve issues beforehand.

    c. The focus of this portion is to evaluate the plan in depth by looking into specifics, addressing gaps, and establishing time-tables for accomplishing both primary and follow-up training.

    d. This is the ultimate test of the plan that includes exercises, movement of personnel, equipment, and the incorporation of internal and external resources.

    e. These should be as realistic as possible and should be constructed in such a way as to allow for note-taking and evaluation of performance of personnel and equipment.

149. In emergency planning, damage assessment and impact evaluation should include which of the following?

    a. A comprehensive survey of the facility in conjunction with insurance underwriters and government officials

    b. Itemized lists of structural and nonstructural damage, including photographic documentation, a written summary of the damage, cost estimates, and recovery schedules

    c. Determining the need for temporary relocation and a time frame for return to the facility

    d. Identifying the need for contracted services, labor, material, and restoration of operations

    e. All of the above

150. Which of the following causes a tsunami?

    a. Tornados

    b. Displacement of a large volume of water

    c. Lightning

    d. Displacement of a large volume of air

    e. Sunspots

CHAPTER 8 ANSWERS

1. e. Employees familiar with the work area where the bomb is reportedly located
2. a. To meet the negotiated demands of the terrorists
3. b. Mutual aid association
4. d. Distribution should be limited to senior management.
5. a. Federal Emergency Management Agency
6. c. Fire
7. c. The plant engineering service
8. b. Be put in touch with the person designated in the emergency plan for orderly release of information
9. b. The American Red Cross
10. d. A new organization should be developed to handle emergency situations.

11. d. Any of the above
12. a. Fire loading
13. c. CO_2
14. c. Smoke or heat
15. a. Class A
16. d. Class D
17. c. Class C
18. b. Class B
19. a. Class A fires
20. d. Class D fires
21. d. Fire in closed spaces
22. d. Water fog
23. a. Invisible products of combustion emitted by a fire at its earliest stages
24. d. Thermal detector
25. b. Photoelectric smoke detector
26. e. Employees familiar with threatened areas
27. b. Location of the bomb
28. c. Reported immediately to the designated authorities
29. c. Management
30. b. Report the call immediately to the local police for investigation.
31. c. Professional bomb-disposal personnel
32. e. All of the above
33. a. Evidence of forcible entry
34. d. All of the above.
35. b. Do not cooperate with captors.
36. a. Law enforcement
37. d. An employee at the highest corporate level
38. d. All of the above
39. c. The plant engineering service
40. d. All of the above.
41. d. All of the above
42. b. It should involve the minimum number of people possible in the preparation of the plan.
43. d. Down to the lowest echelons assigned responsibility
44. d. All of the above
45. b. Calmness
46. e. All of the above
47. e. None of the above
48. d. All of the above
49. a. Within a work area under preselected cover
50. a. Lockout
51. c. The police

52. b. Mobilize supervisory personnel into a patrol group.
53. d. All of the above
54. d. The facility's security director
55. e. A specific plan to deal with civil disturbances if conditions dictate
56. d. All of the above
57. b. Plant manager
58. b. FBI
59. e. All of the above
60. b. Restricted only to those responsible for formulating policy in connection with the plan and implementing it
61. d. All of the above
62. c. Local authorities
63. d. Provide armed guards.
64. c. Using uniformed guards from a private security company
65. d. All of the above
66. a. Reducing target accessibility and vulnerability
67. e. Psychological
68. d. All of the above
69. d. To convince the executive being protected of the need for such protection
70. b. Do not use commercial airlines.
71. a. Days to months
72. d. NORAD
73. a. The Emergency Operating Center (EOC) Record Center
74. d. All of the above.
75. e. All of the above
76. c. Conversion hysteria
77. b. Don't emphasize discipline.
78. c. Tell only top executives of the plan.
79. b. Carbon copies
80. b. Vaulting
81. e. All of the above.
82. a. Tens of millions
83. d. All of the above.
84. b. Roentgen
85. c. 3 to 5 min wavering sound on sirens, a series of short blasts, whistle, etc.
86. e. 3 to 5 min steady blast on sirens
87. d. Telephone the nearest civil defense office for more information.
88. e. Give the person alcohol to drink.
89. e. All of the above
90. d. National Oceanic and Atmospheric Administration

91. a. If outside, immediately go inside.
92. d. All of the above
93. a. 2%
94. a. There is reasonable suspicion that a bomb is present
95. d. All of the above
96. c. Notify the police anyway
97. a. Some plants or facilities just are not vulnerable to natural disasters and therefore should not be involved in the planning.
98. b. Coastal areas where winds of 74 mph or higher are expected
99. d. Tornados only occur in the middle plains, southeastern states, and some Middle Atlantic states.
100. a. Institute appropriate emergency notification procedures as this means that a tornado has actually been sighted in the area or is indicated by radar.
101. a. If employees are outside, proceed to the nearest building and head for the basement promptly.
102. c. The actual movement of the ground in an earthquake is usually the direct cause of injury or death.
103. e. To make certain that mutual assistance agreements have been developed with local governments, other plants, and nearby federal installations
104. c. The US Department of Transportation
105. e. The US Department of Commerce
106. d. The chief of police must make the decision whether or not to evacuate the building after a bomb threat has been received.
107. a. Promptly consider evacuation.
108. c. The services of a bomb-disposal unit should be requested.
109. a. Types of targets for sabotage, as a rule, cannot be predicted with any degree of accuracy.
110. d. Special emergency response capabilities have been established by the Environmental Protection Agency for coping with accidents involving nuclear weapons.
111. a. An experimental nuclear device exploded in the Aleutian Islands in November 1971 had an estimated yield of more than 5 megatons, which means it released more energy than the explosion of 50 million tons of TNT.
112. c. In an all-out nuclear attack against US military, industrial, and population centers, it is estimated that severe to moderate damage from the blast and heat effects would occur in about 50% of the nation's area.
113. b. As a result of the national fallout shelter survey, it was determined that very few existing buildings contain usable shelter space.

114. d. A 3- to 5-min wavering sound on sirens or a series of short blasts on whistles, horns, or other devices as necessary

115. b. Because this signal means that an actual enemy attack against the United States has been detected, protective action should be taken immediately.

116. d. Providing for a special stockholder meeting immediately after the attack to provide for methods of operation

117. e. Utilize a chain of command and execute proper power-of-attorney papers for the top three officials so the most senior could execute legal affairs if the board is not functioning.

118. d. Responsibility for day-to-day operations is vested in the officers.

119. a. 2%

120. b. Personal identification fingerprints of employees

121. b. The vital-records protection program is an administrative device for preserving existing records.

122. a. A nuclear detonation produces an electromagnetic pulse (EMP) that could cause considerable damage. However, well-tested EMP-protective devices are available.

123. d. Make sure all unused wiring, including telephone cables, is neatly stored in the computer room.

124. d. The test period should not be limited in time but should be extended as long as needed.

125. c. Appoint an emergency coordinator at the corporate level.

126. c. Enough names so as to make sure that at least one person on the list would always be available during an emergency

127. c. The recreational coordinator

128. a. It means that you are prepared to react promptly to save lives and protect property if your plant is threatened or hit by a major emergency or disaster of any type.

129. c. There should be a listing of types of emergencies limited to those experienced by the company in the past.

130. c. Maintenance employees on each shift who handle these procedures on a regular basis

131. b. Time should not be wasted in attempting to move critical or valuable items inside.

132. a. Information disseminated to management should be prepared no differently from that contained in a general employee announcement.

133. c. Relying on their own self-help organization and equipment and joining hands with other plants in the community for mutual aid

134. b. Capital outlay and operating costs are usually modest.

135. a. Take personal charge of all operations at the disaster scene.

136. ·a. Do not clutter this manual with such minor items as the geographic location of the plant, site plans, floor plans, and utilities layouts.
137. c. Plenty of advance notice should be given so all possible preparations can be made.
138. a. Mitigation, preparedness, response, and recovery
139. b. The focus of this training is to evaluate the plan, detect possible problems, and resolve issues beforehand.
140. a. The pre-event efforts undertaken by the company to lessen the impact of the event
141. e. These should be as realistic as possible and should be constructed in such a way as to allow for note-taking and evaluation of performance of personnel and equipment.
142. e. All of the above
143. c. The focus of this portion is to evaluate the plan in depth by looking into specifics, addressing gaps, and establishing timetables for accomplishing both primary and follow-up training.
144. b. The efforts exerted to prepare the staff for response and recovery requirements
145. d. This is the ultimate test of the plan that includes exercises, movement of personnel, equipment, and the incorporation of internal and external resources.
146. c. The activities necessary to address situations as they arise in the course of an emergency
147. d. After the emergency has occurred, the actions to be taken to return the business to full, pre-event operations
148. a. The focus of this training is to become familiar with the emergency response plan.
149. e. All of the above
150. b. Displacement of a large volume of water

CHAPTER 9: GUARD FORCE

1. What is considered an advantage of requiring minimum training requirements of security officers?
    a. Productivity increases dramatically with proper training.
    b. There is a sales and service advantage if trained guards are provided.
    c. It builds professionalism.
    d. Promotions are more easily made.
    e. Both a and c.
    f. All of the above.

2. Which of the following procedures is recommended to motivate nighttime guards?
    a. Give the night shift an elite status.
    b. Pay for nighttime guards should be higher than for daytime guards.
    c. People should be "promoted" to being on the night shift.
    d. Make night jobs as attractive as possible.
    e. All of the above.

3. Which of the following constitutes a prime responsibility entrusted to the guard force of a museum?
    a. Protection of objects of art against all hazards
    b. Enforcement of the institution's rules and regulations
    c. The safety and well-being of visitors and the employees of the museum
    d. All of the above
    e. None of the above

4. The Bank Protection Act specifies that each banking institution:
    a. Must have a security officer at each location
    b. Is not required to have a designated security officer
    c. Must have a security officer but not necessarily at each location
    d. Must have at least two security officers at each location
    e. None of the above

5. Which of the following is considered to be an advantage of contracting for guard services?
    a. Lower payroll costs
    b. Fewer administrative headaches
    c. No absenteeism problems
    d. No collective bargaining
    e. All of the above

6. Which of the following factors should be evaluated in considering the need for security officers to have weapons?
    a. The type of encounter to be faced by the security officer
    b. The nature of the potential threat
    c. The operational objective of the security officer
    d. All of the above
    e. None of the above

7. Which of the following would be an argument against the use of nonlethal weapons by the security officer?
    a. They do not pose a substantial risk of death if used properly.
    b. They provide an alternative to guns where the situation requires less-than-lethal force.

    c. Use of nonlethal weapons reduces the risk of death to innocent bystanders.

    d. It might escalate confrontations with security officers because offenders would feel less threatened.

    e. None of the above.

8. The issuance of weapons to guards is usually *not* justified:

    a. In a situation where deterrence is needed in handling a large amount of cash

    b. In situations in which terrorism is a real threat

    c. In a situation where there would be a greater danger to life without weapons than with them

    d. In a situation where there seems to be no danger to life without weapons

9. In issuing policy statements regarding the handling of disturbed persons, the primary consideration is:

    a. Legal liability to the disturbed

    b. Reducing the disturbed person to a form of benevolent custody and eliminating the immediate danger

    c. Legal liability to employees and third persons if restraint is not achieved

    d. Employee–community public relations

    e. None of the above

10. The argument usually used by contract guard representatives as a selling point in their services is that:

    a. They are nonunion

    b. There are no administrative problems

    c. They are better trained

    d. They provide a reduction in cost

    e. Their objective is carrying out duties

11. The most important written instructions for the security guard are known as:

    a. Memoranda

    b. Operational orders

    c. Staff orders

    d. Post orders

12. Which of the following should be a required criterion of the security guard's post orders?

    a. The order should be written at the lowest level possible.

    b. Each order should deal with multiple subjects.

    c. The order should be detailed.

    d. The order should be indexed sparingly.

    e. None of the above.

13. The security guard's primary record of significant events affecting facility protection is known as the:`
   a. Ingress log
   b. Egress log
   c. Security log
   d. Daily events recorder log
   e. Supervisor's log

14. Estimates as to the number of security officers—both contract and proprietary—in the United States is approximately:
   a. 250,000
   b. 300,000
   c. 500,000
   d. 700,000
   e. 1,000,000+

15. A major study on private security was prepared by the:
   a. American Society for Industrial Security
   b. International Association of Chiefs of Police
   c. Private Security Task Force of the National Advisory Committee on Criminal Justice Standards and Goals
   d. Brookings Institute
   e. Harvard Symposium in Private Security

16. The number of security guards required for a facility is determined by the:
   a. Number of personnel
   b. Number of entrances and hours of operation
   c. Physical complexity of a facility
   d. Number of security guards required to protect the facilities
   e. Number of escorts or special assignments required
   f. All of the above

17. What is the primary function of the security officer?
   a. Patrol of buildings and perimeters
   b. Inspection of security and fire exposures
   c. Access control
   d. Being a bodyguard
   e. Bomb threats

18. Guard patrols are generally divided into what two categories?
   a. Specialized patrols and security patrols
   b. Night-watch patrols and day-watch patrols
   c. Foot patrols and vehicle patrols
   d. None of the above

19. Which of the following is *not* true of post orders?
   a. Most are important written instructions to the security force.
   b. They summarize the required security officers' duties.

c. They express the policies of the facility being protected.

d. They provide clear instructions.

e. Most post orders include oral instructions to the security officer.

20. Which of the following is *not* a true characterization of the guard operation?

a. Security guards are costly.

b. Security guards are generally recognized as an essential element in the protection of assets and personnel.

c. Security guards are the only element of protection that can be depended on to give complete security.

d. Security guards can also perform as public relations representatives when properly trained.

21. Each guard post that is manned 24 h/day, 7 days a week, requires:

a. Two guards

b. Three guards

c. Four and a half guards

d. Five guards

e. Six guards

22. The occupation of a uniformed security officer is psychologically:

a. Extraordinarily high stress

b. High stress

c. Medium stress

d. Low stress

e. An easy occupation

23. One supervisor can effectively control only a limited number of people, and that limit should not be exceeded. This principle is called:

a. Unity of command

b. Supervisory limits

c. Span of control

d. Line discipline

24. An important principle of organization is that an employee should be under the direct control of one and only one immediate superior. This principle is:

a. Unity of command

b. Supervisory limits

c. Span of control

d. Line discipline

25. As a rule, which department of the company administers the recruiting activity?

a. Security department

b. Administrative department

    c. Personnel department

    d. Internal affairs

26. In non-entry-level recruiting, the recommended technique is:

    a. "Blind ad"

    b. Open advertisement in newspaper

    c. Advertisement in trade journal

    d. Word of mouth on a selective basis

27. Every applicant's first interview should be with:

    a. The security manager or director

    b. The security supervisor

    c. A security line employee

    d. A personnel interviewer

28. The heart of personnel selection is a(n):

    a. Polygraph test

    b. Review of application

    c. Interview

    d. Background investigation

29. Discipline is primarily the responsibility of:

    a. The supervisor

    b. The employee

    c. The security manager or director

    d. The inspection division

30. Among classical theories of human behavior in the work environment, one emphasizes negative aspects of employee behavior, which is known as:

    a. The autocratic theory

    b. The custodial theory

    c. The supportive theory

    d. McGregor's "Theory X"

31. Among classical theories of human behavior in the work environment is one that suggests that employees do not inherently dislike work and will actually seek responsibility and better performance if encouraged to do so. It is known as:

    a. McGregor's "Theory Y"

    b. McGregor's "Theory X"

    c. The supportive theory

    d. The motivational theory

32. Dr. Frederick Herzberg developed a position that motivation comes from work itself, not from factors such as salary and job security. This theory is known as:

    a. The supportive theory

    b. The work motivation theory

    c. The custodial theory

    d. McGregor's "Theory X"

33. In conducting background investigations, it is good policy to:

    a. Not let prospective employees know an investigation is being conducted

    b. Restrict the investigation to "confidential" record checks

    c. Restrict the investigation to employment checks

    d. Advise the applicant of forthcoming investigation and secure his or her permission

34. The behavioral scientist whose key concept is that every executive relates to his or her subordinates on the basis of a set of assumptions termed Theory X and Theory Y was formulated by:

    a. Abraham Maslow

    b. Douglas McGregor

    c. Warren Bennis

    d. B.F. Skinner

35. The term *knowledge worker* is used to describe those workers:

    a. Whose primary task is to use information to produce value

    b. Who have a detailed knowledge of the physical tasks that they perform

    c. With a PhD

    d. Whose education has progressed to at least a master's degree

36. Motivational theory that argues that the strength of a tendency to act in a certain way depends on the strength of an expectation that the act will be followed by a given outcome and on the attractiveness of that outcome to the individual is known as:

    a. Goal-setting theory

    b. Manifest-needs theory

    c. Learned-needs theory

    d. Expectancy theory

37. A line-item budget is the traditional and most frequently used method of budgeting. Two other commonly used budgeting techniques include:

    a. Management and program budgets

    b. Capital and program budgets

    c. Program and exception-item budgets

    d. Fund allocation and capital budgets

38. A management tool wherein there is a systematic method of achieving agreed-upon goals set in advance is known as:

    a. Matrix management

    b. Proactive management

    c. Scheduling management

    d. Management by objective (MBO)

39. The activity concerned with proposals for the future, an analysis of those proposals, and methods for achieving them is known as:
    a. Effective management
    b. Evaluation techniques
    c. Planning
    d. Budgeting
40. Stewardship means:
    a. The function of serving passengers on a cruise ship
    b. Serving as the head of the wine cellar in a quality restaurant
    c. To hold something in trust for another
    d. To serve on the board of directors in an enterprise
41. Administrative management does not:
    a. Expressly state the objectives of the security organization
    b. Indicate organizational relationships, responsibilities, and authority
    c. Identify the regular and extraordinary methods of communication
    d. Provide required financial resources
42. When an assets protection program is planned or implemented, input should be sought from:
    a. Experienced security personnel only
    b. Anyone with whom the protection organization has a relationship
    c. Local law enforcement personnel only
    d. Anyone within the enterprise being protected
43. In a protection program, a prime objective should be to motivate which of the following to become a part of the protection team?
    a. All management personnel
    b. Senior management
    c. Local law enforcement personnel
    d. All employees
44. Any plan that no longer serves a useful purpose should be:
    a. Revised
    b. Abandoned
    c. Reviewed
    d. Filed for historical reference
45. Which of the following techniques would not contribute directly to cost-effective management?
    a. Doing things in the least expensive way
    b. Maintaining the lowest costs consistent with required results
    c. Maintaining a high level of personnel training
    d. Ensuring that amounts spent generate high returns

46. Which of the following is *not* a benefit of technology over the use of manpower?
    a. They do not take vacations.
    b. They remove the problem of human error.
    c. They do not call in sick.
    d. They do not save money in the long term.
    e. They can document incidents more efficiently (via videotape).
47. An in-house security guard force should have which of the following insurance coverages?
    a. False-arrest insurance
    b. Defamation-of-character insurance
    c. False-detention insurance
    d. Assault-and-battery insurance
    e. All of the above
48. When scheduling, what is the optimum span of control ratio of supervisors to officers?
    a. One supervisor for every five officers
    b. One supervisor for every ten officers
    c. One supervisor for every fifteen officers
    d. One supervisor for every twenty officers
    e. One supervisor for every twenty-five officers
49. If you have a 168 h schedule to cover, which is one standard week of 24 h coverage for 7 days a week, how many persons will be needed to cover that shift utilizing a standard 8 h shift?
    a. 5.0 persons
    b. 4.5 persons
    c. 5.5 persons
    d. 6.0 persons
    e. 6.5 persons
50. Benefits of using outside security include the following *except*:
    a. More flexibility in emergency situations
    b. No payroll taxes and insurance costs
    c. Usually higher turnover of personnel
    d. No benefit package costs
    e. No bookkeeping or payroll preparation cost

CHAPTER 9 ANSWERS

1. f. All of the above.
2. e. All of the above.
3. d. All of the above

4. c. Must have a security officer but not necessarily at each location
5. e. All of the above
6. d. All of the above
7. d. It might escalate confrontations with security officers because offenders would feel less threatened.
8. d. In a situation where there seems to be no danger to life without weapons
9. b. Reducing the disturbed person to a form of benevolent custody and eliminating the immediate danger
10. d. They provide a reduction in cost
11. d. Post orders
12. a. The order should be written at the lowest level possible.
13. c. Security log
14. e. 1,000,000+
15. c. Private Security Task Force of the National Advisory Committee on Criminal Justice Standards and Goals
16. f. All of the above
17. c. Access control
18. c. Foot patrols and vehicle patrols
19. e. Most post orders include oral instructions to the security officer.
20. c. Security guards are the only element of protection that can be depended on to give complete security.
21. c. Four and a half guards
22. b. High stress
23. c. Span of control
24. a. Unity of command
25. c. Personnel department
26. a. "Blind ad"
27. d. A personnel interviewer
28. c. Interview
29. a. The supervisor
30. d. McGregor's "Theory X"
31. a. McGregor's "Theory Y"
32. b. The work motivation theory
33. d. Advise the applicant of forthcoming investigation and secure his or permission
34. b. Douglas McGregor
35. a. Whose primary task is to use information to produce value
36. d. Expectancy theory
37. b. Capital and program budgets
38. d. Management by objective (MBO)
39. c. Planning
40. c. To hold something in trust for another

41. d. Provide required financial resources
42. b. Anyone with whom the protection organization has a relationship
43. d. All employees
44. b. Abandoned
45. c. Maintaining a high level of personnel training
46. d. They do not save money in the long term.
47. d. Assault-and-battery insurance
48. a. One supervisor for every five officers
49. b. 4.5 persons
50. c. Usually higher turnover of personnel

CHAPTER 10: LEGAL ASPECTS

1. The basic or "organic" law of the United States is:
   a. Common law
   b. The US statutes at large
   c. The US Constitution
   d. Supreme Court decisions
   e. The Bill of Rights

2. The only crime mentioned in the US Constitution is:
   a. Treason
   b. Murder
   c. Extortion
   d. Fraud against the government
   e. None of the above

3. In substance, a crime is:
   a. A violent act
   b. A violation of one's property
   c. An act or omission prohibited by law that provides a punishment
   d. A public wrong
   e. A private wrong

4. The federal criminal law is contained in:
   a. Title 1 of the US Code
   b. Title 12 of the US Code
   c. Title 18 of the US Code
   d. Title 20 of the US Code
   e. Title 48 of the US Code

5. The federal definition of a felony is:
   a. Any offense that calls for imprisonment
   b. Any offense punishable by death
   c. Any offense for which the minimum penalty is $500
   d. Any offense punishable by death or imprisonment for a term exceeding 1 year

6. In general, an act will not be criminal unless the person engaged in the act has:
   a. *Mens rea*
   b. The necessary motive
   c. Knowledge of the criminal statute
   d. *Actus rea*
   e. None of the above

7. Whoever has knowledge of the actual commission of a felony cognizable by a court of the United States but conceals and does not, as soon as possible, make known the same to some judge or other person in civil or military authority is guilty of the following violation:
   a. Subornation of perjury
   b. Obstruction of justice
   c. Misprision of felony
   d. White-collar crime
   e. None of the above

8. In federal courts, the usual prosecutor is known as:
   a. The district attorney
   b. The state's attorney
   c. The commonwealth attorney
   d. The US attorney
   e. The special prosecutor

9. The main purpose of a grand jury is to:
   a. Determine whether an individual has committed a crime or not
   b. Determine guilt
   c. Determine whether there is probable cause that a crime has been committed
   d. Determine the nature of punishment
   e. Give the accused the chance to face his or her accuser

10. After an indictment has been returned by a grand jury, the person named must be taken into custody and appear personally before the appropriate court. This process is called a(n):
    a. Arraignment
    b. First appearance
    c. Preliminary hearing
    d. Magistrate's hearing
    e. Pretrial hearing

11. The purpose of bail is to:
    a. Confine the accused pending trial
    b. Take dangerous offenders off the street
    c. Make certain each accused person is offered his or her constitutional right to put up security in order to gain release

    d. Ensure the appearance of the accused in court

    e. None of the above

12. In a criminal trial, the burden of proof required to find guilt is:

    a. Preponderance of evidence

    b. Beyond a reasonable doubt

    c. Reasonableness of presentation

    d. The amount necessary to convince a majority of jurors

    e. None of the above

13. The release of a convicted person under certain conditions without having to be imprisoned is known as:

    a. Probation

    b. Parole

    c. *Corpus juris*

    d. Detainer

    e. Commutation

14. The release from confinement of a person who has served part of a sentence is called:

    a. Probation

    b. Parole

    c. Reprieve

    d. Commutation

    e. Pardon

15. The process of a lower court abiding by a decision of a higher court is known as:

    a. *Corpus delicti*

    b. *Habeas corpus*

    c. *Ex post facto*

    d. *Stare decisis*

    e. *Mens rea*

16. The crime that consists of an unlawful entry into or remaining within a building with the intent to commit some crime therein is:

    a. Robbery

    b. Trespassing

    c. Burglary

    d. Embezzlement

    e. Shoplifting

17. Which of the following elements elevates the crime of larceny to robbery?

    a. Wrongful taking of the property of another

    b. The use of force or threat of force

    c. Intent to deprive the owner of the use of certain property

    d. Unlawful appropriation of property

18. In order to make the proof of intent easier in proving shoplifting, many stores have a policy that:
    a. Requires apprehension of the suspect to be done after the accused leaves the premises
    b. Requires apprehension of the suspect as soon as the theft occurs
    c. Requires apprehension of the suspect as soon as the material is concealed
    d. Requires apprehension only upon issuance of a warrant
    e. None of the above

19. Deadly force can only be used:
    a. In reasonable anticipation that fatal force has been threatened or is imminent against the person seeking to justify
    b. In prevention of a crime or apprehension of a criminal when a deadly weapon was employed in the commission of or attempt to commit the crime
    c. In defense of premises or property when a burglary is attempted or committed and physical force is threatened against some occupant
    d. All of the above
    e. None of the above

20. The private citizen generally may arrest without a warrant:
    a. For a felony
    b. For a misdemeanor
    c. For a crime committed in his or her presence
    d. When he or she has "reasonable cause" to believe the person arrested committed the crime
    e. None of the above

21. The Supreme Court decision that holds that no suspect, in a custodial environment, may be asked any questions until he or she has first been warned that he or she need not make any statement and advised of certain other rights is the:
    a. McNabb decision
    b. Mallory decision
    c. Ennis decision
    d. Miranda decision
    e. Terry decision

22. The amendment to the US Constitution that deals with searches and seizures is the:
    a. First Amendment
    b. Fourth Amendment
    c. Fifth Amendment
    d. Sixth Amendment
    e. Eighth Amendment

23. As a general rule, searches can be made of employee lockers and desks located on the premises of the company:
    a. If consent is given by employees
    b. Under no circumstances
    c. If done by the local police
    d. If done by the security manager
    e. If done by the plant manager
24. When a law enforcement agent induces the commission of an offense not otherwise contemplated, the accused may use an affirmative defense known as:
    a. Hearsay
    b. Illegally induced crime
    c. *Ex post facto* law
    d. Bill of attainder
    e. Entrapment
25. The imputation of another's negligence to the employer is described as:
    a. Gross liability
    b. Vicarious liability
    c. Agency liability
    d. Net liability
    e. Tort liability
26. A willful or negligent wrong done to one person by another is:
    a. A crime
    b. A misdemeanor
    c. A felony
    d. A tort
    e. A malfeasance
27. The following action can be considered a tort:
    a. Battery
    b. False imprisonment
    c. Fraud
    d. All of the above
    e. None of the above
28. The agency created by the Civil Rights Act of 1964 and specifically charged with investigating charges of employment discrimination that violate Title VII of the Civil Rights Act is the:
    a. Equal Employment Opportunity Commission
    b. Community Relations Commission
    c. Office of Compliance of Civil Rights
    d. Human Relations Council
    e. Civil Rights Division of the Department of Justice

29. The area of civil law dealing with the creation and activities of independent agencies and of some executive departments of government, both federal and state, is called:
    a. Agency law
    b. Tort law
    c. Administrative law
    d. Constitutional law
    e. None of the above

30. The codified regulations of the administrative agencies are contained in:
    a. Statutes at large
    b. The Code of Federal Regulations (CFR)
    c. The US Code (USC)
    d. The Federal Register
    e. None of the above

31. The practice of not considering evidence illegally obtained is called:
    a. The silver platter doctrine
    b. The exclusionary rule
    c. The McNabb–Mallory rule
    d. The Miranda rule
    e. The best-evidence rule

32. The privilege against self-incrimination is found in the following amendment:
    a. Fifth
    b. Tenth
    c. Second
    d. Sixth
    e. Fourteenth

33. *Corpus delicti* means:
    a. The dead body
    b. The body of the crime
    c. A command to produce the body
    d. Criminal intent
    e. Criminal actions

34. An example of a *mala prohibitum* crime is:
    a. Rape
    b. Illegal parking
    c. Murder
    d. Kidnapping
    e. Assault

35. Many offenses that do not require proof of intent are called:
    a. Strict liability crimes
    b. Common-law crimes
    c. True crimes
    d. *Mala in se* crimes
    e. None of the above

36. Sometimes an intent to do one act will establish the intent element for another offense, even though the act that was intended did not occur. This is:
    a. Transferred intent
    b. Felonious intent
    c. General intent
    d. Specific intent
    e. None of the above

37. When homicide is committed by accident and misfortune in doing any lawful act by lawful means with usual ordinary caution, it is known as:
    a. General homicide
    b. Justifiable homicide
    c. Excusable homicide
    d. Voluntary manslaughter
    e. Involuntary manslaughter

38. A situation whereby there was adequate provocation by the victim to arouse passion and an unlawful killing took place is called:
    a. Negligent manslaughter
    b. Involuntary manslaughter
    c. Murder
    d. Voluntary manslaughter
    e. Excusable homicide

39. Battery that mutilates or causes permanent loss of the use of a part of the body of the victim is called:
    a. Aggravated assault
    b. Aggravated battery
    c. Felonious assault
    d. Felonious battery
    e. Mayhem

40. Whoever, without lawful authority, restrains an individual from going about as he or she wishes may be guilty of:
    a. False imprisonment
    b. Extortion
    c. Seduction

    d. Assault

    e. Battery

41. The probable cause necessary to constitute a prerequisite to arrest and search by law enforcement officers is:

    a. A high degree of suspicion

    b. Evidence that will prove guilt

    c. Those facts that would lead a reasonable person to believe that the accused committed the offense

    d. A preponderance of evidence

    e. None of the above

42. The federal agency that has primary jurisdiction over those who print and pass counterfeit money is:

    a. The FBI

    b. The Bureau of Alcohol, Tobacco, and Firearms

    c. The Secret Service

    d. The US Marshal Service

    e. None of the above

43. The federal kidnapping statute provides that:

    a. Primary jurisdiction is in the hands of the Secret Service

    b. The FBI cannot enter the case until evidence is developed that the victim was taken across a state line

    c. The FBI has full jurisdiction in all kidnappings, regardless of interstate transportation of the victim

    d. A presumption is created that if the victim has not been returned within 24 h following abduction, he or she has been moved interstate

44. The unlawful taking of property by force or threat of force constitutes the crime of:

    a. Burglary

    b. Robbery

    c. Assault and battery

    d. Larceny

    e. False pretenses

45. The term used to refer to the body of the crime and all the elements necessary to prove that a crime has been committed is:

    a. *Habeas corpus*

    b. *Corpus delicti*

    c. *Mens rea*

    d. *Actus rea*

    e. None of the above

46. One who is actually or constructively present, aiding and abetting in the commission of the crime, is generally known as a(n):

    a. Principal in the first degree

    b. Principal in the second degree

    c. Accessory before the fact

    d. Accessory after the fact

    e. None of the above

47. One who has knowledge of the commission of a felony and renders personal assistance to the felon, such as hiding him or her, is generally liable as a(n):

    a. Principal in the first degree

    b. Principal in the second degree

    c. Principal in the third degree

    d. Accessory before the fact

    e. Accessory after the fact

48. Which of the following is not an element of a serious crime that must be proved for conviction?

    a. Motive

    b. Criminal intent

    c. Criminal act

    d. Concurrence between act and intent

    e. None of the above

49. An offense that was not a common-law crime but created by statute is termed a(n):

    a. *Mala in se* crime

    b. *Mala prohibitum* crime

    c. Felony

    d. Misdemeanor

    e. Infraction

50. Legislative enactments establishing arbitrary time periods in which the state must initiate criminal proceedings or not act at all are known as:

    a. Legal defenses

    b. Bills of attainder

    c. Statutes of limitation

    d. Statutes of fraud

    e. None of the above

51. The act of inducing a person to commit a crime for the purpose of having him or her arrested is known as:

    a. Solicitation

    b. Entrapment

    c. *Nolo contendere*

    d. Misprision

    e. Legal suggestion

52. As a general rule, deadly force is justified in which of the following cases?
    a. An unarmed robbery
    b. An armed robbery
    c. Observation of a man entering a second-story window of a house in the early hours of the morning
    d. In effecting the arrest of one who has committed a misdemeanor
    e. All of the above

53. A homicide committed while attempting to effect an arrest or to prevent an escape can only be justified in:
    a. Effecting the arrest of one who has committed a misdemeanor
    b. Effecting the arrest of a fleeing felon
    c. Atrocious felony cases as an absolute last resort
    d. Effecting the arrest of any felon
    e. All of the above

54. Deadly force may be used to defend oneself if:
    a. One reasonably believes deadly force is necessary to protect himself or herself or another from unlawful use of deadly force of a third party
    b. One's home is broken into
    c. One is protecting one's own property
    d. All of the above
    e. None of the above

55. Giving or attempting to give to another person an instrument known to be false with intent to defraud is:
    a. Forgery
    b. False pretenses
    c. Counterfeiting
    d. Uttering
    e. None of the above

56. The unlawful restraint by one person of the physical liberty of another person is the crime of:
    a. Kidnapping
    b. Unlawful restraint
    c. Abduction
    d. False imprisonment
    e. None of the above

57. In some states, it is a crime to begin a criminal case without probable cause in bad faith and with the intent of harassing or injuring the other party. The crime is:
    a. Felonious intent
    b. Felonious harassment
    c. Malicious prosecution

     d. Misprision of a felony

     e. None of the above

58. When a person in his or her private capacity and not as a public official uses written or oral threats of force or fright and demands money or property to which he or she is not entitled, the crime committed is:

     a. Blackmail

     b. Criminal defamation

     c. Bribery

     d. Misprision of a felony

     e. None of the above

59. The corrupt procurement of another to commit perjury is:

     a. Perjury

     b. Solicitation

     c. Bribery

     d. Subornation of perjury

     e. Misprision of a felony

60. The Federal Bureau of Investigation is under the:

     a. Treasury Department

     b. Department of the Interior

     c. Department of Defense

     d. Department of Justice

     e. State Department

61. Federal trial courts are called:

     a. District courts

     b. Courts of Appeal

     c. Chancery courts

     d. Superior courts

     e. County courts

62. The United States Supreme Court consists of:

     a. 5 members

     b. 12 members

     c. 16 members

     d. 7 members

     e. 9 members

63. The prohibition against being tried twice for the same crime is found in the:

     a. First Amendment of the US Constitution

     b. Third Amendment of the US Constitution

     c. Fifth Amendment of the US Constitution

     d. Fourteenth Amendment of the US Constitution

     e. None of the above

64. In a criminal prosecution, the measure of evidence used to find the accused guilty is:

    a. Beyond a reasonable doubt

    b. Probable cause

    c. Suspicion

    d. Preponderance of evidence

65. "Strict liability in tort" is also known as:

    a. Gross negligence

    b. Comparative negligence

    c. Intentional liability

    d. Last clear chance

    e. Liability without fault

66. Which of the following is a *mala prohibitum* offense?

    a. Rape

    b. Robbery

    c. Burglary

    d. Forgery

    e. Speeding

67. Richard Roe came home early from work and found his wife in bed with another man. Roe become immediately incensed and killed both. He is probably guilty of:

    a. Premeditated murder

    b. Involuntary manslaughter

    c. Voluntary manslaughter

    d. Second-degree murder

    e. None of the above

68. The US Supreme Court case that established the accused's right to be informed of his or her constitutional right to remain silent, to have a lawyer present, and to be informed of the state's duty to provide a lawyer when the accused cannot afford one is:

    a. *Gideon v. Wainwright*

    b. The McNabb case

    c. The Mallory case

    d. *United States v. Silver Thorne*

    e. *Miranda v. Arizona*

69. A principal will be liable for the contracts entered into by his or her agents in emergency situations under the theory of:

    a. Agency by operation of law

    b. Agency by estoppel

    c. Constructive agency

    d. Implied agency

    e. None of the above

70. The theory of law that vicariously imposes liability on the principal for acts of his or her agent is known as:

    a. Plain agency

    b. Master servant

    c. Strict liability

    d. Respondeat superior

    e. Common law

71. An employer is responsible for the acts of his or her employee committed within:

    a. The employee's scope of employment

    b. The area of the place of business

    c. The employer's area of primary activity

    d. The employee's area of primary activity

    e. None of the above

72. The doctrine that states that an employer is not liable for injuries inflicted by one employee upon another while both are engaged in the same general enterprise is called:

    a. Last clear chance

    b. *Caveat emptor*

    c. *Respondeat superior*

    d. Fellow-servant rule

    e. Workman's compensation

73. The relationship in which two parties agree that one will act as a representative of the other is known as a(n):

    a. Contractual relationship

    b. Fiduciary relationship

    c. Partnership relationship

    d. Agency relationship

    e. None of the above

74. An agent ordinarily can act for the principal in such a way to make the principal legally responsible provided that:

    a. The agent is authorized by the principal to act that way

    b. The agent acts reasonably

    c. The agent notifies the principal within 24 h

    d. The agent is 18 years of age

    e. All of the above

75. An agent can become liable while acting for the principal if:

    a. The agent violates any duties owed to the principal

    b. The agent exceeds actual authority

    c. The agent assumes liability for a particular transaction

    d. All of the above

    e. None of the above

76. If the agent commits a tort:

    a. The agent is personally responsible to the injured party

    b. The agent is not liable if the agent was working for the principal at the time

    c. The agent is not liable if acting within the scope of employment

    d. The agent is not liable if the agent has a written contract with the employer

    e. None of the above

77. As a general rule, the employer is *not* liable for a tort committed by:

    a. The servant if committed in the scope of the servant's employment for the master

    b. The independent contractor

    c. One hired to do a job that is inherently dangerous

    d. None of the above

    e. All of the above

78. If S, a subordinate, while acting within the scope of employment, injures T and T dies, S's superior:

    a. Can be held liable in a civil suit for damages

    b. Can be subject to criminal liability

    c. Can be held liable for both a civil suit and criminal action

    d. Can be criminally liable if the act is malicious

    e. Can be criminally liable if the act is a "true" crime

79. The requirement that certain types of contracts be in writing in order for a contract to be enforceable in a lawsuit is known as a:

    a. Contingency contract

    b. Voidable contract

    c. Statute of frauds

    d. Strict liability contract

    e. None of the above

80. A law that sets forth a maximum time period from the occurrence of an event for a legal action to be properly filed in court is known as:

    a. The statute of frauds

    b. The statute of limitations

    c. The doctrine of estoppel

    d. *Stare decisis*

    e. None of the above

81. A legal theory under which a person can be held liable for damage or injury even if not at fault or negligent is known as:

    a. *Caveat emptor*

    b. The no-fault statute

    c. Strict liability

    d. *Actus reus*

    e. None of the above

82. The Uniform Crime Reports are published by:

    a. The US Department of Justice

    b. The Secret Service
    c. The Census Bureau
    d. The Law Enforcement Assistance Administration
    e. The FBI

83. Crimes that do not require any *mens rea* (guilty intent) or negligence are commonly described as:
    a. Common-law crimes
    b. True crimes
    c. Statutory crimes
    d. Strict liability crimes
    e. None of the above

84. It is generally held that a crime cannot be committed by a child under the age of:
    a. 6
    b. 7
    c. 9
    d. 10
    e. 12

85. The statute of limitations for the crime of murder is:
    a. 3 years
    b. 5 years
    c. 7 years
    d. 10 years
    e. None of the above

86. The statute of limitations does not apply to the following:
    a. Felonies
    b. Misdemeanors
    c. While a defendant is a fugitive
    d. White-collar crimes
    e. None of the above

87. Generally, deadly force may *not* be used:
    a. To solely protect property
    b. Against a mere trespasser
    c. Against a thief who steals a car
    d. All of the above
    e. None of the above

88. In making an arrest, the authority of a private citizen is:
    a. Not as broad as a police officer's
    b. The same as a police officer's
    c. Nonexistent if the arrested person turns out to be innocent
    d. Based on the "probable cause" theory
    e. All of the above

89. Cases in which the defendant intended to kill or inflict serious bodily injury but did not have malice because of the existence of provocation is:
    a. Voluntary manslaughter
    b. Involuntary manslaughter
    c. First-degree murder
    d. Second-degree murder
    e. Third-degree murder
90. Cases of criminal homicide in which the actor lacked an intent to kill or cause bodily injury is:
    a. First-degree murder
    b. Second-degree murder
    c. Voluntary manslaughter
    d. Involuntary manslaughter
    e. Justifiable homicide
91. Theft involves the crime of:
    a. Robbery
    b. Embezzlement
    c. Larceny
    d. False pretenses
    e. All of the above
92. The legal standard that must be met to sustain an arrest is known as:
    a. Proof beyond a reasonable doubt
    b. Probable cause
    c. Suspicion
    d. Preponderance of evidence
    e. None of the above
93. The amendment that provides that no person shall be denied life, liberty, or property without due process of law is the:
    a. First Amendment
    b. Second Amendment
    c. Fifth Amendment
    d. Eighth Amendment
    e. Fourteenth Amendment
94. The right to have the assistance of counsel for one's defense is provided by the:
    a. Second Amendment
    b. Fifth Amendment
    c. Sixth Amendment
    d. Eighth Amendment
    e. Tenth Amendment

95. Police are allowed to conduct a frisk-type search where there was reason to believe that the person stopped was armed according to the Supreme Court decision of:
   a. *Terry v. Ohio*
   b. *Mapp v. Ohio*
   c. *Kirby v. Illinois*
   d. *Massiah v. U.S.*
   e. *Wong Sun v. U.S.*

96. A legal search may be made:
   a. Without a warrant
   b. Incident to lawful arrest
   c. With consent
   d. For inventory purposes
   e. All of the above

97. For a search warrant to be valid, it must conform to the following requirement(s):
   a. It may be issued only for certain objects.
   b. It must be issued on probable cause.
   c. The place to be searched and things to be seized must be particularly described.
   d. All of the above.
   e. None of the above.

98. Which of the following is an exception to the general rule that a search and seizure requires a warrant?
   a. Waiver
   b. Movable vehicle
   c. Seizure without a search (plain view)
   d. All of the above
   e. None of the above

99. Two famous Supreme Court rulings resulted in a rule of law that states that a person, upon arrest, shall be taken before a judicial officer for arraignment without unnecessary delay. The rule is called the:
   a. McNabb–Mallory rule
   b. Miranda rule
   c. *Terry v. Ohio* rule
   d. Escobedo rule
   e. Katz rule

100. Which of the following procedures has been held to violate the self-incrimination provisions of the Fifth Amendment?
   a. Fingerprinting for identification purposes
   b. Photographing for identification purposes
   c. Preindictment lineup

    d. All of the above

    e. None of the above

101. Which of the following is *not* considered to be personal property?

    a. Cars

    b. Animals

    c. Money

    d. Furniture

    e. House

102. Which of the following crimes would be considered a white-collar crime?

    a. Tax evasion

    b. False advertising

    c. Mail fraud

    d. All of the above

    e. None of the above

103. What is the crime when a person, knowing an object to be false, attempts to pass it off as the real thing?

    a. Forgery

    b. False pretenses

    c. Uttering

    d. Larceny by trick

    e. None of the above

104. The investigative jurisdiction for the federal crime of counterfeiting is in the hands of the:

    a. FBI

    b. Secret Service

    c. Internal Revenue Service

    d. Bureau of Alcohol, Tobacco, and Firearms

    e. None of the above

105. To combat the crime of loan sharking, the US Congress passed:

    a. The Organized Crime Control Act

    b. The Extortionate Credit Transactions Act

    c. The Omnibus Crime Act

    d. The Federal Crime Act

    e. None of the above

106. Which of the following is *not* considered to be an inchoate crime?

    a. Attempt

    b. Solicitation

    c. Conspiracy

    d. Embezzlement

    e. All of the above

107. The procedure by which a defendant in a criminal case petitions the court to allow an inspection of certain items in the possession of the prosecution is known as:
    a. Venue
    b. Estoppel
    c. *Voir dire*
    d. Discovery
    e. None of the above
108. The term *venue* refers to:
    a. The authority of the court to deal with a particular case
    b. The place at which the authority of the court should be exercised
    c. The process of jury selection
    d. The process of appeal
    e. None of the above
109. The examination of prospective jurors on the jury panel is commonly referred to as:
    a. Discovery
    b. *Voir dire*
    c. Venue
    d. Peremptory challenge
    e. Mittimus
110. A challenge of a prospective juror for no specific reason is known as:
    a. Discovery
    b. Examination in chief
    c. Peremptory challenge
    d. Challenge without cause
    e. *Voir dire*
111. Which of the following is *not* recommended as a witness in a court of law?
    a. Sit erect, with ankles crossed and hands folded on your lap.
    b. Look up to the judge from time to time.
    c. Seek opportunity to smile genuinely.
    d. Fold your arms across your chest.
    e. Watch the attorney as he or she frames a question.
112. The attitude of the US Department of Justice with regard to introducing polygraph results as evidence is that the:
    a. Justice Department opposes it
    b. Justice Department will allow it
    c. Justice Department feels it is okay if a waiver is given
    d. Justice Department feels that failure to take a polygraph is evidence of guilt
    e. Judge should be present during the polygraph examination

113. Occupational Safety and Health Administration (OSHA) regulations have been in force since:
    a. 1940
    b. 1951
    c. 1970
    d. 1971
    e. 1980

114. OSHA is administered by the:
    a. Department of Health and Human Resources
    b. Department of Labor
    c. Department of the Interior
    d. Department of Justice
    e. Department of Commerce

115. As a practical matter, the OSHA Act covers
    a. Only federal workers
    b. Nongovernmental employers that manufacture hazardous materials
    c. Nongovernmental employers whose activities affect commerce
    d. Those employers in the mining industry only
    e. None of the above

116. Which of the following was not provided by the OSHA Act?
    a. An effective enforcement program
    b. Reporting procedures
    c. Research
    d. Authorization for the Secretary of the Interior to set mandatory standards
    e. Development of safety standards

117. Under the OSHA Act, a national consensus standard was defined as one that is:
    a. Adopted and issued by a nationally recognized standard-producing organization such as NFPA
    b. Developed after consideration of conflicting or differing views
    c. In the nature of a practice designated by the secretary of labor after consultation with other federal agencies
    d. All of the above
    e. None of the above

118. The OSHA Act allows states to continue their present safety and health enforcement activities provided that:
    a. The state program is "at least as effective" as the federal program
    b. The secretary of labor signs a certificate of authorization
    c. The attorney general, after hearing, approves
    d. Litigation is pursued in the federal court system
    e. None of the above

119. A *de minimis* violation of the OSHA Act is:
    a. One that is serious
    b. One that is serious and willful
    c. One that is willful
    d. One that has no immediate or direct relationship to safety or health
    e. One that is repeated
120. Citations issued by an OSHA area director are:
    a. Written
    b. Mailed by US certified mail
    c. Required to be posted at or near the place of violation
    d. All of the above
    e. None of the above
121. Which of the following is *not* required by OSHA regulations?
    a. A serious violation must be assessed a monetary penalty.
    b. A nonserious violation may be assessed a proposed penalty.
    c. All notices, including *de minimis* notices, must be posted.
    d. Written notices must be sent to the employer whenever penalties are proposed.
122. Under OSHA regulations, a serious violation must be assessed some monetary penalty, but the amount should not exceed:
    a. $100,000
    b. $1,000,000
    c. $50,000
    d. $10,000
    e. $1000
123. Unless appealed, payment of penalties under OSHA must be made within:
    a. 10 working days
    b. 5 working days
    c. 15 working days
    d. 30 working days
    e. 2 months
124. In order to enforce compliance with health and safety standards under OSHA, employees are:
    a. Required to comply within 5 days of written notice
    b. Required to pay $10,000 per day for each day of noncompliance
    c. Required to comply or to forfeit their job
    d. All of the above
    e. None of the above
125. The OSHA law requires the maintenance of three basic types of injury and illness records by each establishment that employs:
    a. 5 or more employees

    b. 8 or more employees

    c. 15 or more employees

    d. 50 or more employees

    e. 200 or more employees

126. Under OSHA regulations, the employer is responsible to see that every recordable injury or illness is listed on the log within:

    a. 4 days of learning of occurrence

    b. 6 days of learning of occurrence

    c. 14 days of learning of occurrence

    d. 15 days of learning of occurrence

    e. 30 days of learning of occurrence

127. The law that prohibits the armed forces from executing civil law in the United States, its territories, and possessions is:

    a. Title 18, US Code

    b. The Delimitations Agreement

    c. The Armed Services Act of 1950

    d. The Posse Comitatus Act

    e. None of the above

128. The federal criminal law is set forth in the following title of the US Code:

    a. Title 5

    b. Title 12

    c. Title 18

    d. Title 28

    e. Title 50

129. According to the US Code, a felony is:

    a. Any offense punishable by death

    b. Any offense punishable by imprisonment of 1 year or more

    c. Any offense punishable by imprisonment exceeding 1 year

    d. Any offense punishable by death or imprisonment for a term exceeding 1 year

    e. None of the above

130. The act of concealing the commission of a felony cognizable by a US court by someone having knowledge of the felony is a violation called:

    a. Misprision of felony

    b. Accessory

    c. Subornation of perjury

    d. Obstruction of justice

    e. None of the above

131. The Fourth Amendment of the US Constitution does *not* apply to:

    a. Secret Service agent searches

    b. US Customs agent searches

    c. A search by a private person

    d. A search by an FBI agent

    e. A search by local police

132. When a law enforcement agent induces the commission of an offense, the process is called:

    a. Accessory before the fact

    b. Misprision of a felony

    c. Entrapment

    d. *Stare decisis*

    e. *Corpus delecti*

133. Statements by persons that things done or said by them are actually as they are described or said to be constitute:

    a. Expressed contracts

    b. Warranties

    c. Implied contracts

    d. All of the above

    e. None of the above

134. The actual use of force against another, which involves physical touching, is a willful tort called in common law:

    a. Assault

    b. Battery

    c. Felonious assault

    d. Aggravated assault

    e. None of the above

135. Wrongful appropriation of the personal property of another for the use of the taker is a tort called:

    a. Conversion

    b. Larceny

    c. Trespassing

    d. Embezzlement

    e. None of the above

136. Rules issued by administrative agencies are published in the:

    a. Congressional Record

    b. Federal Register

    c. US Code

    d. Statutes at large

    e. None of the above

137. Rules promulgated by administrative agencies are ultimately published in the:

    a. Code of Federal Regulations

    b. US Code

    c. Federal Register

    d. Statutes at large

    e. Congressional Record

138. A writ issued by a court directing the recipient to appear and testify is a:
    a. Warrant
    b. Subpoena
    c. Writ of *mandamus*
    d. Writ of prohibition
    e. None of the above

139. The process whereby the determinations and actions of an administrative agency are reviewed by the courts is:
    a. *Stare decisis*
    b. *Certiorari*
    c. *Mandamus*
    d. Judicial review
    e. None of the above

140. The act that deals with the release and disclosure of certain kinds of information by the federal government is:
    a. The Freedom of Information Act
    b. The Privacy Act
    c. The Administrative Procedures Act
    d. The Federal Communications Act
    e. None of the above

141. The Freedom of Information Act, passed in 1966, applies to:
    a. State governments
    b. State and federal governments
    c. Private industry
    d. The federal government only
    e. None of the above

142. Which of the following is *not* subject to public disclosure under the Freedom of Information Act?
    a. Classified information
    b. Internal personnel rules
    c. Personal medical records
    d. Confidential informants
    e. All of the above

143. When guards are deputized, it is customary and prudent to:
    a. Encourage the guard to assist law enforcement off the premises
    b. Take out additional liability insurance
    c. Limit the scope of the guard's authority to actual guard duties
    d. All of the above
    e. None of the above

144. An arrest made by a guard who has not been deputized is called:
    a. A citizen's arrest
    b. A conservator's arrest
    c. An illegal arrest
    d. A detention
    e. None of the above

145. The general rule as to the amount of force a guard is permitted to use in order to accomplish a lawful arrest is:
    a. The amount needed to ensure the guard is not injured
    b. Up to and including deadly force
    c. The maximum amount
    d. Only such force as is reasonably necessary

146. The authority of a private person to make an arrest is usually:
    a. Unlimited
    b. Limited to those cases where a warrant is obtained
    c. A matter of state law
    d. The same as that of a deputized guard
    e. None of the above

147. Which of the following is *not* true of common law?
    a. It originated in France.
    b. It was brought to America by English colonists.
    c. It basically was unwritten law.
    d. All of the above.
    e. None of the above.

148. The makeup of a federal grand jury is:
    a. 16–23 jurors
    b. 12 jurors
    c. 12–18 jurors
    d. 5 jurors
    e. 9 jurors

149. Which of the following is *not* correct with regard to the grand jury?
    a. A federal grand jury consists of 16–23 jurors.
    b. A witness may be accompanied by his or her attorney.
    c. The proceedings are secret.
    d. Its main responsibility is to find probable cause.
    e. None of the above.

150. If a grand jury determines that probable cause exists and that the accused committed a crime, the grand jury then:
    a. Issues information
    b. Issues an indictment
    c. Issues a *mittimus*
    d. Enters a finding of guilty
    e. None of the above

151. A case that is proved "on the face of it" is known as:
    a. A *corpus delicti* case
    b. A *prima facie* case
    c. The case in chief
    d. A directed verdict
    e. None of the above

152. Which of the following would be considered a primary tort relevant to security officers?
    a. Battery
    b. Assault
    c. False imprisonment
    d. All of the above
    e. None of the above

153. Limitations may be imposed on authority of a security force by:
    a. Licensing laws
    b. Administrative regulations
    c. Specific statutes
    d. All of the above
    e. None of the above

154. A legal doctrine that holds that the master is responsible for the actions of his or her servant while the servant is acting in the master's behalf is known as:
    a. *Caveat emptor*
    b. Vicarious liability
    c. Strict liability
    d. *Respondeat superior*
    e. None of the above

155. Which of the following torts affects private security and investigative personnel?
    a. False imprisonment
    b. Malicious prosecution
    c. Invasion of privacy
    d. Trespassing on personal property
    e. All of the above

156. Which of the following is generally *not* true with regard to the constitutional limitation on arrest powers of private police?
    a. A private police agent operates under the same constitutional limitations as public police.
    b. A private policeman's authority is essentially the same as a private citizen's.
    c. Regulation of authority of private police will usually be based on state law.

    d. All of the above.

    e. None of the above.

157. A police officer may make an arrest without a warrant:

    a. When he or she witnesses a misdemeanor or felony

    b. When a felony is committed and the officer has reasonable cause to believe a suspect committed it

    c. When he or she has reasonable cause to believe a felony was committed and reasonable cause to believe the suspect committed it

    d. When he or she has reasonable cause to believe the suspect is an escaped convict

    e. All of the above

158. Which of the following is *not* true with regard to arrest by a private citizen?

    a. Private citizens may arrest for a misdemeanor only if they witnessed it.

    b. Private citizens may arrest if a felony has been committed and they have reasonable cause to believe a suspect has committed it.

    c. Private citizens may make an arrest if they have reasonable cause to believe a felony has been committed.

    d. All of the above.

    e. None of the above.

159. The most common charge placed against someone who has made an erroneous arrest is:

    a. Kidnapping

    b. False imprisonment

    c. Assault and battery

    d. Malicious prosecution

    e. None of the above

160. Which of the following is true with regard to the power of detention?

    a. Detention differs from arrest.

    b. It is lawful as long as it is for a reasonable time and conducted reasonably.

    c. There is no one standard to apply.

    d. All of the above.

    e. None of the above.

161. Which of the following is true with regard to the law of arrest?

    a. Force may be used if it is reasonable and necessary.

    b. The deputized private agent has powers similar to those of the police.

    c. Citizen's arrest is not a right; it is a privilege.

    d. The private security agent should understand what his or her powers and limitations are according to law.

    e. All of the above.

162. A private citizen may arrest in which of the following cases?

    a. When a felony has been committed and he or she has reason to believe that a suspect has committed it

    b. When he or she has reasonable cause to believe that a felony has been committed and reasonable cause to believe that the suspect committed it

    c. When he or she has reason to believe that a suspect is an escaped convict or has violated parole or probation

    d. All of the above

    e. None of the above

163. Defenses and immunities that protect a person from liability resulting from a private arrest include:

    a. Self-defense

    b. Defense of property

    c. Crime prevention

    d. All of the above

    e. None of the above

164. Generally, a private citizen has the right to initiate arrest for a misdemeanor if:

    a. The misdemeanor was, in fact, committed

    b. The misdemeanor was committed in the arrester's presence

    c. The private citizen's rights to arrest do not apply to misdemeanors

    d. All of the above

    e. None of the above

165. When armed with a pistol, the private security officer should use it to immobilize a suspect:

    a. At the first sign of resistance

    b. Only as a last resort

    c. Under no circumstances

    d. All of the above

    e. None of the above

166. If a private security officer violates the restriction of the laws of arrest that apply to him or her, he or she may:

    a. Jeopardize the case against the subject

    b. Be subject to criminal charges

    c. Be held liable for damages in a civil suit

    d. All of the above

    e. None of the above

167. A preliminary examination in a court proceeding to determine if a prospective juror is qualified to sit on a jury panel is called:
  a. Arraignment
  b. Preliminary hearing
  c. *Voir dire*
  d. Discovery
  e. None of the above

168. A sworn statement of a party or witness taken outside the court after notice is given to the opposing side, which provides information or evidence to a court, is:
  a. An affidavit
  b. A deposition
  c. A writ of *mandamus*
  d. A writ of *certiorari*
  e. None of the above

169. For a search with voluntary consent to be valid, the person being searched must:
  a. Be aware of his or her rights
  b. Not be coerced in any way
  c. Be the person giving the consent
  d. Give consent in writing whenever possible
  e. All of the above

170. A valid arrest must contain the following elements:
  a. Intent of taking the person into physical custody
  b. Authority on the part of arresting officer
  c. Physical control by the arresting officer
  d. Understanding by the person who is being arrested
  e. All of the above

171. A crime can be described as:
  a. A violent act
  b. A violation of one's privacy
  c. An act or omission prohibited by law for which a penalty is provided
  d. A public wrong

172. The federal definition of a felony is any offense:
  a. That calls for punishment
  b. That is punishable by death
  c. For which the minimum penalty is $500
  d. That is punishable by imprisonment for a term exceeding 1 year

173. In federal system, the chief prosecutor is:
  a. The district attorney
  b. The state's attorney

c. The commonwealth attorney

d. The US attorney

174. The process in which a court abides by a previous court decision is known as:

   a. *Corpus delicti*

   b. *Habeas corpus*

   c. *Ex post facto*

   d. *Stare decisis*

175. The crime of unlawful entry into or remaining within a building with intent to commit some crime therein is:

   a. Robbery

   b. Trespass

   c. Burglary

   d. Embezzlement

176. The term *foreseeability* refers to:

   a. Illegal action

   b. Whether a harm is likely to occur

   c. Administrative law

   d. Strict liability

177. Which is not considered a comprehensive environmental compliance program?

   a. Disciplining wrongdoers

   b. Establishing an incentive program

   c. Auditing and monitoring all activities outside the company

   d. Evaluating the whole effort by retaining an outside expert

178. If an employee, while acting within the scope of his or her employment, injures another party, and that party dies, the employee's employer can be:

   a. Held liable in a civil suit for damages

   b. Subject to criminal liability

   c. Held liable for both civil and criminal action

   d. Criminally liable if the act is malicious

179. Which amendment protects citizens against being compelled to testify against themselves; double jeopardy; depriving someone of life, liberty, or property without due process; and holding someone for a serious crime without presentation to a grand jury for indictment?

   a. First Amendment

   b. Second Amendment

   c. Fourth Amendment

   d. Fifth Amendment

   e. Sixth Amendment

180. Which of the following is *not* a component of a law?
     a. A statute
     b. The body of principles, standards, and rules put out by a government
     c. A moral wrong
     d. That which must be obeyed
     e. A set of regulations governing the relationship between man and his fellow men and between man and state

181. Larceny is defined as:
     a. The taking of something of value from a person through the use of force or fear of force
     b. The taking and carrying away of personal property of another with the intent to deprive the owner permanently of the property
     c. The conversion of personal property by a person to whom the property was entrusted
     d. The taking of something from a person through the fear of a future harm
     e. The attempt to influence a public officer in the discharge of his or her official duties by the offer of a reward or other consideration

182. Which amendment provides for freedom of speech, religion, and press and the right of peaceful assembly for redress of grievances?
     a. First Amendment
     b. Second Amendment
     c. Fourth Amendment
     d. Fifth Amendment
     e. Sixth Amendment

183. Malicious mischief is defined as:
     a. The unlawful taking of a person against his or her will
     b. Deliberately and knowingly testifying falsely, under oath, to a material matter in a court proceeding
     c. The unlawful violation of the person or property of another
     d. The actual damage or destruction of property belonging to another being done voluntarily and knowingly
     e. The willful and deliberate burning of a dwelling or outbuildings of another

184. Which of the following in *not* a component of a crime?
     a. Any violation of a government's penal law
     b. An unethical act
     c. An illegal act or failure to act
     d. A public wrong
     e. An act or omission forbidden by law for which a state prescribes a punishment

185. Which amendment prohibits excessive bail, excessive fines, and cruel and unusual punishment?
    a. Fourth Amendment
    b. Fifth Amendment
    c. Sixth Amendment
    d. Seventh Amendment
    e. Eight Amendment

186. Embezzlement is defined as:
    a. The taking of something of value from a person through the use of force or fear of force
    b. The taking and carrying away of personal property of another with the intent to deprive the owner permanently of the property
    c. The conversion of personal property by a person to whom the property was entrusted
    d. The taking of something from a person through the fear of a future harm
    e. The attempt to influence a public officer in the discharge of his or her official duties by the offer of a reward or other consideration

187. Trespass on real property is defined as:
    a. The unlawful taking of a person against his or her will
    b. Deliberately and knowingly testifying falsely, under oath, to a material matter in a court proceeding
    c. The unlawful violation of the person or property of another
    d. The actual damage or destruction of property belonging to another being done voluntarily and knowingly
    e. The willful and deliberate burning of a dwelling or outbuildings of another

188. Which amendment prohibits unreasonable searches and seizures?
    a. First Amendment
    b. Second Amendment
    c. Fourth Amendment
    d. Fifth Amendment
    e. Sixth Amendment

189. Kidnapping is defined as:
    a. The unlawful taking of a person against his or her will
    b. Deliberately and knowingly testifying falsely, under oath, to a material matter in a court proceeding
    c. The unlawful violation of the person or property of another
    d. The actual damage or destruction of property belonging to another being done voluntarily and knowingly

e. The willful and deliberate burning of a dwelling or outbuildings of another

190. Robbery is defined as:
   a. The taking of something of value from a person through the use of force or fear of force
   b. The taking and carrying away of personal property of another with the intent to deprive the owner permanently of the property
   c. The conversion of personal property by a person to whom the property was entrusted
   d. The taking of something from a person through the fear of a future harm
   e. The attempt to influence a public officer in the discharge of his or her official duties by the offer of a reward or other consideration

191. Which amendment prohibits the government from interfering with the right to keep and bear arms?
   a. First Amendment
   b. Second Amendment
   c. Fourth Amendment
   d. Fifth Amendment
   e. Sixth Amendment

192. Extortion is defined as:
   a. The taking of something of value from a person through the use of force or fear of force
   b. The taking and carrying away of personal property of another with the intent to deprive the owner permanently of the property
   c. The conversion of personal property by a person to whom the property was entrusted
   d. The taking of something from a person through the fear of a future harm
   e. The attempt to influence a public officer in the discharge of his or her official duties by the offer of a reward or other consideration

193. Which amendment provides for a speedy trial by an impartial jury, your right to be informed of charges against you, your right to present defense, and your right to confront witnesses against you?
   a. First Amendment
   b. Second Amendment
   c. Fourth Amendment
   d. Fifth Amendment
   e. Sixth Amendment

194. Bribery is defined as:
    a. The taking of something of value from a person through the use of force or fear of force
    b. The attempt to influence a public officer in the discharge of his or her official duties by the offer of a reward or other consideration
    c. The taking and carrying away of personal property of another with the intent to deprive the owner permanently of the property
    d. The conversion of personal property by a person to whom the property was entrusted
    e. The taking of something from a person through the fear of a future harm

195. Perjury is defined as:
    a. The unlawful taking of a person against his or her will
    b. Deliberately and knowingly testifying falsely, under oath, to a material matter in a court proceeding
    c. The unlawful violation of the person or property of another
    d. The actual damage or destruction of property belonging to another being done voluntarily and knowingly
    e. The willful and deliberate burning of a dwelling or outbuildings of another

196. Which amendment provides for a trial by jury?
    a. Fourth Amendment
    b. Fifth Amendment
    c. Sixth Amendment
    d. Seventh Amendment
    e. Eight Amendment

197. What are the first 10 amendments of the US Constitution known as?
    a. The Declaration of Independence
    b. The Bill of Rights
    c. Due Process
    d. The Constitution of the United States
    e. None of the above

198. Arson is defined as:
    a. The unlawful taking of a person against his or her will
    b. Deliberately and knowingly testifying falsely, under oath, to a material matter in a court proceeding
    c. The unlawful violation of the person or property of another
    d. The actual damage or destruction of property belonging to another being done voluntarily and knowingly
    e. The willful and deliberate burning of a dwelling or outbuildings of another

Chapter 10 Answers

1. c. The US Constitution
2. a. Treason
3. c. An act or omission prohibited by law that provides a punishment
4. c. Title 18 of the US Code
5. d. Any offense punishable by death or imprisonment for a term exceeding 1 year
6. a. *Mens rea*
7. c. Misprision of felony
8. d. The US attorney
9. c. Determine whether there is probable cause that a crime has been committed
10. a. Arraignment
11. d. Ensure the appearance of the accused in court
12. b. Beyond a reasonable doubt
13. a. Probation
14. b. Parole
15. d. *Stare decisis*
16. c. Burglary
17. b. Through the use of force or threat of force
18. a. Requires apprehension of the suspect to be done after the accused leaves the premises
19. d. All of the above
20. c. For a crime committed in his or her presence
21. d. Miranda decision
22. b. Fourth Amendment
23. a. If consent is given by employees
24. e. Entrapment
25. b. Vicarious liability
26. d. A tort
27. d. All of the above
28. a. Equal Employment Opportunity Commission
29. c. Administrative law
30. b. The Code of Federal Regulations (CFR)
31. b. The exclusionary rule
32. a. Fifth Amendment
33. b. The body of the crime
34. b. Illegal parking
35. a. Strict liability crimes
36. a. Transferred intent
37. c. Excusable homicide
38. d. Voluntary manslaughter

39. e. Mayhem
40. a. False imprisonment
41. c. Those facts that would lead a reasonable person to believe that the accused committed the offense
42. c. The Secret Service
43. d. A presumption is created that if the victim has not been returned within 24 h following abduction, he or she has been moved interstate
44. b. Robbery
45. b. *Corpus delicti*
46. b. Principal in the second degree
47. e. Accessory after the fact
48. a. Motive
49. b. *Mala prohibitum crime*
50. c. Statutes of limitation
51. b. Entrapment
52. b. An armed robbery
53. c. Atrocious felony cases as an absolute last resort
54. a. One reasonably believes deadly force is necessary to protect himself or herself or another from unlawful use of deadly force of a third party
55. d. Uttering
56. d. False imprisonment
57. c. Malicious prosecution
58. a. Blackmail
59. d. Subornation of perjury
60. d. Department of Justice
61. a. District courts
62. e. 9 members
63. c. Fifth Amendment of the US Constitution
64. a. Beyond a reasonable doubt
65. e. Liability without fault
66. e. Speeding
67. c. Voluntary manslaughter
68. e. *Miranda v. Arizona*
69. a. Agency by operation of law
70. d. *Respondeat superior*
71. a. The employee's scope of employment
72. d. Fellow-servant rule
73. d. Agency relationship
74. a. The agent is authorized by the principal to act that way
75. d. All of the above
76. a. The agent is personally responsible to the injured party
77. b. The independent contractor

78. a. Can be held liable in a civil suit for damages
79. c. Statute of frauds
80. b. The statute of limitations
81. c. Strict liability
82. e. The FBI
83. d. Strict liability crimes
84. b. 7
85. e. None of the above
86. c. While defendant is a fugitive
87. d. All of the above
88. c. Nonexistent if the arrested person turns out to be innocent
89. a. Voluntary manslaughter
90. d. Involuntary manslaughter
91. e. All of the above
92. b. Probable cause
93. c. Fifth Amendment
94. c. Sixth Amendment
95. a. *Terry v. Ohio*
96. e. All of the above
97. d. All of the above.
98. d. All of the above
99. a. McNabb–Mallory rule
100. e. None of the above
101. e. House
102. d. All of the above
103. c. Uttering
104. b. Secret Service
105. b. The Extortionate Credit Transactions Act
106. d. Embezzlement
107. d. Discovery
108. b. The place at which the authority of the court should be exercised
109. b. *Voir dire*
110. c. Peremptory challenge
111. d. Fold your arms across your chest.
112. a. Justice Department opposes it
113. d. 1971
114. b. Department of Labor
115. c. Nongovernmental employers whose activities affect commerce
116. d. Authorization for the Secretary of the Interior to set mandatory standards
117. d. All of the above
118. a. The state program is "at least as effective" as the federal program

119. d. One that has no immediate or direct relationship to safety or health
120. d. All of the above
121. c. All notices, including de minimis notices, must be posted.
122. e. $1000
123. c. 15 working days
124. e. None of the above
125. b. 8 or more employees
126. b. 6 days of learning of occurrence
127. d. The Posse Comitatus Act
128. c. Title 18
129. d. Any offense punishable by death or imprisonment for a term exceeding 1 year
130. a. Misprision of felony
131. c. A search by a private person
132. c. Entrapment
133. b. Warranties
134. b. Battery
135. a. Conversion
136. b. Federal Register
137. a. Code of Federal Regulations
138. b. Subpoena
139. d. Judicial review
140. a. The Freedom of Information Act
141. d. The federal government only
142. e. All of the above
143. c. Limit the scope of the guard's authority to the actual guard duties
144. a. A citizen's arrest
145. d. Only such force as is reasonably necessary
146. c. A matter of state law
147. a. It originated in France.
148. a. 16–23 jurors
149. b. A witness may be accompanied by his or her attorney.
150. b. Issues an indictment
151. b. A *prima facie* case
152. c. False imprisonment
153. d. All of the above
154. d. *Respondeat superior*
155. e. All of the above
156. a. A private police agent operates under the same constitutional limitations as public police.
157. e. All of the above

158. c. Private citizens may make an arrest if they have reasonable cause to believe a felony has been committed.
159. b. False imprisonment
160. d. All of the above.
161. e. All of the above.
162. a. When a felony has been committed and he or she has reason to believe that a suspect has committed it
163. d. All of the above
164. b. The misdemeanor was committed in the arrester's presence
165. b. Only as a last resort
166. d. All of the above
167. c. *Voir dire*
168. b. A deposition
169. e. All of the above
170. e. All of the above
171. c. An act or omission prohibited by law for which a penalty is provided
172. d. That is punishable by imprisonment for a term exceeding 1 year
173. d. The US Attorney
174. d. *Stare decisis*
175. c. Burglary
176. b. Whether a harm is likely to occur
177. c. Auditing and monitoring all activities outside the company
178. a. Held liable in a civil suit for damages
179. d. Fifth Amendment
180. c. A moral wrong
181. b. The taking and carrying away of personal property of another with the intent to deprive the owner permanently of the property
182. a. First Amendment
183. d. The actual damage or destruction of property belonging to another being done voluntarily and knowingly
184. b. An unethical act
185. e. Eight Amendment
186. c. The conversion of personal property by a person to whom the property was entrusted
187. c. The unlawful violation of the person or property of another
188. d. Fifth Amendment
189. a. The unlawful taking of a person against his or her will
190. a. The taking of something of value from a person through the use of force or fear of force
191. b. Second Amendment
192. d. The taking of something from a person through the fear of a future harm

193. e. Sixth Amendment
194. b. The attempt to influence a public officer in the discharge of his or her official duties by the offer of a reward or other consideration
195. b. Deliberately and knowingly testifying falsely, under oath, to a material matter in a court proceeding
196. d. Seventh Amendment
197. b. The Bill of Rights
198. e. The willful and deliberate burning of a dwelling or outbuildings of another

CHAPTER 11: LIAISON

1. According to the Hallcrest I study, published in 1985, employees in various facets of private security in the United States number about:
   a. 500,000
   b. 700,000
   c. 1,000,000
   d. 3,000,000
2. According to Hallcrest I, the common ground for interaction between law enforcement and private resources is:
   a. Education
   b. Patriotism
   c. Career enhancement
   d. Crime
3. According to estimates made by the Fireman's Fund Insurance Company, about one-third of all business failures are caused by:
   a. Thefts by outsiders (nonemployees)
   b. Thefts by employees
   c. Mismanagement
   d. Poor quality of product
4. Private security relies on both commercial security services and government agencies for intelligence gathering and crisis management planning. Which of the following agencies has overall coordinating responsibility for the federal government in the event of a large-scale disruption of social, economic, or political significance due to a massive terrorist or nuclear incident?
   a. The CIA
   b. The FBI
   c. FEMA
   d. The Secret Service
5. Hallcrest I stated that the major item conspicuously absent from police-based crime prevention programs was:

    a. A comprehensive training program

    b. Manpower dedicated to crime prevention concepts

    c. The input of a huge number of persons employed in private security

    d. The use of updated technology

6. According to Hallcrest I, what was the most frequent recommendation made by both law enforcement and security managers to improve private security officials and their working relationships with the police?

    a. Higher entry-level pay

    b. Upgrading the quality of security personnel

    c. A planned educational program involving both police and private security

    d. Requirement of being armed

7. Hallcrest I indicates that the most frequently shared resource between law enforcement and private security is:

    a. A CCTV system and other surveillance equipment

    b. Personnel

    c. "Buy money" for stolen goods

    d. Reward money

8. The main objective of private security is:

    a. To apprehend those who steal property from their firms

    b. To protect assets and prevent losses

    c. To assist police in investigation of crimes

    d. To prevent unauthorized persons from entry on firm's property

9. What is the most frequently investigated crime by private security?

    a. Employee theft

    b. Shoplifting

    c. Bad checks

    d. Embezzlement

10. As a general rule, local law enforcement has very little effect on many crimes against business. However, there are some crimes that would be the exception. Which of the following would be the exception to this general rule?

    a. Shoplifting

    b. Employee theft

    c. Embezzlement

    d. Burglary

11. Approximately what percentage of medium and large security departments deputize private security personnel or give them special police powers?

    a. 10%

    b. 25%

    c. 50%

    d. 60%

12. A Hallcrest I survey was made relative to private security perceptions of law enforcement cooperation of criminal incidents and
assistance calls. The survey showed that proprietary security managers perceived the degree of law enforcement cooperation to be:

    a. Don't cooperate

    b. Cooperate reluctantly

    c. Cooperate fully

    d. Interfere with the private security investigation

13. According to Hallcrest I, approximately what percentage of proprietary security employees feel that the public police are satisfied with their current level of involvement in problems referred by
security personnel?

    a. 10%

    b. 20%

    c. 40%

    d. 60%

14. Hallcrest I revealed that operational law enforcement employees
rated their overall relationships with private security as:

    a. Very good or excellent

    b. Bad

    c. Poor

    d. Just moderately good

15. Hallcrest I revealed that chiefs and sheriffs rated their overall relationships with private security as:

    a. Excellent

    b. Very good

    c. Extremely bad

    d. Poor or less than good

16. According to Hallcrest II, American businesses' losses to crime in
1990 were estimated at:

    a. $114 billion

    b. $53 billion

    c. $241 billion

    d. $16 billion

17. A national crime survey for the years 1975–1988 reported that the
percentage of households touched by crime had:

    a. Increased by 25%

    b. Decreased by 23%

    c. Increased by 7%

    d. Decreased by 5%

18. For the past 20 years, the two major components of economic crime have been:
    a. Employee theft and corporate bribery
    b. Fraud and embezzlement
    c. White-collar crime and ordinary crime
    d. Computer crime and ordinary crime

19. According to the White House Conference for a Drug-Free America, approximately how many Americans had used an illegal drug in 1987?
    a. 1 in 20
    b. 1 in 2
    c. 1 in 7
    d. 1 in 40

20. According to a 1989 Gallup Poll, what percentage of American workers have personal knowledge of coworkers using illegal drugs on the job?
    a. 5%
    b. 10%
    c. 25%
    d. 50%

21. The percentage of the world's production of illegal drugs consumed in the United States is approximately:
    a. 5%
    b. 25%
    c. 60%
    d. 95%

22. The total annual cost to the United States for drug abuse due to resulting crime, lost productivity, absenteeism, health care costs, and so forth is most closely represented by:
    a. $50 million
    b. $100 million
    c. $100 billion
    d. $400 billion

23. According to a 1989 Department of Labor study, the percentage of employees in America working for a company that has a drug-testing program for employees or plans to have a drug-testing program is:
    a. 1%
    b. 10%
    c. 50%
    d. 80%

24. To improve cooperation and communications between private security and law enforcement, the authors of Hallcrest II recommend that:
    a. Cooperative programs be established in every metropolitan area
    b. Cities and counties enact ordinances providing for the police to regulate security
    c. Secondary employment of law enforcement officers in security work be prohibited
    d. Police academies teach security officers more about police work

25. The percentage of computer security incidents resulting from "insider" attacks by dishonest and disgruntled employees is approximately:
    a. 10%
    b. 35%
    c. 50%
    d. 80%

26. The percentage of computer security incidents that are annually believed to be attributed to hackers is closest to:
    a. 1%
    b. 10%
    c. 20%
    d. 50%

27. A 1990 National Institute of Justice study indicated that what percentage of computer crimes are *not* prosecuted?
    a. 10%
    b. 25%
    c. 70%
    d. 90%

28. The practice of preventing unauthorized persons from gaining intelligent information by analyzing electromagnetic emanations from electronic equipment, such as computers, is often termed:
    a. Tempest
    b. Veiling
    c. Bugging
    d. Hardening

29. According to Hallcrest II, North American incidents of terrorism represent what percentage of worldwide incidents?
    a. Less than 1%
    b. About 10%
    c. Almost 25%
    d. 40%

CHAPTER 11 ANSWERS

1. c. 1,000,000
2. d. Crime
3. b. Thefts by employees
4. c. FEMA
5. c. The input of a huge number of persons employed in private security
6. b. Upgrading the quality of security personnel
7. b. Personnel
8. b. To protect assets and prevent losses
9. a. Employee theft
10. d. Burglary
11. b. 25%
12. c. Cooperate fully
13. d. 60%
14. a. Very good or excellent
15. d. Poor or less than good
16. a. $114 billion
17. b. Decreased by 23%
18. c. White-collar crime and ordinary crime
19. c. 1 in 7
20. c. 25%
21. c. 60%
22. c. $100 billion
23. b. 10%
24. a. Cooperative programs be established in every metropolitan area
25. d. 80%
26. a. 1%
27. d. 90%
28. a. Tempest
29. a. Less than 1%

Appendix B: Security Survey

PART I. EXTERIOR PHYSICAL CHARACTERISTICS

A. GROUNDS

1.	Are there natural and man-made barriers?	Yes	No
2.	Is the fence strong and in good repair?	Yes	No
3.	Type of fence: _____		
4.	Is there a top guard on the top of the fence (examples: barbed wire, concertina, etc.)?	Yes	No
5.	What gauge of wire has been installed on the fence? _____		
6.	Fence height: _____		
7.	Is it designed so that an intruder cannot crawl underneath it?	Yes	No
8.	Is it designed so that an intruder cannot crawl over it?	Yes	No
9.	Distance, fence from building: _____		
10.	Are boxes or other material placed at a safe distance from the fence?	Yes	No
11.	Are there weeds or trash near or around the building? If yes, describe: _____	Yes	No
12.	Are stock, crates, or merchandise allowed to be piled near the building?	Yes	No
13.	Is there a cleared zone or area on both sides of the fence?	Yes	No
14.	Are unsecured overpasses or subterranean passageways near the fence?	Yes	No
15.	Are fence gates solid and in good repair?	Yes	No
16.	Are fence gates properly locked?	Yes	No
17.	Are fence gate hinges secure and nonremovable?	Yes	No
18.	What type of lock and chain are used to secure access gates? _____		
19.	Are access gates equipped with an alarm or under surveillance?	Yes	No
20.	Have unnecessary gates been eliminated?	Yes	No
21.	Are all locked gates regularly checked?	Yes	No
22.	Are all locking devices verified that they are authentic and not replaced by an intruder?	Yes	No
23.	Are blind alleys near buildings protected?	Yes	No
24.	Are all fire escapes and exits designed for quick exits but difficult entry?	Yes	No
25.	Is the perimeter reinforced by protective lighting?	Yes	No
26.	Has shrubbery near windows, doors, gates, garage, and access roads been kept to a minimum?	Yes	No
27.	What are the physical boundaries of the facility's grounds? _____		
28.	Does lighting illuminate all roads?	Yes	No

29. Is there a procedure to identify vendors, subcontractors, and   Yes   No
     visitors before they enter the gate?
30. Are there security personnel or guards?   Yes   No
     If yes, how many? _____
31. Number of employees: _____
32. How many entrances and exits into the facility? _____
     Are they controlled?   Yes   No
     How? _____
     _____
33. Is the entire perimeter under control?   Yes   No
     If no, explain: _____

B. Parking Areas

1.   Are vehicles permitted to park anywhere on the grounds?   Yes   No
     List areas: _____
2.   Are there designated parking lots?   Yes   No
     Where? _____
3.   Are the parking areas fenced in or monitored by security?   Yes   No
4.   Are there any controls established to protect vehicles from   Yes   No
     vandalism or theft?

C. Exterior Doors

1.   Are all doors strong and formidable, and do they appear secure?   Yes   No
2.   Are all door-hinge pins located on the inside?   Yes   No
3.   Are all door hinges installed so that it would be impossible to   Yes   No
     remove closed doors without seriously damaging doors or jambs?
4.   Are all doorframes well constructed and in good repair?   Yes   No
5.   Are the exterior locks either double-cylinder locks, dead bolts, or Yes   No
     jimmy-proof or pickproof types of locks?
     Describe: _____
     _____
6.   Can the breaking of glass or a door panel allow the person to open   Yes   No
     the door?
7.   Are all locks working properly?   Yes   No
8.   Are all doors properly secured or reinforced?   Yes   No
9.   Are all doorframes reinforced to resist prying, spreading, etc.?   Yes   No
10. Are all unused doors kept locked and secured?   Yes   No
11. Are all keys in the possession of authorized personnel?   Yes   No
12. Are keys issued only to personnel who actually need them?   Yes   No

| 13. | Are the padlocks, chains, and hasps heavy enough? | Yes | No |
| 14. | Are the hasps installed so that the screws cannot be removed? | Yes | No |

D. EXTERIOR WINDOWS

1.	Are nonessential windows either bricked up or protected with steel mesh, iron bars, grills, etc.?	Yes	No
2.	Are all windows within 18 ft. of the ground equipped with protective coverings?	Yes	No
3.	Are all windows less than 14 ft. from trees, poles, adjoining buildings, etc. equipped with protective coverings?	Yes	No
4.	Are the bars or screens mounted securely?	Yes	No
5.	Are the window locks designed so that they cannot be opened by breaking the glass?	Yes	No
6.	Are small or expensive items left in windows overnight?	Yes	No
7.	Are there security-type glass panes used in any of the windows?	Yes	No
8.	Are windows that are located under loading docks or similar structures protected?	Yes	No
9.	Are windows removable without breaking them?	Yes	No
10.	Are unused windows permanently closed?	Yes	No
11.	Are windows connected to an alarm system adequately protected?	Yes	No
12.	Are windows that are not secured by bars or alarms kept locked or otherwise protected?	Yes	No
13.	Have windows and doors been reinforced (examples: burglar-resistant glass, Lexan, Plexiglas, etc.)? Describe: _____	Yes	No
14.	Are all windows properly equipped with locks or reinforced glass or with decorative protective bars or sturdy shutters?	Yes	No
15.	Are all vents and similar openings that are larger than 96 ft.^{2} secured or reinforced with protective coverings?	Yes	No

E. EXTERIOR LIGHTING

1.	Is the lighting adequate to illuminate critical areas (alleys, fire escapes, ground-level windows, etc.)?	Yes	No
2.	Is illumination sufficient for at least 100 yd.?	Yes	No
3.	Is there adequate candlepower at ground level for horizontal viewing?	Yes	No
4.	Is there sufficient illumination over entrances?	Yes	No
5.	Are the perimeter areas lighted to assist police surveillance of the area?	Yes	No

6.   Are the protective lighting system and the working lighting system   Yes   No
     on the same level?
7.   Is there an auxiliary power source for protective lighting?   Yes   No
8.   How often is the auxiliary power system tested?
     Explain: _____

     _____

9.   Is the auxiliary power system designed to go into operation   Yes   No
     automatically when needed?
10. Are the protective lights controlled by an automatic timer, photo   Yes   No
     cells, or manual operation?
     Explain: _____

     _____

11. During what hours of the day is this lighting used?_____
12. Is either the switch box(es) or the automatic timer secured from   Yes   No
     attack?
13. Can protective lights be compromised easily (i.e., unscrewing of   Yes   No
     bulbs, breaking, etc.)?
14. Is lighting weatherproof?   Yes   No
15. What types of lights are installed around the property?_____
16. Are they cost-effective?   Yes   No
17. Are the fixtures vandal-proof?   Yes   No
18. Is there a glare factor?   Yes   No
19. Is there an even distribution of light?   Yes   No

F. OTHER OPENINGS

1.   Are there manhole covers that allow direct access to the building or   Yes   No
     to a door that a burglar could easily open?
2.   Are manhole covers that are 10 in. or more in diameter secured?   Yes   No
3.   If manholes or similar openings are no longer in use, are they   Yes   No
     permanently closed?
4.   Are the sidewalk doors or gates locked properly and secured?   Yes   No
5.   Are the sidewalk doors or grates securely in place so that frames   Yes   No
     cannot be pried open?
6.   Are accessible skylights protected with bars or an intrusion alarm?   Yes   No
7.   Are there any unused skylights that need to be eliminated?   Yes   No
8.   Are exposed roof hatches properly secured?   Yes   No
9.   Is there an alarm attached to the roof hatch to alert of an intrusion? Yes   No
10. Are fan openings or ventilator shafts protected?   Yes   No
11. Is there a service tunnel or sewer connected to the building?   Yes   No
12. Do fire escapes comply with city and state fire regulations?   Yes   No
13. Are the fire exits or escapes designed so that a person could leave   Yes   No
     easily but would have difficulty in reentering?

14. Do fire exit doors have portable alarms mounted, to communicate   Yes   No
    if doors are opened, or are they connected to the intrusion alarm?
15. Can entrance be gained from an adjoining building?   Yes   No

Comments:_____
_____
_____
_____

PART II. INTERIOR PHYSICAL CHARACTERISTICS

Name of site:_____
_____
_____

Address:_____
_____
_____

Administrative officer (exact title and full name):_____
_____

Telephone:_____
Surveying officer:_____
Security liaison (exact title and full name):_____
_____

Specific security problem with site:_____
_____

General purpose of site:_____
_____

Range of hours in use:_____

High-activity use (hours/days):_____

Number of people who have access (watchman, staff, cleaners, etc.):
_____

Is the site normally opened to the public?_____
Number of rooms occupied by the various departments and offices:

Who performs maintenance?_____

Maintenance schedule:_____
_____

Estimated dollar value of equipment and property in department/office:

_____

Area of highest dollar value:_____

A. INTERIOR LIGHTING

1. Is there a backup system of emergency lights?   Yes   No
2. Is the lighting provided during the day adequate for security purposes? Yes   No
3. Is the lighting at night adequate for security purposes?   Yes   No
4. Is the night lighting sufficient for surveillance by the local police   Yes   No
    department?
5. Can the lighting in restrooms not be turned on or off, except by   Yes   No
    maintenance or security personnel?

B. INTERIOR DOORS

1. Are doors constructed of a sturdy material?   Yes   No
2. Are doors limited to an essential minimum?   Yes   No
3. Are outside door-hinge pins spot-welded or bradded to prevent   Yes   No
    removal?
4. Are there hinges installed on the inward side of the door?   Yes   No
5. Is there at least one lock on each outer door?   Yes   No
6. Is each door equipped with a locking device?   Yes   No

C. OFFICES

1. Can entrances be reduced without loss of efficiency?   Yes   No
2. Are office doors locked when unattended for long periods of time?   Yes   No
3. Is there a clear view from the receptionist's desk, stairs, and elevators? Yes   No
4. Are maintenance personnel, visitors, etc. required to show   Yes   No
    identification, and is there a log kept of visitation?
5. Are desks and files locked when the office is unattended?   Yes   No
6. Are items of value left on desks or in an insecure manner?   Yes   No
7. Are all typewriters, computers, etc. bolted down or secured by   Yes   No
    steel cables?
8. Are floors free of projections, cracks, and debris?   Yes   No
9. During normal business hours, is the storage facility kept locked   Yes   No
    when not in use?
10. How many people have keys to the storage facility? _____

11.   How are important documents destroyed? _____
12.   Are important documents shredded before being discarded?   Yes   No

D. CAFETERIA

1.   Are coolers and food storage areas properly locked?   Yes   No
2.   Where are the cash registers located? _____
3.   How are they operated by employees? _____
4.   Does the cafeteria have a lot of customers?   Yes   No
5.   Do personnel leave the cash registers open for long periods of time? Yes   No
6.   Is the amount of cash kept in the registers kept to a minimum?   Yes   No
7.   Are there vending machines?   Yes   No
     If yes, where? _____
8.   Are the vending machines in an area where they can be easily   Yes   No
     broken into or vandalized?
9.   Are there security cameras monitoring the area?   Yes   No

E. LOCKER ROOMS

1.   Are there employee locker rooms?   Yes   No
2.   Are there periodic unannounced locker checks?   Yes   No
3.   Is there a direct outside access from the locker rooms?   Yes   No
4.   Are there security cameras monitoring the area?   Yes   No

F. KEYS

1.   Total keys issued: _____
2.   What is the basis of issuance of keys? _____
     _____
3.   Is there a key control system?   Yes   No
4.   Is an adequate log maintained of all keys that are issued?   Yes   No
5.   Are key holders allowed to duplicate keys?   Yes   No
6.   Are keys marked "do not duplicate"?   Yes   No
7.   If master keys are used, are they devoid of markings identifying   Yes   No
     them as such?
8.   Are losses or theft of keys promptly reported to the security office Yes   No
     or police department?
9.   Whose responsibility is it to issue and replace lost keys? _____
     _____

10.   When was the last visual key audit made (to ensure keys were not loaned, lost, or stolen)? _____

11.   Were all keys accounted for?   Yes   No
       If not, how many were missing? How often is a key audit conducted?

12.   Are the duplicate keys stored in a secure place?   Yes   No
       Where? _____

13.   Are keys returned when an employee resigns, is discharged, or is   Yes   No
       suspended?
       If no, why not?_____

G. Locks

1.   Are all entrances equipped with secure locking devices?   Yes   No
2.   Are they always locked when not in active use?   Yes   No
       If no, why not? _____

3.   Are locks designed or frames built so that doors cannot be forced   Yes   No
       by spreading the frames?
4.   Are all locks in working order?   Yes   No
5.   Are the screws holding the locks firmly in place?   Yes   No
6.   Are bolts protected or constructed so that they cannot be cut?   Yes   No
7.   Are the locks' combinations changed or rotated immediately when   Yes   No
       an employee who possesses a master key resigns, is discharged,
       or is suspended?
       If no, why not?_____
8.   Are the locks changed once a year regardless of transfers or known   Yes   No
       violations of security?
       If no, why not?_____
9.   When was the last time the locks were changed or rekeyed? _____

H. Petty Cash

1.   The amount of petty cash kept: _____
2.   Who are the employees who have access to the cash? _____

3.   Are funds kept to a minimum?   Yes   No
4.   Where is the petty cash stored? _____

5.	Are blank checks also stored there?	Yes	No
6.	Are checks pre-signed?	Yes	No
7.	Is the accounting system adequate to prevent loss or pilferage of funds accessible to unauthorized persons at any time?	Yes	No
8.	Are funds kept overnight in a safe, locked desk, or file cabinet?	Yes	No
9.	Is this area secured?	Yes	No
10.	Are locks in this area replaced when keys are lost, missing, or stolen?	Yes	No

I. SAFES

1.	What methods are used for protecting safe combinations? _____ _____		
2.	Are combinations changed or rotated immediately when an employee who possesses a combination resigns, is discharged, or is suspended?	Yes	No
3.	Are the safes approved by Underwriters Laboratories?	Yes	No
4.	Are the safes designed for burglary protection as well as fire protection?	Yes	No
5.	Where are the safes located? _____		
6.	Are the rooms containing safes well lit at night?	Yes	No
7.	Can the safes be seen from outside the building?	Yes	No
8.	Is money kept in the safes?	Yes	No
9.	Is cash kept to a minimum by banking regularly?	Yes	No
10.	Is care taken when working the combination so that it is not observed?	Yes	No
11.	Do you "spin" the dial rather than leaving it on "day lock"?	Yes	No
12.	Is there a policy making certain that the safes are properly secured and that the room(s), door(s), and window(s) are locked; night light(s) on; and no one has hidden inside the room(s)?	Yes	No
13.	Are the safes secured to the floor or wall?	Yes	No
14.	Are combinations changed every 6 months? When was the last time? _____	Yes	No
15.	Are there protective theft alarms for each safe? Is it local or central? _____	Yes	No
16.	When was the system last tested? _____		

J. INTRUSION ALARMS

1.	Does the facility utilize any alarm devices? How many? _____ What type? _____ Where are they located? _____	Yes	No

2.   Are the alarms monitored by a proprietary company, a central station, or the
      police department? _____

      _____

      List the types of sensors: _____

      _____

3.   Are there regular recorded tests?   Yes   No
      How often? _____

K. Closed-Circuit Television (CCTV)

1.   Is CCTV utilized?   Yes   No
2.   What is CCTV used for (surveillance, access control, etc.)? _____

      _____

3.   Is the CCTV monitored continuously?   Yes   No
      If not, is there a recorder to monitor later? _____
4.   Are the lights compatible with the lighting requirements of the   Yes   No
      CCTV cameras stationed around the facility's grounds?

L. Inventory Control

1.   When was the last time an inventory of business equipment was made that listed
      serial numbers and descriptions? _____
2.   Were any items missing or unaccounted for?   Yes   No
      What were they? _____

      _____

      _____

3.   Are signed authorizations required?   Yes   No
4.   Are employees required to sign a receipt for the items checked out?   Yes   No
5.   Are late returns followed up on?   Yes   No
6.   Has all equipment been bolted down or otherwise secured?   Yes   No
7.   Is all business equipment marked?   Yes   No
8.   Is all expensive business equipment stored in a security cabinet or room?   Yes   No

M. Product Controls

1.   Is there an inspection and a review of all controls on shipping and   Yes   No
      receiving?
2.   How many people are responsible for checking the merchandise? _____

      _____

List the personnel: _____

_____

3.	Are vendors allowed to wander freely in the facilities?	Yes	No
4.	Is there a waiting room for vendors?	Yes	No
5.	Is there surveillance, CCTVs, or a supervisor on duty at all times?	Yes	No
6.	Has there been a review of facility loss, returns, and breakage?	Yes	No

If no, why not? _____

7. What is the rate of loss, returns, and breakage for the facility? _____

_____

8.	Are there spot checks on shipments and receiving?	Yes	No
9.	Are waste and trash receptacles spot-checked?	Yes	No

If yes, how often? _____

10.	Are shipments made after closing hours?	Yes	No

N. Contract Services

1.	Are there independent contractors?	Yes	No

2. What types of contractors (examples: janitorial, maintenance, cleaners, etc.)? _____

_____

_____

3. What are their schedules? _____

4. Are they permitted full access to the facility, or is access restricted? _____

_____

5.	Do independent contractors have their own keys to the facility?	Yes	No
6.	Are they allowed to enter and exit without security supervision?	Yes	No
7.	Are they monitored by a CCTV system?	Yes	No

O. Computers and Database Information

1. Are computers locked down, or can they be carried out? _____

2.	Are computers positioned so that proprietary information cannot be seen on the screen from outside windows or by other people?	Yes	No
3.	Do employees leave their computers unattended with information on the screen?	Yes	No
4.	Has the facility had problems in the past with hackers?	Yes	No
5.	Does security monitor the computer room during night hours?	Yes	No

6. What kind of system is in place to guard access to a company's database? _____

_____

7. How often are passwords changed? _____

8.	Are passwords shared among personnel?	Yes	No
9.	Are passwords written down anywhere?	Yes	No
10.	How often are systems checked for viruses? _____		
11.	Are personnel allowed to bring in their own software for use on the company's computers?	Yes	No
12.	Where is the company's backup software stored? _____		

13. How is the company's sensitive information (such as customer lists and pricing) protected? _____

14.	Are there personnel training programs that explain the importance of protecting and guarding the company's proprietary information?	Yes	No

P. Personnel Screening

1.	Is a written, signed employment application required?	Yes	No
2.	Is all information listed on an employment application (past employers, addresses, dates, positions, performance, education, etc.) verified?	Yes	No
3.	Are there background investigations conducted for criminal activities?	Yes	No
4.	Are credit history investigations done on personnel who are put in sensitive positions?	Yes	No
5.	How is sensitive information (employee records, medical information) for personnel protected? _____		

Q. Educational Programs

1.	Are all newly assigned or employed personnel given a security orientation?	Yes	No
2.	Are follow-up security instructions given?	Yes	No
3.	If none are given, would employed personnel be interested if a security orientation were offered?	Yes	No
4.	What areas would employee personnel like to see covered? _____		
5.	Are personnel given written and verbal instructions on what to do if there is an emergency?	Yes	No
6.	Are there test emergency drills for the employees?	Yes	No

7.   What means are in place to alert employees of an emergency situation or
      condition? _____
      _____
      _____

8.   Are personnel aware of where all emergency kits (first-aid kits, fire   Yes   No
      extinguishers, etc.) are located?

PART III. FIRE PREVENTION

	Construction Type	**(Check)**
1.	Fireproof	_____
2.	Semifireproof	_____
3.	Heavy timber and masonry	_____
4.	Light wood and masonry	_____
5.	Metal frame	_____
6.	Wood frame	_____

Number of building stories: _____
_____

Do the building stories vary in height? Explain and attach pictures.

_____
_____

Height: _____
Width: _____
Depth: _____
Ceiling height (space above drop ceiling measurement):

_____

Number of guest rooms or occupants: _____
Certificate of occupancy: _____
Certificate for places of assembly (list locations and approved capacity):

_____
_____

Fire department license, permits, or flameproofing certificates:

_____
_____

Are they up-to-date?   Yes   No
Other: _____
List names and addresses of maintenance contacts:_____
_____

Maintenance Performance Schedules

For cleaning range hoods, ducts, etc.:

_____

_____

For maintaining fire alarm system:

_____

_____

Fire Alarm System

Type (local, central, etc.): _____

Was it tested during this inspection?   Yes   No

When? _____

Did it operate properly?   Yes   No

Was the software or configuration revised?   Yes   No

When? _____

Did it operate properly?   Yes   No

Is there a municipal, automatic, ADT, etc. alarm box on the premises?

_____

Is it connected to the local alarm system?   Yes   No

Will a responsible person be available 24 h/day to transmit an alarm?   Yes   No

What means are provided for notifying the fire department of a fire?

_____

_____

Type of Transmission	**Service**
____ McCulloh	_____ Weekly
____ Multiplex	_____ Monthly
____ Digital	_____ Quarterly
____ Reverse Priority	_____ Semiannually
____ Radio frequency (RF)	_____ Annually
____ Other (specify)	_____ Other (specify)

_____

_____

Panel manufacture and model number: _____

_____

Circuit styles: _____

Number of circuits: _____

Software used: _____

Are there any features to this system that should be noted (prealert, manual trip, etc.)?

_____

_____

Supervisory Signal Initiating Devices and Circuit Information

Quantity	Circuit Style
_____	_____ Building temperature
_____	_____ Site water temperature
_____	_____ Site water level
_____	_____ Fire pump power
_____	_____ Fire pump running
_____	_____ Fire pump auto position
_____	_____ Fire pump/controller trouble
_____	_____ Generator in auto position
_____	_____ Generator/controller trouble
_____	_____ Switch transfer
_____	_____ Generator engine running
_____	_____ Other

System Power Supplies

Main or Primary: _____ Voltage   _____ Amps

Overcurrent protection: _____ Type   _____ Amps

Location: _____

_____

Disconnecting location: _____

_____

Standby or Secondary: _____ Amp/hour rating

Storage battery: _____

_____

Battery condition: _____

_____

Battery test (i.e., load voltage, discharge, charger, specific gravity):

_____

_____

Capacity to operate system in hours: _____

_____

Engine-driven generator dedicated to fire alarm system: _____

_____

Location of fuel storage: _____

_____

Transient suppressors: _____

_____

Remote annunciators: _____

_____

Notification systems (i.e., audible, visible, speakers, voice clarity, etc.):

_____

Were initiating and supervisory devices tested and inspected?	Yes	No
Did they operate properly?	Yes	No

EMERGENCY LIGHTING

Type of system: _____

Are all units operational?	Yes	No
If no, explain: _____		

Are all areas covered systematically?	Yes	No
If no, explain: _____		

Is the system regularly inspected and tested as required bylaw?	Yes	No
How often? _____		

By whom? _____

Are records maintained of such tests?	Yes	No
Are fire drills held for employees?	Yes	No
If yes, how often? _____		

SPRINKLER SYSTEMS

Are they complete or partial sprinkler systems? _____

Are there any areas not covered that should be?	Yes	No
If yes, diagram and explain: _____		

What supervises the system? Is it electronic, manual, or both?

_____

Are sprinkler valves open?	Yes	No
Are the gauges registering properly?	Yes	No
Are the sprinkler heads free and unobstructed?	Yes	No
Where does the sprinkler alarm sound?_____		

STANDPIPE AND HOSE SYSTEM

Condition of hose and nozzle: _____

_____

Location of fire department standpipes: _____

_____

FIRE EXTINGUISHER

Is there an extinguisher for every 1500 ft.^{2} of floor area?	Yes	No
Is the type provided suitable for the hazards?	Yes	No

Condition of extinguishers: _____

_____

Have they been recharged yearly as required?	Yes	No
Are they accessible?	Yes	No

EXITS

Are there two independent exits from each floor?	Yes	No

Are there any obstructions to, or in, doors, stairs, landings, or corridors?

_____

_____

Do exit doors open out?	Yes	No
Are fire doors kept closed?	Yes	No

Is there any location where additional exits are necessary? _____

_____

_____

Location of exit and directional signs (natural or artificial lighting):

_____

_____

Are there barred windows?	Yes	No
Are there locked doors?	Yes	No
Are enclosed stairs or fire towers available?	Yes	No

Location: _____

_____

Self-closing doors: _____

_____

Proper lighting: _____

_____

Type of emergency lighting: _____

_____

Handrails: _____

_____

Are there any transoms over room doors?   Yes   No
Location: _____

Interior Finishes of Floors, Walls, and Ceilings

Is any acoustical ceiling tile used?   Yes   No
Location of use: _____

Is any questionable wall covering (wood paneling, tile, fabric, etc.) used?   Yes   No
Location of use: _____

Which type of floor covering is used? _____

Do floor and wall materials meet fire code requirements?   Yes   No
(Note: Samples of same should be obtained if possible and submitted for testing. Burden
of proof is on the occupant.)

General Check—Any Area

Is there an accumulation of wastepaper, rubbish, furniture, etc.?   Yes   No
Where? _____

Housekeeping deficiencies: _____

Stairs, ramps, elevators, vents, dumbwaiters, and other shafts:
Are they enclosed?   Yes   No
Are doors self-closing?   Yes   No
Do they have noncombustible interior coverings?   Yes   No
Do all chutes, including for rubbish and laundry, have self-closing doors?   Yes   No
Are there noncombustible linings? (The building code requires a 1 h
fire-resistant rating.)   Yes   No
Is there an automatic sprinkler installation in chutes?   Yes   No
Is there a fire detection unit provided?   Yes   No
Are venting facilities provided that extend through the roof?   Yes   No
Are they adequate?   Yes   No
Are there instances of temporary wiring, extension cords, or the use of
electrical equipment that should be corrected?   Yes   No
Are covered metal containers provided for rubbish, oily waste, and
other materials?   Yes   No
If no, what type is used? _____

What methods are used to dispose of rubbish? _____
_____

Is rubbish removed daily?   Yes   No
If no, how often? _____
_____

(Note: Plastic baskets and barrels cannot be used for rubbish.)

MAINTENANCE SHOPS

	Violations Found	**Corrections Made**
Carpentry	_____	_____
Plumbing	_____	_____
Electrical	_____	_____
Upholstery	_____	_____
Paint	_____	_____

INCINERATOR

Location: _____
_____

How is it cut off from the rest of the building? _____
_____

Is it an approved type?   Yes   No
Do feed hoppers close tightly?   Yes   No
Does it have a spark arrestor?   Yes   No
How is rubbish handled in its transfer from chutes? _____
_____

HEATING EQUIPMENT

Location: _____
_____

How is it cut off from the rest of the building? _____
_____

Are all openings to the unit kept closed?   Yes   No
Type of fuel used: _____

Where and how is fuel stored? _____

_____

Individual responsible for this equipment: _____

_____

What defects were noted? _____

_____

KITCHEN

Location: _____

Type of fuel for cooking: _____

Condition of ranges, hoods, ducts, etc.: _____

_____

Fire protection equipment available: _____

_____

Can personnel use equipment properly?   Yes   No

Refrigerating equipment used: _____

_____

Does it have separate enclosures?   Yes   No

If no, should it? Explain: _____

_____

Refrigerant used: _____

_____

Condition of motors etc.: _____

_____

Is the area vented?   Yes   No

How? _____

_____

To where? _____

_____

LAUNDRY

Location: _____

_____

How is it cut off from the rest of the building? _____

_____

Are dryers and controls properly installed? _____

_____

Are vents kept free and clear?   Yes   No

Do electrical devices including irons have automatic controls,
and are they operating properly?   Yes   No

Do pilot lights operate adequately?   Yes   No

EMERGENCY ELECTRICAL SERVICES

Type: _____

_____

Location: _____

_____

How and when is it placed in operation? _____

_____

_____

UTILITY GAS SERVICE

Location: _____
Size: _____
Shutoff location: _____

ELECTRICAL SERVICE

Location: _____
Shutoff location: _____

HEAVY FUEL OIL SHUTOFF

Location: _____
Is it operable?   Yes   No

OUTSIDE MEANS OF EGRESS

Number and type: _____
Location: _____
Condition: _____
Do exits open out?   Yes   No

OUTSIDE ENTRANCES TO BASEMENTS

Location: _____
Do they open out?   Yes   No

STEAMER CONNECTIONS

Location: _____
What do they supply? _____
Are they accessible?   Yes   No

Air-Conditioning

Is system complete or partial? _____

Location of intake: _____

Shutoff control: _____

Dampers (automatic where passing through walls, floors, etc.):

_____

Refrigerant used: _____

Inspector Checks for the Following Part of the Form Are from Outside the Building

Location of nearest city fire alarm box, number and location of hydrants in relation to building: _____

_____

City hydrants:_____

_____

Private hydrants: _____

_____

Condition, width, and grade of streets: _____

_____

Drives or approaches to hotels/motels: _____

_____

Can apparatus approach for emergency evacuation?   Yes   No

Clarify: _____

_____

Building areas that are accessible: _____

_____

Building areas that are not accessible: _____

_____

Factors or obstructions influencing or hampering accessibility for department operations (such as narrow drives, tunnels, grades, overhead wires, fences, walls, gates, parked cars, building set back, etc.):

_____

_____

_____

_____

_____

Exposures to This Building

Adjacent buildings: _____

Grass, rubbish, brush, etc.: _____

Combustible sheds, other: _____

Buildings that this building might expose: _____

Remarks: _____

Recommendations: _____

Note: Briefly describe the existing stairways, including the number, type of enclosure, termination point, etc.:

Appendix C: Physical Security and Legal Glossary of Terms

WINDOWS

Burglar-resistant glazing: Any glazing that is more difficult to break through than the common window or plateglass. It is designed to resist burglary attacks of the smash-and-grab type.

Double glazing: Two-layered thickness of glass that is separated by an airspace and framed in an opening designed to reduced heat transfer or sound transmission. Usually referred to as *insulating glass*. The airspace between the layers of glass is desiccated and sealed airtight.

Dry glazing: A method of securing glass in a frame by use of a preformed resilient gasket.

Face glazing: A method of glazing in which the glass is set in a L-shaped frame, the glazing compound is finished off in the form of a triangular bead, and no loose stops are used.

Glazing: Any transparent or translucent material used in windows or doors to admit light.

Glazing bead: A strip of trim or a sealant such as a caulking or glazing compound that is placed around the perimeter of a pane of glass or other glazing to secure it to the frame.

Glazing compound: A soft, doughlike material used for filling and sealing the spaces between a pane of glass and its surrounding frame and/or stops.

Laminated glass: A type of glass made from two layers of glass with a transparent bonding layer between them. Also known as *safety glass*.

Wet glazing: The sealing of glass or other transparent material in a frame by the use of a glazing compound or sealant.

Window guard: Strong metal grid-like assemblies that can be installed on a window or other opening for reinforcement, such as metal bars, metal mesh grilles, sliding metal gates, etc.

LOCKS

Ace lock: A type of pin-tumbler lock where the pins installed in a circle around the axis of the cylinder move perpendicularly to the face of the cylinder. This type of lock is operated with a push key.

Antifriction latch: A latch bolt that incorporates any device that reduces the closing friction between the latch and the strike.

Armored faceplate: A plate or plates that are secured to the lock front of a mortised lock by machine screws in order to prevent tampering of the cylinder set screws. Also known as an *armored front*.

Auxiliary lock: Also known as a *secondary lock*, used as extra security to the primary installed lock. It can be a mortised, bored, or rim lock.

Back plate: A plate on the inside of a door through which the cylinder connecting screws and tailpiece is passed.

Backset: The horizontal distance from the edge of a door to the center of a lockset.

Barrel key: A key with a bit projecting from a hollow cylindrical shaft that fits on a post in the lock.

Bevel: (1) Pertaining to a latch bolt, indicates the direction in which the latch bolt is inclined; regular bevel for doors opening in and reverse bevel for doors opening out. (2) Pertaining to a lock front, indicating the angle of a lock front when not at a right angle to the lock case. This allows the front to be flush with the edge of a beveled door.

Bicentric pin-tumbler cylinder: A cylinder having two cores and two sets of pins, each having different combinations. The cylinder requires two separate keys used simultaneously to operate it.

Bilock: A pin-tumbler cylinder lock consisting of two parallel rows of pin tumblers and two sidebars operated by a U-shaped key.

Bit: A blade projecting from a key shank that engages and operates the bolt or level tumblers of a lock.

Bit key: A key with a bit projecting from a solid cylindrical shaft. The bit has cuts to bypass the wards or operate levers in the correct lock. Similar to the **barrel key**, but it is solid rather than a hollow cylinder.

Bit key lock: A warded or lever lock that uses bit keys.

Bitting: See **cut**.

Blade: The portion of the key that is inserted into the lock.

Blank: Any key before any cuts have been made, or an unfinished key from the manufacturer.

Bolt: The part of the lock that, when projected or "thrown" from the lock into a strike plate, prevents moving or opening of a window, door, or drawer.

Bolt attack: A category of intruder attacks in which force is directed against the bolt in an attempt to break or disengage it from the strike.

Bolt throw (projection): The distance from the edge of the door at the bolt centerline to the furthest point on the bolt in the thrown position.

Bottom pins: See also **lower pins**.

Bow: The handle of a key.

Buttress lock: A lock that secures a door by wedging a bar between the door and the floor.

Bypass tool: A device designed to neutralize the security of a locking device, or its application hardware, that takes advantage of a design weakness.

Cam: The part of a lock or cylinder that rotates to operate the bolt or latch as the key is turned.

Cam lock: A lock that has an attached cam that serves as the lock's bolt. Often used on cabinets, file cabinets, and drawers.

Case: The housing or body of a lock.

Case ward: Protrusions that stick out of the sides of the keyway to allow entry of only the correct type of key blank.

Chain bolt: A vertical spring-loaded bolt mounted at the top of a door. It is manually operated by a chain.

Change index: The point on a key changeable combination lock dial ring to which the old and new combinations must be dialed when changing the combination.

Change key: The key that operates on a lock in a master-keyed system.

Code: A series of numbers or digits on a key, or lock, that specifies or refers to the particular cuts of the key to operate a lock.

Combination: (1) The sequence and depth of cuts on a key. (2) The sequence of numbers to which a combination lock is set.

Control key: A key used to remove the core from an interchangeable core cylinder.

Control shear line: The shear line that allows operation of the control lug of an interchangeable core.

Control sleeve: The part of an interchangeable core-retaining device that surrounds the plug.

Cross bore: A hole drilled into the face of a door where a bored or interconnected lockset is to be installed.

Cuts: A cut, or a series of cuts, on the bit or blade of a key. Also known as *bitting*.

Cylinder: Generally used to refer to the lock or to the shell, plugs, and pins as a single unit. A double cylinder has a cylinder on both the interior and exterior of the door.

Cylinder guard ring: A hardened metal ring surrounding the exposed portion of a lock cylinder that protects the cylinder from being wrenched, turned, pried, cut, or pulled with attack tools.

Cylinder housing: The external case of a lock cylinder, also known as a *cylinder shell*.

Cylinder key: A key for use with pin-tumbler or wafer-tumbler locks.

Cylindrical lockset: A bored lockset whose latch or bolt locking mechanism is contained in the portion installed through the cross bore.

Dead bolt: A lock bolt, usually rectangular in shape, that has no spring action and becomes locked against end pressure when fully projected.

Dead latch: A spring-activated latch bolt with a beveled end that can be automatically or manually locked against end pressure when projected.

Deadlock: A lock equipped with dead bolt.

Deadlocking: Pertaining to any feature that, when fully engaged, will attempt to resist moving the latch or bolt in the unlocking direction through direct pressure.

Deadlocking latch: A latch bolt with a deadlocking mechanism.

Depth: The depth of a cut is measured from the bottom of the blade up to the bottom of a cut. Depths are numbered starting with the number 0, or sometimes the number 1, as the highest depth.

Depth key: A special key that enables a locksmith to cut blanks made from a particular lock according to a key code.

Door bolt: A rod or bar manually operated without a key that provides a way to secure the door.

Double-acting lever tumbler: A tumbler that must be lifted to a precise amount, neither too little or too much, to allow movement of a bolt.

Double cylinder: Pertaining to a lock with two keyed cylinders.

Double-cylinder deadlock: A dead-bolt lock whose bolt may be operated by a key from either side.

Double-throw bolt: A bolt than can be projected beyond its first position, into a second or fully extended position.

Double-throw lock: A lock that has a double-throw bolt.

Drivers: The pins in a lock that sit on top of the lower pins and rest against the springs.

Dummy cylinder: A mock cylinder without an operating mechanism that is used for appearance only.

Electric strike: An electrically operated device that allows a door to be opened using electric switches at remote locations.

Euro profile cylinder: The shape of a standard lever lock keyway in central Europe that manufacturers use; the same lever lock case is a basis for the Euro lock cylinder. The cylinder is normally fitted with the pins upside down to allow the cam on the cylinder to reach the lever lock mechanism.

Fence: A metal pin that extends from the bolt of a lever lock and prevents retraction of the bolt unless it is aligned with the gates of the lever tumblers.

Flat steel key: A key that is completely flat on both sides; usually used for warded or lever-tumbler locks.

Flush bolt backset: The vertical distance from the centerline of the lock edge of a door to the centerline of the bolt.

Full mortise: Usually pertaining to a method of installation where only the faceplate and trim are exposed. The lock case is installed in a pocket in the door or drawer.

Gate: A notch in the end of a lever tumbler, which, when aligned with the fence of the lock bolt, allows the bolt to be withdrawn from the strike.

Grooves: Long, narrow, milled-out areas along the sides of the blade to allow the blade to bypass the wards in the keyway.

Hasp: A hinged metal strap designed to be passed over a staple and secured in place.

Heel: Pertaining to the part of a padlock shackle, which is retained when in the unlocked position.

Heel-and-toe locking: A padlock that has locking dogs at both the heel and toe of the shackle.

Hollow-post key: A key with a bit projecting from a hollow cylindrical shaft.

Hook bolt: A lock bolt shaped in the general outline of a hook. Usually used on sliding doors or where spreading of the frame and door can possibly be attacked.

Impressioning: A way of fitting a key directly to the lock cylinder by manipulating a blank in the keyway and cutting the blank where the tumblers have made marks.

Interconnected lockset: A lockset where the trim provides a way of simultaneous retraction of two or more bolts that may be operated independently.

Interlocking strike: A strike that receives and holds a vertical, rotary, or hook dead bolt.

Jamb: The inside vertical face of a doorway.

Jamb peeling: A technique used in forced entry to deform or remove portions of the jamb to disengage the bolt from the strike.

Jimmying: A technique used in forced entry to pry the jamb away from the lock edge of the door to disengage the bolt from the strike.

Key: A tool or other piece of equipment used to operate a lock bolt or latch into the locked or unlocked position.

Key code: A series of numbers or digits on a key or lock that specifies or refers to the particular cuts of the key to operate a lock.

Keyway: The part of the plug where you insert the key.

Keyway grooves: Long, narrow, milled-out areas along the sides of the blade to allow the blade to bypass the wards in the keyway.

Latch: A mechanical device that automatically keeps a door closed until a deliberate action is used to retract it.

Lever lock: Lock with levers that are each lifted to the correct level by a bit key or a flat metal key to enable the lock to operate.

Lever pack: A set of lever tumblers.

Lever tumbler: Normally a flat, spring-loaded tumbler that pivots on a post.

Lock: Any device that can prevent access or use by requiring special knowledge or equipment.

Lock backset: The horizontal distance from the vertical centerline of the faceplate to the center of the lock cylinder keyway.

Lock pick: A tool, other than the designed key, that is made for the purpose of manipulating a lock into a locked or unlocked position.

Locking dog: The part of the padlock mechanism that engages the shackle and holds it in the locked position.

Lower pins: The pins of a lock that contact the cuts on the key. They determine the combination of a pin-tumbler cylinder; also referred to as *bottom pins*.

Mortise cylinder: A lock cylinder that has a threaded housing that screws directly into the lock case with a cam or other mechanism engaging the locking mechanism.

Padlock: A detachable and portable lock with a hinged or sliding shackle or bolt, usually used with a hasp-and-staple system.

Pin stack: The combination of a lower pin sitting beneath an upper pin. In master-keyed locks, additional master pins may be located between the lower and upper pins.

Pin-tumbler cylinder: A lock cylinder that uses metal pins, or tumblers, to prevent the rotation of the core until the correct key is inserted into the keyway. Small coil compression springs hold the pins in the locked position until the key is inserted.

Plug: The part of the lock that you put the key into that turns to operate the lock.

Pressed padlock: A padlock whose outer case is pressed into shape from sheet metal and then riveted together.

Privacy lock: A lock that is usually used for an interior door and is secured by a button or thumb turn and requires no key.

Removable core cylinder: A cylinder whose core may be removed by the use of a special key.

Rim cylinder: A lock cylinder that is held in place by tension against its rim applied by screws from the interior face of the door.

Rim lock: A lock or latch typically mounted on the surface of a door or drawer.

Rotary interlocking dead-bolt lock: A type of rim lock where the extended dead bolt is rotated to engage with the strike.

Shackle: The part of a padlock that passes through an opening in an object or fits around an object and is locked into the case.

Shear line: The dividing line between the plug and the shell, or the height to which the tops of the lower pins must be raised to open the lock.

Shell: The outer part of the lock that surrounds the plug.

Shoulder: The edge of the key that touches the face of the lock to define how far the key is inserted into the lock.

Single-acting lever tumbler: A lever tumbler that must be moved to a minimum distance to allow travel of the bolt but cannot be moved too far so as to restrict the bolt's travel.

Skeleton key: Any noncylinder key whose bit, blade, and/or post is cut away enough to allow it to enter and turn in different warded locks.

Spool pin: A pin that has a groove cut around its outer limits or edge. The groove is intended to catch at the shear line as a deterrent to picking.

Stop: A button or other device that serves to lock and unlock a latch bolt against operation by the outside knob or thumb piece.

Strike: A metal plate attached to or mortised into a doorjamb to receive and hold a projected latch bolt or dead bolt in order to secure the door to the jamb.

Strike backset: The distance from the doorstop to the edge of the strike cutout.

Tail piece: The unit on the core of a cylinder lock that operates the bolt or latch.

Tension wrench: A tool used in picking a lock. It is utilized to apply torsion to the cylinder core.

Three-point lock: A locking device required on A-label fire double doors to lock the active door at three points: the normal position plus top and bottom.

Tip: The very end of the key that is put into the lock first.

Toe: The part of the shackle that may be removed from the padlock's body.

Top master key: The highest-level master key that fits all the locks in a multilevel master-keyed system.

Top pins: The pins in a lock that sit on top of the pin stack.

Tubular key cylinder: A cylinder whose tumblers are arranged in a circle and are operated by a tubular key.

Tubular lockset: A bored lockset whose latch or bolt locking mechanism is contained in the component installed into the edge bore.

Tumbler: Generally used to refer to the pins or wafers in a lock. It is a movable obstruction in a lock that must be adjusted to a particular position before the bolt can be thrown, as by a key.

UL listed: Listed in a directory as having passed specific Underwriters Laboratories testing.

Unit lock: A lock that has all the parts assembled into a unit at the manufacturer and, when installed into the rectangular section cutout of the door at the lock's edge, requires little or no assembly. Also known as a *preassembled lock*.

Vertical bolt lock: A lock that has two dead bolts that move vertically into two circular receivers in the strike area of the lock attached to the doorjamb.

Ward: Protrusion that sticks out of the sides of the keyway to restrict entry from the wrong key entering or turning the lock unless the correct type of key blank is used.

LIGHTING

Brightness: Refers to the ratio of illumination that is being observed. High brightness causes glare, while low brightness on some backgrounds causes difficulty in observation.

Candlepower: 1 candlepower is the amount of light emitted by one standard candle.

Foot-candle: 1 foot-candle equals 1 lumen of light per square foot of space, or the illuminant produced on a surface, all points of which are at a distance of 1 ft. from a directionally uniform point source of one candela. The density or intensity of illumination is measured in foot-candles. The more intense the light, the higher the rating.

Illuminant: The density of the luminous flux incident on a surface.

Light level: The intensity of incident light measured in foot-candles or lux.

Lumen: The lamps (lightbulbs) that are used in various lighting systems are rated in lumens. The lumen is used to express the output of a light source. 1 lumen is the amount of light required to light an area of 1 ft.^{2} to 1 candlepower.

Luminaire: A complete lighting unit consisting of a lamp or lamps together with the parts designed to distribute the light, to position and protect the lamps, and to connect the lamps to the power supply.

Lux: The metric unit of illuminant equal to 1 lumen incident upon 1 m^2. 1 lux is equal to 0.0929 foot-candle.

Reflector: Basically a parabolic mirror used to redirect the light by the process of reflection in various ways.

Restrike: If there is a voltage interruption, there are varying times, depending on the light source, required to reenergize or relight. Depending on the type of lighting use, the restrike time varies.

Watt: A term used to measure the amount of electrical energy consumed.

ALARM MONITORING SYSTEMS

Access control: The control of pedestrian and vehicular traffic through entrances and exits of a **protected area** or premises.

Access mode: The operation of an **alarm system**, such as no **alarm signal** being given when the **protected area** is entered; however, a signal may be given if the **sensor, annunciator,** or **control unit** is tampered with or opened.

Accumulator: A circuit that accumulates a sum. For instance, in an audio alarm control unit, the accumulator sums the amplitudes of a series of pulses, which are larger than some threshold level; subtracts from the sum at a predetermined rate to account for random background pulses; and initiates an alarm signal when the sum exceeds some predetermined level. This circuit is also called an *integrator*; in digital circuits, it may be called a *counter*.

Active intrusion detection sensor: An intrusion detection sensor that emits a signal from a transmitter and detects changes in, or reflections of, that signal by means of a receiver. See also **passive intrusion detection sensor**.

Active intrusion sensor: An active sensor that detects the presence of an intruder within the range of the sensor. Some examples are an **ultrasonic motion detector**, a **radio-frequency motion detector**, and a **photoelectric alarm system**. See also **passive intrusion detection sensor**.

Actuating block: One part of a magnetic contact, consisting of a magnet in a case.

Actuator: A manual or automatic button, switch, or sensor such as a **holdup button, magnetic switch**, or thermostat, which causes a system to transmit an **alarm signal** when manually activated or when the device automatically senses an intruder or other suspicious conditions.

Air gap: The distance between two magnetic elements in a magnetic or electromagnetic circuit, such as between the core and the armature of a relay.

Alarm: A warning from a sensor or sensor system that a sensor has been triggered or activated; usually signaled by light or sound. It may indicate a nuisance, false alarm, or valid alarm.

Alarm assessment: The process of determining an alarm condition status; the credibility, reliability, accuracy, or usefulness of an indicated alarm.

Alarm circuit: An electrical circuit of an alarm system that produces or transmits an **alarm signal**. This may be done via an electrical circuit that transmits the alarm signal over telephone or fiber-optic lines, or through airwaves.

Alarm condition: A threatening condition, such as an intrusion, fire, or holdup, sensed by a detector.

Alarm discrimination: The ability of an alarm system to distinguish between those stimuli caused by an intrusion and those that are part of the environment.

Alarm line: A wired electrical circuit used for the transmission of alarm signals from the protected premises to an alarm monitoring system.

Alarm signal: A signal produced by a **control unit**. Alarm signals **alert** someone that the **alarm system** has been activated to an alarm condition. The alarm signal may be a bell, horn, siren, or **local alarm**, or a signal may be transmitted to a remote location, the **central station**, via self-dialing phone, punch tape, or telephone lines. Every alarm system must have an alarm signal.

Alarm station: (1) A manually actuated device installed at a fixed location to transmit an **alarm signal** in response to an **alarm condition**, such as a concealed **holdup button** in a bank teller's cage. (2) A well-marked emergency **control unit**, installed in fixed locations usually accessible to the public, used to summon help in response to an **alarm condition**. The **control unit** contains either a manually actuated switch or telephone connected to fire or police headquarters, or a telephone **answering service**. See also **remote alarm system**.

Alarm system: A network or wires and devices connected for the purpose of detecting an **alarm condition** requiring urgent attention, such as unauthorized entry, fire, temperature rise, etc. The system may be local, at the police department, at the central station, or proprietary.

Alert: Communication that informs all security personnel of an establishment emergency and of the location of the emergency.

Annunciator: An electrical alarm monitoring device that has a number of visible signals that show the status and location of the detectors in an alarm system or systems. When an **alarm condition** is indicated, a signal is visibly or audibly reported, or both.

Answering service: A business that is set up with subscribers to answer incoming telephone calls after a specified delay, or when scheduled to do so. It may also provide other services, such as relaying a fire or intrusion alarm to the proper authorities.

Area protection: Protection of the inner space, rather than an object, by means of photoelectric, ultrasonic, or microwave alarm systems.

Area sensor: A sensor with a detection zone that approximates an area, such as a wall surface or the exterior of a safe.

Assessment: The determination of the cause of an alarm and information regarding the threat.

Audible alarm device: A noisemaking device, such as a siren, bell, or horn, used as part of a local alarm system to indicate an alarm condition. This device can also serve as a part of an annunciator to indicate a change in the status or operating mode of an alarm system.

Audio frequency (sonic): Sound frequencies within the range of human hearing, approximately 15 to 20,000 Hz.

Audio monitor: An arrangement of amplifiers and speakers designed to monitor the sounds transmitted by microphones located in the **protected area**. Similar to an **annunciator**, except that supervisory personnel can monitor the protected area to interpret the sounds.

Authorized-access switch: A device used to make an alarm system or some portion or zone of a system inoperative in order to permit authorized access through a protected port. A **shunt** is an example of such a device.

Beam divergence: In a **photoelectric alarm system**, the angular spread of the light beam.

Biometric device: Automatic device that can verify an individual's identity from a biological measurement of a feature.

Bistatic: Refers to an active intrusion detection sensor in that the transmitter and the receiver are in separate units.

Break alarm: A condition signaled by the opening or breaking of an electrical circuit, and/or a signal produced by a break alarm condition. Sometimes referred to as an open-circuit alarm or trouble signal that is designed to indicate possible system failure.

Burglar alarm (BA) pad: A supporting frame laced with fine wire or a fragile panel located with **foil** or fine wire and installed so as to cover an exterior opening in a building, such as a door or skylight. Entrance through the opening breaks the wire or foil and initiates an **alarm signal**. See also **grid**.

Burglar alarm system: A sensing system designed to detect an attempt to compromise or unlawfully break into a **protected area**, and transmit an **alarm signal** to control and/or annunciation components.

Burglary: The forcible breaking into a structure with the intent to commit a felony or theft therein while the structure is unoccupied or without having a confrontation with an occupant of the structure.

Buried-line sensor: A passive intrusion detection sensor that employs a buried transducer to detect seismic and/or magnetic disturbances. Ported coaxial cables are an active intrusion detection sensor.

Bypass: A sensor defeat mode in which an intruder defeats a sensor by avoiding its detection zone or detection method.

Cabinet-for-safe: A wooden enclosure having closely spaced electrical grids on all inner surfaces and contacts on the doors. It surrounds a safe and initiates an alarm signal if an attempt is made to open or penetrate the cabinet.

Capacitance: The property of two or more objects that enables them to store electrical energy in an electrostatic field between them. The capacitance varies with the distance between the objects; hence, the change of capacitance with relative motion is greater the nearer one object is to another. The basic measurement unit is farads.

Capacitance alarm system: An alarm system in which a protected object is electrically connected as a **capacitance sensor**. The approach of an intruder causes sufficient change in **capacitance** to upset the balance of the system and initiate an **alarm signal**. Also called **proximity alarm system**.

Capacitance sensor: A sensor/device that responds to a change in **capacitance** in a field containing a protected object or in a field within a protected area.

Carrier current transmitter: A device that transmits **alarm signals** from a sensor to a **control unit** via the standard alternating current (AC) power lines.

CCTV: Closed-circuit television. A television system in which the signal distribution is limited or restricted, usually by cable.

Central station: A control center to which alarm systems in a subscriber's premises are connected, where circuits are supervised, and where personnel are maintained continuously to record and investigate alarm or trouble signals. Facilities are provided for the reporting of alarms to police and fire departments or to other outside agencies.

Central station alarm system: An alarm system, or group of systems, that transmits the **alarm signal** to the **central station**. This differs from a proprietary alarm in that the central station is owned and operated independently of the subscriber.

Circumvention: The defeat of an alarm system by the avoidance of its detection devices, such as by jumping over a pressure-sensitive mat, by entering through a hole cut in an unprotected wall rather than through a protected door, or by keeping outside the range of an **ultrasonic motion detector**. Circumvention contrasts with **spoofing**.

Clear zone: An area within the site perimeter and/or around the boundary of the site free of all obstacles, topographical features, and vegetation exceeding a specified height. The zone is designed to facilitate detection and observation of an intruder, to deny protection and concealment to an intruder, to maximize effectiveness of the security personnel, and to reduce the possibility of a surprise attack.

Closed-circuit system: A system in which the sensors of each zone are connected in series so that the same current exists in each sensor. When an activated sensor breaks the circuit or the connection wire is cut, an alarm is transmitted for that zone.

Coded alarm system: An alarm system in which the source of each signal is identifiable. This is usually accomplished by means of a series of current pulses that operate audible or visible annunciators to yield a recognizable signal. This is usually used to allow the transmission of multiple signals on a common circuit.

Coded transmitter: A device for transmitting a coded signal when manually or automatically operated by an **actuator**. The actuator may be housed with the transmitter, or a number of actuators may operate a common transmitter.

Combination senor alarm system: An alarm system that requires the simultaneous activation of two or more sensors to initiate an **alarm signal**.

Conductor: Material that transmits an electrical current. Examples are wire, cable, and the like.

Constant-ringing drop (CRD): A relay that, when activated even momentarily, will remain in an **alarm condition** until reset. A key is often required to reset the relay and turn off the alarm.

Contact microphone: A microphone designed for attachment directly to a surface of a **protected area** or object; usually used to detect surface vibrations.

Contactless vibrating bell: A vibrating bell whose continuous operation depends upon application of an alternating current, without circuit-interrupting contacts such as those used in vibrating bells operated by direct current.

Contacts: A device that, when actuated, opens or closes a set of electrical contacts, such as a switch or relay. Means of protecting a door or other opening. A pair of metallic parts of a switch or relay that, when touching, make or, when separating, break the electrical current path.

Control unit: A device, usually electronic, that provides the interface between the alarm system and the operator and produces an **alarm signal** when its programmed response indicates an **alarm condition**. Also known to be the terminal box for all sensors.

Cross alarm: An **alarm condition** signaled by crossing or shorting an electrical circuit.

Crossover: An insulated electrical path used to connect foil across window dividers, such as those found on multiple-pane windows, to prevent grounding and to make a more durable connection.

Dark current: The current output of a **photoelectric sensor** when no light is entering the sensor.

Defeat: The frustration, counteraction, or thwarting of an alarm device so it fails to signal an **alarm** when a **protected area** is entered. Defeat includes both **circumvention** and **spoofing**.

Delay: The element of a physical protection system designed to impede adversary penetration into or exit from the protected area.

Detection: Determining that an unauthorized action has occurred or is occurring; includes sensing the action, communicating the alarm to a control center, and assessing the alarm. Detection is not complete without **assessment**.

Detection zone: A volume of space or surface area under surveillance of one or more intrusion detection devices from which an **alarm** is produced when the volume or surface area is subject to an **alarm condition**.

Dialer: See **telephone dialer, automatic**.

Differential pressure sensor: A sensor used for perimeter protection that responds to the difference between the hydraulic pressures in two liquid-filled tubes buried just below the surface of the earth around the exterior perimeter of the **protected area**. The pressure difference can indicate an intruder walking or driving over the buried tubes.

Digital telephone dialer: See **telephone dialer, digital**.

Direct connect alarm system: A security system in which signaling devices at the **protected area** are connected by means of a supervised transmission circuit to an **annunciator** installed in municipal headquarters, such as police headquarters, fire department, etc.

Direct wire circuit: A wired electrical circuit used for the transmission of **alarm signals** from the **protected area** to a **monitoring station**.

Door cord: A short, insulated cable with an attaching block and terminals at each end used to conduct current to a device, such as **foil**, mounted on the movable portion of a door or window.

Door trip switch: A **mechanical switch** mounted so that movement of the door will operate the switch.

Doppler effect (shift): The apparent change in frequency of sound or radio waves when reflected or originating from a moving object. Utilized in some types of **motion detectors**.

Double-circuit system: An alarm circuit in which two wires enter and two wires leave each sensor.

Duress alarm system: A system that produces either a **silent alarm** or a **local alarm** under a condition of personnel stress, such as holdup, fire, illness, or other panic or emergency. The system is normally manually operated and may be fixed or portable.

E-field sensor: A **passive intrusion detection sensor** that detects changes in the earth's ambient electric field caused by the movement of an intruder. See also **hi-field sensor**.

Electric-field sensor: An **active intrusion detection sensor** that generates an electric field and senses changes in **capacitance** caused by an intruder.

Electromechanical bell: A bell with a prewound spring-driven striking mechanism that is initiated by the activation of an electric tripping mechanism.

Electronic: Related, or pertaining to, electrons or semiconductors, and to devices that utilize components such as microchips and transistors that control and direct electric currents.

End-of-line resistor: See **terminal resistor**.

Entrance delay: The time between actuating a sensor on an entrance door or gate and the sounding of a **local alarm** or transmission of an **alarm signal** by the **control unit**. This delay is used if the **authorized-access switch** is located within the **protected area** and permits a person with the control key to enter without causing an **alarm**. This delay is provided by a timer within the control unit.

EOL: End of line.

Exit delay: The time between turning on a **control unit** and the sounding of a **local alarm** or transmission of an **alarm signal** upon actuation of a sensor on an exit door. This delay is used if the **authorized-access switch** is located within the **protected area** and permits an authorized person with the control key to turn on the **alarm system** and leave through a protected door or gate without causing an **alarm**. The delay is provided by a timer within the control unit.

Fail safe: A feature of a system or device that initiates an **alarm** or trouble signal when the system or device either malfunctions or loses power.

False alarms: An **alarm signal** that is received without the presence of an **alarm condition**. False alarms can be caused by many factors, such as environmental conditions like rain, fog, wind, lighting, temperature changes, etc.; animals; insects; human-made disturbances like electromagnetic interference, vehicles, etc.; equipment malfunctions like transmission errors, component failure, operator error, etc.; and the unknown.

Fence alarm: Any of several types of sensors used to detect the presence of an intruder near a fence or any attempt by them to climb over, go under, or cut through a fence.

Field: The space or area in which there exists a force such as that produced by an electrically charged object, a current, or a magnet.

Foil: Thin metallic strips that are cemented to a protected surface, usually glass in a window or door, and connected to a closed circuit. If the protected material is broken so as to break the foil, the circuit opens, initiating an alarm signal. A window, door, or other surface to which foil has been applied is said to be taped or **foiled**.

Foil connector: An electrical terminal block used on the edge of a window to join interconnecting wire to a window foil.

Footrail: Foot-operated **holdup alarm device** used to unobtrusively initiate an **alarm signal**. Most often seen at cashier windows, in which a foot is placed under the rail, lifting it, thus triggering an alarm signal.

Frequency-division multiplexing (FDM): A signaling method characterized by the simultaneous noninterfering transmission of more than one signal in a communication channel. Signals from one another by virtue of each signal being assigned to a separate frequency, also called a channel, or combination of frequencies.

Full-band jamming: A jamming signal with a bandwidth greater than or equal to the bandwidth of the signal being jammed.

Glass-break vibration detector: A **vibration detection system** that employs a **contact microphone** attached to a glass window to detect cutting or breakage of the glass.

Grid: (1) Area of coverage. (2) A screen or metal plate, connected to earth ground, sometimes used to provide a stable ground reference for objects. (3) A lattice or wooden dowels or slats concealing fine wires in a closed circuit, sometimes called a protective screen. (4) An arrangement of electrically conducting wire, screen, or tubing placed in front of doors or windows or both, which is used as part of a **capacitance sensor**.

Guards: On-site security personnel who comprise the response function for an intrusion detection system.

Hardening: Enhancing a wall or door to make it more difficult to penetrate.

Heat sensor: A sensor designed to respond to infrared radiation from a remote source, such as a person.

Hi-field sensor: A passive sensor that detects changes in the earth's ambient magnetic field caused by the movement of an intruder. See also **e-field sensor**.

Holdup alarm device: A device that signals a holdup. The device is usually **surreptitious** and may be manually or automatically actuated or fixed, or portable.

Holdup alarm system, automatic: An alarm system that employs a holdup alarm device, in which the signal transmission is initiated by the action of the intruder, such as a money clip in a cash drawer.

Holdup alarm system, manual: A holdup alarm system in which the signal transmission is initiated by the direct action of the individual attacked or of an observer of the attack.

Holdup button: A manually actuated mechanical switch used to initiate a duress alarm signal; usually constructed to minimize accidental activation.

Hood contact: A switch that is used for the supervision of a closed safe or vault door. Usually installed on the outside surface of the protected door.

Identification: The positive assessment of a recognized object as a specific person, animal, or thing.

Impedance: The opposition to the flow of alternating current in a circuit. May be determined by the ratio of an input voltage to the resultant current.

Impedance matching: Making the **impedance** of a **terminating device** equal to the impedance of the circuit to which it is connected in order to achieve optimum signal transfer.

Infrared (IR): Light or energy in the portion of the electromagnetic spectrum having a longer wavelength than visible light.

Infrared motion detector: A sensor that detects changes in the **infrared** light radiation from parts of the **protected area**. When objects or intruders move positions, their radiation likewise changes the infrared light intensity from that direction.

Insider: A person who, by reason of official duties, has knowledge of the establishment's operations and/or physical security systems and who is in a position to significantly enhance the likelihood of successful bypass of or defeat of the security measures of the establishment.

Interior perimeter protection: Protection along the interior boundary of a protected area including all points through which entry can be affected.

Intrusion alarm system: An alarm system for signaling the entry or attempted entry of an unauthorized person or an object into the area protected by the system.

Intrusion detection system: The combination of components including sensors, control units, transmission lines, and monitor units integrated to operate in a specified manner.

IR: See **infrared**.

Jack: An electrical connector that is used for frequent connect and disconnect operations. For example, connecting an alarm circuit to an overhang door.

Jamming: An intruder's attempts to prevent radio communications through physical destruction of communications equipment or through insertion of unwanted signals into the frequency channel of a communications system for the purpose of masking desired signals.

Keyed alarm controls: The alarm is either activated or deactivated with an alarm key from the exterior area of the **protected area**. A signal is transmitted only upon an **alarm condition** and not upon opening, closing, or nonscheduled entries.

Lacing: A network of fine wire surrounding or covering an area to be protected, such as a safe, vault, or glass panel, and connected into a **closed-circuit system**. The network of wire is concealed by a shield such as concrete or paneling in such a manner that an attempt to break through the shield breaks the wire and initiates an alarm.

Line amplifier: An audio amplifier that is used to provide preamplification of an audio alarm signal before transmission of the signal over an alarm line. Use of an amplifier extends the range of signal transmission.

Line sensor (detector): A sensor with a **detection zone** that exhibits detection along a line, such as a **photoelectric sensor** that senses a direct or reflected light beam.

Line supervision: Electronic protection of an **alarm line** is accomplished by sending a continuous or coded signal through the circuit. A monitor will detect a change in the circuit's characteristics, such as a change in **impedance** due to the circuit being tampered with. The monitor initiates an alarm if the change exceeds a predetermined amount.

Local alarm: An alarm that, once activated, makes a loud noise or floods the site with lights or both at or near the **protected area**. See **audible alarm device**.

Local alarm system: An alarm system that, when activated, produces an audible or visible signal in the immediate vicinity of the **protected area** or object.

Loop: (1) A signal path. (2) An alarm communication and display term that refers to a series of multiplexers connected via dual communication paths to two microprocessors.

Magnetic alarm system: An alarm system that will initiate an alarm when it detects changes in the local magnetic field. The changes could be caused by motion of metals containing iron, such as guns, tools, etc., near the magnetic sensor.

Magnetic buried-line sensor: A buried-line sensor that generates an electrical signal when ferromagnetic material passes near the transducer.

Magnetic sensor: A sensor that responds to changes in a magnetic field. See also **magnetic alarm system**.

Magnetic switch: A switch that consists of two separate units: a magnetically actuated switch and a magnet. The switch is usually mounted in a fixed position, such as a doorjamb or window frame, opposing the magnet, which is fastened to a hinged or sliding door, window, etc. When the movable section is opened, the magnet moves with it, actuating the switch.

Magnetic switch, balanced: A balanced switch that operates using a balanced magnetic field in such a manner as to resist **defeat** with an external magnet. It signals an alarm when it detects either an increase or decrease in magnetic field strength.

Matching network: A circuit used to achieve **impedance matching**. It may also allow audio signals to be transmitted to an **alarm line** while blocking direct current used locally for **line supervision**.

Mat switch: A flat area switch used on open floors or under carpeting. It may be sensitive over an area of a few square feet or several square yards.

McCulloh circuit (loop): A supervised single-wire **loop** connecting a number of coded **alarm signals** to a **central station** receiver.

Mechanical switch: A switch in which contacts are opened and closed by means of a depressible plunger or button.

Mercury switch: A switch operated by tilting or vibrating, which causes an enclosed pool of mercury to move, making or breaking physical and electrical contact with conductors. Used on tilting doors and windows and on fences.

Microwave frequency: Radio frequencies in the range of approximately 1.0 to 300 GHz.

Microwave motion detector: An active intrusion detection sensor that transmits microwave signals and detects changes in the signal caused by a moving object.

Microwave reflector: A planar metallic surface or grid designed for passive reflection of a microwave beam and used for the purpose of directing the beam.

Monitoring station: The central station, proprietary station, or other area at which security personnel, police, etc. observe **annunciators** and report on the conditions of the alarms.

Motion detector: A sensor that responds to the motion of an intruder and generates an **alarm**. See also **ultrasonic motion detector**, **microwave motion detector**, and **infrared motion detector**.

Multiplexing: A technique for the concurrent transmission of two or more signals in either or both directions over the same wire, carrier, or other communication channel. The two basic multiplexing techniques are time division multiplexing and **frequency-division multiplexing**.

Multiplexing, frequency division (FDM): The **multiplexing** technique that assigns to each signal a specific set of frequencies (called a channel) within the larger block of frequencies available on the main transmission path in much the same way as many radio stations broadcast at the same time but can be separately received.

Multiplexing, time division (TDM): The multiplexing technique that provides for the independent transmission of several pieces of information on a time-sharing basis by sampling, at frequent intervals, the data to be transmitted.

Nonretractable (one-way screw): A screw with a head designed to permit installation with an ordinary flat-bit screwdriver but that resists removal. They are used to install alarm system components so that removal is inhibited.

Normally closed switch: A switch in which the **contacts** are closed when no external forces act upon the switch.

Normally open switch: A switch in which the **contacts** are open or separated when no external forces act upon the switch.

Nuisance alarm: Any alarm that is not caused by an intrusion. See **false alarm**.

Object protection: Protection of objects such as safes, files, or anything of value that could be damaged or removed from the premises. Also known as spot protection.

Open-circuit alarm system: A system in which the sensors are connected in parallel. When a sensor is activated, the circuit is closed, permitting a current that activates an **alarm signal**.

Passive intrusion detection sensor: These sensors detect some type of energy that is emitted by the intruder, or detect the change of some natural field of energy caused by the intruder. **Passive sensors** include those based on vibration, heat, sound, and capacitance.

Passive sensor: A sensor that detects natural radiation or radiation disturbances, but does not itself emit the radiation on which its operation depends.

Passive ultrasonic alarm system: An alarm system that detects the sounds in the **ultrasonic frequency** range caused by an attempted forcible entry into a protected structure. The system consists of microphones, a **control unit** containing an amplifier, filters, an **accumulator**, and a power supply. The unit's sensitivity is adjustable so that ambient noises or normal sounds will not initiate an **alarm signal**; however, noise above the preset level or a sufficient accumulation of impulses will initiate an alarm.

Perimeter protection: Protection of access to the outer limits of a **protected area** by means of physical barriers, sensors on physical barriers, or exterior sensors not associated with a physical barrier.

Permanent circuit: An **alarm circuit** that is capable of transmitting an **alarm signal** whether the alarm control is in **access mode** or **secure mode**. Used, for example, on foiled fixed windows, **tamper switches**, and supervisory lines. See also **supervisory alarm system**, **supervisory circuit**, and **permanent protection**.

Permanent protection: A system of alarm devices such as **foil, burglar alarm pads**, or **lacings** connected in a permanent circuit to provide protection whether the **control unit** is in the **access mode** or **secure mode**.

Photoelectric alarm system: An **alarm system** that employs a light beam and a **photoelectric sensor** to provide a line of protection. The photoelectric sensor will pick up any interruption to the beam by an intruder. Mirrors may be used to change the direction of the beam. The maximum beam length is limited by many factors, some of which are the light source intensity, number of mirror reflections, detector sensitivity, **beam divergence**, fog, and haze.

Photoelectric alarm system, modulated: A photoelectric alarm system in which the transmitted light beam is modulated in a predetermined manner and in which the receiving equipment will signal an alarm unless it receives the properly modulated light.

Photoelectric sensor: A sensor that detects a visible or invisible beam of light and responds to its complete or nearly complete interruption. See also **photoelectric alarm system** and **photoelectric alarm system, modulated**.

Police station alarm: The direct link by which an alarm system is connected to an annunciator installed in a police station.

Portable duress station: A device carried on a person that may be activated in an emergency to send an **alarm signal** to a **monitoring station**.

Positive noninterfering (PNI) and successive alarm system: An **alarm system** that employs multiple alarm transmitters on each **alarm line**, like a **McCulloh circuit (loop)**, so that in the event of simultaneous operation of several transmitters, one of them takes control of the alarm line, transmits its full signal, and then releases the alarm line for successive transmission by other transmitters, which are held inoperative until they gain control.

Pressure alarm system: An **alarm system** that protects a vault or other enclosed spaces by maintaining and monitoring a predetermined air pressure differential between the inside and outside of the space. Equalization of pressure resulting from opening the vault or by cutting through the enclosure will be sensed, initiating an **alarm signal**.

Printing recorder: An electromechanical device used at a **monitoring station** that accepts coded signals from alarm lines and converts them to an alphanumeric printed record of the signal received.

Proprietary alarm: An **alarm system** that is similar to a **central station alarm system** except that the **annunciator** is owned and located at the establishment that is constantly maintained by security personnel. Security personnel will monitor the system and respond to all **alarm signals** or alert the proper authorities.

Protected area: An area monitored by an **alarm system** or security personnel, or enclosed by a physical barrier.

Proximity alarm system: An intrusion detection system that protects metal objects such as safes, file cabinets, etc. It is attached to the metal object and surrounds it with radiation several inches or feet away. If the metal object is touched or the radiation is penetrated, the alarm sounds. See also **capacitance alarm system**.

Radar alarm system: An **alarm system** that employs a **radio-frequency motion detector**.

Radio-frequency motion detector: A sensor that detects the motion of an intruder through the use of a radiated radio-frequency electromagnetic field. The device operates by sensing a disturbance in the generated radio-frequency (RF) field caused by intruder motion, typically a modulation of the field referred to as the **Doppler effect** that is used to initiate an **alarm signal**. Most radio-frequency motion detectors are certified by the Federal Communications Commission (FCC) for operation as field disturbance sensors at one of the following frequencies: 0.915 GHz (L-band), 2.45 GHz (S-band), 5.8 and 10.525 GHz (X-band), 22.125 GHz (K-band). Detectors operating in the **microwave frequency** range are usually called **microwave motion detectors**.

Reed switch: A type of **magnetic switch** consisting of contacts formed by two thin movable magnetically actuated metal vanes or reeds held in a normally open position within a sealed glass envelope.

Register: An electromechanical device that makes a paper tape in response to signal impulses received from transmitting circuits. A register may be driven by a prewound spring mechanism, an electric motor, or a combination of both.

Register, inking: A register that marks the tape with ink.

Register, punch: A register that marks the tape by cutting holes in it.

Register, slashing: A register that marks the tape by cutting V-shaped slashes in it.

Remote alarm: An **alarm signal** that is transmitted to a remote **monitoring station**. See also **local alarm**.

Remote alarm system: An **alarm system** that employs remote **alarm stations** usually located in building hallways or on city streets.

Retard transmitter: A **coded transmitter** in which a delay period is introduced between the time of actuation and the time of signal transmission.

Robbery (holdup): The felonious or forcible taking of property by violence, threat, or other overt felonious act from another person.

Safe cover: A magnetic cover that fits over the dial of a safe. It is connected to the **alarm system**, and when removed without first deactivating it, an **alarm signal** is initiated.

Secure mode: The condition of an **alarm system** in which all sensors and **control units** are ready to respond to an intrusion.

Seismic sensor: A sensor, generally buried under the surface of the ground for **perimeter protection**, that responds to minute vibrations generated as an intruder walks or drives within the **detection zone**.

Sensor: A device that is designed to produce an **alarm signal** or indicate a response to an event or stimulus within the **detection zone**.

Service: The repair and maintenance of an alarm system. UL-listed central stations must provide 24 h, 7-day/week service.

Shunt: (1) A deliberate shorting-out of a portion of an electric circuit. (2) A key-operated switch that removes some portion of an **alarm system** for operation, allowing entry into a **protected area** without initiating an **alarm signal**. A type of **authorized-access switch**.

Shunt switch: A key-operated switch often provided at the **protected area** to allow authorized personnel to remove the door contact from the protection circuit temporarily and allow entrance without generating an **alarm**. See also **shunt**.

Silent alarm: A **remote alarm** transmitted without the obvious bells and horns.

Silent alarm system: An **alarm system** that signals a remote station by means of a **silent alarm**.

Single-circuit system: An **alarm circuit** that routes only one side of the circuit through each **sensor**. The return may be through the ground or a separate wire.

Solid state: (1) An adjective used to describe electronic devices such as semiconductor transistors, diodes, resistors, and capacitors. (2) A circuit or system that does not rely on vacuum or gas-filled tubes to control or modify voltages and currents.

Sonic motion detector: A **sensor** that detects the motion of an intruder by the disturbance of an audible sound pattern generated within the protected area.

Sound-sensing detection system: An **alarm system** that detects the audible sound caused by an attempted forcible entry into a **protected**

area. The system consists of microphones and a **control unit** containing an amplifier, **accumulator**, and power supply. The system's sensitivity is adjustable so that ambient noises or normal sounds will not initiate an **alarm signal**. However, noises above this preset level or a sufficient accumulation of impulses will initiate an **alarm**.

Sound sensor: A **sensor** that responds to sound; a microphone.

Spoofing: Any technique that allows the intruder to pass through the sensor's normal detection zone without generating an **alarm** by tricking or fooling its detection system. Methods that can be employed include short-circuiting part or all of a series circuit, cutting wires in a parallel circuit, reducing the sensitivity of a **sensor**, and/or entering false signals into the system. Spoofing contrasts with **circumvention**.

Spot protection: Protection of objects of value that can be damaged or removed from an establishment.

Spring contact: A device employing a current-carrying cantilever spring that monitors the position of a door or window.

Spring-driven mechanism: A mechanism that is powered by a spring-wound mechanical energy source. It is completely independent of any electrical power source.

Standby power supply: Equipment that supplies power to a system in the event the primary power is lost. The equipment may consist of batteries, charging circuits, auxiliary motor generators, or a combination of these.

Strain-gauge alarm system: An **alarm system** that detects the stress caused by the weight of an intruder as he moves about the building. Typical uses include placement of the **strain-gauge sensor** under a floor joist or stairway tread.

Strain-gauge sensor: A **sensor** that, when attached to an object, will provide an electrical response to an applied stress upon the object, such as bending, stretching, or compressive force.

Strain-sensitive cable: An electrical cable that is designed to produce a signal whenever the cable is strained by a change in applied force. Typical uses include mounting it to a wall to detect an attempted forced entry through the wall, fastening it to a fence to detect climbing on the fence, or burying it around a perimeter to detect walking or driving across the perimeter.

Subscriber: The alarm company's term for a customer.

Supervised lines: Interconnecting lines in an **alarm system** that are electrically supervised against tampering. See also **line supervision**.

Supervisory alarm system: An alarm system that monitors conditions and/or persons and signals any deviation from an established norm or schedule.

Supervisory circuit: An electrical circuit that sends information on the status of a sensor to an **annunciator**. For **intrusion alarm systems**, this circuit provides **line supervision** and monitors **tamper-resistant devices**.

Surreptitious: Covert, hidden, concealed, or disguised.

Surveillance: (1) Control of premises for security purposes through the use of alarm systems, CCTVs, or other monitoring methods. (2) Monitoring industrial operations whose conditions could cause damage if not corrected, such as sprinkler water pressure, temperature, or liquid levels.

System: An assembly of components that operate as a functional unit to provide sensing, transmission, and action functions.

Tamper-resistant device: A device that is electrically supervised to ensure that it will not be improperly altered or changed by an intruder to defeat protection.

Tamper switch: (1) Any device, usually a switch, that is used to detect an attempt to gain access to the alarm components, such as removing the switch cover, control box doors, etc. The alarm component is then often described as being tampered with. (2) A monitor circuit to detect any attempt to modify the alarm circuitry, such as cutting a wire.

Telephone dialer, automatic: A device that, when activated, automatically dials one or more preprogrammed telephone numbers, such as the police or fire department, and relays a recorded voice or coded message giving the location and nature of the **alarm**.

Telephone dialer, digital: An automatic telephone dialer that sends its message as a digital code.

Terminal resistor: A resistor used as a **terminating device**.

Terminating device: A device that is used to terminate an electrically supervised circuit. It makes the electrical circuit continuous and provides an end-of-line resistor against which changes are measured. A sensor, tampering, or other circuit trouble may cause the changes.

Transducer (transmitting and receiving): A device by means of which energy can be made to flow from one or more transmission mediums. The energy may be in any form, such as electrical, mechanical, or acoustical.

Trap: An **intrusion detection system** or device that detects passage through doors, windows, floors, ceilings, or specified interior areas.

Trickle charge: A continuous direct current, usually very low, which is applied to a battery to maintain it at peak charge or to recharge it after it has been partially or completely discharged. Usually applied to nickel cadmium (NICAD) or wet-cell batteries.

Trip-wire switch: A switch that is actuated by breaking or moving a wire or cord installed across a floor space.

Trouble signal: A signal indicating trouble of any nature, such as the opening or breaking of an electrical circuit, or possible system failure.

UL: See **Underwriters Laboratories.**

UL certificated: A certification or certain types of products that have met UL requirements. A certificate is provided, which the manufacturer may use to identify quantities of material for specific job sites or to identify field-installed systems.

UL listed: Signifies that production samples of the product have been found to comply with the established **Underwriters Laboratories** requirements and that the manufacturer is authorized to use the laboratory' listing marks on the listed products that comply with the requirements, contingent upon follow-up services as a check of compliance.

Ultrasonic: Pertaining to a sound wave having a frequency above that of audible sound, approximately 20,000 Hz. Used in **ultrasonic motion detectors**.

Ultrasonic frequency: Sound frequencies that are above the range of human hearing, approximately 20,000 Hz or higher.

Ultrasonic motion detector: A sensor that detects the motion of an intruder through the use of **ultrasonic** generating and receiving equipment. The device operates by filling a space with a pattern of ultrasonic waves. The modulation of the waves by a moving intruder or object is detected and initiates an **alarm signal**.

Underwriters Laboratories (UL): A private independent research and testing laboratory that tests and lists various items meeting good practice and safety standards.

Uninterruptible power supply (UPS): A battery-powered, alternating-current source that will maintain power to vital equipment if all site power is lost.

Vibration detection system: An **alarm system** that employs one or more **contact microphones** or **vibration sensors**, which are fastened to the surfaces of the area or object being protected to detect excessive levels of vibration. The contact microphone system consists of microphones, a **control unit** containing an amplifier and an **accumulator**, and a power supply. The unit's sensitivity is adjustable so that ambient noises or normal vibrations will not initiate an **alarm signal**. In the vibration sensor system, the sensor responds to excessive vibration by opening a switch in a **closed-circuit system**.

Vibration sensor: A sensor that responds to vibrations of the surface on which it is mounted. It has a **normally closed switch** that will momentarily open when it is subjected to a vibration with sufficiently large amplitude. Its sensitivity is adjustable to allow for the different levels of normal vibration, to which the sensor should not respond, at different locations. See also **vibration detection system**.

Volumetric sensor: A sensor with a **detection zone** that extends over a volume such as an entire room, part of a room, or passageway. **Ultrasonic motion detectors** and **sonic motion detectors** are examples of volumetric sensors.

Walk test light: A light-on-motion detector that comes on when the detector senses motion in the area. It is used while setting the sensitivity of the detector and during routine checking and maintenance.

Watchman's reporting system: A **supervisory alarm system** arranged for the transmission of a patrolling watchman's regularly recurrent report signals from stations along the patrol route to a central supervisory agency.

Zoned circuit: A circuit that provides continual protection for parts of zones of the **protected area**, while normally used doors and windows or **zones** may be released for access.

Zones: Smaller subdivisions into which large areas are divided to permit selective access to some areas while keeping other areas secure, and to permit pinpointing of the specific location from which an **alarm signal** is transmitted.

LEGAL TERMINOLOGY

Affidavit: A written or printed declaration or statement of facts, taken before an officer having authority to administer oaths.

Arraign: To bring a prisoner before the court to answer the indictment.

Arrest: The taking of a person into custody to answer to a criminal charge.

Arson: The willful and deliberate burning of a dwelling or outbuildings of another. This also covers the burning of any building to defraud an insurer.

Assault: The intentional unlawful use of force by one person upon another.

Bill of rights: The first 10 amendments of the US Constitution are known as the Bill of Rights. The key amendments from the security standpoint are as follows:

- The First Amendment provides for freedom of speech, religion, and press, and the right of peaceful assembly for redress of grievances.
- The Second Amendment prohibits the government from interfering with the right to keep and bear arms.
- The Fourth Amendment prohibits unreasonable search and seizure.

- The Fifth Amendment protects citizens against being compelled to testify against themselves; double jeopardy; being deprived of life, liberty, or property without due process; and being held for a serious crime without presentation to a grand jury for indictment.
- The Sixth Amendment provides for a speedy trial by an impartial jury, your right to be informed of charges against you, your right to present a defense, and your right to confront witnesses against you.
- The Seventh Amendment provides for a trial by jury.
- The Eighth Amendment prohibits excessive bail, excessive fines, and cruel and unusual punishment.

Bribery: The attempt to influence a public officer in the discharge of his or her official duties by the offer of a reward or other consideration.

Burglary: Breaking and entering or remaining in a building with the intent to commit a felony therein.

Civil court: Courts established for private parties and enforcement of private rights.

Concurrent: Sentences that run at the same time.

Consecutive sentences: Sentences that are served one after another.

Conviction: The result of a trial that results in a judgment or sentence of guilt.

Corpus delicti: The body of the crime.

Defendant: The party charged with a crime.

Due process of law: The Fifth and Fourteenth Amendments are considered the due-process amendments. Although the Supreme Court has not specifically defined due process, it has, in a number of cases, stated the following as fundamental rights coming within the purview of the due-process clauses:
- Freedom of speech and the press.
- Unreasonable searches and seizures.
- The right to have counsel.
- The right against self-incrimination.
- The right to have a jury trial.
- Protection against double jeopardy.

Embezzlement: The conversion of personal property by a person to whom the property was entrusted.

Extortion: The taking of something from a person through the fear of a future harm.

False imprisonment: The unlawful restraint by a person of another.

Foreseeability: Should have been able to see an event could happen. This is an element of proximate cause in a tort claim.

Homicide: The illegal and unjustified taking of a human being's life. Homicide can also be justified and legal, such as in self-defense or in wartime by armed forces. Lesser offenses include manslaughter and criminally negligent homicide.

Indigent: A person who has no funds or source of income.

Kidnapping: The unlawful taking of a person against his or her will.

Larceny: The taking and carrying away of personal property of another with the intent to deprive the owner permanently of the property.

Larceny by false pretense: Obtaining personal property of another with the intent of depriving them permanently by use of false pretenses in misrepresenting a past or present fact.

Malicious mischief: The actual damage or destruction of property belonging to another and this being done voluntarily and knowingly.

Misprision of a felony: The active concealment and failure to report a federal felony in which the accused is not involved.

Parole: Is an administrative act following incarceration. It is the release of a prisoner from prison but not from the legal custody for rehabilitation outside of prison walls.

Perjury: Deliberately and knowingly testifying falsely, under oath, to a material matter in a court proceeding. This also covers signing documents, under oath, which are known to contain falsehoods.

Plea of guilty: A confession of guilt in the open court.

Plea of nolo contendere: "No contest." Has the same effect as a plea of guilty, but cannot be used against the defendant in a civil suit.

Plea of not guilty: A plea denying the guilt of the accused to the offense.

Probable cause: Reasonable cause. Having more evidence for than against.

Probation: The release of a defendant by a court under conditions imposed by the court.

Prosecutor: Prosecutes another for a crime in the name of the government.

Public defender: An attorney designated by law or appointed by the court to represent indigent defendants.

Receiving stolen property: Receiving or concealing stolen property, knowing the property to be stolen.

Robbery: The taking of something of value from a person through the use of force or fear of force.

Tort: A civil wrong for which a remedy may be obtained relative to damages awarded in a court of law.

Tort feasor: A person who commits a tort or wrongful act.

Trespass on real property: The unlawful violation of the person or property of another. Trespass is a tort as well as a crime.

Uttering: When a person draws a check on an account knowing that there are insufficient funds to cover the check.

Bibliography

Blount, Ernest C., *Occupational Crime: Deterrence, Investigation, and Reporting in Compliance with Federal Guidelines*, CRC Press, Boca Raton, FL, 2002.

Bolz, Frank, Jr., Kenneth J. Dudonis and David P. Schulz, *The Counterterrorism Handbook: Tactics, Procedures, and Techniques*, 3rd ed., CRC Press, Boca Raton, FL, 2005.

Collins, Larry R. and Thomas D. Schneid, *Physical Hazards of the Workplace*, CRC Press, Boca Raton, FL, 2001.

Corcoran, Michael H. and James S. Cawood, *Violence Assessment and Intervention: The Practitioner's Handbook*, CRC Press, Boca Raton, FL, 2003.

Della-Giustina, Daniel E., *Motor Fleet Safety and Security Management*, CRC Press, Boca Raton, FL, 2004.

Devlin, Edward S., *Crisis Management Planning and Execution*, Auerbach Publications, Boca Raton, FL, 2006.

Di Pilla, Steven, *Slip and Fall Prevention: A Practical Handbook*, CRC Press, Boca Raton, FL, 2003.

Ferraro, Eugene, *Investigations in the Workplace*, Auerbach Publications, Boca Raton, FL, 2005.

Gustin, Joseph F., *Facility Manager's Handbook*, Taylor & Francis, Boca Raton, FL, 2002.

Gustin, Joseph F., *Disaster and Recovery Planning: A Guide for Facility Managers*, 3rd ed., Taylor & Francis, Boca Raton, FL, 2004.

Gustin, Joseph F., *Bioterrorism: A Guide for Facility Managers*, Taylor & Francis, Boca Raton, FL, 2005.

Kairab, Sudhanshu, *A Practical Guide to Security Assessments*, Auerbach Publications, Boca Raton, FL, 2004.

Kirschenbaum, Alan, *Chaos Organization and Disaster Management*, CRC Press, Boca Raton, FL, 2003.

Lack, Richard, *Safety, Health, and Asset Protection: Management Essentials*, 2nd ed., CRC Press, Boca Raton, FL, 2001.

Peltier, Thomas R., Justin Peltier and John A. Blackley, *Information Security Fundamentals*, Auerbach Publications, Boca Raton, FL, 2004.

POA Publishing, *Asset Protection and Security Management Handbook*, Auerbach Publications, Boca Raton, FL, 2002.

Reese, Charles D., *Office Building Safety and Health*, CRC Press, Boca Raton, FL, 2004.

Schroll, R. Craig, *Industrial Fire Protection Handbook*, 2nd ed., CRC Press, Boca Raton, FL, 2002.

Sonne, Warren J., *Criminal Investigation for the Professional Investigator*, CRC Press, Boca Raton, FL, 2006.

Sterneckert, Alan B., *Critical Incident Management*, Auerbach Publications, Boca Raton, FL, 2003.

Tipton, Harold F. and Micki Krause, *Information Security Management Handbook*, 5th ed., Auerbach Publications, Boca Raton, FL, 2003.

Index

A

Absenteeism
  employee, 92–93
  substance abuse and, 123
Access control, 549
  in emergency planning, 247–248
Access control systems
  biometric based, 164
  credential based, 163–164
  knowledge based, 164
  objectives, 163
  other methods, 165
Access mode, 549
Accessory after the fact, 479
Accident investigations, *see* Traffic
      accident investigations
Accumulator, 549
Accuracy, investigative services, 38
Ace lock, 542
Acid flashbacks, as hallucinogens side
      effects, 137
Acoustic detector, 396
Acrylic glazing, 172
  for storefront window, 395
Active infrared sensors, 201
Active intrusion detection sensor, 549
Active intrusion sensor, 549
Active sensors, 198, 549
Actuating blocks, 549
Actuator, 549
Actus rea, 274
Addressable/intelligent fire alarm systems,
      211, 213–215
Administrative law, 476
Admission statement, 64
ADP systems, 350
Affidavit, 567
Age Discrimination in Employment Act
      (1967), 80, 325, 413
Agency by operation of law, 482
Agency relationship, 483
Aggression, workplace causes of, 414
Air-conditioning, fire prevention survey, 538

Air gap, 549
Air-sampling smoke detectors, 222–223
Alarm, 549
Alarm assessment, 549
Alarm circuit, 550
Alarm condition, 550
Alarm discrimination, 550
Alarm line, 550
Alarm monitoring system, 207–209
  central alarm system, 208–209
  grades of service, 207–208
  local alarm system, 208
Alarm polling, 209
Alarm sensors, 197–198
Alarm signal, 550
Alarm station, 550
Alarm system, 17, 141, 206–207, 260, 550
  fire prevention survey, 530
Alcohol, 139
Alert, 550
Alibi defense, 277
Alkaloids, from opium, 129–130
The American Medical Directory, 40
American National Standards Institute
      (ANSI), 175
American Red Cross, 425
American Society for Industrial Security
      (ASIS), 1, 3–4, 142, 303, 390
Americans with Disabilities Act (ADA),
      80, 210
Amphetamines, 136–137, 371
Amytal, 133
Ancillary services, by contract guard
      agencies, 266
Animal barriers, 158
Annunciators, 398, 400, 550
Annunciator status panels, in fire alarm
      systems, 212
Answering service, 550
Antagonists, narcotic, 132
Antifriction latch, 542
Applicant investigation, 239
Area protection, 551
Area sensor, 551

Printed in the United States
by Baker & Taylor Publisher Services